Letters from John, Paul, and Peter

A super-expanded translation of ten New Testament letters

ROY JONES

ISBN: 9798672611938

He who began in you a work which is good will bring it to a successful conclusion

CONTENTS

An introduction

I have always had a love for the Bible from the first time I read it nearly forty years ago back in 1982. Recently I have tried to find the most accurate translation of the New Testament.

The difficulty is that the Greek language, being rich in concepts and meaning, does not lend itself easily to a comprehensive, but at the same time readable translation. In these pages I have attempted to produce such a translation.

The means I have used to achieve this is as follows:

Imagine one of the writers, John say, arrives at your group, having previously sent you his letter.

You say to John, "We got your letter. Could you please explain it for us."

Then John reads through the letter a sentence or so at a time.

After each sentence he looks up and tells the group about his motives and his thinking in what he had written in that part of the letter.

His explanations, as imagined here, are still true to the original language and not a contemporary paraphrase of the Bible text.

I've done this by amalgamating Wuest's Expanded New Testament (bold italics) and a much reduced version of the accompanying notes in his Word Studies (plain text), making it a kind of Super-Expanded translation of these letters.

So what I've produced here is not from my own research into the Greek language, but is based on those works of Kenneth Wuest. Although this is not a complete translation of the New Testament, it is nevertheless a translation of nearly half of the New Testament letters text.

I gained a lot of understanding in compiling this translation, so hopefully you will also increase your understanding as you read this.

Enjoy.

Roy

From John

That which was from the beginning,

I am referring here to Jesus, from the time of the Creation until His appearing on earth.

that which we have heard with the present result that it is ringing in our ears,

I heard Jesus speak at length, over and over, so often, that I have no doubt as to His reality and humanity.

that which we have discerningly seen with our eyes with the present result that it is in our mind's eye,

I saw Jesus and came to understand what I was looking at and seeing, with a growing sense of wonder.

that which we gazed upon as a spectacle, and our hands handled with a view to investigation,

I touched Jesus and felt His body, repeatedly, throughout His time on earth, and after His resurrection, when He invited us to handle Him to assure us that He was real and alive again in the flesh.

that which is concerning the Word of life - and this aforementioned life was made visible, and we have seen it with discernment and have it in our mind's eye,

I came to realise from all that I heard and saw and felt of Jesus, that He is the totality of God as seen through a human form, the invisible God in concrete form in humanity, with a human body with its limitations, living a life on earth by the power of the Holy Spirit. In the same way that invisible light can be split into its constituent colours, so He revealed the constituent love, grace, humility and kindness of God, through His human life here i.e. He lived out what 'the Word became flesh' actually results in, before our eyes and ears, so that we humans could understand it with our physical senses.

and are bearing witness and are bringing back to you a message concerning the life, the eternal life,

Jesus is without beginning or end, He always has been and always will be, deity. And the life of deity is not merely a characterless animation, but an ethical and spiritual life, whose qualities have now been communicated by

Jesus to all sinners whose faith is in Him, energising and transforming them to live a Christian life. Indeed it is essential that these qualities are shown in us who now have this same life in us, the qualities exhibited in Jesus' life being our pattern for living.

which is of such a nature as to have been in fellowship with the Father

Jesus and the Father have a joint participation in Their common deity.

and was made visible to us. That which we have seen with discernment and at present is in our mind's eye, and that which we have heard and at present is ringing in our ears, we are reporting also to you, in order that as for you also, you may be participating jointly in common with us [in our firsthand knowledge of the life of our Lord].

So my desire in writing this to you is that you might share with me in my experience of Jesus, as you read this under the guidance of the Holy Spirit, that you might have a supernatural firsthand knowledge of Jesus and a more real, actual and intimate companionship with Him, since you need to 'see' Jesus in order to have companionship with Him, and so that you come to have common likes, dislikes, loves, hates, nature and character with Him, as well as also sharing the same Father with Him.

And the fellowship indeed which is ours, is with the Father and with His Son, Jesus Christ. And these things, as for us, we are writing in order that our joy, having been filled completely full in times past may persist in that state of fullness through the present time.

Our fellowship with Jesus and the Father is our joint participation with Them in Their life, the God life. I want you to have our same joy of intimate, intelligent companionship with Jesus, to see, hear and touch Him through these words, as the Holy Spirit ministers my writing to you.

And it is this message which we have heard from Him and at present is ringing in our ears and we are bringing back tidings to you, that God as to His nature is light, and darkness in Him does not exist, not even one particle.

This message was declared to me and others. By 'light' I mean that He is physically glorious, intellectually true, morally holy, pure, loving, full of life, having no earthly material substance, but an eternal spirit.

If we say that things in common we are having with Him, and thus fellowship, and in the sphere of the aforementioned darkness are habitually ordering our behaviour, we are lying, and we are not doing the truth.

We can't compromise with sin and still have things in common i.e. fellowship, with God, we need to have the same interests and be involved in the same activities as Him. No child of God would sin to the exclusion of righteous acts, and one whose actions are encircled by sin cannot be a companion of God, as nothing of God ever enters the circle of sin.

But if within the sphere of the light we are habitually ordering our behaviour as He himself is in the light, things in common and thus fellowship we [the believer and God] are having with one another, and the blood of Jesus His Son keeps continually cleansing us from every sin.

But for Christians who are walking in the light of God by habit; your actions are encircled by light, so you do have companionship with God, and He becomes a companion to you too! While in this fellowship with God, in order for it to remain intact, Jesus' blood keeps cleansing us from our sins of omission and ignorance, which we are too immature in grace as yet to be aware of ourselves.

If we say that [indwelling] sin we are not having, ourselves we are leading astray [nobody else], and the truth is not in us.

Some say there is no sin principle in us, no sinful nature passed down from Adam. A Christian who believes that their evil nature has been eradicated is deceiving them self.

If we continue to confess our sins, faithful is He and just to forgive us our sins and to cleanse us from every unrighteousness.

We believers need to agree with God about our each single act of sin that is known to us, that we have committed it and that it is God against whom it has been committed, so we should hate each such act and feel guilt and contrition for it, and a determination to change. I'm talking here about infrequent, isolated sins in an otherwise well-ordered life. We should moreover be eager for the Holy Spirit to discover sin in our life so that it can be confessed and put out by His power. By forgiving us, God is keeping faith with Himself and man, fulfilling His promises and the purpose for which He called man, to remit the debt and put away the sin. Firstly on the basis of the Law's demands being satisfied at the Cross i.e. all sins, whether past when unsaved or future when saved, were legally forgiven for all who would put their faith in Jesus. Secondly, sin in a Christian's life is now not a matter between lawbreaker and judge, but between child and father, as it grieves the Father's heart when we sin. So His forgiveness is also a matter of His guarding those who trust in Him, it is His righteous dealing with those who partake of His nature and walk, so that once we agree with Him and put away the sin, our fellowship with our Father, that was broken by that sin, is restored. His nature rules in us as far as we confess our sins.

If we say that we have not sinned and are now in a state where we do not sin, a liar we are making Him, and His word is not in us.

Some say no acts of sin were committed in the past, so none can be committed now. This is just a stifling of the conscience, turning a deaf ear to the inward voice of our souls, and shows an ignorance of His Word.

My little children [born-ones, bairns], these things I am writing to you in order that you may not commit an act of sin. And if anyone commits an act of sin, One who pleads our cause we constantly have facing the Father, Jesus Christ the righteous One. And He himself is an expiatory satisfaction for our sins, and not only for ours but also for the whole world.

So why not sin, since we can never be holy in this life and since Jesus' blood cleanses us? Though this is true, it is still far better not to sin. But if we do sin occasionally, not habitually, we have an advocate in Jesus Who champions our cause and Who is a Friend of the accused. If we do cherish our sin and don't confess it, Jesus still pleads our cause through His blood to bring us back into fellowship with the Father, in that He faces the Father with our sin, which wounds His heart. Our judge becomes our advocate by removing the obstacle of alienation, able to remove the sin and guilt because on the Cross He was both priest and sacrifice. By His sacrifice on the Cross Jesus offers the choice of life or death to everybody.

And in this we know experientially that we have come to know Him experientially and are in that state at present, if we are continually having a solicitous, watchful care in safeguarding His precepts by obeying them. He who keeps on saying, I have come to know Him experientially and as a present result am in that state, and His precepts is not habitually safeguarding with solicitous care, is a liar, and in this one the truth does not exist. But whoever habitually with a solicitous care is keeping His word, truly, in this one the love of God has been brought to its completion with the present result that it is in that state of completion.

If we observe Him carefully and walk as He walked, all of His attention as mentioned above, is on us. We just need to practice and increase our knowledge day by day by experience. We know that we have come to know Him, so now we need to know that we know Him, having not just a desire not to disobey, but a desire to obey perfectly, with a self distrust and vigilance against temptation and high-mindedness, not wanting to dishonour the Word. The precepts I refer to here are those given by Jesus when on earth, and later through the disciples, not those given through Moses in the Law. A believer habitually obeys the Word.

In this we have an experiential knowledge that in Him we are. He who is constantly saying that he as a habit of life is living in close fellowship with and dependence upon Him is morally obligated just as that One conducted himself, also himself in the manner spoken of to be conducting himself.

Personal experiential knowledge of Jesus is available to all. An obedient child of God is not characterised by the quality of his own personality, but as a subject of divine love's work working perfectly, showing the truth is in him. We are to be a manifestation of God's love. He loves us and lives in us, and also our love for Him is part of His love's work, as perfect love is only possible if it is mutual i.e. both parties loving each other. We obey Jesus because we love Him, and we live restrained by the love that is produced in our hearts by the Holy Spirit, harmoniously, in communion and dependence and friendship, moment by moment. We love as a debt to His love.

Divinely loved ones, no commandment new in quality am I writing to you, but a commandment, an old one, which you have had constantly from the beginning. The commandment, the old one, is the Word which you heard.

When I say 'Walk with Jesus', I am not giving you a Christian exhortation of a newer quality than what you have had previously, namely 'Love one another'. It does not supplant that.

Again, a commandment, one new in quality, I am writing to you, which fact is true in him and in you, because the darkness is being caused to pass away, and the light, the genuine light, already is shining.

What I am writing is new though, because, by practice of loving one another is developed power, meaning and obligation. So the commandment is old in teaching but new in practice. Walking with Jesus is putting an old commandment into practice, making it fresh and new in every experience... Our eyes are getting accustomed to the light of Gospel revelation. Sin's darkness and unbelief are passing by like a parade, and like a parade it will come to an end. Whatever is not in fellowship with God is darkness. Satan covers his darkness with a fake, superficial light, whereas God is light, to the core.

He who is saying that in the light he is, and is habitually hating his brother [Christian] is in the darkness up to this moment.

Anyone not in fellowship with God walks in darkness and hatred. Determined hatred, not just an instinctive hateful reaction, is opposed to all levels of love whether self-sacrificial or just fondness.

He who is habitually loving his brother [Christian] in the light is abiding, and a stumbling block in him there is not.

Loving in dependence on Jesus is self-sacrificial, attending to the well-being of the other, being the overflow of His love for us. Walking thus leads to there being no trap in our path, to trip us up or to cause others to stumble.

But he who as a habit of life hates his brother [Christian] is in the darkness, and in the sphere of the darkness is habitually ordering his behaviour, and he does not know where he is going, because the darkness blinded his eyes.

Less than an active loving benevolence is hatred. There is no middle way. Similar to how indifference to the Gospel is a rejection of it... The darkness is such that not only can that person not see, but it also causes them to go blind. Such is the case of an unsaved person who professes Christianity.

I am writing to you, little children [born-ones, bairns], because your sins have been put away for you permanently because of His Name.

You young believers, your sins were put away at the Cross, never more to be remembered, for His Name's sake i.e. because of what Jesus was in His Person. The Father put away our sins, recognising and accepting the atonement Jesus offered on the Cross.

I am writing to you, fathers, because you have come to know experientially the One who is from the beginning, and as a present result are possessors of that knowledge. I am writing to you, young men, because you have gained the victory over the Pernicious One and as a present result are victorious over him. I write to you, little children under instruction, because you have come to know the Father experientially, with the present result that you are possessors of that knowledge.

You fathers are mature Christians, in that you have more experiential knowledge and are well-rounded with a permanent faith. Young men, you are those who have won a permanent victory after a conflict, victorious by the power of the Holy Spirit, such that you stand in a place of consistent victory over the one who seeks to drag everyone else down with him in his downfall, namely Satan. Little children, you of lower authority, see what I wrote here.

I write to you, fathers, because you have come to know experientially the One who is from the beginning, and are as a present result possessors of that knowledge. I write to you, young men, because you are strong with endowed strength and the word of God in you is abiding, and you have gained the victory over the Pernicious One, and as a present result are victorious over him.

Fathers, see what I wrote here. Young men, see what I wrote here, you are strong in Jesus with salvation strength, the Word being at home in you, unhindered and welcome, plus, by the power of the Holy Spirit, you have the victory over Satan, who sought to drag you down with him.

Stop considering the world precious with the result that you love it, and the things in the world. If anyone as a habit of life is considering the world precious and is therefore loving it, there does not exist the Father's love [i.e., the love possessed by the Father] in him. Because everything which is in the world, the passionate desire of the flesh [the totally deprived nature], and the passionate desire of the eyes, and the insolent and empty assurance which trusts in the things that serve the creature life, is not from the Father as a source but is from the world as a source. And the world is being caused to pass away, and its passionate desire. But the one who keeps on habitually doing the will of God abides forever.

By the world I mean human life in the ordered world, as headed by Satan and consequently hostile to God, and earthly things that seduce us from God, including demons and the unsaved. Also I mean all that is religious, cultured, refined, and intellectual but anti-God, the spirit of the age, the moral atmosphere which we constantly inhale and exhale, comprising thoughts, opinions and hopes. Don't have a heart-love for the world since this will exclude your love for God, as love to God cannot co-exist with love to the world, meaning that God's love is not then in you. Your body is not evil in itself, but can be energised by evil cravings associated with the world, Satan, and your own evil nature. Do not have a vain assurance in your own resources or in the stability of earthly things, as that shows a contempt for divine laws. The world is passing by. God will end it.

Little children under instruction, it is a last hour in character. And even as you heard that Antichrist comes, even now, antichrists, many of them have arisen and are here; from which fact we know by experience that it is a last hour in character.

It is a critical time. The Antichrist is he who proposes to do the work of Christ, in defiance of Christ. He denies the Word, hates worship and everything called God, and destroys every religion and every submission to a higher power than man, telling man that he is God, and seeking to establish his own throne. He can also appear as a false Christ, come in fulfilment of God's promises and man's expectations, proclaimed as the world's saviour and blessing his adherents with earthly enjoyments. The same as all of this is true of antichrists, but to a lesser degree. These are established in the church already and will animate Antichrist.

Out from us they departed [doctrinally], but they did not belong to us as a source. For if they had belonged to us, they would in that case have remained with us. But they departed in order that they might be plainly recognised, that all do not belong to us as a source.

The antichrists departed doctrinally from the Church with respect to the Person of Jesus. They showed only mental assent to doctrines, but no heart acceptance of Jesus Himself. Though members of the visible organised church, they are not part of the Body of Jesus, posing as Christians, every one of them.

But as for you [in contradistinction to the antichrists], an anointing you have from the holy One, and all of you have the capacity to know [spiritual truth]. I am not writing to you because you do not know the truth, but because you know it, and because every lie is not out of the truth as a source.

You were anointed with the Holy Spirit, the Father sending the Spirit to you in answer to Jesus' prayer for all believers, this anointing being manifested on the occasion of your accepting Him. Thus was the Spirit in position in you, ready, but of no help to you until you yielded to and trusted the Spirit to assist you. Then He was able to teach you, giving you the ability to know God's truth absolutely and correctly, and to detect error.

Who is the liar if not the one who is denying that Jesus is the Christ? This one is the antichrist, the one who is denying the Father and the Son. Everyone who denies the Son, not even does he have the Father. The one who confesses the Son also has the Father.

The liar is the one who impersonates all that is false, habitually denying Christ. Jesus means Yahweh saves, so 'Jesus' points to the One Who is deity and humanity. Only Yahweh could offer the sacrifice, and it had to include human nature but without its sin, as deity cannot die, and deity acting as a priest for sinners must also partake of the nature of the human beneficiaries. So denial of the Son is to say that the Person called Jesus is neither God nor man and that he did not offer an atonement for sin on the Cross i.e. a denial that there are two Persons in the Godhead, Father and Son, a denial that the Son is deity and the son of Yahweh. The one who agrees with the Word, is he who regards the unique sonship of Jesus with respect to God the Father, so acknowledges that Jesus is equal with God.

As for you, that which you heard from the beginning, in you let it be constantly abiding. If in you there abides that which from the beginning you heard, both in the Son and in the Father you will abide. And this is the promise which He himself promised us, the life, the eternal life. These things I am writing to you concerning those who are leading you astray. But as for you, the anointing which you received from Him remains in you. And no need are you constantly having that anyone be constantly teaching you. But even as His anointing teaches you concerning all things, and is true and is not a lie, and even as He [the Holy Spirit, the anointing] taught you, be constantly abiding in Him.

But you, don't divert from the doctrines you were taught. Let them be at home in you, giving them access to every part of your life. By living a holy life and by a determination to remain true to these doctrines, you will nurture them and cause them to grow and become stable. Adhering to what you heard from the beginning shows that you are saved, and assures that you will continue to abide in the Son and in the Father. The Holy Spirit stays in you forever. Teaching pastors are of worth, but you are not to be at their mercy. No teacher is the only and ultimate source of instruction, but only the Holy Spirit and the Word, as you abide in Jesus.

And now, little children [born-ones, bairns], be continually abiding in Him, in order that whenever He is made visible, we may have instant freedom of speech and not be made to shrink away from Him in shame at His coming and personal presence. If you know in an absolute manner that He is righteous, you know experientially that everyone who habitually does this aforementioned righteousness [which God is], out from Him has been born, with the present result that that one is a born-one.

Be ready for Jesus' coming at the Rapture, so that there is nothing between you and Him when He comes, no known sin. Perform a daily check-up for sin in your life. Maintain a constant yieldedness to and dependence on the Holy Spirit, for Him to show you the sin in your life, and give you the grace to judge it and put it out. That way, the sudden appearance of Jesus will just be a continuation of the fellowship that you had with Him on earth, with not even a momentary separation through shame of any conscious guilt. We believers are born of Christ, since Jesus is divine. We are children of God by birth, permanently in relationship with our Father, and His presence in us keeps us righteous with His righteousness, as produced by the Holy Spirit. That is the sign of new birth.

Behold what exotic [foreign to the human heart] love the Father has permanently bestowed upon us, to the end that we may be named children [born-ones, bairns] of God. And we are. On this account the world does not have an experiential knowledge of us, because it has not come into an experiential knowledge of Him.

The love God has for us is not found in humanity, it is unearthly, other worldly. We are permanent objects of His love, and given His character. The people of the world system of evil do not understand or appreciate our nature since they have no fellowship with God. We are foreigners to the world, strangers to it.

Divinely loved ones, now born-ones of God we are. And not yet has it been made visible what we shall be. We know absolutely that whenever it is made visible, like ones to Him we shall be, because we shall see Him just as He is.

Now and eternally we are children of God, we have within us the germ of all the possibilities of eternal life. What we shall be like in eternity has never yet manifested on any occasion, but we shall be something unspeakable, contained in the likeness of God. Since we are His children we shall be like Jesus, we know this now, as a promise. We shall have a physical likeness to Him then, as well as the spiritual likeness that we have now, as our outward expression will reflect what is within us. At the Rapture we will experience the glorification of our physical bodies. Through eternity we will grow in likeness to Jesus through the Holy Spirit, but we will never equal Him since we are finite where He is infinite. We will have an outer covering of glory, as now covers Jesus' body, such that our mortal eyes cannot look on His glory. We need our bodies and our eyes to be transformed to the immortal, to be like Him, in order to see Him as He is.

And everyone who has this hope continually set on Him is constantly purifying himself just as that One is pure.

Resting our hope in Jesus of our becoming like Him, we can maintain our purity with effort and fearfulness, amid the defilements and allurements of this world. Jesus, because of His human experience, appeared before God, presenting His work to the King so as to purify Himself. We will to purify ourselves, stirred up by this hope to be like Him, as a result of our Christian state. God ministers the power to carry out our will to self-purification from all defilement of flesh and spirit i.e. the hope of being like Jesus inspires a determination in us to be pure like Him, so we will to carry that resolve into action, in dependence on the Holy Spirit, to put sin out of our life and to keep it out.

Everyone who habitually commits sin, also habitually commits lawlessness; and sin is lawlessness. And you know absolutely that that One was manifested in order that He might take away our sins; and sin in Him does not exist. Everyone who in Him is constantly abiding is not habitually sinning. Everyone who is constantly sinning has not with discernment seen Him, nor has he known Him, with the result that that condition is true of him at present. Little born-ones, stop allowing anyone to be leading you astray. The one who habitually does righteousness is righteous, just as that One is righteous. The one who is habitually committing sin is out of the devil as a source, because from the beginning the devil has been sinning. For this purpose there was manifested the Son of God, in order that He might bring to naught the works of the devil.

A child of God cannot continue in sin. The purpose of Jesus' sacrifice was to atone for sins of the past, that they be lifted up and carried away, and also to prevent future sins. Your habitual actions denote your character. Are you habitually abiding in Jesus or habitually sinning? Sin is to be the exception, not the rule, for a believer, so that he now does righteousness, though he may sin at times. Righteous character is expressed in righteous conduct. Christ is our type, we must be like Him. He that makes sin his business and practice, is subject to his depraved nature inherited from Adam, whose source is in the devil. The devil has been sinning from the beginning of his career, has never ceased to sin from that beginning, and still sins now. Jesus came to destroy, loosen and dissolve the seeming solid front of the works of the devil. Jesus revealed their complete insubstantiality and undid the seeming bonds by which they were held together. Jesus paid for sin by His blood and made a way of escape for us. He defeated the devil's purposes and will bring about his complete downfall.

Everyone who has been born out of God with the present result that he is a born-one of God does not habitually commit sin because His seed remains in him. And he is not able habitually to sin, because out of God he has been born with the present result that he is a born-one of God. In this is apparent who are the born-ones of God and the born-ones of the devil. Everyone who is not habitually doing righteousness is not of God, also the one who is not habitually loving his brother [Christian] with a divine and self-sacrificial love.

The act of our regeneration is complete. The divine nature and life have been imparted to us so that now we are spiritually alive. His seed is the principle of divine life in us, which makes it impossible for us to live habitually in sin because the divine nature causes us to hate sin and to love righteousness, and it also gives us the desire and power to do God's will. This seed grows gradually. There are occasional retardations, but there is sure growth, leading to full fruition. No growth means no life. We can sin, but we are not able to habitually sin. Those born of the devil inherit a totally depraved nature, as he has. We are to love our fellow Christian brothers.

Because this is the message which you heard from the beginning, namely, We should habitually be loving one another with a divine and self-sacrificial love; not even as Cain [who] was out of the Pernicious One, and killed his brother by severing his jugular vein. And on what account did he kill him? Because his works were pernicious and those of his brother righteous. Stop marvelling, brethren, if, as is the case, the world hates you. As for us, we know absolutely that we have passed over permanently out of the death into the life, because we are habitually loving the brethren with a divine and self-sacrificial love. The one who is not habitually loving in this manner is abiding in the sphere of the death. Everyone who habitually is hating his brother [Christian] is a manslayer. And you know absolutely that no manslayer has life eternal abiding in him.

There is an evil in people that is in active opposition to good, so as to drag the good down with them when they fall. Cain shed much blood when he killed his brother in the same way that an animal is sacrificed. Though the world hates us, it is not our business or intention to be hated by the world, but rather to commend Jesus to the world, so as to win it. The world's hostility to us doesn't necessarily imply our goodness. It could be that they are justifiably hostile due to our being unamiable or tactless. The test of our goodness is not in the world's hatred of us, but in our love for it. We are in the life, so are separated from the death, since man is either in death or in life. Our self-sacrificing love for others is the evidence of our being saved. Those not in life are dead in their trespasses and sins. Our spirit man is incapable of indifference, so if we banish brotherly love, then automatically we are abandoned to the rule of hate. Love and hate, light and dark, life and death, these all replace and exclude each other. A hater is a potential murderer.

In this we have come to know by experience the aforementioned love, because that One on behalf of us laid down His soul. And, as for us, we have a moral obligation on behalf of our brethren to lay down our souls.

Jesus laid down His life that we may receive salvation. We know this with a permanent, enduring knowledge. He suffered physical death and abandonment from God because human sin was laid on Him. Our ego has to be crucified as we deny self for our brothers, though the laying down of our lives for others does not bring any atonement.

But whoever has as a constant possession the necessities of life, and deliberately keeps on contemplating his brother constantly having need, and snaps shut his heart from him, how is it possible that the love of God is abiding in him?

The necessities of life are food, clothing and shelter. How can you observe someone's lack of these with interest and purpose over a long period, but then shut the door against any compassionate feelings or merciful actions toward them? We are called to lay down our life in little things, in day-to-day small sacrifices and self denials that go unnoticed by the world.

Little born-ones, let us not be loving in the sphere of word, nor even in the sphere of the tongue, but in the sphere of deed and truth.

Warm words are to be accompanied by warm deeds. Don't just appear generous, exercise generosity.

In this we shall know experientially that we are out of the truth, and in His presence shall tranquilize our hearts in whatever our hearts condemn us, because greater is God than our hearts and knows all things.

Am I as loving as I ought to be? Does my heart condemn me? Our worst is known by God already and still He cares for us and desires us. He can see the deepest thing in us that is real, a desire for goodness, as well as the failure on the surface to act out that desire. Do we want to be judged by God Who sees everything and makes allowance for us all, or to be judged by our own conscience? So pacify and soothe the alarm that stirs in your heart. God is greater than our hearts, but not greater in judgement, to condemn us more than our hearts do. Rather He is greater in compassion, so that we can quiet our condemning heart, knowing that we are in God's hands, at the mercy of He Who surpasses us in love and compassion.

Divinely loved ones, if our hearts are not condemning us, a fearless confidence we constantly have facing God the Father, and whatever we are habitually asking we keep on receiving from Him, because His commandments we are habitually keeping with solicitous care, and the things which are pleasing in His penetrating gaze we are habitually doing.

Our hearts do not condemn us if, as far as we know, there is no unconfessed sin in our lives, nothing between us and Jesus, and we are yielded habitually to the Holy Spirit, living in close fellowship with Jesus. Then we can be free, unreserved, confident, cheerful, bold and assured in our relationship with the Father. We can ask day after day for our desires to be met, knowing that day after day we are keeping His commandments and doing the things that please Him.

And this is His commandment, namely, We should believe the Name of His Son Jesus Christ, and be habitually loving one another even as He gave a commandment to us. And the one who as a habit of life exercises a solicitous care in keeping His commandments, in Him is abiding, and He himself is abiding in him. And in this we know experientially that He is abiding in us, from the Spirit as a source whom He gave to us.

Viewing the entire course of a Christian's life in one panoramic shot, the whole tenor of that life is to be Christward. You believed on the name of Jesus, now believe the Name of Jesus i.e. believe all that Jesus is in His wonderful Person. Give assent to all that the Bible says is true of Jesus and submit your heart to Him personally. Allow God to be a home to you and be the home of God. Abide in Him and let God abide in you. The Holy Spirit bears witness, in connection with our human spirit, as energised by Him, that we are born of God.

Divinely loved ones, stop believing every spirit. But put the spirits to the test to see whether they are of God and for the purpose of approving them if they are, and finding that they meet the specifications laid down [as to orthodoxy in doctrine], put your approval upon them, because many false prophets are gone out into the world.

Test each person to ascertain the spirit that is in them. False teachers have a demonic spirit in them that leads to heresy, as also do some pastors and evangelists. Such as these have gone out and are at present in the world of mankind and are becoming established there.

In this you know experientially the Spirit of God. Every spirit who agrees [to the doctrinal statement] that Jesus Christ has come in the sphere of the flesh [i.e. in incarnation] and still remains incarnate [in human form] is of God; and every spirit who does not confess this aforementioned Jesus [agree to the above teaching concerning Him] is not of God. And this is the spirit of the Antichrist which you have heard that it comes, and now is already in the world.

Does the spirit in the teacher agree with the Bible that Jesus is come in the flesh i.e. that the God of the Old Testament in His Son Jesus became incarnate as a human but without flesh's sin, died on the Cross to satisfy the Law's just demands which man had broken, and raised Himself from the dead in that same body in which He died to become the living Saviour of all who place their faith in Him by accepting what He did for them on the Cross? Those who teach this are activated by the Holy Spirit. Those who do not teach this are not of God, but are activated by the spirit of Antichrist.

As for you, out of God you are, little born-ones and you have gained a complete victory over them and are still victors, because greater is He who is in you than he who is in the world.

In contradistinction to those false teachers, you are of God. You have overcome them and are a conqueror, not being taken in by them. You are solid in an attitude of victory with your eyes wide open to that victory's source and nature i.e. that you have gained the victory because of the Holy Spirit Who is in you. He is greater than the fallen angel Satan who is in and ruling the world system of evil.

They themselves are out of the world as a source. On this account out of the world as a source they are constantly speaking, and the world listens to them. As for us, out of God we are.

The source of false doctrines is the world, inspired by demons who are the source of all heresy. The world accepts these false teachers as they are speaking from within the world, so the world recognises its own language as spoken by them.

The one who is knowing God in an experiential way is listening to us. He who is not out of God is not listening to us. From this we know experientially the Spirit of the truth and the spirit of the error.

Our knowing of God is progressive and not yet complete, but habitually and ever more clearly we are perceiving and recognising God, as our

Christian life unfolds... One's attitude to the message of the incarnate Saviour decides whether that one is on God's side or the world's. This message is to be spoken by us in love, graciously. There must be nothing in or about ourselves that causes this message to be rejected. The Holy Spirit teaches truth, the devil teaches error.

Divinely loved ones, let us be habitually loving one another with a divine and self-sacrificial love, because this aforementioned love is out of God as a source; and everyone who is in this manner habitually loving, out of God has been born with the present result that he is regenerated and knows God in an experiential way. The one who is not habitually loving in this manner has not come to know God, because God as to His nature is love.

Those loved by God should love one another habitually. This love should be returned in each case i.e. there should be reciprocal self-sacrificial love amongst you... The new birth is permanent. Each child of God remains a child of God forever... Those who do not love like this do not know God since they did not get to know Him, in fact they never knew Him. God's nature, His essence and character, is love. That is to say He is loving and it is His nature to be loving.

In this was clearly shown the love of God in our case, because His Son, the uniquely begotten One, God sent off into the world on a mission in order that we may live through Him.

Jesus is the only begotten, meaning He is the single One of His kind, the only Son of God. In that sense He has no brethren. He proceeds by eternal generation from the Father as God the Son in a birth that never took place because it always was, Jesus possessing the essence of deity co-eternally with the Father and the Spirit. Jesus was sent to perform duties; to die for sinners, and to provide salvation on the basis of justice satisfied, to all who would place their faith in Him as their Saviour. That salvation is available now, still.

In this is the love, not that we have loved God, but that He himself loved us, and sent off His Son, an expiatory satisfaction concerning our sins.

The human race has not loved God, and still now it does not possess any love for Him. God has always loved sinners. He needs no gift to appease His supposed wrath against man, since He loves man from His heart, spontaneously. Good works cannot placate His wrath against sin. Only by inflicting the penalty of sin, death, can the demands of His holy Law be satisfied, so that His government is maintained, and so that a proper basis is provided for His bestowal of mercy upon us. Jesus' sacrifice fully satisfies the demands of the broken Law.

Divinely loved ones, since in that manner and to that extent did God love us, also, as for us, we are under moral obligation to be constantly loving one another.

This was an act of infinite love and infinite sacrifice on the part of the Father and the Son. The Father's heart was pierced when sin was laid on His Son and then His holiness demanded that He abandon the Son. Consequently, in view of this, we should continuously show self-sacrificial love to our brothers.

God in His [invisible] essence no one has ever yet beheld, with the result that no one has the capacity to behold Him. If we habitually are loving one another, God in us is abiding, and His love has been brought to its fullness in us and exists in that state of fullness.

We cannot view God attentively or contemplate Him visually, since He is deity. But His nature has been brought to human fullness and completion in us who walk in love. If we love by the Spirit, this nature of God has accomplished its purpose in us, by making us loving and self-sacrificial.

In this we know experientially that in Him we are dwelling and He himself in us, because He has given us from His Spirit as a source [spiritual gifts and their operation] as a permanent gift.

Has Jesus given us any testimony of His presence in us? Yes, in making us partakers of His Spirit. This is our internal proof of the external act of the sending of the Son. We experience the work of the Spirit within us when He is at home in us. He is a gift to us so that we can dwell in God permanently and He in us. Each of us receives the Holy Spirit in His entirety. Out of that fullness we operate in spiritual gifts, certain ones, out of the total number. These gifts outworking in our Christian life are also an evidence of the Spirit in us.

And as for us, we have deliberately and steadfastly contemplated, and we are testifying that the Father has sent off the Son as Saviour of the world.

In contradistinction to certain others, we viewed as a process, not just momentarily, Jesus, and that process is now complete, resulting in the abiding fact that we know that it is Jesus Who is the Saviour of the world, not Caesar, though he goes by that title.

Whoever agrees with the statement that Jesus is the Son of God, God in him dwells and he himself in God.

This is our lifetime confession, sustained by our attitude of heart; Jesus is the Son of God, so God the Son. This confession implies a life of surrender and obedience to Him, rather than just lip-service.

And as for us, we have known experientially the love which God has in our case, and have that knowledge at present, and we have believed and at present maintain that attitude. God is, as to His nature, love, and he who dwells in the aforementioned love in God is dwelling, and God in him is dwelling.

Ours is the sphere in which God's love operates.

In this has been brought to completion the aforementioned love which is in us [produced by the Holy Spirit], which love exists in its completed state, resulting in our having unreservedness of speech at the day of the judgement, because just as that One is, also, as for us, we are in this world.

His love is with us, produced in our hearts by the Holy Spirit, as a present reality. The fullness of His nature in us results in a life devoted entirely to Jesus, so there is nothing to hide or be ashamed of at the Rapture. Then we will approach the judgment seat of Christ boldly, freely and confidently. His life in us also results in our Christ-like life, making us, as we dwell in the midst of a world of sinful people, resemble Jesus now. There will be no condemnation for those who were like Him while they lived on earth.

Fear does not exist in the sphere of the aforementioned love. Certainly, this aforementioned love which exists in its completed state throws fear outside, because this fear has a penalty, and the one who fears has not been brought to completion in the sphere of this love, and is not in that state at present.

We should not have a fear like that of a slave in fear of their master, or like a criminal before a judge awaiting correction or penalty. The only kind of fear we experience is not like this at all, but is a holy fear of displeasing the Father through sin. Divine love does not produce fear of rebuke in the heart of a yielded saint. We are to have no fear of correction or loss of reward at Christ's judgement seat. Fearfulness implies we didn't experience the fullness of His nature in us, meaning that we didn't maintain a Spirit-filled life on earth.

As for us, let us be constantly loving because He himself first loved us. If anyone says, I am constantly loving God, and is as constantly hating his brother [Christian], he is a liar. For the one who is not constantly loving his brother [Christian] whom he has seen with discernment and at present has within the range of his vision, God whom he has not seen with discernment and at present does not have within the range of his vision he is not able to be loving. And this commandment we have from Him, [namely], The one who is constantly loving God should constantly be loving also his brother [Christian].

The amazing love of God in Christ is the inspiration of all the love that stirs in our hearts. It awakens within us an answering love, a grateful love for Him, manifesting in self-sacrificial love for our brothers. As we walk in His love, by the Holy Spirit, we fully 'see' God, with abiding results.

Everyone who believes that Jesus is the Christ, out from God has been born and as a result is His child. And everyone who loves the One who begot loves the one who has been begotten out from Him.

Every child of God accepts Jesus as being God incarnate; His humanity, His substitutionary death, His salvation that brings mercy through justice satisfied. Such a one is born of God and begotten of God. All who love God as father, love His children because of a family relationship i.e. having a common Father. So believers are all children in the same family.

In this we know experientially that we are habitually loving the born-ones of God, whenever God we are habitually loving and His commandments are habitually obeying.

Love the brethren on every occasion. Obedience of God's commandments puts us in right relationship with our brothers, resulting in our acting in love towards them. We obey Him carefully, with a jealous safe-keeping of His commandments lest they be violated, because we are concerned with His honour and glory, and with our testimony to Him.

For this is the love of God, namely, that we are habitually and with solicitous care guarding and observing His commandments.

Our love for God is shown by our keeping His Word. We are to have a self-sacrificing love for Him. His commandments are not severe or stern or cruel in any way. The love for God that the Holy Spirit energises in us makes keeping His commandments a delight.

And His commandments are not burdensome, because everything that has been born of God is constantly coming off victorious over the world. And this is the victory that has come off victorious over the world, our faith. Who is he who is constantly coming off victorious over the world but the one who believes that Jesus is the Son of God?

His commandments are not burdensome because obedience to them enables us to overcome the world. Every child of God is victorious in battle over the world system of evil, comprising the flesh and the depraved nature, the devil, and the pernicious world system's atmosphere by which we are surrounded. Thus there is incessant warfare against us attempting to ruin our Christian life and testimony. Our habit of life is to gain victory over the world. Defeat is the exception, not the rule. We are victorious now, in that we are winning the fight that is in progress, and we come off victorious, in that triumph is assured, by clinging to eternal realities. Our heart-belief in Jesus' incarnation as the Son of God results in our victory over the world.

This is the One who came through the instrumentality of water and blood, Jesus Christ; not in the sphere of the water only, but in the sphere of the water and the blood. And the Spirit is the One who is constantly bearing witness, because the Spirit is the truth. Because three there are that are constantly bearing testimony, the Spirit and the water and the blood. And the aforementioned three concur in the one thing.

The Advent of the Son of God and His embracing of human nature but without its sin since by virgin birth, and His atonement for sin, were made effective through water and blood. At His water baptism He declared His purpose; to fulfil all righteousness and to shed His blood and die on the Cross for the sin of the world. The Holy Spirit, Whose characteristic is truth, is the third witness to Jesus' incarnation, shown by the visible anointing in the form of a dove at Jesus' baptism. The blood, the water and the Spirit contribute to one and the same result, converging upon the one truth; Jesus Christ, the Son of God, came in the flesh and we have life in Him.

Since the testimony of men we are habitually receiving, the testimony of God is greater, because this is the testimony of God, [namely], that He has borne testimony concerning His Son, and this testimony is on record.

If we receive someone's testimony, we appropriate it to our self as something to be depended on as the truth. So we should receive God's testimony, when He bore it concerning His Son with an audible 'This is My Son' at Jesus' baptism.

The one who believes on the Son of God has the testimony in himself. The one who does not believe God has made Him a liar, and as a result considers Him to be such because he has not believed the testimony which God has given concerning His Son, which testimony is on record, with the result that he is in a settled state of unbelief.

We believe God, we accept His testimony concerning His Son, not only by the voice at Jesus' baptism, but also in the works that Jesus did. We believe in the Son and surrender ourselves to His Person, which is our reasonable and inevitable response. His inward testimony to us by the Holy Spirit, satisfies the deepest need of our nature. Our soul rises up and greets Him, as being all its salvation and all its desire. Thus His testimony goes from an external event in history to an inward experience, so is unquestionable.

And this is the testimony, that life eternal God gave us. And this life is in His Son. The one who has the Son has the life. The one who does not have the Son of God the life he does not have.

The life which God is and which He offers to us, is for those who place their faith in Jesus. Believers know that the Son is God. Unbelievers need to know that it is God Himself that they don't know, if they reject the Son.

These things I write to you in order that you may know with an absolute knowledge that life you are having, eternal life, to you who believe on the Name of the Son of God.

In my previous writing about the life of Jesus, being my reporting of the Gospel as inspired by the Holy Spirit, I exhibited Jesus to you, that you might believe in His divinity incarnated as a man and so have eternal life i.e. I assumed His humanity and proved His deity to you. In this letter, I have written and wrote that I am commending Jesus to you in His humanity, so as to assure you that you might know beyond any doubt that you have eternal life in Him, by believing that all that Jesus is in His Person entered fully into humanity i.e. I have assumed His deity and have proved His humanity to you, from my experiential knowledge of Him when we saw and heard and touched Him.

And this is the assurance which we are having toward Him, that if we keep on asking anything for ourselves, [which is] according to His will, He hears us. And if we know with an absolute knowledge that He hears us, whatever we are asking for ourselves, we know with an absolute knowledge that we have the things which we have asked from Him.

We have a prayer-hearing, prayer-answering God, and in Jesus we can have fearless confidence to approach Him cheerfully, boldly and assuredly, as we keep on asking for something for ourselves. Our prayers are always heard and never go unanswered, but He answers in His own way, not necessarily according to our wishes, so we pray with the proviso, whether implicit or explicit, 'If it be Your will'. We have our requests, not always according to how we pray, but as we would pray were we wiser. He gives us what we really need, which may not be what we ask for.

If anyone sees his brother sinning a sin which is not in its tendency towards death, he should ask, and He will give him life, to those who are sinning not with a tendency towards death. There is a sin which tends towards death. Not concerning that one [sin] do I say that he should ask. Every unrighteousness is sin. And there is a sin which does not tend towards death.

The sin leading to death is a rejection of the Son. These antichrists don't have the Son and are the Son's enemies, meaning they deny both the Father and the Son. They deny that Jesus is the incarnate Son of God. Their denial is the opposite of salvation i.e. of believing Jesus with the heart and confessing Him with the mouth, since they deny Christ with their mouth and in their heart do not believe in Him.

We know absolutely that everyone who has been born of God and as a result is a regenerated individual does not keep on habitually sinning. But He who was born of God maintains a watchful guardianship over him, and the Pernicious One does not lay hold of him.

All children of God are taken care of and guarded by Jesus. Our security is not in our grip on Christ, but in His grip on us.

We know with an absolute knowledge that out of God we are, and the whole world is lying in the Pernicious One.

The world is passive and in an unprogressive state under Satan. In contrast, we are new born, proceeding by faith, and have experienced a change of state.

We know with an absolute knowledge that the Son of God has come and is here, and that He has given us a permanent understanding in order that we may be knowing in an experiential way the One who is genuine. And we are in the Genuine One, in His Son, Jesus Christ. This is the genuine God and life eternal.

The assurance and guarantee of the totality of our faith and belief, is the incarnation of Jesus, an overwhelming demonstration of God's interest in us and of His concern for our highest good. He has come and He has given to us and He gives to us, all an abiding ongoing operation, rather than a historical fact. Our faith is a matter of personal and growing acquaintance with God through the enlightenment of Christ's Spirit. We experience His coming, His arrival, and His personal presence, that He is here with us, having come and having arrived. He departed in His glorified body to Heaven, but is here in His presence in the Church, as He remains in His followers on earth.

Little children [born-ones, bairns], guard yourselves from the idols.

Be on guard and keep watch. Your heart must be guarded against insidious assailants from without. This is a time of crisis and we need to decisively repulse them. Idols are heresies and substitutes for the Christian conception of God. Guard against everything which occupies the place of God.

From Paul to Colossae

Paul, an ambassador of Christ Jesus through the will of God, and Timothy our brother, to the saints in Colossae, even the faithful brethren in Christ. [Sanctifying] grace to you and [tranquilizing] peace from God our Father.

I am writing to you as a divinely appointed ambassador of Jesus, the Anointed of God, the Person chosen from the Godhead to be the anointed Prophet, Priest and King, so as to accomplish the purposes of God in the plan of salvation. I am writing to you who are set apart for God, having been elected by Him to salvation, taking you out of the first Adam and placing you into the last Adam, in view of which there is a demand that you separate yourselves from the world system of evil, from everything that would interfere in the least with your worship and service that is due to Him to Whom you have been set apart. I am writing to you, true and steadfast members of the brotherhood of believers at Colossae who have put your trust in Jesus. I know there are those among you who are pondering defecting in their allegiance to you, and these I seek to warn that they should remain steadfast and unswerving in their companionship with you. I bring to you a message in light of God's dealings with us; we were His bitter enemies, undeserving of salvation, deserving punishment for sins, but He has given free-heartedly to us out of His bounty, in an unlimited way, offering without any expectation of return, His salvation, something which we could never earn but which we can only accept by faith in Jesus Christ as our personal Saviour, being procured by His infinite personal sacrifice at the Cross where He poured out His precious blood. Such is grace. And there is an ongoing grace which we experience, to the extent that we are yielded to the Spirit and dependent upon His ministry for us... Having been so set apart, He has now joined Himself to us and is living in harmony with us, since Jesus concluded peace through His blood shed on the Cross, allowing the righteous and holy God to bestow mercy upon us believing sinners without violating His justice, and so binding us together again as father and child. Now the law of God has nothing against us and we can look up into the Father's face unafraid and unashamed. Such is peace.

I am giving thanks to God the Father of our Lord Jesus Christ concerning you, constantly offering petitions, having heard of your faith in Christ Jesus and of the divine, self-sacrificial love which you constantly have for all the saints because of the hope which is laid aside for you in Heaven, concerning which you heard before in the word of the truth of the good news which is present with you even as also it is in all the world constantly bearing fruit and increasing, just as it is also among you from the day when you heard it and came to know experientially the grace of God in the sphere of truth; even as you learned from Epaphras, the beloved, our fellow bondslave, who is faithful on your behalf as a servant of Christ, who also declared to us your love in the sphere of the Spirit.

I am always giving thanks for you and talking face to face with God concerning your needs and circumstances. Having placed your faith in the Lord Jesus as your Saviour, I am pleased to hear that your faith now rests in Him. And also that the love of each one of you reaches into the very hearts of all the others of you. You love because of the hope of reward which has been set before you, the oil of your hope feeding the flame of your love and of your faith in Jesus, making that flame burn ever more intensely. Your reward has been reserved for you in past times, and is now stored up and awaiting you in Heaven, out of reach of all enemies and sorrows, to be enjoyed by you in the future life. These things you heard about in the beginning, when Epaphras brought you the Gospel message, having heard it from me, which message snuggled up close to you, and you took it into your hearts. In the same way, the message is being universally accepted wherever it is proclaimed, since the Gospel message is such that it is a seed with a reproductive energy within itself, being about the grace of God in its genuine simplicity.

Because of this, we also, from the day we heard, do not cease on behalf of you offering our petitions and presenting our definite requests, that you might be filled with the advanced and perfect experiential knowledge of His will in the sphere of every kind of wisdom and intelligence which is spiritual, so that you may order your behaviour worthily of the Lord with a view to pleasing Him in everything, in every work which is good constantly bearing fruit and increasing by means of the advanced and perfect experiential knowledge of God,

Since I am hearing such good things about you, I am motivated to continue to pray for you, desiring that things be given to all of you, in particular, a greater and more thorough knowledge of His will for you with respect to the conduct of your lives, that you may grasp and penetrate into His will for you, that you might have this knowledge and be filled with it. From the inspiration of the Holy Spirit proceed both spiritual wisdom and insight into what is false and what is true. Having thus every kind of wisdom and intelligence, you can conduct yourselves worthily of the Lord, having as weighty a character as that of Jesus i.e. He is to be your example in life and the copy, you, must be like the example. Wisdom and insight is not an end in itself, but must lead to right living. Then we can please God in all our ways. Fruit bearing for example, not here meaning that the fruit is an increase in the knowledge of God, since knowledge is the motive and energy to bear fruit, rather that by means of the knowledge of God are we to bear fruit.

by every enabling power being constantly strengthened in proportion to the manifested power of His glory, resulting in every patience and forbearance, with joy constantly giving thanks to the Father who qualified you for the portion of the share of the inheritance of the saints in the sphere of the light;

The inherent power of God gives us the ability to do all that He asks of us, as He constantly strengthens us. He is the one source of all our highest strength, as He adapts His supply to our need. Then we have the ability not to be easily provoked or to be subject to a blazing anger, but are able to bravely bear up under a great siege of trials or difficulties or hardships, not losing heart or courage, but holding out long in our minds before giving room to action, or more normally, to anger or another passion. It is necessary to add joyfulness to our patience and longsuffering, so as to avoid becoming gloomy or of a sour disposition. On the contrary, we should be so filled with joy as to be able to meet all our trials with a buoyant sense of mastery... We always thank the Father who has rendered us fit to be partakers of the saints' inheritance which is situated in light, whether that light be in Heaven or on earth, by placing us in Christ and so making us objects of His grace. It has been assigned to us by lot to enjoy future blessedness, not only in the future heavenly life, but also while here on earth.

who delivered us out of the tyrannical rule of the darkness and transferred us into the kingdom of the Son of His love,

The Father has drawn us to Himself, rescuing and delivering us by His strong arm, as a mighty conqueror. We have been saved and brought out of the lawless, disorderly kingdom of darkness, whose capricious unruly rulers are Satan and his demons. Now there has been a wholesale transportation of peoples, so that we have been made subjects in a well-ordered, sovereign Kingdom, ruled by the Son, the object of the Father's love, to Whom therefore, the Kingdom was given

in whom we are having our liberation, procured by the payment of ransom, the putting away of our sins;

Our release and rescue from bondage was effected by payment of a ransom, resulting in sin being sent away from God. That payment was the act of God on the Cross, bearing the penalty of human sin, so satisfying the just demands of His holy law, then bidding sin to go away, never to be seen again.

who is a derived reproduction and manifestation of absolute deity, the invisible deity, who [the Son] has priority to and sovereignty over all creation,

Jesus is supreme over the natural, created universe. He is the manifestation of the unseen God in the creation and government of the world. He encompasses all the ways by which God makes Himself known to man in His purpose, design and revelation. Jesus mediates between God and His creation. Jesus is the imprint of God, being a precise reproduction of God in every respect. Jesus is the Son to the Father, derived by eternal generation in a birth that never took place because it always was. Jesus enables us to see God with our physical senses, as well as with the inner eye of our understanding. Since Jesus existed before all created things, He must be uncreated, and therefore eternal, and therefore God, so sent by God and is God Himself.

because in Him were created all things in the heavens and upon the earth, the visible things and the invisible ones, whether they are thrones or lordships or principalities or authorities. All things through Him as intermediate agent and with a view to Him stand created.

Jesus is outside of creation. All things, with no exception, were created in Him i.e. the creative will and energy is within the sphere of His personality, and in that sphere the creative act takes place. Thus the whole of creation is dependent on Him, in all locations whether in Heaven or on earth, and of all essences, whether material or immaterial, including all angels, both holy and fallen, and demons and man. All things, since they had their beginning in Him, tend to Him as their consummation, to depend on Him and to serve Him. The abiding result of this creation is that all things now exist in Him.

And He himself antedates all things, and all things in Him cohere.

Jesus is absolute in His existence, before all things in time. He is the principle of cohesion in the universe. He impresses upon creation that unity and solidarity which makes it an ordered system, a cosmos, rather than it being chaotically unformed. For example, gravity, which keeps things either fixed in their place or regulated in their movement, is an expression of His mind.

And He himself is the Head of His Body, the Church. He is the originator [i.e., the creator], the firstborn out from among the dead, in order that He might become in all things himself the One who is pre-eminent,

Jesus is supreme over the moral, newly created Church. He inspires, rules, and guides His Body with His sustaining power, being the mainspring of its activity, the centre of its unity, the seat of its life. He began the new spiritual life in the Church, being its originating power, by His resurrection. He came forth from among the dead as the first-born issues from the womb. While He is Head of the universe in virtue of His absolute and eternal Being, He became Head of the Church through His incarnation and resurrection.

because in Him [God] was well pleased that all the fullness be permanently at home.

Jesus is supreme over both creation and the Church, so that in all things He is pre-eminent. Jesus dwells absolutely in both, so the reconciliation and harmony of all things must be affected in Him. In Jesus dwells the sum total of the divine powers and attributes i.e. the fullness of God as deity is at home in Him permanently, as part of His essential Being and His very constitution.

And [God was well pleased] through His agency to reconcile all things to himself, having concluded peace through the blood of His cross, through Him, whether the things upon the earth or the things in the heavens.

Thus in Jesus there is an absolute and complete reconciliation of universal nature to God, affected through the mediation of Himself, the incarnate Word, since, of necessity, He is fully God, and He was also, of necessity, born into the world as a man. On the Cross, Jesus, by His death, bound together again harmoniously, a holy God, and sinful man who places his faith in the Saviour. God is reconciled in that justice has been satisfied at the Cross, while sinful man is reconciled in that his enmity towards God is changed to friendship, he having believed in Jesus. Also, the curse placed upon the material universe because of sin, will one day be removed through that same precious blood.

And you who were at one time those who were in a settled state of alienation, and hostile with respect to your intents in the sphere of your works which were pernicious, yet now He reconciled in the body of His flesh through His death, in order that He might present you holy and without blemish and unchargeable before His searching and penetrating gaze;

You were permanently estranged from God, actively in a state of enmity towards Him, which was exhibited in your outward behaviour. Only by putting to death a body composed of man's flesh, could a reconciliation between God and man be effected. Now Jesus can place us in the Father's presence, near to Him, and present us as a redeemed and now perfect child before Him, separated to God and from worldly defilement, without any defect and unreprovable. The Father looks down inside us, to the very core, and is pleased with what He sees.

assuming indeed that you are adhering to the Faith, having been placed upon a foundation with the present result that you are on that foundation, firmly established, and that you are not being shifted away from your hope held out by the good news which you heard, that good news which was proclaimed in all creation which is under Heaven, of which, I, Paul, became one who ministers.

I am writing to you members of the brotherhood at Colossae who are in the faith as you were taught it, and so are saved, not accepting that any supplements to the Gospel are needed to attain salvation. You were placed on the only, true foundation, the Lord Jesus, when you put your faith in Him, so that you are now grounded on Him alone. So respect this Foundation by Whom you are supported as a believer as being all sufficient, and go on in the inward strength which He supplies and which you now possess as a believer.

I now am rejoicing in my sufferings on your behalf, and on my part am filling up the things lacking of the afflictions of the Christ in my flesh for the sake of His Body which is the Church,

I am now in the midst of imprisonment and sufferings, after having become a minister of the Gospel, and having preached it. If ever I have been disposed to despair at my lot, if ever I have felt my cross almost too heavy to bear, yet now, when I contemplate the lavish wealth of God's mercy, when I see all the glory of bearing a part in this magnificent work, I who am not worthy to be a representative of Christ, my sorrow is turned to joy. I rejoice that I should be allowed to share and even supplement and fill up on my part His sufferings, by which I mean in His humiliation prior to the Cross, His suffering for righteousness' sake, His sufferings through exhausting service, and His heart-sufferings due to the opposition of, and persecution by, sinners. These sufferings were curtailed by reason of His limited time on earth, and need to be continued in His servants if the work of preaching the Word is to be carried on. These sufferings are for the sake of the assemblies of Christians everywhere who gather for worship.

of which I became a servant according to the stewardship of God which was given to me for you, to fulfil the word of God,

I am called to be a house steward, given the responsibility of administering the laws regulating the proper conduct of affairs in the household of the Church, preaching the Word of God and giving complete development to it, and seeing to it that it is guided rightly in its initial impact upon the world. I fully discharge this office of mine, so that the divine intent is fully carried out in the preaching of the Gospel to the Gentiles, no less than to the Jews.

the mystery which has been kept hidden from the ages and from the generations, but now was made known to His saints,

The Christian mysteries, paradoxically, are fully communicated to all. There are no secrets and no reserve in what I preach, simply the revealing of truths which were once hidden. For example, the free admission now of the Gentiles, on equal terms, to the privileges of the covenant that Jesus has made, by His blood shed on the Cross for all men. Before the beginning of the ages of the world, the counsel of God was ordained, but not concealed, since there were no humans from whom to conceal it. The concealment, the mystery, began from the beginning of the world, with the appearance of subjects to whom it could be a fact.

to whom God desired to make known in an experiential way what is the wealth of the glory of this mystery among the Gentiles, which is Christ in you, the hope of the glory,

It was by God's grace that the mystery was made known, not because of any merit in us. The richness of the mystery is that the dispensation of this grace is to Gentile as well as Jew, so not limited by national lines, or those of caste or race. Judaism was beggarly by comparison, since the treasures of that covenant sufficed only for a few. The mystery is Christ, revealed to the Gentiles and received by them, though the full glory of the inheritance of Christ in us is a hope, which hope will only be realised at Christ's coming.

whom we are constantly announcing, admonishing every man and instructing every man in every wisdom in order that we may present every man spiritually mature in Christ Jesus,

Our job is to present Jesus as Saviour to everyone, warning them to change their mind and heart so as to have faith in Him, and to then instruct them in the faith. I emphasise to you the universality of the Gospel; it is for every man, without exception. There are no secret truths that are known only to a select few, nor any exclusive religious observances to be followed. The fullest wisdom is offered to all alike, as in Christ, every believer is fully initiated, and the character of the teaching is as free from restriction as are the qualifications to be a recipient. Every believer is admitted to the faith as an eye-witness to its most profound secrets. Our aim is to fully instruct everyone with a view to their attaining a state of spiritual maturity and completeness.

to which end also I am constantly labouring to the point of exhaustion, engaging in a contest in which I am controlled by His energy which operates in me in power.

I work like an athlete in training who strives to contend in the games, but I have the superhuman power of God energising me. This power is increased in me, in and through exercising it. So my struggle is carried on not in proportion to my natural powers, but according to the mightily working energy of Christ within me.

For I desire you to know how great a conflict I am having in your behalf and in behalf of those in Laodicea, and as many as have not seen my face in the flesh,

This struggle and contending for you that I am engaged in is an inward one, as I wrestle and fight in prayer for you whom I have yet to meet.

in order that their hearts may be encouraged, having been knit together in the sphere of love and resulting in all the wealth of the full assurance of the understanding, resulting in an advanced and perfect experiential knowledge of the mystery of God, Christ, in whom are all the hidden treasures of the wisdom and knowledge.

Let love bind your hearts, as opposed to false teaching about who Jesus is, which tends to the creation of divisions amongst you. In Him are not just some, but all wisdom and knowledge. There are no other sources of these, so do not waste your time or be led astray looking for these things outside of Him. This wisdom and knowledge in Him is hidden only in the sense that it is not 'on the surface', but must be sought for earnestly, as men seek for hidden treasure. They are not matters of external observances and rituals, but are to be apprehended by deep and serious meditation.

This I am saying in order that no one may be leading you astray by false reasoning in the sphere of specious discourse.

So do not be led astray by those who speak of another knowledge, or of other mysteries. They reckon wrongly and would beguile you, to delude you and persuade you into error.

For if, as is the case, I am in fact absent in my flesh, yet I am with you in my spirit, rejoicing and beholding your orderly array and the solid front of your faith in Christ.

Though not with you physically, I see you in my spirit, and am satisfied with what I see, that you are lined up and ready to go into battle for the faith, united, together, and so I am caused to rejoice over you.

In the same manner, therefore, as you received the Christ, Jesus, the Lord, in Him be constantly ordering your behaviour, having been rooted with the present result that you are firmly established, and constantly being built up in Him and constantly being established with reference to the Faith, even as you were instructed, abounding in it in the sphere of thanksgiving.

You received by instruction the teaching regarding the Person and work of Jesus, so accordingly, conduct yourselves in life as you were taught. So I am saying to you; from an orderly starting point, walk in such a way so as to build yourselves up strong and abundantly in the faith, building within the sphere of Him, because the whole upbuilding of the Church proceeds within the compass of His personality, life and power.

Be ever on your guard lest there shall be someone who leads you astray through his philosophy, even futile deceit, which is according to the tradition of men, according to the rudimentary teachings of the world, and not according to Christ,

Keep a watchful eye ever open to imminent events, as there is a serious danger you could be carried off as booty and as a prey to false teaching. It is false as it is mere vain, deceitful speculation, futile and devoid of truth, and fruitless, comprising practices of abstinence, ceremonies, diets, washings, initiatory rites and so on, that have been handed down from generation to generation. These things are all without effect, so will not succeed, as they are to do with material, external things, and not the Person of Christ.

because in Him there is continuously and permanently at home all the fullness of absolute deity in bodily fashion.

Christ is the fountain-head of all spiritual life. The fullness of the Godhead, being the totality of the divine powers and attributes, dwelt in Him before His incarnation, indeed dwelt in Him from all ages and to all ages. That fullness dwells now in His glorified humanity in Heaven in a bodily way i.e. He is clothed with a body, a human body. Before His incarnation, He was in the form of God. The human body was taken out by Him in the fullness of time when He became in the likeness of men, when the Word became flesh. The fullness of the Godhead dwelt in His Person from His birth to His ascension. He carried His human body with Him into Heaven, and in His glorified body now and ever dwells the fullness of the Godhead. God's power and majesty can be seen in the created universe and in His works, but He can only be personally known by the revelation of Himself in His Son. Jesus is not merely One Who is gilded or lit up for a season by rays of divine glory, with a splendour not His own. He is absolute and perfect God.

And you are in Him, having been completely filled full with the present result that you are in a state of fullness, in Him who is the Head of every principality and authority,

In Jesus dwells the fullness. Being in Him, you are filled, your fullness coming from His fullness, transfused into you by virtue of your incorporation in Him, so that you find the satisfaction of your every spiritual want. It is not that you become divine yourself, but that you share His holiness and righteousness, having been born anew in His image. So there is no need to seek mystical angelic powers, as all you need you have in Christ.

in whom you were circumcised by a circumcision not effected by hand, in the putting off and away from yourselves the body of the flesh in the circumcision of Christ,

You do not need to be circumcised in the flesh, as you have received the circumcision of the heart. This circumcision is an inward work, wrought by the Holy Spirit, depriving of power the whole corrupt, carnal nature, and is a work of Christ Himself. The old clothing of the depraved sinful nature has been stripped off of you and laid aside, so that you are no longer under the constant control of that nature, it having been rendered inoperative by this spiritual circumcision, so that it now only has the power that you allow it to have. Christ's circumcision enables you, by the Holy Spirit, to live in a physical body and be dominated by the divine nature.

having been entombed with Him in the placing into [Christ by the Holy Spirit], in which act of placing into [Christ] you were also raised with Him through your faith in the effectual working energy of the God who raised Him out from among the dead.

When you believed in Jesus and identified with Him in His death, this broke the power of indwelling sin in you. When you identified with Him in His resurrection, the divine nature was imparted to you. So were you resurrected from your sinful state into divine life.

And you being dead with reference to your trespasses and the uncircumcision of your flesh, He gave life together with Him having in grace forgiven you all your trespasses,

You were physically alive but spiritually dead, due to your wrong doings and deviations from the truth. Your lives were not upright, being devoid of the life of God and activated by a totally depraved nature. Your outward uncircumcision, in a way, symbolised your unchastened carnal mind. But when Jesus was raised from the dead, in the mind and purpose of God you believers were identified with Jesus in His resurrection and potentially given divine life, a potential realised when you put your faith in Him as your Saviour.

having obliterated the hand-written document consisting of ordinances, the one [which was] against us, which was directly opposed to us, and He removed it out of the midst with the result that it is no longer there, having nailed it to the cross;

We had broken not only the law of Moses, but also the moral law of God in general. We consequently had a legally binding bill of debt against us which none of us could ever repay, and which was hostile towards us; accusing us and revealing our guilt to us, but giving us neither the inclination nor the power to do what was necessary to pay the debt, but rather threatening and giving us foretastes of penalty and pain, first setting the standard, then accusing, and finally avenging. This bill was perpetually before us our whole life, but Jesus took it away from our sight and, moreover, abolished it, paying the debt in full by His death on the Cross.

having stripped off and away from himself the principalities and authorities, He boldly made an example of them, leading them in a triumphal procession in it.

Jesus, after His death on the Cross, needed to present Himself at the Mercy Seat in Heaven in His bloodless body glorified, as the great High Priest, thus completing the atonement for human sin. To do this He had to pass through the kingdoms of Satan in the earth's atmosphere. The demons in these kingdoms in the air attempted to oppose Jesus' passage, but He stripped them off and away from Himself and took them captive, leading them in triumph in His ascension as He left the tomb.

Stop therefore allowing anyone to be sitting in judgement upon you in eating or drinking or in the matter of a feast day or a new moon, or a Sabbath day, which things are a shadow of those things about to come. But the body belongs to Christ.

So do not go back to trying to obey the demands of that bill of debt that Jesus has now abolished. Do not listen to those who would take you to task over eating and drinking, whether to partake or to abstain of wine and of meat, or whether to observe the new moon festival with its blowing of trumpets, special sacrifices and feasting, so carefully and precisely observed as to its timing, and the weekly Sabbath. These were but a preceding shadow of the real substance that has now appeared, being the Christian economy, derived from Him, and only realised through union with Him.

Let no one as a judge declare you unworthy of a reward, taking delight in a self-imposed humility and worship of the angels, scrutinising minutely the things he has seen, being futilely puffed up by the mind of the flesh, and not holding fast the Head, out from whom all the Body, through the instrumentality of the joints and ligaments being constantly supplied with nourishment and being constantly compacted together, increases with the increase wrought by God.

False teachers, in their vain enthusiasm, would actually deprive you of your reward at the Judgement Seat of Christ, should you allow them to lead you astray. They would have you believe that you cannot approach God directly. Self-conscious humility has no value, and the teaching of angel worship is a perversion of the truth. They boastfully talk of their imaginings and supposed visions, claiming to be guided by higher reason, but in fact it is carnal, nothing more than the mind of the flesh. In following these teachers, rather than growing to a spiritually higher order, you would rather loosen your hold on Christ, so preventing any spiritual growth at all, since He, as the Head of His Body, is the very channel of spiritual life, and has a constant awareness and sensitivity to all of the parts in His Body, and to all of their relationships to each other. When we lose fellowship with the Head we suffer instant paralysis in our spiritual life and service. Jesus inputs life and energy to all His Body, preserving unity and order within it. He is the source of all communications to His Body, but the channels of communication are the different members of His Body in their relation one to another. By this two-fold means of contact and attachment, nutriment is diffused to the entire Body and structural unity attained, but these are only intermediate processes, the end result is growth. In this growth the finite is truly united with the Infinite, this uniting being the yearning of the human heart and that for which the human intellect is feeling.

In view of the fact that you died with Christ from the rudimentary things of the world, why, as living in the world, are you subjecting yourselves to ordinances [such as], do not begin to touch, neither begin to taste, nor begin to handle, which things are all destined for corruption in their consumption; [ordinances] which are according to the precepts and teachings of men, which things as a class have a reputation for wisdom in a self-made, self-imposed worship and [an affected, hypocritical] humility and an unsparing and severe treatment of the body, [ordinances which are] not of any value as a remedy against the indulgence of the flesh?

You died with Christ at the Cross so are separated from all these worldly teachings. To follow them would be inconsistent with what you were first taught. You died to your old relations; to sin, to law and legalism, to guilt, and to the world which is alienated from and hostile to God and would seek to seduce you from God. So do not rekindle any of these relations. Avoidance of oil, wine, meat, strangers, religious inferiors and so on, brings no spiritual benefit. The very using of these ordinances brings destruction. These are forms of worship that men have devised and prescribed for themselves, so are contrary to the contents and nature of the faith which ought to be directed to Christ. They appeal to men as being indications of superior wisdom and piety, but they are not of any value to remedy indulgence of the flesh.

In view of the fact, therefore, that you were raised with Christ, the things above be constantly seeking, where Christ is, on the right hand of God, seated.

You were spiritually resurrected out from among the spiritually dead, from a state of spiritual death into that of spiritual life, actuated for you when you placed your faith in Jesus as your Saviour. So seek heavenly things now, from that higher place where a glorified Man, Himself God the Son, is seated, His work of salvation being finished.

The things above be constantly setting your mind upon, not the things on the earth; for you died, and your life has been hidden with Christ in God.

Whenever the Christ is made visible, our life, then also you with Him shall be manifested in glory.

Direct your mind so that you not only seek Heaven but also think Heaven, so that not only your practical striving but also your inward impulse and disposition are directed at things above. You have been separated from your former life, and from everything of an evil nature that pertained to it. Your new spiritual life is no longer in the sphere of the earthly and the sensual, but is with the life of the risen Christ, Who is unseen, in union with God. Hence we are in union with God in Christ i.e. our life is not just shared with Christ, it is Christ. This life will be made visible when Jesus appears from Heaven, with all His glorified saints, in glory, His manifestation including the manifestation of those who are one with Him. Then the veil which now shrouds your higher life from others will be withdrawn, so that the world which now persecutes, despises and ignores, will be blinded with the dazzling glory of the revealing of Christ and His Body of believers.

By a once-for-all act, and at once, put to death your members which are upon the earth; fornication, impurity, depraved passion, wicked craving, and avarice which is of such a nature as to be idolatry; because of which things there comes the wrath of God; in the sphere of which things also you ordered your behaviour at one time when you were living in them.

Carry out the principle of death that is in Christ and kill everything that is mundane and carnal in your being. The heavenly life in Christ has the power to kill the whole carnal man, in contradistinction to following a code of numerous minute ordinances, striving to do the same but in vain. In salvation, God has broken the power of the evil nature over your physical body. Now you are charged with the responsibility of maintaining that state of liberation in your Christian walk. As the behests of the evil nature come before you, you are to put them to death by refusing to obey them, by the power of the Holy Spirit Who is in you. So have nothing to do with illicit sexual intercourse, with moral uncleanness, with lustful, luxurious, profligate living, or with a greedy desire to have more, being the worship of Mammon. At one time you did these things. Your entire lives were circumscribed by these sins, so that not a ray of light from God, not a single good thing in the sight of God, penetrated that circle. You were living a life of total depravity.

But now put away once for all, and at once, also all these things; a habitual, revengeful anger, violent fits of anger, malignity, slander, obscene speech out of your mouth.

Also strip yourselves of these vices; a settled habitual anger, a boiling, angry agitation of the feelings, ill will, a desire to injure, speech that maligns another's good name, and crude, foul words.

Stop lying to one another, having stripped off and away from yourselves and for your own advantage the old, antiquated, outworn, decrepit, useless man [that person you were before you were saved] with his evil practices, and having clothed yourselves with the new man [the person you are after you are saved] who is constantly being renewed, with a resulting advanced and perfect experiential knowledge which is according to the image of the One who created him; in which state there cannot be Greek or Jew, circumcision or uncircumcision, Barbarian, Scythian, slave, or free man, but Christ is all things and in all things.

You have carried over the sin of lying into the new life. Stop doing this, since true knowledge and all truth is in Christ. You are a new creation. Your spiritual man in your heart is created after God's image, analogous to the primal man's creation in the beginning of the world. You have been recreated in God's image and your subsequent life must be a deepening of this image that has been stamped upon you, so put on the new man and fully embrace the life to which you are called. As we all grow into Him, Christ, it is impossible for human distinctions to remain. These have disappeared in our new life together and we are all one, regardless of national, ritual, intellectual or social diversities. Christ has dispossessed and obliterated all distinctions of religious prerogative and intellectual pre-eminence and social caste, He has substituted Himself for all these, occupying the whole sphere of human life, and He permeates all its developments.

Put on therefore as your spiritual apparel, as chosen-out ones of God, saints and beloved ones, a heart of compassion, bearing with one another and forgiving one another if anyone has a matter of complaint against anyone. Even as and in the degree that the Lord forgave you, in the same manner also you forgive.

Become so possessed of the mind of Christ, purposing in thought, feeling, and action to resemble Him, that you reproduce the life He lived. Do this now. See that your manner of life is befitting the kind of life the elect of God should live. You stand in His grace, loved self-sacrificially by God, and now and always loved by Him. Have a gentle, gracious disposition, with a humble opinion, each one of you, of yourself, accepting God's dealings with you as good. Out of this attitude of meekness before God, also have this same attitude in the face of men, even evil men, knowing that the insults and injuries which they may inflict are permitted and employed by God for the chastening and purifying of His elect. Be patient under the ill-treatment of others, and show yourselves gracious, kind, and benevolent to grant forgiveness, to the degree that He forgave you, being full forgiveness.

And upon all these, put on divine and self-sacrificial love which is a binding factor of completeness.

On top of all, clothe yourselves with self-sacrificial love, as this will hold all other virtues in place, so that perfection is the result i.e. full-grown maturity in Christ. This love is to permeate all that you do, so that it fuses with the other virtues as it binds them together into one harmonious whole and makes them usable.

And the peace of Christ, let it be acting as umpire in your hearts, into which also you were called in one Body. And be constantly thankful persons.

Jesus left tranquillity of heart as a legacy to His disciples. Whenever we are faced with a conflict of motives or impulses or reasons, this peace steps in to decide which is to prevail. As members of the One Body of Christ we are also to enjoy peace, not just in our individual hearts, but amongst the members of the Body in our relations one to another, so peace in the sphere of oneness. Disunion in the Body is incompatible with the peace of individual members.

The word of Christ, let it be continually at home in you in abundance; with every wisdom teaching and admonishing each other by means of psalms, hymns, spiritual songs, with the grace singing in your hearts to God. And all, whatever you do in the sphere of word or deed, do all in the Name of the Lord Jesus, constantly giving thanks to God the Father through Him.

Be so yielded to Christ's words, those spoken by Him on earth and also as He speaks through us new covenant writers, that they are at home in you. Let them have unrestricted freedom in your life. You need to develop a good knowledge of His Word, since the Holy Spirit uses it, to the extent that you know it, as He talks to you and guides your life, so the more you know the Word, the more efficiently He can talk to you. Teach and warn each other through the medium of spiritual verse, whether musically accompanied or not, whether written down or spontaneously given. Sing with thanksgiving and with the grace supplied by the Holy Spirit to your yielded hearts, in a way that glorifies God, not your own talents.

Wives, be constantly subjecting yourselves with implicit obedience to your husbands as you ought to do in the Lord. Husbands, be loving your wives with a divine love which impels you to deny yourselves for their benefit, and stop being bitter and harsh to them. Children, be obeying your parents in all things, for this is commendable in the Lord. Fathers, stop irritating your children, lest they become disheartened. Slaves, be constantly obedient in all things to your human masters, not with eye-service as men-pleasers, but with an undivided heart, fearing the Lord.

Wives, you should have each been submitting to your husband as an obligation from the time you entered into the Christian life, which is a self-evident obligation, being arrived at from reasoning regarding the proper relation of the wife to the husband in salvation in Christ. Husbands, you are each to love your wife self-sacrificially, by the power of the Holy Spirit, submitting your own wishes in the interest of the well-being of your wife. Children, you can each please the members of the Body by submitting to your parents. Fathers, do not be too exacting with your children, causing them to be broken in spirit and to lose heart, rather submit any feelings of irritation or anger to the need to encourage them as you should. Slaves, though you are now free in Christ, nevertheless submit to your master for the sake of the constitution of society, until such time that Christian principles on slavery can be asserted successfully. Determine to please your Lord, Jesus, by conscientious performance of the tasks set you by your earthly master.

Whatever you are doing, from your soul do it diligently as to the Lord and not to men, knowing that from the Lord you will receive back the just recompense which consists of the inheritance. The [heavenly] Master, Christ, you are serving. For the one who is doing wrong will get back that which he did which is wrong. And there is no showing of partiality. Masters, that which is just and equitable be rendering on your part to your slaves, knowing that you also have a Master in Heaven.

Work at your tasks as though you are doing them at the request of Jesus Himself. Your earthly master may well reward you for your service, but Jesus will reward you justly, being the heavenly inheritance you will receive. If as a slave you do wrong, you shall be punished, but the master who does wrong will also not be excused, for with the Lord there is no respect of persons. In society you slaves have no rights, but in Christ you are treated with justice and equity, and your claims are as real as the claims of your master. Masters, you are each to treat your slaves with an attitude of brotherly equality, submitting yourself to the Christian truth that in Jesus there is neither bond nor free.

Be giving constant attention to prayer, constantly vigilant in it with thanksgiving, praying at the same time also for us, that God would open for us a door for the Word, that we may speak the mystery of the Christ, because of which [mystery] also I have been bound, in order that I may make it plain as it is necessary in the nature of the case for me to speak.

Persevere in prayer, and be in constant readiness to pray, lest through being remiss or lazy some destructive calamity overtake you. Remain awake and alert as you pray, remembering also Timothy, Epaphras and myself, asking that an opportunity for preaching the Gospel would arise, and for announcing the unification of Jew and Gentile in the Body of Christ, the Church. I am still bound in prison, twenty-four hours a day, for declaring these things, but long to be freed so that I may resume doing so once again.

In wisdom be ordering your behaviour towards those on the outside, buying up for yourselves the strategic, opportune time.

Be wise in your relations to unbelievers so as not to give them an unfavourable impression of the Gospel. Make wise and sacred use of every opportunity for doing good, using your zeal and well-doing as currency, by which you may buy the moment, making it your own.

Your word, let it always be with graciousness, with salt thoroughly seasoned, to the end that you know how it is necessary in the nature of the case to answer everyone.

Be pleasant, sweet, and courteous in your conversation, also wise, so as to favourably impress unbelievers and give flavour to each discourse, as salt improves the flavour of food to the palate, and renders it wholesome.

All the things that relate to me, Tychicus will make known to you, the beloved brother and faithful servant and my fellow bondslave in the Lord, whom I am sending to you for this same purpose, in order that you may come to know the things concerning us and in order that he may encourage your hearts; [sending him] with Onesimus the faithful and beloved brother who is one of you All things to you they will make known, the things here.

Tychicus, who is bringing copies of a letter from me to the principal assemblies in proconsular Asia, will also visit you as you are near to Laodicea, to bring this letter to you. Onesimus you once knew as a slave, but now as a brother, no more dishonest and faithless but now trustworthy, no more an object of contempt but now of love.

There greet you Aristarchus, my fellow prisoner, and Mark, the cousin of Barnabas, concerning whom you received orders; if he comes to you, receive him, and Joshua, the one called Justus, who are of the circumcision. These are my only fellow workers with respect to the kingdom of God who are of such a character as to have become a solace to me.

Aristarchus' friendship with me has resulted in him being a prisoner here with me. Mark, though once he abandoned me, I commend to your kindness. Joshua was devoted to the law, being a convert from Judaism, as was Aristarchus. These three brothers are steadfast in their allegiance to me, and bring me comfort, consolation and encouragement, so that they are a medicine to me.

There greets you Epaphras, the one who is one of your number, a bondslave of Christ Jesus, always contending on your behalf in his prayers, to the effect that you may stand fast, spiritually mature ones, and those who have been brought to the place of full assurance in everything willed by God; for I bear witness to him that he has much toil on your behalf and on behalf of those in Laodicea, and those in Hierapolis.

Epaphras, who brought the Gospel message to you, has served me exceptionally. He has wrestled inwardly and outwardly, with dangers, and difficulties antagonistic to the Gospel, on your behalf, that you might become full-grown and carry through to the end everything in the will of God for each of you, being fully convinced of His purpose in you.

There greet you Luke, the physician, the beloved one, and Demas.

Luke is my personal physician and I have great gratitude for his services as such, as well as his being a companion and friend to me. Demas, though with me now, is about to forsake me it seems.

Greet the brethren in Laodicea, and Nymphas, and the [local] assembly [which meets] in her home.

Extend my greetings to the assembly of the saints that meet in Nymphas' home for worship.

And when this letter is read in your presence, see to it that also it is read in the assembly of the Laodiceans, and the letter from Laodicea, see to it that you also read it.

Make sure now that you also read my letter to the assemblies in Asia, of which there are copies in Laodicea and Ephesus, and that those assemblies also read this letter.

And say to Archippus, Be ever keeping a watchful eye upon the ministry which you received in the Lord, that you discharge it fully.

Archippus has an important calling, similar to that of Timothy. It is a serious calling, so he should give it his full attention and energy.

The greeting by my hand, the hand of Paul. Be remembering my bonds. The grace be with you.

I have dictated this letter, due to the eye disease I contracted in Pamphylia and which worsened in Galatia, and which induces semi-blindness in me as well as making me repulsive to look at. But I write this sentence myself so that you may know that this letter is genuinely from me and is not a forgery. I am a prisoner in chains, I who care so deeply for you and love you, and who am anxious for you to remain true to the doctrines you were taught from me, and for you to have a deep regard for my words to you. Remember me with affection and pray for me.

From Paul to Asia, being the copy for Ephesus

Paul, an ambassador of Christ Jesus through the will of God, to the saints, the ones who are [in Ephesus], namely, believing ones in Christ Jesus. Grace to you and peace from God our Father and the Lord Jesus Christ.

I am writing to you as a divinely appointed ambassador of Jesus, the Anointed of God, the Person chosen from the Godhead to be the anointed Prophet, Priest and King, so as to accomplish the purposes of God in the plan of salvation. I am writing to you who are set apart for God, having been elected by Him to salvation, taking you out of the first Adam and placing you into the last Adam, in view of which there is a demand that you separate yourselves from the world system of evil, from everything that would interfere in the least with your worship and service that is due to Him to Whom you have been set apart. I am writing to you, true and steadfast members of the brotherhood of believers at Ephesus, though this same letter is also being sent to other assemblies, who have put your trust in Jesus, in that you have taken yourselves out of your own keeping and entrusted yourselves into the keeping of the Lord Jesus. I bring to you a message in light of God's dealings with us; we were His bitter enemies, undeserving of salvation, deserving punishment for sins, but He has given free-heartedly to us out of His bounty, in an unlimited way, offering without any expectation of return, His salvation, something which we could never earn but which we can only accept by faith in Jesus Christ as our personal Saviour, being procured by His infinite personal sacrifice at the Cross where He poured out His precious blood. Such is grace... Having been so set apart, He has now joined Himself to us and is living in harmony with us, since Jesus concluded peace through His blood shed on the Cross, allowing the righteous and holy God to bestow mercy upon us believing sinners without violating His justice, and so binding us together again as father and child. Now the law of God has nothing against us and we can look up into the Father's face unafraid and unashamed. Such is peace. So we have an untroubled, undisturbed tranquillity and wellbeing produced in our hearts as we yield to the Holy Spirit and are intelligently conscious of and dependent upon His ministry for us. This grace and peace come from the Father and from Jesus, since both co-eternally possess the same essence of deity, being uniquely related to each other and being of the same rank, the Father having adopted you as children, Jesus being your Lord as Head of the Church, having won the right to your loving obedience and honour.

May the God and Father of our Lord Jesus Christ be eulogised, the One who conferred benefactions upon us in the sphere of every spiritual blessing in the heavenly places in Christ, even as He selected us out for himself in Him before the foundations of the universe were laid, to be holy ones and without blemish before His searching, penetrating gaze;

Always speak well of the Father, He is of the greatest repute. In Jesus' humanity, the Father is His God. Note that the Persons of the Godhead recognise each other as co-equal deity and address each other as God. Also the Father is Jesus' own, private, peculiar, individual Father, in a different way to that in which He is the Father of believers... When God blesses us, it is in deed and positive effect, when we bless Him, it is in word and thought. He blesses us with blessings produced and given to us by the Holy Spirit as He works upon the human spirit, being blessings of grace and of a divine order, for example the assurance of immortality, the promise of the resurrection, the inheritance of the Kingdom of Heaven, and the privilege of adoption. These blessings having their seat where God Himself is and where Christ reigns, we will enjoy in Heaven, and even some of the blessings we are enjoying on earth now. These blessings are in Christ, having their ground and reason in Christ, so that apart from Him they could have no relation to us i.e. they are ours by reason of our being in Him as our Representative and Head. In Jesus lay the reason that God has now blessed us with every spiritual blessing, since Jesus' act of redemption is the meritorious cause of this divine bestowal of blessing. The blessing proceeded out from His divine election, and took effect in accordance with that, having its foundation in eternity, so neither an incidental thing nor an afterthought of God... We were chosen by God for Himself, for the purpose of being channels through which the knowledge of salvation might be brought to the rest of mankind, so that those who put their trust in Jesus as Saviour might be saved. It is not that any are rejected or refused salvation, or that we have any prominence over or preference to others not already chosen. So the saving work of the Godhead is; the Father selects out from among mankind in the setting apart work of the Holy Spirit, the Spirit bringing them to the act of faith in Jesus, which faith is answered by the act of Jesus cleansing him in His precious blood and conferring His righteousness, holiness and life upon him. God's choice was made even before He threw down a harmonious universe into space, speaking it materially into existence where it had not been in existence before, so an eternal choice, a determination of the divine Mind before all time. Thus the name of every Christian is as eternal as God is, for God has held each individual in His heart for salvation as long as He has been in existence, and that salvation will extend through time and into and throughout the eternity that is after time ceases. Once saved we are forever children of God, eternally placed by the Father in Christ, where now the Holy Spirit sees right down into our innermost being, through all of the superficialities, hypocrisies and shams of our human existence. He is not looking for faults, but rather contemplates, with satisfaction and delight, the reflection of the holiness and spotlessness of the Lord Jesus in our new character, which character makes us near to Him and dear to Him, and gives us a foretaste of our future standing, before the throne of God, when we will be similarly contemplated by the Father.

in love having previously marked us out to be placed as adult sons through the intermediate agency of Jesus Christ for himself according to that which seemed good in His heart's desire,

God's motive in foreordaining us and so determining our destiny was due to His love. He took us as believing sinners, regenerated us to make us His children, and legally placed us as adult sons, joint-heirs of God with Christ, so inheriting jointly with Jesus all that He possesses as an heir of God the Father by virtue of His Sonship and His work on the Cross. This, and our being conformed to the image of Jesus, are the objects of God's predestination. Predestination follows election, not in point of time, for the acts were simultaneous, but in point of divine economy or logical order. As He sees it, our adoption and being made holy, and how and by what means this should be brought about, because it could only be thus brought about, is all of one essence. Jesus was the intermediate agent of the Father to bring to fruition His purpose of placing believers as adult sons, through His work on the Cross that satisfied the just requirements of God's law which we broke. This made it possible for the Father to bestow mercy on believing sinners on the basis of justice satisfied, enabling Him to lavish His love on us as His sons, that He might be glorified in saving us and glorified as we worship and serve Him. This was all done in grace, being His sovereign, unmerited acts, not due to any desert in us or anything outside God Himself, but acts of His own pure goodness, originating wholly in the freedom of His own thoughts and loving counsel.

resulting in praise of the glory of His grace which He freely bestowed upon us in the Beloved,

Glory is an attribute of grace, in which grace grandly and resplendently displays itself. Praise is called forth from the children of God by this divine glory which thus appears in grace. In praising God for what He does, we learn to praise Him for what He is. See the splendour of the mystery of redemption; our adoption results in the glorious nature, the brightness, majesty, kindliness and beauty of His grace, causing us to praise it, it being beyond description and infinite, and ourselves being its objects. He graced us with this grace in Jesus, the One the Father has always loved with an absolute love, being a permanent attitude on His part. This grace could not operate in our salvation apart from the atoning death of Jesus, for God is not only a loving God, but a righteous and just God Who cannot pass by sin, but must require that it be paid for. Only then can He manifest His grace.

in whom we are having our redemption through His blood, the putting away of our trespasses according to the wealth of His grace

We have been purchased by Jesus. He bought us for Himself in the slave market of sin by His blood poured out at the Cross to make us His bondslaves. Now we are His possession forever, never to be put up for sale in any slave market ever again. We are now set free from the guilt and power of sin, finally to be set free from the presence of sin at the Rapture. Like a prisoner that has been pardoned and set free, we have been released from sins, from our lapses and deviations, as if they had never been committed, hence there is now no penalty to pay. So sinners are lost now not because they sin, but because they have not availed themselves of the salvation which is in Christ Jesus. Sin has now been put away judicially, with the guilt and penalty remitted, but this redemption needs to be individually received by personally accepting Jesus as Saviour by faith in what He did for them on the Cross. God's forgiveness is complete and unchanging since it is controlled by His plenteous, abundant, indeed infinite, grace.

which He caused to superabound to us in the sphere of every wisdom and understanding,

His grace to us is over and above measure, more than enough to save us and to keep us saved for time and eternity, and is available for every sinner who comes to God in Jesus. This grace is not only directed towards us, but grips us in its irresistible working, drawing and bringing us into salvation. This grace operates within the circle of the highest and noblest wisdom, being God's supreme intelligence. God's wisdom and prudence is bestowed upon us recipients of His grace, so that we can have insight into the true nature of things, His gift of spiritual discernment allowing us access to the deep things of the divine counsel and the divine revelation.

having made known to us the mystery of His will according to that which seemed good to Him, which good thing He purposed in himself,

This abounding of His grace was in His making known to us His secret purposes and counsels in and for His Kingdom. Previously His will, which comes from His wisdom and His heart of love, was not understood, as it was not revealed, but now revealed, it is not difficult to be understood by any Spirit-enlightened believer. God's purposed, determined, gracious will is controlled by His delight, pleasure and satisfaction in blessing us, in His seeking that which would contribute most to our well-being and prosperity i.e. what He does for us is dictated by what is good for us.

with respect to an administration of the completion of the epochs of time to bring back again to their original state all things in the Christ, the things in the heavens and the things on the earth, in Him,

The purpose of God is with regard to His administration and management of the completion of the seasons of human history i.e. with a view to His plan for His dealings with humanity, once all that has been ripening through long ages is mature and complete and so comes to a close. We now live in the Age of Grace, it having replaced the Age of Law, the next season being the Messianic Kingdom. Subsequent to that age, at its completion, having judged all lost human beings, fallen angels and demons, God will gather together again in one, all created beings and things, in and around Christ, things in Heaven and things on earth, in perfect unity in Him. The material universe will be brought back to its pristine state, comprising a new Heaven and a new earth, in which saved men shall dwell in righteousness and glory. Then the endless eternal ages will begin.

in whom also we were made an inheritance, having been previously marked out according to the purpose of the One who operates all things according to the counsel of His will,

God's purpose was also fulfilled in us in that we were made His own, His heritage, His portion and possession. The God of the chosen is the God of the universe, so our being made His heritage and possession has behind it both the sovereignty and the efficiency of His will. It is this will that energises and is operative in absolutely all things, being governed by a reasoned, intelligent and deliberate process, this reasoning being proper to the Highest Mind and Most Perfect Moral Nature, and being the free determination of the divine will.

with a view to our being to the praise of His glory who had previously placed our hope in the Christ,

Our being made God's heritage is so that, in our position in Christ, we Jewish Christians are to the praise of God's glory, so that through us His glory is set forth.

in whom also, as for you, having heard the word of the truth, the good news of your salvation, in whom also having believed, you were sealed with the Spirit of the promise, the Holy Spirit,

And you Gentiles, having believed, were sealed and marked with the Spirit of the promise, permanently, showing that everything is in order for you to be presented to the Father, and that no one can interfere with your salvation. The transaction is complete and now you are owned and eternally secure.

who is the token payment of our inheritance guaranteeing the full payment of all, looking forward to the redemption of the possession which is being preserved with a view to the praise of His glory.

The Holy Spirit is deposited in us as earnest money, being God's part payment in the salvation He gives us believing sinners, so guaranteeing full delivery of all parts of the salvation to be given to us; the removal of guilt and sin's penalty and the bestowal of His righteousness, Jesus Christ, on our putting our faith in Him as Saviour, the progressive work of the Spirit in our lives to eliminate sin from our experience and to produce His own fruit, and the transforming of our present bodies into perfect, sinless, deathless bodies. So the Holy Spirit's indwelling us is God's earnest money, guaranteeing to us the future glorification of our bodies, our souls and spirits having already become the recipients of His saving grace. Until that time, God preserves us for Himself, in readiness for the Rapture, when our bodies will also experience His saving grace, resulting in praise of His glory.

On account of this, I also, having heard of the faith in the Lord Jesus which is among you and of your love to all the saints, do not cease giving thanks for you as I constantly make mention of you in my prayers,

In view of all of this, particularly of your being sealed with the Spirit, I pray for your day by day faith, as exercised in Jesus, for daily living, and am ever thankful to hear that you are indeed practicing this faith, as exhibited in your self-sacrificial love toward all believers, that love being produced by the Holy Spirit in hearts that are yielded to Him.

that the God of our Lord Jesus Christ, the Father of the glory, might give to you a spirit of wisdom and revelation in the sphere of a full knowledge of Him,

As I said before, Jesus, in His humanity, worships and is obedient to the Father, to Whom glory belongs... I ask that the Father give you a special gift of wisdom and revelation, as an outcome of your spirit being indwelt and energised by His Spirit, this gift being within the knowledge of Him. I desire gifts for you that are of a spiritual order and that enhance your acquaintance with God Himself.

the eyes of your heart being in an enlightened state with a view to your knowing what is the hope of His calling, what is the wealth of the glory of His inheritance in the saints,

This gift of wisdom and revelation will enhance your spiritual understanding, reasoning and intelligence, and this enlightening will be a permanent work of the Holy Spirit in your spirit, so that you will know three things; firstly what is our hope, being an assured attitude of mind about our expectation as Christians, secondly what is God's inheritance in us, being a knowledge of how precious and valuable we are in His eyes, our being part of His wealth and dearer to Him than anything else in His creation.

and what is the superabounding greatness of His inherent power to us who are believing ones as measured by the operative energy of the manifested strength of His might, which might was operative in the Christ when He raised Him from among the dead and seated Him at His right hand in the heavenly places,

And thirdly what is the exceeding greatness of His power towards us who believe, being beyond measure, it working in reference to our salvation, not only in the future but also now as it ministers to our spiritual needs. This power is of His inherent natural ability, and manifests the strength of His might in its exercise, as when it operated in Christ in raising Him from the dead and then making Him to sit down at His side.

over and above every government and authority and power and lordship and every name that is constantly being named, not only in this age, but also in the one about to come.

Jesus is exalted far above the holy angels and all earthly and heavenly authorities. Whatever name can be uttered, He is above it, both in the present state of things and in the future state of things.

And all things He put in subjection under His feet, and Him He gave as Head over all things to the Church, which is of such a nature as to be His Body, the fullness of the One who constantly is filling all things with all things.

Following Christ's being made to sit at the Father's right hand, all things will be made to submit to Him so that He has absolute dominion consequent to His being exalted. Jesus is also the Father's love gift to the Church of saved believers, who are subject to Him and animated by Him as His power operates in the Church. So the Church is not merely an institution ruled by Jesus, but a Society which is in vital connection with Him, having the source of its life in Him, sustained and directed by His power, by which power He works. Christ's Spirit is in it and it embraces all believers, existing wherever any such are found. It is filled with God, with His life and presence, His power and energy, His agency and graces, His gifts and riches. His fullness abides in it and is exemplified by it. Such is the Church... The whole system of things, made by Christ, also having their grounding, order and continuance in Him, is filled with the material universe itself and all the things that comprise its fullness.

And you being dead with reference to your trespasses and sins, He made alive;

This same power that raised Jesus is applied to you believers, causing you to live, giving you life and making you alive with His divine life, where previously you were spiritually dead; you were inactive with respect to doing right, but being given up to sins and deviations from truth and wanderings from the right path, always missing the mark and going wrong and failing in your purpose, being energised by the totally depraved nature, so separated from God and His life.

in the sphere of which trespasses and sins at one time you ordered your behaviour as dominated by the spirit of the age in this world system, as dominated by the leader of the authority of the lower atmosphere, the source also of the spirit that is now operating in the sons of the disobedience

Previously you walked about and conducted yourselves within the circle of trespasses and sins, all your thoughts, words and deeds being ensphered by sin. Not one of your acts ever got outside this circle of sin, but, when viewed from above, your whole life was lived in total depravity. Your behaviour was dominated and controlled by the course of this world system with all its atmosphere of wicked thoughts and opinions that are alienated from and hostile to God, since it is a system headed up and ruled by Satan and his demons, with the unsaved as his slaves, whom he preys upon. His kingdom is in the lower, denser atmosphere where human beings are, as opposed to the rarer atmosphere above the mountain tops. Satan is the prince of the spirit that works in the children of disobedience, whose character is also to be impersuasible and uncompliant, so having a tendency to evil in thought and deed, in particular in the original sin of Adam i.e. it is the spirit of the unsaved. Satan dominates and controls this spirit in man.

among whom also we all ordered our behaviour in the sphere of the cravings of our evil nature, continually practicing the desires of our evil nature and of our thoughts, and were continually children of wrath by nature, as also the rest.

You were numbered amongst these children of disobedience, impersuasible, driven by the lusts of your flesh and dominated by the totally depraved nature, having only evil thoughts, and swayed by your unreasoning emotions. This was your continuous condition from the moment of your birth. God has a holy hatred of sin, being essentially antagonistic to everything evil. This is not inconsistent with His love, but is the reaction of that love against the denial of its sovereign rights of responsive love. So you were subject to divine wrath, not merely by your deeds nor by circumstance, but by your very nature. There was a law of sinning at work in you. The divine wrath operates only where sin is.

But God, being wealthy in the sphere of mercy, because of His great love with which He loved us, and we, being dead with respect to our trespasses, made us alive together with the Christ; by grace have you been saved completely in past time, with the present result that you are in a state of salvation which persists through present time, and raised us with Him and seated us with Him in the heavenly places in Christ Jesus,

You were dead in your sins and condemned before God, but He is a God of grace, His disposition towards those who are dead through trespasses and sins being one of mercy, a mercy that is rich and exhaustless and supplied abundantly to us. His own love, called out of His heart by our preciousness to Him, led Him, in mercy, to sacrifice Himself for our benefit at the Cross of Jesus, making us alive with divine life, imparted to us as we identify with Him in His resurrection. Now we believers are in a state of unending salvation comprising; our putting our faith in Jesus as Saviour so attaining our eternal position, His eliminating of sin from our lives and His producing of His fruit in us so that gradually, both now and through eternity He is conforming us to Jesus' image, and His glorifying of our bodies at the Rapture. Our spiritual, moral resurrection has already happened, our bodily resurrection we look forward to. Our position now and eternally is that we are made sharers with Him in dignity and dominion, alive and complete in Him as our Representative and our Head so that even now, in a foretaste of our future exaltation, our life and thought are raised to the heavenlies where He reigns.

in order that He might exhibit for His own glory in the ages that will pile themselves one upon another in continuous succession, the surpassing wealth of His grace in kindness to us in Christ Jesus.

He saved us so that He might show us the exceeding riches of His glory, displayed through His grace and kindness to us who were once dead in sins. He raised us with new life in order to satisfy His love for us. We will be on display before the angelic world, basking in the sunshine of God's smile, enjoying the riches of His blessings, all in order that He might be glorified by the angelic hosts. Such will it be in eternity, from after the universe is returned to its pristine glory, and throughout the endless ages which will come rolling in one after another.

For by the grace have you been saved in time past completely, through faith, with the result that your salvation persists through present time; and this [salvation] is not from you as a source; of God it is the gift, not from a source of works, in order that no one might boast; for we are His handiwork, created in Christ Jesus with a view to good works which God prepared beforehand in order that within their sphere we may order our behaviour.

The grace of God leading to salvation is apprehended by faith. Salvation cannot be earned by us but is a gift of God, with no strings tied to it. Works would glorify man, but grace glorifies God. We ourselves are a work of God, made anew by Him in Christ, so our salvation is due to Him and can only take place following a union of Jesus and ourselves. This making anew is with a view to our then doing good works, so our works are a product of His grace as well. These works are a necessary outcome of faith, their character and direction having been made ready by God, being within His prearranged circle of moral action within which we are to live and walk. They spring from His purpose for us and are explained by His purpose in us. The very domain of our life is to be these good works of His, which we can only perform now that we have been made a new creation in Christ.

On this account be remembering that at one time, you, the Gentiles in the flesh, the ones habitually called uncircumcision by that which is called circumcision in the flesh made by hand, that you were at that time without a Messiah, alienated from the commonwealth of the Israel and strangers from the covenants of the promise, not having hope and without God in the world.

See how much God has done for you in delivering you from your past and how great is your current privilege, which should lead you to be all the more careful to walk in the good works of God. Your Gentile, uncircumcised bodies proclaim your heathen character, causing you to be looked down upon because of this, even though the distinction is nothing more than an outward manual act performed on the bodies of those who despise you, and not essential to salvation. Nevertheless it remains a social barrier between Jew and Gentile. Five things were true of you Gentiles; firstly you had no covenant connection with the promised Christ, so were sadly inferior to the Jews who are waiting for their Messiah, secondly you were strangers to Israel having no claim to citizenship nor possessing any rights within its constitution under which God made Himself known to the Jews, thirdly you had no share in the covenants with Abraham and his descendants, fourthly you had no hope of salvation, nothing to hope for beyond this world, and fifthly you had no knowledge of the true and living God, but only knew the life of this evil world system which is hostile to Him.

But now in Christ Jesus you, who at one time were far off, have become near by the blood of the Christ.

Now though, with the coming of the Christ into the world, Jesus, as your Saviour, your alienation and being distanced from the things of God, are in the past.

For He himself is our peace, the One who made the both one, having broken down the middle wall of the partition,

Jesus has joined together Jew and Gentile, making them one. Now, in the blood of Christ, they in the Church have been joined. Jesus, and no other, in His own Person, made peace i.e. apart from Him we cannot have this peace, it being made by Him and it being in Him, created and concluded by His knocking down the separating fence of the whole economy of Moses.

the enmity, in His flesh having rendered inoperative the law of the commandments in ordinances, in order that the two He might create in himself, resulting in one new man, making peace,

The whole law of Moses that stood in between was made inoperative and so abolished by Jesus' death on the Cross. Now Jew is no longer Jew, and Gentile is no longer Gentile, as the old distinctions are lost in a new third order of mankind, Christian man, being new in quality, this new creation and new union being created, grounded and patterned in Jesus.

and in order that He might reconcile the both in one body to God through the Cross, having put to death the enmity by it,

So are Jew and Gentile brought into a state of unity, and both are now reconciled to God, mankind's state being restored to that which had been lost i.e. to its original sinless state, at one with God, and also with no distinct Jewish nation. Jews and Gentiles are now made one unified Body, in right relation to God by His Cross, sin having been put away for all believing sinners.

and having come, He proclaimed glad tidings of peace to you who were far off, and to you who were near, because through Him we have our entrée, the both of us, by one Spirit into the presence of the Father.

Jesus has announced peace to the world of sinners by His atoning work of salvation on the Cross, whether to distant Gentiles or to nearby Jews. He has thus opened to us a way of access to the Father, that we might have the privilege of conversing with Him, taken into His presence by the ministry of the Holy Spirit.

Now then, no longer are you aliens and foreign sojourners, but you are fellow citizens of the saints and householders of God, having been built up upon the foundation of the apostles and prophets, there being a chief cornerstone, Jesus Christ himself,

Now in one unified Body that is at peace with God, none of us are strangers in God's sight or unwelcome in His Kingdom, but we have been made full citizens. Before, our totally depraved nature made us hostile outsiders, foreigners camped alongside, but with none of the rank or privileges of a citizen.

in whom the whole building closely joined together grows into a holy inner sanctuary in the Lord, in whom also you are being built together into a permanent dwelling place of God by the Spirit.

In Jesus, the Church, being the Body of believers brought into salvation from when the day of Pentecost was fulfilled and until the Rapture occurs, is being fitly framed together architecturally into the temple of God, where He will be pleased to dwell and make His home eternally.

On this account I, Paul, the prisoner of the Messiah, Jesus, on behalf of you, the Gentiles,

As you are so being built together, I am conscious that I have been given authority to preach Christ to you Gentiles, I who am currently one made prisoner by Christ Jesus for you, due to the enmity of the Jews, but it is for your sake and your good, and helpful to your Christian life, since my afflictions are your glory.

assuming that you heard of the administration of the grace of God which was given to me for you , that by revelation there was made known to me the mystery even as I wrote above in brief,

I remind you, by the way, that I was given the responsibility of the oversight and management of publicising the grace of God to you Gentiles, having been given the revelation of this grace and the task of properly preaching and teaching it. This previously secret purpose of God was uncovered and laid bare before me, so that it can now be understood by all Spirit-taught believers.

in accordance with which you are able when you read to understand my insight into the mystery of the Christ which in other and different generations was not made known to the sons of men as now it has been revealed to His holy apostles and prophets by the Spirit,

So I do have insight and a mental apprehension, indeed a critical understanding, of this long-hidden but now revealed mystery regarding Christ, that He is not for Israel only but also for the Gentiles. The Spirit kept this fact hidden from men's understanding previously, but in these times He has revealed it.

that the Gentiles are fellow heirs, and belong jointly to the same body, and are fellow partakers of His promise in Christ Jesus, revealed through the good news

Gentiles belong jointly to the same Body as the Jews and share inheritance with them of the blessings of salvation as fellow members of the Body of Christ, since there is no line of separation in this new creation, but all members are equal partakers of the promises which are in Christ Jesus Who became the Saviour at the Cross. Such are the facts of the mystery. It was known previously that the Gentiles would be saved, but the forming of the Church by the baptism with the Holy Spirit and in which the earthly distinction of Jew and Gentile disappears was a mystery hidden in God. The revelation of this mystery was foretold by Jesus but not explained by Him. That task was committed to me, His bondslave for this purpose, to declare the doctrine, position, walk and destiny of the Church.

of which I became one who ministers according to the gift of the grace of God, which grace was given to me according to the operative energy of His power. To me, the one who is less than the least of all saints, there was given this grace, to the Gentiles to proclaim the good news of the incomprehensible wealth belonging to the Christ,

I am a servant of Jesus, seen in my activity as I minister the Gospel, in His gracious gift to me of apostleship to the Gentiles, according to the working of His power in me. What grace that He would use me since I am more least than all the saints... The riches of Christ, those that He has and those that are contained in Him, being the whole wealth of salvation which He bestows, cannot be traced out, but are inexhaustible, not able to be fully comprehended by men.

and to bring to light what is the administration of the mystery which has been kept covered up from the beginning of the ages in the God who created all things,

In my apostleship, it was given to me to make visible to men the way this mystery of the Gentiles being on equal terms with the Jews was to be administered.

in order that there might be made known now to the principalities and powers in the heavenly places through the intermediate agency of the Church the much-variegated wisdom of God,

So was I raised up, that you members of the Church should then make this wise, many-coloured plan of His salvation known to heavenly powers, teaching the angels themselves about His grace and the mysteries of His plan of redemption.

according to the eternal purpose which He carried into effect in the Christ, Jesus our Lord, in whom we are having our freedom of speech and entrée in perfect confidence through faith in Him.

The purpose through the course of the duration of the ages was fulfilled in Jesus' work on the Cross. Now we are in a settled state of utter confidence with unreservedness of speech, having had a way made whereby we are in a friendly relation to God, accepted by Him, and assured that He is favourably disposed towards us.

Wherefore, I am asking in my own interest, that you do not lose heart by reason of my tribulations on your behalf which are of such a nature as to be your glory.

Since such great trust has been put in me in my apostleship to the Gentiles, I can rejoice in my tribulations in carrying out this calling on my life, and I am content to so suffer. So I urge you to take the view that, given the greatness of the office that has been graced to me, the more do my afflictions endured on your behalf redound to your honour, and I would ask that you understand my situation, so as to not give way to any weakness and discouragement, as that would cause me concern in addition to my suffering here.

On this account I bow my knees to the Father from whom every family in Heaven and on earth is named,

Since Jew and Gentile have become one Body in Christ and this Body is growing into a holy inner sanctuary for the dwelling-place of God, I face the Father in prayer, fully confident that He is listening to me. He is the Father from Whom all related orders of intelligent beings, human and angelic, each by itself, get the significant name of family or community, since He created them all. We are all related to God, He being the common Father of our origin, and only in virtue of that relation has any of us the name of family.

that He would grant to you according to the wealth of His glory, with power to be strengthened through the Spirit in the inward man,

My prayer is that out of the totality of God's revealed perfections, He would impart and infuse His power into you, through the workings of the Holy Spirit in His fullness, directing His power to you and pouring it into your conscious essence and moral personality.

that the Christ might finally settle down and feel completely at home in your hearts through your faith; in love having been firmly rooted and grounded in order that you may be able to grasp with all the saints what is the breadth and width and height and depth, and to know experientially the love of the Christ which surpasses experiential knowledge in order that you may be filled up to the measure of all the fullness of God.

This strengthening by the Spirit is so that the Person of Jesus may make His home and dwell in your hearts i.e. if you make room for the Holy Spirit, He will make room for Jesus, since He eliminates sinful things and worldly things from your lives, enabling Jesus, Heaven's King, to have fellowship with you. So have faith in the Lord Jesus for the fullness of the Holy Spirit, believing on Jesus as the One Who grants the fullness of the Spirit and so fills you with Him. So are you securely settled and deeply founded in love, as produced by the Spirit. This Spirit-strengthening enables you to understand the love of Christ, though not fully grasping its full implications, nevertheless laying hold of it and making it your own, this vast love of His. You begin to know by experience this love as you live out your earthly lives, and find that it is beyond being fully known, as no matter how much you experience of the love of Jesus, yet there are oceans of love in the great heart of God that have not been touched by your experience. As Jesus dwells in your heart, God imparts His fullness to you, so that you are filled with the fullness of the Godhead.

Now to the One who is able to do beyond all things, superabundantly beyond and over and above those things that we are asking for ourselves and considering, in the measure of the power which is operative in us, to Him be the glory in the Church and in Christ Jesus into all the generations of the age of the ages. Amen.

God can do all things, and above all things. He can do more than necessary, having exhaustless power, and then more power on top of that. So anything that we can ever ask, or consider asking, for ourselves, He is able to answer in a way that is beyond overflowing, according to the efficiency, richness, and power of the working of the Spirit in our lives, in proportion to our yieldedness to Him i.e. God is unlimited in what He is able to do, but we can limit what He actually can do in and through us... Glory is due to the Father in the Church, being the domain in which the praise that belongs to Him is to be rendered to Him. Let praise be given to Him and let His glorious perfections be shown forth, both in the Church, the Body, as chosen by Him, and in Jesus, the Head, as given, raised, and exalted by Him. Let praise be given to Him eternally. So let it be.

I beg of you, please, therefore, I, the prisoner in the Lord, order your behaviour in a manner worthy of the divine summons with which you were called, with every lowliness and meekness, with longsuffering, bearing with one another in love, doing your best to safeguard the unanimity of the Spirit in the bond of peace.

I now want to move on to urging and encouraging you to lead a Christian life, having up to this point established the doctrine from which you can obtain the necessary power and technique so as to obey these exhortations of mine i.e. I have shown you that God says 'You have been made saints', now I want to help you in obeying Him as He says 'Live a saintly life'. I might use my apostolic authority over you, but rather I plead with you to consider your obligations, given your blessings and exalted positions in salvation which you enjoy. I, as a prisoner solely because of my connection with Jesus, in which I rejoice, urge you to see to it that the weight of your Christian life and experience should be as much as the weight of the profession of Christianity that you make, that your experience measures up to your standing in grace, that you practice what you preach. You have a heavenly calling to be saints, so live saintly lives. Think truly of yourselves, with a small estimation of yourselves and not too highly, not disputing with God, but accepting His dealings with you as always good. Also be patient and bear up with courage in your dealings with people who are hostile to you so as to not be easily provoked by them. As the love shown on the Cross was a forgiving love, so should your love be. This love is produced in your hearts by the Holy Spirit as you yield to Him. Take care then and do your best to guard that unity and agreement which is yours in the Body of Jesus, bound by His peace. Unity will be yours in so far as you make peace the relation which you maintain one to another, walking together in harmony.

There is one Body and one Spirit, even as also you were called in one hope of your calling, one Lord, one Faith, one placing into [the Body of Christ by the Holy Spirit], one God and Father of all, the One above all and through all and in all.

You are to be in unity, as oneness is the common factor of every aspect of your salvation. This divine oneness is the basis, the reason and the fact on which I urged you to walk in meekness and patience, as this results in your unity. You all believed in the same saving work of Jesus on the Cross, and were all placed by the same Holy Spirit into the same Body of Jesus.

But to each one of us there was given the grace in the measure of the gift of the Christ.

Unity of the Body is nevertheless consistent with there being a variety of gifts and offices working in us all. We each experience getting the grace which Jesus has to give, and each gets it in the proportion in which He, the Giver, is pleased to bestow it. But all get from the same Hand and with the same purpose; to serve Him in His Body.

Wherefore He says, Having ascended on high, He led away captive those taken captive and gave gifts to men.

Jesus also gave gifts to specific people, for the benefit of the Church... He ascended to Heaven, following His resurrection from the dead, so as to present Himself in the Holy of Holies as High Priest, completing the atonement for men's sins by proving that He had paid the penalty for sin with His own blood. To go from earth to Heaven He had to pass through the air, being the territory of Satan and His demons. Having tried to keep Jesus from going to the Cross and having tried to keep Him in the tomb, being unsuccessful in these attempts, Satan then tried to bar His progress through the air. But Jesus stripped the opposing demons who tried to cling to His Person, off and away from Himself. These He then led in a triumphal procession through the air, making a bold display of His captives.

Now, the fact that He ascended, what is it except that also He descended into the nether parts of the earth? The One who descended himself is also the One who ascended above all the heavens, in order that He might fill all things.

So by descending into the depths and ascending above all, He entered upon His function of filling the whole universe, in virtue of which function He distributes gifts to men. Following His death on the Cross, Jesus went to two places in the unseen world; firstly Tartarus, the prison house of fallen angels where in His human spirit He proclaimed to those non-persuasible spirits His triumph, and secondly Paradise, where as the Man Christ Jesus He went to be with the righteous dead.

And He himself gave some, on the one hand, as apostles, and, on the other hand, as prophets, and still again some as bringers of good news, and finally, some as pastors who are also teachers, for the equipping of the saints for ministering work with a view to the building up of the Body of Christ,

These are the gifts given to men, given by Jesus Himself and no other; those who proclaim the Word, those who preach and expound the Word, travelling missionaries, and shepherds of God's flock who also teach the Word to them as rich food. These gifted men are given to the Church that it might be built up, both by additions to its membership in lost souls being saved, and by the building up of individual saints, equipping them for Christian service.

until we all attain to the unity of the Faith and of the experiential, full, and precise knowledge of the Son of God, to a spiritually mature man, to the measure of the stature of the fullness of the Christ,

These gifts are for the purpose of, and for the duration of the time until and when all members of the Church have come to their proper unity and maturity in Jesus their Head, having a oneness of faith in Him with respect to clearness and purity of faith, each thoroughly knowing Him as the highest and most dignified Son of God. Then will we each be imaged and likened to the sum of the graces and qualities which make Him what He is, achieving the goal that He set before us all, though we can never, not even in eternity, equal Him, since His perfections are so wonderful that we will only ever bear but a dim reflection of them, being the distance between finiteness and infinity.

in order that we no longer may be immature ones, tossed to and fro and carried around in circles by every wind of teaching in the cunning adroitness of men, in craftiness which furthers the scheming deceitful art of error,

Let us not be like infants, or like those who can be easily agitated mentally and have their unstable souls blown about in every direction by crafty philosophies or religious quackery. These teachers would play dice with your souls, attempting to deceive you and lead you away from the faith and knowledge of Jesus. This is their deliberate plan, for which they lie in wait for you, to get you to follow them and so stray fatally from the truth.

but speaking the truth in love, may grow up into Him in all things, who is the Head, Christ, from whom all the Body constantly being joined closely together and constantly being knit together through every joint of supply according to the operative energy put forth to the capacity of each part, makes for increased growth of the Body resulting in the building up of itself in the sphere of love.

So then, being in truth and following after it, while at the same time operating in love, let us cement brotherly love by our walking in truth. Then, as we grow following Jesus' example, we shall resemble Him, which is our goal, since He is the source from which the grace and power comes that makes it possible for us to grow. In this process, the members of His Body are growing together in a vital, organic union, since the joints of supply that bind us together in love are the channels through which the supply of life from Him, the Head, is brought to us various members of the Body. The power He supplies to each member is determined and measured off according to each member's ability to hold it and to allow it to operate in them, being in proportion to their fellowship with Him and with their fellow saints. This building up of the Body promotes Christian wisdom, piety and holiness.

This, therefore, I am saying and solemnly declaring in the Lord, that no longer are you to be ordering your behaviour as the Gentiles order their behaviour in the futility of their mind,

I appeal to you now with an exhortation as being one made by Jesus Himself; have nothing more to do with aimless, futile living that is given over to things devoid of worth or reality, whether intellectually, morally, or spiritually.

being those who have their understanding darkened, who have been alienated from the life of God through the ignorance which is in them, through the hardening of their hearts,

Their minds have been blinded and are still blind, permanently, through sin, which affects their understanding, their feeling and their desiring. So have they become strangers to the true life, the life of God, the life that He has in Himself and which He imparts to the believing sinner. They are culpably ignorant of divine things both moral and spiritual, stemming from the calloused state of their heart and from their nature, having an arrogance in them, being inexcusably lacking in knowledge, and having about them a deep rooted arrogance and moral blindness.

who, being of such a nature as to have become callous, abandoned themselves to wantonness, resulting in a performing of every uncleanness in the sphere of greediness.

They are past feeling, morally insensible, their hearts ceasing to respond to the stimuli of their conscience. They have given themselves into the hands of lawless insolence, having no restraints, doing whatever their caprice or wanton petulance suggests, making every kind of moral depravity their business, having a mindset of greed and covetousness.

But as for you, not in this manner did you learn the Christ, since, indeed, as is the case, you heard and in Him were taught just as truth is in Jesus,

You, in contradistinction to the Gentiles as yet unsaved, on being saved, were taught Who the Christ is. And it is a fact that He, the Christ, was the subject and the sum of the preaching that you heard then. In Him, Jesus, your personal Saviour, you then received true instructions through your union and fellowship with Him, as truth is embodied in Him in Whom eternal fact and spiritual reality meet.

that you have put off once for all with reference to your former manner of life the old self who is being corrupted according to the passionate desires of deceit; moreover, that you are being constantly renewed with reference to the spirit of your mind; and that you have put on once for all the new self who after God was created in righteousness and holiness of truth.

You were taught that you put off your old, useless, unsaved self with its totally depraved nature, at the moment when you believed in Jesus as your Saviour. That old self was in a state of progressive corruption, growing ever worse as time went on, controlled by evil cravings and passions. You are now being renovated by an inward reformation in the spirit of your minds i.e. in your God-consciousness in your thinking and your knowing, a work accomplished by the Holy Spirit, in the power of which your mind's entire workings and sphere of operating is radically altered. You have now put on your new self, being new in its quality when compared to your outworn, marred, old self. Now you are dominated by the divine nature, being a new creation after God and according to what God is in Himself i.e. you have been newly created after the pattern of what He is.

Wherefore, having put off the lie once for all, be speaking truth each with his neighbour, because we are members belonging to one another.

Since you are a new creation and are being renewed in your inner self, along with putting off once for all your old self also put off the habit of lying, since you are in union with one another through union with Jesus, and are now to be each other's servants.

Be constantly angry with a righteous indignation, and stop sinning. Do not allow the sun to go down upon your irritated, exasperated, embittered anger.

Anger is only permissible for you when it is your right affection and when guided by reason, it then being a righteous passion, the absence of which anger results in having a placid, apathetic attitude. So, on occasion, your settled attitude of righteous indignation against sin and sinful things is not only permitted but demanded, together with the appropriate actions when conditions make them necessary. You cannot love good unless you hate evil, the two attitudes are inseparable. You must feel the pure wrath of the merciful Son of God, and not allow any over-indulgence of your righteous anger to pass over into sin, or for any sinful element of exasperation to mingle with your righteous anger, but you must only allow the anger to remain that has a right to remain.

And stop giving an occasion for acting [opportunity] to the devil.

No longer give power or occasion to Satan to act.

The one who is stealing, let him no longer be stealing, but rather let him be labouring, working with his own hands that which is good, in order that he may be having that wherewith to be sharing with the one who is having need.

Though stealing is not wholly condemned by society and hence is a temptation for some of you, I urge you rather to work to support yourselves than to thieve and to steal. Then you can truthfully share your honest gain with others, who might otherwise be similarly tempted.

Every word that is rotten and unfit for use, out of your mouth let it not be proceeding, but whatever is good, suitable for edification with respect to the need, in order that it may impart grace to the hearers.

Do not utter words that are worthless or bad, but speak those that spiritually bless and bring benefit to your hearers.

And stop grieving the Spirit, the Holy Spirit of God, with whom you were sealed with a view to the day of redemption.

Evil words are repugnant to the holiness of the Spirit, so restrain from arousing the grief-side of His feelings with regard to His nature and His personal love relationship with you, since He is the seal of God in you, guaranteeing your salvation, which is to be completed at the Rapture when your physical bodies will be glorified.

All manner of harshness and violent outbreaks of wrath and anger and brawling and slanderous speech, let it be put away from you together with all manner of malice.

Have nothing to do with all forms of resentfulness, with anger that boils up soon to subside, and with evil speaking

And be becoming kind to one another, tenderhearted, forgiving each other even as and just as also God in Christ forgave you.

Abandon your mental condition of harshness and begin now to make your way into benevolent, compassionate kindness. Treat each other with favour, being agreeable and pleasant. Be gracious to those who offend you, according to how God manifested Himself and acted on your behalf in the suffering, reconciling Christ, so showing your gratitude to Him Whom you ought to resemble.

Be becoming therefore imitators of God, as children beloved, and be ordering your behaviour within the sphere of love, even as Christ also loved you and gave himself up in our behalf and in our stead as an offering and a sacrifice to God for an aroma of a sweet smell.

As children of God experiencing His love, grow up to become like Him, having a manner of life in accordance with the divine supernatural love produced in your hearts by the Holy Spirit, by allowing this love to become the deciding factor in your choices and the motivating power in your actions. He died instead of us, in our place, substituting Himself for us, receiving the full impact of the divine wrath against sin, offering Himself as a sacrifice to God in full payment of the debt of sin which we owed and which the law demanded, so pleasing the God of justice.

But fornication and uncleanness, every kind of it, or covetousness, let it not be even named among you, just as it is befitting to saints, and obscenity and foolish talking or ribaldry, which things have not been seemly or fitting, but rather giving of thanks,

In the strongest terms I prohibit you from the deadliest of temptations, fornication, whether it be the licensed practice at festivals, the keeping of concubines, or non-Christian marriages i.e. have nothing to do with that which is currently engaged in with moral indifference and without shame or scruple by the mass of the population, even by those who lead otherwise exemplary lives. And do not even speak of greedy desires to have more, since this spirit is of the world, from which you have been separated to God. Also do not engage in immoral conduct and the talk of fools; moronic, godless speech, polished and witty words used as an instrument of sin, being refined and versatile but without the flavour of Christian grace, whether they be sly questions, smart answers, quirky reasoning, shrewd intimations, cunning or clever retorts, tart irony and so on, none of which you learned from Christ.

for this you know absolutely and experientially, that every whoremonger or unclean person or covetous person, who is an idolator, does not have an inheritance in the kingdom of the Christ and of God.

You know beyond doubt and it is self-evident from your experience that every male prostitute or he who indulges in unlawful sexual intercourse, or who is unclean in thought or life, or is eager to have what belongs to others, worshipping Mammon or a false god, has not been separated to God.

Let no one keep on deceiving you by means of empty words, for because of these things there comes the wrath of God upon the sons of the disobedience.

Do not be led astray by hollow words that are without substance of truth or reality, however plausible they sound, since they are designed to disguise the seriousness of these vices or to make them appear to be no vices. Those who hear the truth yet remain unbelieving have a nature of hostility to God.

Stop therefore becoming joint-participants with them; for you were at one time darkness; but now you are light in the Lord. As children of light be habitually conducting yourselves; for the fruit of this light is in the sphere of every beneficence and righteousness and truth, putting to the test and then approving what is well pleasing to the Lord.

Do not lapse into your old vices and so become again what you once were. In Jesus your lives have been transformed so that you are not just enlightened, but you are now light, in virtue of your fellowship with Him. You were born of light so live in light, for your benefit and for the benefit of others, since purity is now your new and proper nature. Be actively good, putting your approval on, and then doing, His will.

And stop having fellowship with the unfruitful works of this darkness, but rather be rebuking them so as to bring out confession and conviction, for concerning the things done in secret by them it is shameful to be speaking.

Do not then, you being light, have common interests and activities with the things they practice that go on in the dark. Do not even speak of these deeds, except as an act of reproof necessitates; convincing them of their error, silencing them, and getting them to acknowledge inwardly the truth of the charge against them. These vices are too abominable even to mention, so the more the need of your open rebuke, instead of your silent overlooking of them or of your connivance with them.

But all the aforementioned things, when they are reproved by the light, are made visibly plain, for everything that is being made plain is light.

These secret sins, when they are reproved by you, are made known and brought out of the dark and into open view. That which is evil seeks to avoid the light, preferring the darkness, but none the less is now brought to the light and appears in its own light.

Wherefore He says, Be waking up, he who is sleeping, and arise from the dead, and there shall shine upon you the Christ.

So, to those who are thus reproved by you, He says, "Stop sleeping and come out of the darkness of sin and into the saving light of Jesus' truth, which He will pour upon you".

Be constantly taking heed therefore how accurately you are conducting yourselves, not as unwise ones but as wise ones, buying up for yourselves the opportune time, because the days are pernicious.

Consider and contemplate exactly how you are behaving, that you are walking faithfully to the Word of God, and making sacred use of every opportunity for doing good, on each occasion making that time your own, purchasing it with the currency of zeal and well-doing, since the world system is evil, being in active opposition to the good.

On this account stop becoming those who are without reflection or intelligence, but be understanding what the will of the Lord is.

Cease from acting rashly or senselessly, but rather think and reflect on His will for you, joining your mind and thinking with His.

And stop being intoxicated with wine, in which state of intoxication there is profligacy. But be constantly controlled by the Spirit, speaking to one another in psalms and hymns and spiritual songs, singing and making melody in your hearts to the Lord, giving thanks always concerning all things in the Name of our Lord Jesus Christ to God, even the Father,

No longer soak yourselves excessively with wine, since this practice has nothing of a saving quality about it, but rather is destructive, leading to an abandoned, debauched life. Instead, moment by moment, be thoroughly flooded and filled up with the Holy Spirit, abounding in Him, and so yielded to Him that you allow Him control over you. Share your joy in salvation with one another, expressing your Spirit-filled lives in spiritual songs, whether accompanied by music or unaccompanied, whether written-down or spontaneous, always giving thanks to God for all the blessings that are yours in Jesus Christ.

putting yourselves in subjection to one another in the fear of Christ.

Under the Spirit's control, arrange yourselves in an array of submission each to the others, subordinating your own desires and wants to theirs, not raising your own voice in selfish vaunting or self assertion, not having an independent, autocratic spirit, but rather desiring to get along with one another and being sweetly reasonable, behaving in a way that befits members of Christ's Body.

The wives, be putting yourselves in subjection with implicit obedience to your own husbands as to the Lord, because a husband is head of the wife as the Christ is Head of the Church, He himself being the Saviour of the Body.

This mutual submission amongst you, I now show you how it is to be displayed with respect to three particular relations that are at the foundation of your social life. Firstly husbands and wives. Wives submit your own private self to your husband, even as you do to Jesus, He being your Lord and Master. Regard your obedience to your husband as an obedience rendered to Jesus, since your husband is neither your lord nor your master, but he is representing to you, as your head, Jesus the Head of the whole Body, though your husband is not your saviour, whereas Jesus is also the Saviour of that whereof He is the Head.

Nevertheless, as the Church subjects itself in obedience to the Christ, in this manner also the wives should subject themselves in obedience to their husbands in all things.

Even though your husband is not your saviour, the question of obedience to him is not affected, so submit to him in everything in the marriage relation.

The husbands, be loving your wives with a love self-sacrificial in its nature, in the manner in which Christ also loved the Church and gave himself on behalf of it, in order that He might sanctify it, having cleansed it by the bath of water in the sphere of the Word, in order that He might present to himself the Church glorious, not having spot nor wrinkle nor any of such things, but in order that it might be holy and unblamable.

Husbands, let the pure love of the Holy Spirit in your hearts, saturate all of your feelings towards your wives, so having a heavenly love towards them, and submitting your own wishes in the interest of the well-being of your wives. Also give the Word full liberty in you so as to displace sin and substitute righteousness in you in its place. Make it then your goal to provide a resource of His righteousness and wisdom to and for your wives, so as to assist them in their progress in purity such that when they meet their Saviour at the Rapture He will be well pleased.

In this manner ought also the husbands to love their wives as their own bodies. The one who loves his own wife loves himself, for no one ever yet hated his own flesh, but nourishes and cherishes it, even as the Christ, the Church, because members are we of His Body.

Husbands, your wife is your body, of which you are the head, as Christ is the Head of His Body, the Church i.e. the wife is part of the husband's self. So the love you have for her is not to be merely dutiful but as part of your very nature.

Because of this a man shall leave behind his father and his mother and shall be joined to his wife, and the two shall become one flesh.

You are to depart from your parents and become glued to your wife so as to become physically one with her in a relationship of most intimate union.

This mystery is great. However, I am speaking with regard to Christ and the Church. Nevertheless, also as for you, let each one in this manner be loving his own wife as himself, and the wife, let her be continually treating her husband with deference and reverential obedience.

Your relation to your wife is a mere semblance of the mysterious relation between Jesus and His Church. Every one of you husbands is to love his wife as himself, none of you is exempt. Wives, be spontaneous in your obedient regard to your husbands.

The children, be always obedient to your parents in the Lord, for this is a righteous thing. Be always honouring your father and your mother, which is a commandment of such a nature as to be the first commandment with a promise, in order that it may be well with you, and in order that you may live long upon the earth.

Secondly parents and children. Children, hear and attend to your parents as being those who you are under authority to, submitting obediently to them, this obedience being within the realm of your fellowship with Jesus i.e. you are to be influenced by religious duty as well as by natural affection. Your obedience to them is to be born out of your honouring them, treating them honestly and with respect, kindness and courtesy.

And the fathers, stop provoking your children to anger, but be rearing them in the discipline and admonition of the Lord.

Fathers, no longer exasperate or irritate your children, arousing them to anger, since this will make them indisposed to be either obedient or honouring of you. Rather submit any feelings of irritation or anger to the need to encourage them as you should. Nurture them to maturity in all areas of their lives by training and educating them in the cultivation of their minds and of their morals, using encouraging exhortations, and reproof, when and if this be required.

The slaves, be constantly obedient to those who, according to the flesh, are your masters, with fear and trembling, in singleness of your heart as to the Christ, not in the way of eye service as men-pleasers, but as Christ's bondslaves, doing the will of God from the soul, with good will rendering a slave's service as to the Lord and not as to men, knowing that each one, whatever good he may do, this he will receive from the presence of the Lord, whether he is a slave or whether he is free.

And thirdly masters and slaves. Slaves, you make up a large part of the society in which we live, slavery being an existing earthly institution which can only be gradually undermined and removed by the progressive operation of the Christian principles i.e. the equality of all men in the sight of God, the common Christian brotherhood, the spiritual freedom of the Christian man, and the Lordship of Christ to which every other lordship is subordinate. Submit then, for the sake of society, to your human masters, they being your masters only so far as earthly and material considerations are concerned. Be anxious not to come short in your duties to them and perform your tasks in sincerity with an undivided heart, not grudgingly or formally, but with hearty readiness, as if you were working for Jesus Himself, He being your spiritual Master. Whatever good you do for your human master, if done as to Jesus, shall be rewarded by Him with an eternal reward.

And the masters, be practicing the same things toward them, giving up your threatening, knowing that also their Master and yours is in Heaven, and there is not partiality with Him.

You Christian masters, show the same consideration to your slaves as the Christian slaves do to you, submitting yourselves to the Christian truth that in Jesus there is neither bond nor free. Jesus will reward you justly, according to your conduct rather than to your position in society, as He will also your slaves.

Finally, be constantly strengthened in the Lord and in the active efficacy of the might that is inherent in Him.

My final exhortation is that you clothe yourselves with Jesus' power, as you live in union with Him.

Clothe yourselves with the full armour of God to the end that you will be able to hold your ground against the stratagems of the devil,

Put on all the weapons that He provides so that you are fully armoured for battle, not lacking any single part, and so ready to meet your spiritual foe who is cunning in his ways, employing deceit, craft and trickery, and so not need to take flight from him.

because our wrestling is not against blood and flesh, but against the principalities, against the authorities, against the world rulers of this darkness, against spirit forces of perniciousness in the heavenly places.

The ones who we seek to hold down by the neck in close combat prior to gouging out their eyes, and the ones who seek to do the same to us, are not human, but are of the spiritual powers of darkness, being Satan and his demons, who rule the lower atmosphere surrounding the earth.

On this account, take to yourself, at once and once for all, the complete armour of God in order that you may be able to resist in the day, the pernicious day, and having achieved all things, to stand.

Since your fight is with such powers, take up the whole armour in order to put it on and use it. Do it now. And keep it on your whole life, never relaxing the discipline necessary in maintaining the constant benefit of all of its protection. Be ready for that day when there will be an onslaught of demons against you in violent temptation and assault, so that you can accomplish your conclusive victory over them and remain standing.

Stand therefore, having girded your loins in the sphere of truth, and having clothed yourself with the breastplate of righteousness, and having sandalled your feet with a firm foundation of the good news of peace; in addition to all these, taking to yourselves the shield of faith by means of which you will be able to quench all the fiery arrows of the pernicious one, and take the helmet of salvation, and the sword of the Spirit which is the word of God;

Stand, having fulfilled your responsibility and fastened your garments in place with your truthfulness, sincerity and reality, practicing no deceits nor attempting any disguises in your fellowship with Jesus. This secures your attitude of battle-readiness and allows you freedom of movement in warfare. The righteousness produced in your heart by the Holy Spirit as you continually yield to Him will proof your heart against the fatal thrust of your spiritual assailants. It is your responsibility also to put on the solid foundation of the courage-inspiring Gospel message that speaks peace to a sinful heart through the atoning work of Jesus on the Cross, as you would put on protecting, studded sandals that give you a firm footing. Also use faith in Jesus for victory over sin and over the hosts of the devil and over Satan himself, who is attempting to drag you down to eternal ruin along with himself through the temptations with which he assails you. So may you be saved from the power of sin in this life and from Satan's onslaughts. Use the Word both for attack and to parry the thrusts of the enemy. It is given to you by the Spirit and He inspires it and aids you in your understanding of it.

through the instrumentality of every prayer and supplication for need, praying at every season by means of the Spirit, and maintaining a constant alertness in the same with every kind of unremitting care and supplication for all the saints,

Standing ready for the combat can be made good only when constant, earnest, spiritual prayer is added to your careful equipping with all the parts of the armour. So be attentive and vigilant to pray, on every occasion, with prayer in general and with special requests, as directed and empowered by the Spirit, persevering always and keeping awake at all times.

and on behalf of me, in order that there might be given me utterance in the opening of my mouth, in every fearless, confident freedom of speaking, to make known the mystery of the good news on behalf of which I am an ambassador in a chain, in order that in it I may speak with every fearless and confident freedom as it is necessary in the nature of the case for me to speak.

Pray that God would give me the words when I open my mouth to speak, and that I may speak those words with boldness and have such confidence that I freely speak all that I am given to say.

But in order that you also might come to know my circumstances, what I am doing, all things to you, Tychicus, the beloved brother and faithful ministering servant in the Lord, will make known, whom I am sending to you for this same purpose in order that you might come to know our circumstances and in order that he might encourage your hearts. Peace to the brethren and love with faith from God the Father and the Lord Jesus Christ. The grace be with all those who are loving our Lord Jesus Christ in sincerity.

Tychicus is bringing copies of this letter from me to you and to the other principal assemblies in proconsular Asia. May your hearts be in a state of tranquillity in knowing Jesus. May the Spirit bring the love and faith of Father and Son to your spirits. May Jesus' favour, presence, ability, strength and help, truly enrich your fellowship with Him.

From Paul to Philippi

Paul and Timothy, bondslaves by nature, the property of Christ Jesus, to all the consecrated and separated ones in Christ Jesus who are in Philippi, together with overseers and deacons. [Sanctifying] grace be to you and [tranquilizing] peace from God our Father and the Lord Jesus Christ.

We are servants by nature, bound to Jesus from the time of our birth in Him by bands of constraining love, and bound forever since He can never die, our wills being swallowed up in the sweet will of God, serving Him with a reckless abandon and not regarding our own interests. Our Master is Jesus, meaning 'Yahweh saves', Whose name declares His deity and His atoning work on the Cross. I am writing to you set apart ones, set apart from sin to holiness, set apart from Satan to God, and who are now consecrated for God's sacred fellowship and service. I am writing to you all, whether or not you personally contributed to the support sent to me, and regardless of any divisions there may be amongst you. I am writing to you, whose new life, interests and activities are in Jesus, so that you live your life within the circle of His guidance and constraints. I am also writing to you who are responsible for and actively involved in the spiritual welfare of your assembly, and to those among you who, as well as caring for the poor and sick among you, also minister the Word to you. I write to you in the light of the favour that God did for you at the Cross, when He stepped down from His judgement throne to take upon Himself the guilt and penalty of human sin, at which time was all of humanity in bitter enmity with Him in their hatred of Him. Thus was His gift of salvation to you, with no strings attached, but given out of the pure generosity of His heart, being an extraordinary action, greatly in excess of what anyone might expect Him to do. And this action of favour to us continues, causing us to grow in likeness to Christ through the ministry of the Holy Spirit. Such is grace... Now we believing sinners are bound to God, bound together in His life, this binding operation continuing so as to bring the believer, in his experience of Him, more and more into harmony with God in his life and service. Such is peace.

I am constantly thanking my God for my whole remembrance of you, always in every prayer of mine making supplication for all of you with joy.

You Philippians form the basis of my thanksgiving to God, as I have no regrets in all of my relationships with you.

I am thanking my God constantly for your joint-participation [with me] in the furtherance of the good news from the first day [when Lydia opened her home for the preaching of the Word] until this particular moment [as characterised by the gift which you have sent],

You support me with your prayers and finances while I am engaged in my missionary labours, and have always done so, for which I thank God repeatedly. You have supported me from the time when I first preached Jesus to you right up until now with this most recent gift from you, for which I am thanking you Philippians also, for all of your help to me, including this latest help.

having come to this settled and firm persuasion concerning this very thing, namely, that He who began in you a work which is good [their financial support of Paul] will bring it to a successful conclusion right up to the day of Christ Jesus.

I am also thanking you for your future support of me which I am confidently led to believe will be the case, since this help of yours is a work of God in you which is ongoing, and will continue until its completion at the imminent Rapture.

Even as it is only just and right on my part to be constantly turning my mind in the direction of this very thing in behalf of all of you [namely, the completion of God's good work in you], because you are holding me in your heart both in my defence and in my confirmation of the good news, all of you being sharers with me in this grace,

It is right that I should believe that you will continue to support me given your affection for me and for the work that I am engaged in. I am defending the faith before Caesar Nero's throne, being the tribunal of the world, the successful outcome of which will result in the confirming and stabilising of the Gospel, its claims having been shown to be true. In this support which you provide for my missionary work and for my defence and establishment of the Gospel, you are my co-sharers in the grace of God, bringing your love and kindness to me in my dark moments.

for my witness is God, how I long after all of you with the tenderheartedness of Christ Jesus.

I solemnly tell you how earnestly I desire you and how strong an affection I have for you, longing for you and longing over you, which longing is not just mine but is also in the heart of Jesus Himself, as if His heart dwelt in me, beating as one with my heart.

And this is the constant purport of my definite petitions, namely, that your love [divine and self-sacrificial in its nature as ministered to you by the Holy Spirit] yet more and more might overflow, but at the same time be kept within the guiding limitations of an accurate knowledge [of God's word] gained by experience, and those [guiding limitations] of every kind of sensitive moral and ethical tact,

I pray with a definite aim, directing my requests consciously to God, aware that I am in His presence and knowing that He is listening attentively to me. What I am praying for you in this manner, is that His love in you might exist in superfluity, this divine love that is like an exotic flower from Heaven planted in the foreign soil of your hearts, that it might overflow into the hearts of others, and that it might increase yet more. I also ask that this overflow of love might be contained within the bounds of a full knowledge and understanding of God's Word that is gained by experience, and within a clearer vision of, and intimacy with, Jesus, in all the beauty and fragrance of His Person, and within both perceptive maturity and delicate tenderness, lest your love work harm rather than, through wise outreach, bring blessing.

so that you may after putting them to the test [of God's word] recognize the true value of the finer distinctions involved in Christian conduct and thus sanction them, in order that you might be unadulterated [by evil] and thus pure and not a stumbling block in view of the day of Christ, having been filled full with the fruit of righteousness and continue in that condition of fullness, which fruit is through Jesus Christ, resulting in the glory and praise of God.

The guiding and constraining of your love is so that you may be able to test which things are excellent so as to give your certifying approval of them, since this requires a deep and keen discernment on your part, in particular where there are delicate matters to do with superior Christian conduct involved i.e. the Spirit-produced love in your hearts, when thus constrained, sharpens your moral and spiritual perception as to the finer qualities of Christian conduct. So will you remain pure, unsullied, and without offence until the Rapture, with no hypocrisy about you, but living openly for all to see, so as not to be a cause of discrediting the Gospel in the sight of others.

Now, after mature consideration my desire is that you gain this knowledge from [my] experience, namely, that the things which are holding me down [those associated with my imprisonment] have come to result rather in the pioneer advance of the good news,

I hear from Epaphroditus that you are concerned that my being in prison is curtailing my missionary work. On the contrary, my being restrained here has only served to advance the Gospel the more. Learn from my experience of how the things that are now dominating me have worked for good; how they have resulted in a path being cleared for the Gospel, as when trees are felled before an advancing army so that it can then proceed through an impenetrable forest where otherwise it could not have gone, so has my imprisonment led to the Gospel being made known in previously impenetrable regions. Learn that God-ordained purposes cannot be thwarted since all circumstances to do with our Christian service are God-permitted, so used by Him in the advance of the Gospel.

so that it has become plainly recognised that my shackles are because of Christ, this recognition of their true meaning existing throughout the whole of the Praetorium Guard and among all the rest.

Since it has become known that I am imprisoned because of my relation to Jesus, this leads to my guards asking the question, 'Who is Jesus?', so giving an opportunity for the Gospel to be told, for which very reason I am imprisoned! These soldiers also hear, since they are permanently chained to me, the conversations concerning the Gospel and the Saviour of sinners that I have with my visitors. They hear me pray. They hear me dictate letters. I talk to them also, about their souls. So the Gospel travels throughout the soldiers' barracks, which could not have happened if I had not been a prisoner here.

And the great majority of the brethren having come to a state of settled confidence in the Lord, having been influenced by the gentle persuasion of my shackles to take that step of confidence, are more abundantly bold, fearlessly breaking their silence and speaking the word of God.

There has also been an increase in the preaching of the Gospel in Rome itself. Few of the believers now hold back from telling the good news, made brave by my example of fearless, joy-filled suffering in this prison.

In fact, certain ones even because of envy and rivalry, but also certain others because of good will are proclaiming the Christ; some indeed out of a spirit of love, knowing that I am appointed for the defence of the good news, but others out of a partisan, self-seeking spirit are proclaiming Christ, not with pure, unadulterated motives, but insincerely, thinking to raise up additional afflictions to my already existing chains.

There are actually two groups that are witnessing to the Gospel, each motivated by their differing attitudes towards me. The Judaizers, envious of the freedom we have from the Jewish law when in Christ, preach with a factious, secondary motive of gaining adherents to the law of Moses, viewing any such converts as a triumph over me. Whilst Gentile converts, being my friends, preach in order to bring me joy, by acting in place of me, my liberty to so preach in the city being currently restricted.

What is my feeling in view of these things? The only thing that follows is that in every manner, whether in pretense or in truth, whether insincerely or sincerely, Christ is being proclaimed. And in this I am rejoicing, and I will certainly continue to be rejoicing.

Jesus is being preached, in every way, so that all the people are getting some knowledge of Him. This is a cause of ongoing joy to me.

For I know positively that this [the fact that Christ is being proclaimed] shall result in deliverance and preservation for me [lest I become discouraged in and because of my imprisonment which restricts my opportunity to proclaim the good news] through your petition and through the full-proportioned support and aid of the Spirit of Jesus Christ. And this is exactly in accordance with my undivided and intense expectancy and hope, namely, that with respect to not even one thing shall I be put to shame [defeated], but in every boldness, courage, and fearlessness of uninhibited freedom of speech as always so also now, Christ shall be conspicuously and gloriously manifested in my body, whether through [a continued] life [on earth] or through [a martyr's] death,

So this preaching is for my well-being, it being like a tonic to my soul, saving me from discouragement, rather spurring me on to greater endeavour in my service to Jesus, plus, most importantly, you are also praying for my spiritual welfare, enabling the Holy Spirit to minister to my needs here in answer to your requests. My head is erect and outstretched, my attention being turned away from all other objects and riveted solely upon remaining free in my speech and on maintaining my desire that Jesus be magnified and made great in me, so that His life in its beauty might be shown in me and that He might get praise through me, whether in my life lived in the fullness of the Spirit, or in my death as a martyr.

for, so far as I am concerned, to be living, both as to my very existence and my experience, [that is] Christ, and to have died, that would be a gain.

Jesus is my life. He is that eternal life which I received in salvation and which operates in me now, being the motivating, energising, pulsating principle of existence that transforms my life, His divine Person living His life in and through me. All of my activities and interests in this life, indeed my very existence, are encircled by Him. And my state after death would be gain to me, since then I would be in His presence in glory.

But if for me [continued] life in this physical existence be my lot, this very thing [namely, continued life on earth] is that in which the fruit of my ministry will be involved and is the condition of that fruit being produced. Then what I shall prefer for myself I do not know.

Though death holds no terror for me, it is probably best for you and me that I remain here, though that involves me having to continue to deal with the encumbrance of my sinful flesh. Only here on earth can I bear fruit for Jesus, as it is here that my apostolic ministry is to be carried out. So I have nothing to say as to my preference with respect to my living or dying.

Rather, I am being held perpendicularly by an equal pull from the two [namely, my desire to remain on earth for further fruit-bearing and my desire to die and be with Christ], so that I am not able to incline towards either one, having the passionate desire towards striking my tent and being with Christ which is by far better, but still to remain in my physical body is more needful for your sakes.

There is an equal pressure being exerted on me from both sides, from the desires of life here on the one hand and of death on the other. I am perplexed, kept back from deciding, due to the equal forces pulling me in opposite directions. My heart desires Heaven and to be with my Saviour, but for your needs I cling to this present life with all of its inconveniences associated with my having a mortal body.

And having come to this settled conviction [namely, that to remain in my physical body is more needful for you] I know positively that I shall remain and continue with all of you for your pioneer advance [in the Christian life] and your joy in the Faith

I have turned this matter over in my mind and, having completed this process, I am persuaded that you need me and my ministry more than I need to go to Heaven just now. So I shall go on serving you here on earth. Whilst I have no active choice in this matter, I believe that Jesus' servants remain here on earth until their work is completed. So, since you still have need of my ministry in order to progress in new paths of Christian conduct and service which would otherwise not be possible, I will not die at this time by the hand of Rome, but will be released and thus able to minister to you and to all the other saints who can also be helped by my ministry.

in order that your rejoicing may abound in Christ Jesus through me by reason of my personal presence with you again.

So shall your progressive trust in Jesus result in the growth of your Christian experience and joy, being yours in the enjoyment of putting your faith in Him, which will then result in your more abundant rejoicing in Him. Jesus makes these blessings possible through His blood shed on the Cross, so that He can become the joy of your life, being the One, the only One, Who completely satisfies. By me coming to you again and by my being beside you, I will be the human instrument through which Jesus works to bring these joys to you.

Only [since my only reason for remaining on earth is for your pioneer advance in the Christian life], see to it that you recognise your responsibility as citizens [of Heaven] and put yourselves to the absolute necessity of performing the duties devolving upon you in that position, doing this in a manner which weighs as much as the good news concerning the Christ, in order that, whether having come and having seen you, or whether being absent, I am hearing the things concerning you, namely, that you are standing firm in one spirit, holding your ground, with one soul contending as a team of athletes do, in perfect cooperation with one another for the Faith [the Christian system of belief], namely, the good news.

Since I am to be released, prepare yourselves to meet me by conducting yourselves, with respect to your public duties as members of the Body of believers Whose Head is Jesus, in a way worthy of the Gospel, more so even than the regard you have for your duties as citizens of your esteemed and specially privileged Roman colony, since you are citizens of Heaven with a heavenly destiny and a privileged position in Him, bearing the responsibility of living a heavenly life in the midst of ungodly people and surroundings, and of bringing to them news of a Saviour. You are living on earth, being a colony of Heaven, so live lives with heavenly standards in order to represent your Sovereign, King Jesus, your manner of life weighing as much as, and corresponding to, the Gospel you profess to believe, and surpassing any duties and submissions required of you to Caesar. You live in hostile territory so stand fast, in one spirit, against any opposition you face, fused and blended together by love, as produced by the Holy Spirit in you. Let your emotions and your reasoning and your wills be united, so that you can fight as one against the forces teamed against you i.e. those that are against believing Christians. To enable you to so live, let me now proceed to exhorting you as to making good the things that are lacking in you and that need to be corrected.

And do not be terrified in even one thing by those who are entrenched in their opposition against you, which failure on your part to be frightened is an indication of such a nature as to present clear evidence to them of [their] utter destruction, also clear evidence of your salvation, and this [evidence] from God.

Do not be startled by those who hate you because you forbid idolatry, being that to which they are very devoted. This lack of fear on your part of their antagonism, will be proof to them of the true nature of the situation, being a post encounter thumbs down for them, while you are already assured of thumbs being turned upward from your heavenly Director, regardless of the desire of a fickle crowd.

And the reason why you should not be terrified is because to you that very thing was given graciously as a favour for the sake of Christ and in His behalf, not only to be believing on Him but also to be suffering for His sake and in His behalf,

Your confidence stems from your having received His gift of salvation. Now you are called to suffer in place of Him, not meaning His suffering on the Cross, but the sufferings He endured for righteousness' sake while on earth. These you are now to suffer, being a result of human antagonism to the preaching of the Gospel. Hence your suffering, when seen in its true light, is a gift of God's grace, as also your placing of your faith in Jesus for salvation is a gift of that same grace.

having the same struggle which you saw in me and now hear to be in me.

Your conflict is the same as mine. We are all God's athletes, to whom He has given the opportunity, each one of us, of showing our prowess in Him, and of our endurance in the battle.

In view of the fact that there is a certain ground of appeal in Christ which exhorts, since there is a certain tender persuasion that comes from divine love, in view of the fact that there is a certain partnership on the part of the Spirit [in which the Spirit gives us aid in the living of our Christian life], since there are certain tenderheartednesses and compassions,

There are four facts in view of which you should be of one accord and one mind; firstly Jesus' wonderful life is an exhortation and encouragement to live in a state of harmony among yourselves, secondly God's comforting, saving love for you is a gentle incentive to persuade you to live in a spirit of unity with one another, while also the Holy Spirit within you produces a love in your hearts impelling you to sacrifice your self, each one of you, for the benefit of the others, thirdly the interests of the Holy Spirit, which are therefore mutual interests of yours as you allow Him to control you and fill you, are to do with the unity of the Body of which you are a part, and fourthly your own hearts, as now influenced by the Spirit, direct you to be merciful and forgiving given the overriding desire you now feel to be at peace with one another, with no estrangements or bickering among you.

fill full my joy by thinking the same thing, by having the same divine self-sacrificial love, being in heart-agreement, thinking the one thing,

Let me hear that you have a unity of affection and sentiment, soul with soul, being of one mind, thinking the one thing, having the same point of view, and with common interests. Then will my joy in you be complete.

doing nothing impelled by a spirit of factiousness, nothing motivated by empty pride, but in lowliness of mind consider one another as excelling themselves, this estimation resting, not upon feelings nor sentiment but upon a due consideration of facts,

Let there be no strife among you. Let none of you be proud or opinionated, as this is futile and has no purpose in the process of building you closer together. Let none of you exalt them self, but rather submit your thinking and feelings, each one of you, to Jesus so as to be humble before God, thinking of yourself no more highly than you should, and thinking of others as above you and surpassing you.

not consulting each one his own interests only, but also each one the interests of others.

Fix your attention not on your own desires alone, but also have an eye for the desires of the rest.

This mind be constantly having in you. [This is the mind] which is also in Christ Jesus,

These qualities of mind, being a part of the mind of Christ, are those which fit your needs at this time. These spiritual graces of humility and of self-denial and an interest in the welfare of others were illustrated in Jesus' act of emptying Himself as He entered the human race, and of His becoming the substitute for us as an atonement for sin on the Cross. Emulate in your own lives these distinctive virtues of His, and in particular, the habitual direction of His mind with reference to denying Himself and to loving others, which direction of mind should also be in you. Let your own minds therefore be a reflection of His, by letting the purpose that was in Him inspire you.

who has always been and at present continues to subsist in that mode of being in which He gives outward expression of His essential nature, that of absolute deity, which expression comes from and is truly representative of His inner being [that of absolute deity], and who did not after weighing the facts, consider it a treasure to be clutched and retained at all hazards, this being on an equality with deity [in the expression of the divine essence],

Jesus has always existed, His Being expressing the very nature and character of God i.e. existing in that mode in which the essential Being of God appropriately expresses itself, that expression proceeding from the very depth of the perfect Being, and into which expression that Being unfolds, as light from fire, apprehensible to angelic spiritual intelligences, but neither apprehensible nor conceivable by human minds. Therefore Jesus is absolute deity Himself, co-participating with the Father and the Holy Spirit in that divine essence which constitutes God, God. When Jesus came to earth He assumed human form but remained in possession of the divine essence, which He still possesses now and always will, just His mode of expression was changed so that we humans could perceive Him through our physical senses. It was in the eternity before the universe was created that Jesus, having reached a judgement based upon the facts, relinquished and laid aside His original expression of the divine essence, waiving His rights to it given the necessity that arose, being the need for Him to enter humanity. He did not lay aside His possession of divine essence, but assumed a human expression of His divine essence as an act of humility and self-denial for the benefit of others.

but himself He emptied, himself He made void, having taken the outward expression of a bondslave, which expression comes from and is truly representative of His nature [as deity], entering into a new state of existence, that of mankind.

Jesus, in His humility, took on the expression of a human in His incarnation and then emptied Himself of self and of His previous, glorious, heavenly expression. It was always in His nature to serve so He was glad to set Self aside, comprising His legitimate and natural desires and prerogatives as deity; that of being glorified. This laying aside of His Self was physically symbolised to us when Jesus knelt and washed the disciples' feet, having laid aside His robes to take on the work of their servant whilst still being their Lord and Master, and when afterwards He put on His outer garments again. Likewise in His incarnation, Jesus took on His work as a human, whilst still being deity, and afterwards, following His resurrection, put on His glorious expression again. Jesus entered a new state of being when He became Man, but this did not exclude His possession of deity. Then and now He possesses two natures; that of absolute deity and that of humanity. His human likeness was a complete copy of humanity, though not expressing the whole of His Being i.e. His manifestation resembled what men are, but His humanity was not all that there was of Him. He was not a man, but the Son of God manifest in the flesh and nature of man. If each of you would in a similar manner set self aside, unity amongst you would prevail.

And being found to be in outward guise as man, He stooped very low, having become obedient [to God the Father] to the extent of death, even such a death as that upon a cross.

Jesus' outward expression as man proceeded from His inner nature of serving, rather than from His nature of deity, so that how He appeared in His incarnation to men, was in contrast to what He was in Himself, God. His humanity was real, He really was a Man, but He was not like others of the human race, all of whom are only man. In His incarnation He was always more than a man, having a single personality but with a dual nature. His deity did not make Him more nor less than a Man, and His humanity did not make Him less than absolute deity. Jesus humbled Himself, resulting in His being humiliated in His ignominious and degrading criminal's death on a cross, and if humiliating in His humanity, how much more humiliating was it in His deity. He died of His own volition, He being always the Master of death, so that He died in a way that no one ever has nor ever will, in that He dismissed His human spirit.

Because of which voluntary act of supreme self-renunciation God also supereminently exalted Him to the highest rank and power, and graciously bestowed upon Him the Name, the name which is above every name, in order that in recognition of the Name [all which the Lord Jesus is in His Person and work] which Jesus possesses, every knee should bow, of things in Heaven, of things on earth, and of things under the earth, and in order that every tongue should plainly and openly agree to the fact that Jesus Christ is Lord, resulting in the glory of God the Father.

Because of Jesus' voluntary act of humility in becoming the sin-bearer on the Cross, also, as a consequence, God freely exalted Him, raising Him to supreme majesty, giving Him The Name that brings with it honour and worship to the One on Whom it is bestowed. The Man Jesus Christ, Who as Very God had laid aside His expression of the glory of deity during His incarnation, now has placed upon His shoulders all the majesty, dignity, and glory of deity itself. The God-Man Who stooped to the depths of humiliation is raised, not as God now, although He is all that, but as Man, to the infinite height of exaltation possessed only by deity, answering Jesus' pre-resurrection payer, "And now glorify Me, Father, beside Yourself, with the glory which I was constantly having with You before the universe existed". It is the glory of deity, not now seen shining in infinite splendour as in His pre-incarnate state, but shining in perfect contrast to and with His glorified humanity that is now raised to a place of equal dignity with deity. It is the ideal and beautiful combination of the exaltation of deity and the humility of deity seen in incarnate deity. It is at The Name that now belongs to Jesus, given to Him in recognition of all that He is in His exaltation, to which every knee will bow and every prayer be offered, not the name 'Jesus' that was given Him at His humiliation. All creation, the entire universe, whether animate or inanimate, will agree with God the Father on the testimony which He has given of His Son, and this testimony; of His Son's supreme majesty, will be publicly declared, with praise and thanksgiving, to all beings everywhere.

Wherefore, my beloved ones, as you always obeyed, not as in my presence only, but now much more in my absence, carry to its ultimate conclusion [likeness to the Lord Jesus] your own salvation with a wholesome, serious caution and trembling, for God is the One who is constantly putting forth His energy in you, both in the form of your being desirous of and of your doing His good pleasure.

So you, being citizens of Heaven, live together in harmony and unity. I have given you reasons for doing this, as well as telling you how unity is in the mind of Jesus, and showing you how He demonstrated this desire for unity in His humility and death on your behalf and how He, as a Man, is now raised to the place of highest honour in the universe. So make humility and self-denial a fact in your own lives, as also you have seen how I have laid down my life for you. Proceed in the salvation which God gave you, working it out fully to its resulting maturity in Jesus, so that you live lives increasingly pleasing to Him, while always maintaining an apprehension of the deceitfulness of the heart and of the insidiousness and power of inward corruption which can so easily be tempted towards evil doing. This remaining vigilant is your responsibility, and this you can do as you submit to the Spirit's working in you, so that you both will to do His pleasure and are also enabled to do it by His power in you. This combination of you taking your responsibility and of His divine enablement must be in evidence in your life, in balance, for you to progress towards His best for you i.e. don't leave everything to Him, waiting for Him to make you holy and defeat sin in you, but take hold with Him in the business of your life, so that as well as being dependant on Him you also say 'No' to sin and exert yourself to doing right, your free will and His grace working together.

All things be constantly doing without discontented and secret mutterings and grumblings, and without discussions which carry an undertone of suspicion or doubt, to the end that you may become those who are deserving of no censure, free from fault or defect, and guileless in their simplicity, God's children without blemish, in the midst of a perverse and distorted generation among whom you appear as luminaries in the world,

I have learned from Epaphroditus that there are disputings amongst you, though his love for you initially led him to cover up your sins until I pressed him further about your progress. There must be no more underlying cliques amongst you, no more secretly distancing yourselves from each other, no more having a show of unity but talking discontentedly when away from the whole group and so undermining it. You must rather resemble your Father, being absolutely pure in that you are of one mind, so that your group is unadulterated with no mixture of conflicting thought. This heavenly quality about you will make you like stars that can be gazed upon and wondered at by those of this crooked, twisted society in which you live.

holding forth the word of life, to the end that I may have a ground for glorying reserved for the day of Christ, this glorying being because of the fact that I did not run in vain nor did I labour to the point of exhaustion in vain.

You are to offer the Gospel to this lost and dying world as you would offer wine to a guest, so that I may have reason to boast about you at the Rapture; that I fulfilled His work in me with regard to you, and into which task I put all of my energy, resulting in the fact that you are engaged in soul-winning.

In fact, if also I am being poured out as a libation upon the sacrifice and priestly service of your faith, I rejoice and continue to rejoice with you all. But as for you, you even be rejoicing in the same thing and continue to rejoice with me.

I will some day die as a martyr, my blood being poured out on the sacrifice of your Christian life and service. I rejoice that I am to be the lesser part of the sacrifice, poured out upon the major part, being your testimony and service to God.

But I am hoping in the Lord Jesus quickly to send Timothy to you, in order that I also may be of good cheer, having come to know of your circumstances. For not even one do I have who is like-souled, one of such a character who would genuinely and with no secondary regard for himself be concerned about your circumstances. For one and all without exception are constantly seeking their own things, not the things of Christ Jesus. But you know from experience his character which has been approved after having been tested, that as a child to a father, with me he served as a slave would do in the furtherance of the good news. This very one therefore I am hoping to send as soon as, having turned my attention from other things and having concentrated it upon my own circumstances, I shall have ascertained my position. But I have come to a settled conviction, which conviction is in the Lord, that I also myself shall come shortly.

Founded on my faith in the Lord, Who is at the centre of all my thoughts, words and deeds, I have a confident hope to send Timothy to you. This will bring well-being to my soul also when I hear about you from him. Only Timothy of those here has a soul like mine, being genuine, faithful, and sincere, self-forgetful and dependable, so he has the same real concern for you that I have. Not one of the others would volunteer to undertake the long journey from Rome to Philippi. You know Timothy personally so have your proof from your experience of knowing him previously that he is of good character. He is my assistant as well as my spiritual child who imitates me, serving with me with oneness of mind and thought in furthering the progress of the Gospel. I have not thought of myself and my own needs while here in prison, so engrossed am I in the welfare of others, but I shall look to my own situation soon. Then, dependant on my own circumstances, I hope to send him to you. Based on Jesus' faithfulness to me, I am sure that I will see you as well soon afterwards.

But after weighing the facts, I considered it indispensable to send to you Epaphroditus, my brother and fellow worker and fellow soldier, but your ambassador, to whom you entrusted a mission, and who in a sacred way ministered to my need.

Epaphroditus is charming by nature as well as that being the meaning of his name. He is like my very brother in closeness to me. He was your messenger to me and I welcomed him as a heavenly citizen, equal with me in all senses. Together we have worked and fought for the Gospel side by side. I have treated him as an honoured apostle, sent from you in order to perform a sacred ministry to my needs. But I have decided that, without any doubt, I have to send him back to you.

For he was constantly yearning after all of you, and was in extreme anguish because you heard that he was ill.

He was homesick, continuously longing for you. And then he had an additional heaviness of soul, like that of Jesus in the garden before His arrest, being troubled and distressed, with a restlessness of heart, due to your hearing that he was ill while away from his home with you, since he knew that you held yourselves in a measure responsible for him, which concern of yours is in itself an evidence of God's grace at work in you.

For truly he was ill, next door to death. But God had mercy upon him, and not upon him alone, but also on me, in order that I might not have sorrow upon sorrow. With increased haste and diligence therefore I am sending him, in order that, having seen him again, you may recover your cheerfulness, and as for myself, my sorrow may be lessened. Receive him to yourselves, therefore, in the Lord with every joy, and hold such ones in honour. Value them highly, and deem them precious, because on account of the work of Christ he drew near to death, having recklessly exposed his life in order that he might supply that which was lacking in your sacred service to me.

He almost died, so I quickly resolved to let you receive him back to yourselves and renew your fellowship with him. Notwithstanding any alienation there has previously been between you and him, now hold him dear since he ventured his life for me here. It was his ministering to me that brought him close to death, as he strenuously served me here in prison in your stead.

As for the rest [of which I wish to say to you] my brethren, be constantly rejoicing in the Lord. To be writing the same things to you is not to me irksome or tedious, while for you it is safe.

Having voiced my concerns about the mild dissensions there are within your group, I now move on to that which is left over; the danger that would assail you from without, being the Judaizers. These are nominal Christians who have accepted Jesus as being the Saviour of Jews only, and who teach that any Gentiles must come through the gate of Judaism in order to be saved. They refuse to accept the setting aside of Israel at the Cross, and the bringing in of the Church at Pentecost, but rather continue to practice living under, and according to, the law of Moses. This is happening in Galatia and I want to forestall it also happening in Philippi. Firstly maintain your joy in Jesus and in what He has done for you. I have previously warned you against these teachers who rejoice rather in man and in his attainments, but I am glad to warn you again, for your ongoing protection.

Keep a watchful eye ever upon the dogs. Keep a watchful eye ever upon the evil-workers. Keep a watchful eye ever upon those who are mutilated, doing this for the purpose of bewaring of and avoiding the same. For, as for us, we are the circumcision, those who by the Spirit of God are rendering sacred service and obedience, and who are exulting in Christ Jesus and who have not come to a settled persuasion, trusting in the flesh [human worthiness and attainment].

Beware these shameless ones, who are like mangy, flea-bitten, vicious, starved scavenger dogs, they who often refer to you Gentiles as dogs. They hammer against the Gospel of Grace so as to beat it out of shape. Theirs is not a true circumcision, just a mutilation of the flesh, and they seek to mutilate the message of the Gospel by adding law to grace. We perform the true service to God in true obedience to Him as believers in the Church, by the Holy Spirit, glorying in Jesus. The Judaizers have come to a settled confidence in the flesh, which, after mature consideration, I refuse to acknowledge as being of any worth.

Although as for myself, I [as a Jew] could be having confidence also in the flesh. If, as is the case, anyone else presumes to have come to a settled persuasion, trusting in the flesh, I could occupy that place, and with more reason;

They trust in human works, following a natural system in which salvation is a work of man for God, whereas we follow a supernatural system in which salvation is a work of God for man. They do not acknowledge the true sacrifice for sin, Jesus, as being the fulfilment, through which salvation is obtained, of the symbolic sacrifices of supernatural Judaism. I myself have many grounds on which to boast of my fleshly standing before God, but I discard all of these and any dependence on them so that I might gain the salvation which is in Jesus. If I don't follow the Judaizers' teaching, neither then should you.

eight days old in circumcision, my origin from Israelitish stock, belonging to the tribe of Benjamin, a Hebrew from true Hebrew parents [i.e., not a Hellenist], with reference to the law, a Pharisee, with regard to zeal, persecuting the Church, with reference to that kind of righteousness which is in the law, become blameless.

I am a pure-blooded Jew, a descendant of Jacob, of the tribe loyal to David, raised by Jewish parents in the Jewish language and customs, practically a Zealot in the way I gladly and energetically hunted down Christians, accurately living under the law of Moses and adhering to it perfectly before men.

But whatever things were to me a gainful asset, these things I have considered a loss when it comes to my acquisition of Christ, and still so consider them.

These things, these fleshly gains, I deem of no account. I have written them off as one joint loss that I might gain Jesus.

Yes, indeed, therefore, at least, even I am still setting all things down to be a loss for the sake of that which excels all others, my knowledge of Christ Jesus my Lord which I have gained through experience, for whose sake I have been caused to forfeit all things, and I am still counting them dung, in order that Christ I might gain,

In the strongest terms I tell you of my conviction that I can not hold on to those things, since in doing so I would fail to appropriate Jesus. And this is my permanent state of mind about this, and about anything else which could come between me and my Lord. The greatest gain is to know Jesus through intimate companionship and communion with Him, to know His heart and His will, for which I have given up wealth, reputation, culture and family. I have lost everything that I might win life with Him, and know His perfections and graces, and the fragrance of His Person.

yes, in order that I might in the observation of others be discovered by them to be in Him, not having as my righteousness that righteousness which is of the law, but that righteousness which is through faith in Christ, that righteousness which is from God on the basis of faith.

I want my life to demonstrate that I am in Christ and for others to see this about me. No more do I desire to have any trace of self-achieved right living as a result of law keeping. I desire now that men see in my life the right living which the Holy Spirit produces in answer to my faith in Jesus, which faith He authored and which faith He also nourishes and maintains, faith given to me by God, with which I appropriate the blessings of grace.

Yes, for His sake I have been caused to forfeit all things, and I count them but dung, in order that I might come to know Him in an experiential way, and to come to know experientially the power of His resurrection and a joint-participation in His sufferings, being brought to the place where my life will radiate a likeness to His death, if by any means I might arrive at the goal, namely, the out-resurrection from among those who are dead.

I have forsaken all else that I might come to know Jesus, progressively becoming more like Him. I want to experience the same resistance-overcoming power which raised Him from the dead, surging through my own being, overcoming sin in my life, and producing His graces in me. I want to come to know jointly with Him His sufferings for righteousness' sake. When these things are fulfilled in me, then will I be brought to the same form with Jesus, having both an inner heart life and an outward expression, in accordance with His nature in me, with respect to His death to self and to His death for others i.e. my desire is that I conform to the spirit and temper of His life, and to His meekness, lowliness and submission. It is my humble but assured hope that I shall arrive at this goal, though I have not attained it yet; the goal of being found by men to be in Christ by the life I live, to have Jesus my Saviour as my righteousness, to come to know Him better all the time by experience, to feel the power that raised Him from the dead coursing through my being, to have a participation in His sufferings for righteousness' sake, and to be made conformable to His death to self.

Not that I already made acquisition or that I have now already been brought to that place of absolute spiritual maturity beyond which there is no progress, but I am pursuing onward if I may lay hold of that for which I have been laid hold of by Christ Jesus.

I shall arrive at this goal of absolute Christlikeness only either at my death or in my participation in the Rapture. I have begun to experience His power in me and I have suffered with Him, and I do radiate to some degree His selflessness, but I have not laid hold of these in the fullest measure. There is room for much growth and improvement and advance in these respects, and in my spiritual maturity, so I press on towards the goal. I am keeping up the chase, as a runner in a race, running towards a fixed point. I will pursue my goal of Christlikeness, intent on catching it and pulling it down and making it my own. This is the same for which Jesus caught me and made me His own, calling me into salvation and giving me the office of apostle so as to reveal Himself in me.

Brethren, as for myself, as I look back upon my life and calmly draw a conclusion, I am not counting myself yet as one who has in an absolute and complete way laid hold [of that for which I have been laid hold of by Christ Jesus]; but one thing: I, in fact, am forgetting completely the things that are behind, and am stretching forward to the things that are in front; bearing down upon the goal, I am pursuing on for the prize of the call from above of God which is in Christ Jesus.

I have deliberated long about my life to reach this conclusion about myself, in contrast to the conclusion some of you have reached about yourselves; that you have already attained perfection. I tell you again in the strongest terms, I have not completely grasped that for which Jesus grasped me; sinless perfection. There is one thing I do above all else; the things I had depended upon to find favour with God I have now completely forgotten. And, as the leading runner in a race forgets his opponents, since if he were to begin to think of those runners behind him and the sound of their pounding feet his pace would slacken, so do I not allow my progress to be hindered by dwelling on the past, full of heartaches, discouragements, and thwarted hopes and plans, but these I completely forget. Instead, like a runner whose eyeing of the runner ahead draws his hand onward, and his hand his foot, I aim at the spiritual target, according to my calling, which is from Heaven and to Heaven, and to which I must ever give heed.

As many therefore as are spiritually mature [in a relative sense], let us be constantly of this mind. And if, as is the case, in anything you are differently minded, and that, in an evil sense, this also will God reveal to you.

Those of you who consider yourselves to be spiritually mature, I exhort you therefore to consider yourselves so only in a relative sense, and to remember that there is much room for further spiritual growth in your lives. You can attain to a maturity in character, being well-rounded and complete, as opposed to spiritual infancy, rather than to you becoming sinless or flawless. You who erroneously believe you have already attained perfection, I leave for God to reveal the truth to you about this matter, if you are willing to be taught.

Only one thing, so far as we have come, let us keep our lives in the same path.

In our Christian progress let us direct our lives so that we reach the same point, arriving together.

Become imitators of me, brethren, and observe attentively those who conduct themselves in a manner which reflects the example which you have in us,

Be joined together with me, as I am compelled to make my own example of living a norm of the new life in Jesus. Fix your attention on me and on those who have followed my example, having a desire to live like us.

for many are going about, concerning whom I often have been telling you, but now also tell you weeping, the enemies [they are] of the Cross of the Christ, whose end is utter destruction, whose god is their stomach, and that which they esteem to be their glory is their shame, who regard the things upon the earth.

I warn you again of those influenced by the Greek school of philosophy which teaches that the satisfying of physical appetites is the highest aim of man. They have allowed their freedom in Christ to degenerate into self-indulgence. They do not understand grace and so think lightly of continuing in sin. They have swung from legalism into lawlessness. They sacrifice to themselves, eating and drinking their own offerings, this way of living being to them the following of their so-called 'god of wise men'.

For the commonwealth of which we are citizens has its fixed location in Heaven out from which we, with our attention withdrawn from all else, are eagerly waiting to welcome the Saviour, the Lord Jesus Christ, and to receive Him to ourselves, who shall transform this body of ours which has been humiliated [by the presence of indwelling sin and by death and decay], so that it will be conformed to His body of His glory, this in accordance with the operation of Him who is able to bring into subjection to himself all things.

We have heavenly obligations and responsibilities along with heavenly privileges, due to our true citizenship. We intensely, yet tenderly, look forward to welcoming Jesus, looking off and away from everything else, concentrating solely on His imminent coming into the air at the Rapture to take His Bride to Heaven with Him. Then will our external expression be changed as we receive our spirit-dominated, glorious, immortal bodies of flesh and bone, devoid of the sinful nature, no more to live in bodies that are subject to weakness and sickness and sin being debilitated and imperfect mediums through which we seek unsuccessfully to express ourselves in the fullest measure, and unfit to fulfil the claims of the spiritual life. At the Rapture our bodies will be made like His glorious body, in substance and nature, being the perfect mediums through which our inner spiritual lives can express themselves, enswathed in glory so not needing to be clothed, with perfectly functioning minds, bodies that are perfect, being free from all the effects of sin. This will be accomplished by His superhuman power by which He is able to bring all things within His divine economy, and to marshal all things under Himself.

Therefore, my brethren, individually loved ones, and individually and passionately longed for, my joy and my victor's festal garland, thus be standing firm in the Lord, beloved ones.

Having this hope, stand firm in Jesus. I love each one of you self-sacrificially with the love produced in me by the Spirit. You are divinely loved and longed-for. You are my victor's crown, awarded me for my Christian service in winning you to Him.

Euodia I exhort, please, and Syntyche, I exhort, please, to be of the same mind in the Lord.

You two women hold prominent positions of leadership and capability within the group, as well as being welcoming to strangers. I humbly beg you to be reconciled, given what I have written here about being of one mind and spirit, and of esteeming others higher than yourselves, and given Jesus' humility, also following the examples of selflessness you hear of in Timothy and Epaphroditus.

Even so, I make request of you also, you who are a genuine yokefellow in deed as well as in name [knowing how to work harmoniously with others], lend a hand with these women in their efforts at settling the differences which they have between themselves, women of such a character that in the good news they laboured and contended in perfect cooperation with me as a team of athletes would, together also with Clement and the rest of my fellow workers whose names are in the book of life.

I am confident the two of them will comply with my request given my authority in Jesus. This contention has put them both out of fellowship with Him, so Syzygus, you who are a true worker joined in double harness with me, I order into action now, to help these women in making up their differences. As in all of Macedonia, the women of Philippi hold superior position, and these two were important members of my team, working strenuously and in perfect harmony, together and with me, in spreading the knowledge of the Word. But now they lead rival factions within your group. There were also many other humble servants of Jesus working with me whose names will never be well known on earth, but who are known in Heaven.

Be rejoicing in the Lord always. Again I say, Be rejoicing.

Ever be full of the joy of the Spirit. I say again, let His joy flow out of you.

Let your sweet reasonableness, your forbearance, your being satisfied with less than your due, become known to all men. The Lord is near [in that His coming may occur at any moment].

Do not keep this joy in your heart only but let it find expression in your conduct, then others will experience its blessings also. Jesus will return soon at the Rapture, so as a consequence be gentle and do not worry.

Stop worrying about even one thing, but in everything by prayer whose essence is that of worship and devotion and by supplication which is a cry for your personal needs, with thanksgiving let your requests for the things asked for be made known in the presence of God, and the peace of God which surpasses all power of comprehension shall mount guard over your hearts and minds in Christ Jesus.

Cease your habit of being anxious. Instead pray with belief. Speak to God with reverence, telling Him of your needs and making appropriate requests. His presence is always surrounding you, so your requests are always in place with Him. Being anxious is out of place in your heavenly Father's presence. His peace, like a sentinel, patrols before your heart's door, keeping worry out.

Finally, brethren, whatever things have the character of truth, whatever things are worthy of reverence, whatever things are righteous, whatever things are pure, whatever things are lovely, whatever things are attractive, whatever excellence there is or fit object of praise, these things make the subject of careful reflection.

Set your attention on those things that are true in character, a due appreciation of which produces a noble seriousness. Ponder actions that can endear you to others, being winsome, pleasing, and amiable in character. Even some things of man's mental excellence, moral quality or physical power can be deemed suitable to reflect on.

The things also which you learned and received and heard and saw in me, these things habitually practice, and the God of peace shall be with you.

Do those things as a habit, that I taught you.

But I rejoiced in the Lord greatly that already once more you let your concern for my welfare blossom into activity again, in which matter you were all along thoughtful, but you never had an opportunity.

Your thoughts for me have flourished again in caring for my interest and I thank you once again for this gift you have sent to me by Epaphroditus, for which I did not ask, it coming purely from your generous spirit towards me.

It is not that I speak as regards a need, for, so far as I am concerned, I have come to learn, in the circumstances in which I am placed, to be independent of these and self-sufficient.

I for my part have come to learn, having previously been brought up in luxury and not knowing want, how to be independent of external circumstances and how to be Christ-sufficient, dependent upon Him alone, my sufficiency being in Him.

I know in fact how to discipline myself in lowly circumstances. I know in fact how to conduct myself when I have more than enough. In everything and in all things I have learned the secret, both to be satiated and to be hungry, and to have more than enough and to lack. I am strong for all things in the One who constantly infuses strength in me.

I do not make the Gospel a means of livelihood, living comfortably on gifts like the one you have just sent. On the contrary, I never seek any financial gain from preaching with the aim of maintaining a certain respectable standard of life. Sometimes I am abased, humiliated, and go hungry, at other times I enjoy affluence and abundance and am filled full with food. I have learned to keep myself low as respects the needs of daily life, living on a very small income, and have also learned how to minister any overflow when having more than I can use. I have been initiated into this mystery so that it has been revealed to me how to so live, Jesus all the while strengthening me by the Spirit.

All the same, you did a beautiful thing when you made yourselves fellow partakers with me in my tribulation.

Having said that I am always sufficient in Jesus, nevertheless your gift to me is most welcome, showing a beautiful goodness in you. You have made yourselves responsible for meeting my needs and, more so even than the gift itself, your heartfelt affection for me while I am here in prison is valued by me.

But you yourselves also know, Philippians, that at the beginning of the good news, when I went out from Macedonia, not even one assembly made itself a partner with me as regards an account of giving and receiving except you only, that even in Thessalonica more than once you sent to relieve my necessity.

From the time of your first gift you have always been generous to me. It has been an expression of your taking a joint role with me in the responsibility of spreading the Gospel. You owed me much since I was the one who, around ten years ago, won you to Jesus and nurtured you in the faith, so I had certain credits on your ledger which you were obligated to honour. I sowed spiritual things into you and I am reaping material things from you. You even supported me when I was in Thessalonica, though they are much wealthier than you.

Not that it is my character to be ever seeking the gift, but I am seeking the fruit which is accumulating to your account.

As I said before, I am not using the Gospel as a means of livelihood. Rather, my gain is noting the interest that is being added to your account due to this work of yours in supporting me, and as you grow in the faith which I planted in you.

But I have all things to the full and overflowing. I have been filled completely full and at present am well supplied, having received at the hands of Epaphroditus the things from you, a fragrant aroma, a sacrifice acceptable, well-pleasing to God.

I give you now, in my words of thanks, a receipt for the gift you sent me. Previously you were so different to me, in origin, training and religion. And you are of a race that looks down upon and despises my race. How great then is your generosity to me, truly a work of the Spirit in you. It is a sacred gift that you have sent me, an offering to God.

But my God shall satisfy to the full your every need in accordance with His wealth in glory in Christ Jesus. Now to God, even our Father, be the glory forever and ever. Amen. Greet every saint in Christ Jesus. The brethren with me send greeting to you. All the saints send greeting to you, especially those of Caesar's household. The grace of the Lord Jesus Christ be with your spirit, with all of you in this respect individually.

Be assured that you have not impoverished yourselves by giving so liberally to the cause of the Gospel. Rather, God shall fill you full, meeting your every need to overflowing, corresponding to your treatment of me in that I am now full to overflowing because of your gift to me i.e. God will do the same for you as you did for me, only His measure of supply is determined by His heavenly wealth, which wealth is in Jesus, being an infinite supply. Glory be to God. The grace of Jesus is with each of you. Love to you from all the believers here.

From Paul to Galatia

Paul, an apostle, not from men nor even through the intermediate agency of man, but through Jesus Christ and God the Father who raised Him from among the dead,

I am one divinely commissioned to preach the Gospel and authorised by God to plant Christianity and with official status to administer the universal Church. My commission does not have a human source nor was it imparted to me by any man. Jesus and God the Father jointly are the source and the agent of my commission, and whereas the other apostles were commissioned by Jesus while He was in His humiliation, I was given my commission by Jesus in His now resurrected, glorified state.

and all the brethren with me, to the assemblies of Galatia.

This letter is from me, and from those who are travelling with me, whom you know, as we teach the Gospel of Grace, so what I say here is also authorised by them. I neither bring you any word of commendation nor refer to you as saints, to emphasise the severe nature of my message to you now, given your defection from the Gospel.

Grace to you and peace from God our Father and from the Lord Jesus Christ

I speak of the grace, as I always do in my letters, being the enabling ministry of the Holy Spirit in believers' lives, which grace you are turning away from in favour of the legalistic teachings of the Judaizers, who say that Christian growth comes from obedience to the law of Moses, in which economy there is no provision for an indwelling, sanctifying Spirit and a dependence upon Him. Rather they teach self-effort, which is of no value with respect to righteousness. How I desire that you would again become recipients of the full work of the Spirit in your lives, meaning that you would also obtain heart peace as a result of His ministry in you. The Father and the Son, jointly, are the source of grace and peace as they cooperate in carrying out the plan of man's redemption.

who gave himself in behalf of our sins so that He might rescue us out from this present pernicious age according to the will of our God and Father, to whom be the glory for ever and ever. Amen.

Jesus' voluntary death in our place with relation to our sins, and His giving of Himself as the Sacrifice that would perfectly satisfy the just demands of God's holy law which the human race has violated, this is the true ground of our acceptance with God, not our works. Thus has Jesus delivered us, plucking us out from our slavery to sin in this current world system, in whose atmosphere we live, and which is ruled by Satan who is intent on destroying all along with himself, even as the Judaizers are intent on pulling down the Church along with themselves. Out from this world and from the clutches of the Judaizers' teachings, Jesus has drawn us to Himself. His rescuing of us has nothing to do with our obedience or with any quality in us, but is according to the Father's sovereign will, and according to the procedure prescribed by Him, so can only be received by faith and as a free gift from Him. Glory be to Him.

I am marvelling that in such a manner suddenly you are becoming of another mind and deserting from Him who called you in the sphere of Christ's grace to a message of good news diametrically opposed to the gospel, which message is not an alternative gospel. Only, there are certain ones who are troubling your minds and are desiring to pervert the gospel of Christ.

I find it extraordinary that you are putting 'another gospel' in place of the Gospel of Jesus, and doing this so quickly and so readily. I expected better of you. I am writing to you so as to arrest the progress of this new doctrinal infection, since you are lending your ears to those who seek your revolt from His grace, and your defection to them and their teaching of salvation by works. God Himself chose you and called you in His grace to participate in the salvation procured by His Son on the Cross, a salvation offered out of the pure generosity and love of His heart with no strings attached, a salvation to be accepted by faith. So you have been put in a position where you are now the objects of His everlasting favour, if indeed you did obey this divine summons and so are called. You are on the verge of abandoning this position of grace i.e. of departing from being objects of the grace of Christ and participants in its benefits, and of putting yourselves under the law of Moses which can only award death to you. Thus this 'other gospel', which is in opposition to the Gospel I preached to you, is a false doctrine and has an evil character, so cannot be good news, whereas the doctrine of grace that you heard from me is God's truth, being the only message of good news. These Judaizers, whom I do not know personally, I have a real contempt for. Their wish is to pervert your faith, reversing it from salvation believed in to salvation earned. Law and grace are incompatible. The two systems have nothing in common.

In fact, even if we or a messenger from Heaven should preach a gospel to you which goes beyond that which we preached to you as good news, let him be accursed.

I and those with me, Barnabas and Silas and Timothy, tell you now in the strongest terms how serious are the differences between my Gospel and the message of the Judaizers. It is not just a controversy between teachers one versus another, but between truth and error. Though someone claims to have come from Heaven, as you once claimed for me when I first preached to you and you declared me to be Hermes and Barnabas Zeus come down in human form, and if that someone also claims to have a message of good news that goes into new regions beyond the limits of the Gospel, let him be an outcast and destined for eternal destruction.

Even as we have said on a previous occasion, indeed, now again I am saying, If, as is the case, anyone preaches a gospel to you which goes beyond that which you took so eagerly and hospitably to your hearts, let him be accursed.

I repeat what we previously said to you some time ago when we warned you of the danger of listening to the Judaizers, which previous warning you will remember us giving you. I repeat it since you did not heed our warning but are actually now listening to these men. Their message is of an opposite nature to my message, which message of mine you were so welcoming of at the time, like a host receiving a guest, such was your response to the Gospel of Grace when it was preached among you by me.

For, am I at this present moment seeking to win the favour of men rather than the approval of God? Or, am I making it my business to be constantly pleasing men? If I still were pleasing men, in that case Christ's bondslave I would not be.

I am being so stern and harsh since I am concerned here about influencing men in God's favour i.e. I would not have said what I did about men being accursed were it just a matter of influencing men in my favour. This harshness of my language proves that I am no flatterer. At this critical moment, as a malevolent attack is being made upon the Church and upon its doctrine of pure grace, it could not possibly be my purpose to curry favour with men rather than to please God, given my calling to administrate the Church. These Judaizers quote me when I said "I became to the Jews as a Jew in order that I may win Jews; to those under law, as one under law, not being myself under law, in order that I may win those under law", and accuse me of changing my message to suit my audience so as to ingratiate myself to their good will. So what do these Judaizers say now about the vehemence of my language? Am I ingratiating myself now to the legalizers? Indeed I preach only one message, regardless of the whims and desires of my hearers, seeking God's approval only, and being one with Him in His desire that, if possible, all might be saved. The only concessions I have made, for example in having Timothy circumcised, were in order to promote harmonious relations between Jewish and Gentile converts, not as an abandonment of my former principles.

For I make known to you, brethren, the message which was announced as good news by me, that it is not as to its nature, human.

I remind you now of what you previously were convinced of, my precious brothers since children of the same heavenly Father as me; the Gospel of Grace, being permanent and unchangeable, is not of human origin, nor is it measured by mere human rules and standards.

For, as for myself, neither did I receive it directly from man, nor was I taught it, but I received it through a revelation given me by Jesus Christ.

And, as I also told you previously, I, by direct communion with God, received a special, exceptional education from Him as to my ministering of the Gospel message. I did not learn it from human teachers, not even from those who had learnt it from Jesus' teaching of it to His disciples, of which group I was not a part. Jesus Himself revealed and disclosed to my mind this Gospel of Grace, bringing me an understanding of it and of the truth of salvation in Him alone, which understanding I would have been incapable of coming to by myself purely through my own human reasoning.

For you heard of my manner of life aforetime in Judaism, that beyond measure I kept on continually persecuting the Church of God and continually bringing destruction upon it,

On the contrary, what I was taught by human teachers was that which is directly opposed to the liberty of the Gospel, being a rigid school of ritualism, a mere ethical cult that bases salvation on the performing of good works and involves the observance of the prescribed sacrifices as a mere form, with no faith in any coming substitutionary atonement for sin as was made by Jesus on the Cross, to all of which I was a staunch adherent. No human could have taught me to change my learnt attitude to the Gospel, such was my intense hatred of it. Only God Himself could have done that, as it needed a total change in my thinking about the whole economy of the Old Testament. Right up to my conversion when Jesus met with me as I approached Damascus, I did my utmost to ruin the assemblies that comprise the Church, so my associations with Christians were not such as would have led me to receive the Gospel. Only at my conversion was it revealed to me by God that He had temporarily set aside the nation of Israel, and was now using the Christian Church as the channel through which He was working.

and I was constantly blazing a pioneer path, outstripping in Judaism many of my own age in my race, being more exceedingly zealous of my ancestral traditions.

I was a leader in Judaism with respect to culture and activity, being recognised amongst my contemporaries as a brilliant pupil of Gamaliel. I was very learned in the oral traditions of my ancestors, traditions that are to do with doctrine, ritual, self-discipline, interpretation of Scripture, and the conduct of life. This was as a result of my thinking being dominated by the Pharasaic teaching, also coming from my Pharisaic father, which teaching is not looking for a needed Christ, since Pharasaic traditions are not only ingrafted to the law of Moses but make that law void. I was more occupied with legal enactments and practices as ingrafted upon and interpreting the Word of God, than I was with the Word of God itself. So Jesus being the Christ and His being needful for salvation was a complete break with all my background and traditions, more so even than if I had been an adherent to the law of Moses, making my reception of the Gospel from human instruction impossible, and thus proving beyond any doubt that neither my office as apostle nor my message came by way of a human channel, but came directly from God. After my conversion I needed to restudy the Old Testament Scriptures in the light of the revelations given me by Jesus, and under the instruction of the Holy Spirit.

But when it was the good pleasure of the One who set me apart before I was born and called me by His grace to give me an inward revelation of His Son in order that I might proclaim Him as glad tidings among the Gentiles, immediately I did not put myself in communication with flesh and blood for the purpose of consultation;

Jesus destined me, before my birth, for His special purpose of sending me with His Gospel message to the Gentiles, calling me and then revealing Himself to me over a period of three days, which is how and when I received the Gospel, so I was neither commissioned by men nor am I subject to any man's control. I needed no one's opinion about this revelation, neither anyone's guidance nor advice. Given mankind's weakness, frailty, and ignorance, and given that my commission and message came to me directly from God, I permitted neither of these to be affected in any way by human intervention.

neither did I go up to Jerusalem to those who were apostles before me, but I went away into Arabia, and again returned to Damascus.

I did not ascend to the heights of Jerusalem to confer with the other apostles who had already received a calling like mine. Instead I spent time alone with God in an arid and sparsely populated place not far from Damascus in order to think, my Pharasaic thought-structure having been completely demolished down to, and including, its very foundations by this revelation from and of Jesus. I used this time alone with God to build a new theological structure on the foundation of this revelation, which would take me many months to do, being led by the Holy Spirit. I restudied the Old Testament, now with the central fact of the Cross of Jesus as the controlling factor in my meditations. From this study came the doctrine which I now preach, and which I have presented in my letter to Rome.

Then, after three years, I went up to Jerusalem to become acquainted with Cephas, and remained with him fifteen days.

After this period alone with God, having had no contact with the other apostles, I went back to Jerusalem in order to become acquainted with them and to assess my sphere of labour having had discussions with them. The disciples though were afraid of me, not believing that I was a disciple, but Barnabas helped me by bringing me to them and telling them of my conversion experience at Damascus. I only spent a brief time with Peter, since firstly, a conspiracy against me from the Greek Jews with the intention of killing me, and then, a command from Jesus ordering me out of Jerusalem when He appeared to me in the Temple, led me to leave there.

But another of the apostles I did not see except James the brother of our Lord.

I also saw Jesus' brother Jacob, an apostle, though not one of Jesus' twelve disciples as he only became a believer after Jesus' resurrection, he being the Moderator of the assembly in Jerusalem.

But the things which I am writing to you, behold, in the sight of God, I am not lying.

I am telling the absolute truth in saying what I just have; that this is the only contact I had with Jesus' disciples, contrary to what the Judaizers are saying about me with regard to this.

Then I went into the regions of Syria and Cilicia,

Then, for about ten years, I preached the Gospel of Grace, ministering in Antioch and Tarsus, also spending time in Cyprus and Asia Minor.

but remained personally unknown to the assemblies of Judaea which are in Christ.

Those believers in Judaea still didn't know me, Judaea being where I would I have been found had I been, as the Judaizers say, just a follower of Jesus' disciples. Rather I was operating as an independent missionary with no supervision from either the Jerusalem assembly or the disciples themselves.

Indeed, they only kept on hearing, The one who used to persecute us at one time now is announcing the glad tidings of the Faith which at one time he was ravaging.

Their only knowledge of me was their continual hearing that I who had previously been intent on destroying the Church and its faith in Jesus, and who had wreaked havoc amongst the believers, breathing in a personally produced atmosphere of threatening and slaughter against the disciples of Jesus in an insane fury against them beyond measure, persecuting them even to foreign cities, and taking pleasure in and applauding their deaths, was now a minister of the Gospel.

And they were continually glorifying God [for that which they found] in me.

So in me, the assemblies of Judaea found reason for which to glorify God, in contrast to the way in which the Judaizers hate me.

Then, after the space of fourteen years, again I went up to Jerusalem, accompanied by Barnabas, having taken along also Titus.

So for the first fourteen years of my Christian life I was independent of Jesus' disciples. Subsequently I went to Jerusalem, with Barnabas, to bring financial aid to the believers in that city. At this time there was a period of persecution during which Jacob and Peter were under the power of Herod and the other apostles were scattered. I spoke to the assembly's council about our right to dispense with the obligation of circumcision in relation to our Gentile converts, which request of ours was agreed to by the council. So rather than my submitting to and acknowledging my inferiority to the apostles, as the Judaizers claim, I was received by Jacob, Peter, and John as a brother and accorded full recognition by them as the apostle to the Gentiles. I also brought Titus with me, who was uncircumcised, as a test case, showing the determined, independent spirit with which I came to the council meeting.

And I went up in accordance with a revelation. And I laid before them for their consideration the gospel which I am preaching among the

Gentiles, but privately to those of recognised eminence, lest by any means I should be running or had run in vain.

The assembly at Antioch commissioned me to go to Jerusalem and also the Holy Spirit spoke to me directly that I should go there. In Jerusalem I set forth the Gospel of Grace to them, being that which I now preach, in separate small discussions with those in divine authority whom I have just listed and whom I honour and whose opinion I value, prior to the main council meeting. This was to confirm that I was not running my race in error and that my previous work was not therefore a failed endeavour on my part. I desired to know that my work should not in any way be disowned by them, as their denying that the economy of Moses had been set aside at the Cross would have greatly handicapped my work in establishing a Church free from all connections with legalism, and would have resulted in there being a division of the Church into a Jewish and Gentile branch.

But not even Titus who was with me, although he was a Gentile, was compelled to be circumcised.

Having previously won the argument on circumcision in Antioch, and having been sent from there for validation of that ruling by the Jerusalem assembly, I felt bold to bring Titus with me as a test case in person. My boldness was rewarded since, despite strong pressure being brought to bear upon the assembly that Gentile believers should be circumcised, the final ruling of the Jerusalem council sustained the Antioch decision to the effect that circumcision was not to be required of Gentile converts.

Now it was because of the false brethren who had been surreptitiously brought in, those of such a character that they sneaked in for the purpose of spying out our liberty which we are having in Christ Jesus, with the expectation of reducing us to abject slavery;

Judaizers secretly infiltrated the council meeting, entering by the back door, being those who had previously intruded into other Christian assemblies, and whose presence the leaders were unaware of. They urged the council to require that we circumcise our Gentile converts so as to bring both Jew and Gentile under the law of Moses. These false 'brethren' accept Jesus as their long-awaited Messiah, but know nothing of salvation through Jesus' precious, atoning blood shed on the Cross, instead clinging to legalistic Judaism and its system of salvation by works, which system they desire to bring into the Church itself. With hostile intent they scrutinise us, looking for any weak points by which they can gain entry. At the council meeting, they were assured in their minds that they would in fact gain such entry.

to whom not even for an hour did we yield with reference to the particular voluntary submission demanded, in order that the truth of the gospel might abide for you.

The Church was on the verge of a potentially great crisis. The entire status of Gentile Christianity was at stake, centred upon the case of Titus i.e. whether it was to be merely a modified form of legalistic Judaism, or a system of pure grace. Salvation and justification by faith was on trial, since a requirement for circumcision would have set grace aside. With their ruling, the council announced that the Gospel of Grace, as you received it from me, is fully approved by all of the Christian leadership, and so it is your firm and secure possession. Do not let anyone tell you that it is in error or that there is a superior 'alternative gospel'.

But to be something at the hands of those who were of repute, whatever they were aforetime, is of no importance to me. God accepts not man's person. For those who were of repute imposed nothing on me.

Not only did the council agree with us on the matter of circumcision, but they imposed no other restrictions or commands or burdens of doctrine or practice related to this matter on us. Their apostolic authority differs to mine and I am independent of them, but on this issue we were all agreed. Their agreeing with me, they being those with an apostolic commission, doesn't matter to me, as I received my commission direct from Jesus. Though they talked with Jesus while He was here on earth, that gives them no position of pre-eminence in the Church, since God does not show any partiality because of man's natural ability, position or possessions within human society.

But on the contrary, when they saw that I had been entrusted with [the responsibility of preaching] the gospel to the uncircumcised as Peter with [the responsibility of preaching] the gospel to the circumcised -

Rather than the Judaizers getting their way, the apostles came over strongly to our side after they had heard and discussed the issue in those private talks with me, their endorsement coming from what they learned from me. They agreed that we were preaching the same Gospel, but to distinct sets of hearers; Jews and Gentiles, and that we were on an equal footing, working in unison as imperial secretaries of the King of kings Himself, and entrusted with the writing and proclaiming of the same Gospel message.

for He who worked effectively for Peter with respect to his apostolate to the circumcision also worked effectively for me with respect to the Gentiles -

Peter's apostleship and mine both have a divine source. The experience of our preaching is equal and of the same character in our efforts, he among the Jews, I among the Gentiles. Both of us have been recipients of the blessing of God in our work for Him, as He gave recognition to each of us as an apostle divinely appointed, with souls being saved, both Jews and Gentiles.

and having come to perceive the grace which was given to me, James, and Cephas, and John, those who in reputation were looked upon as pillars, gave to me and Barnabas the right hand of fellowship, to the end that we should preach the gospel to the Gentiles and they themselves to the circumcision;

It was important that these men of distinction fully accept us, these men who were thought of by the Jerusalem assembly as being prominent upholders of the Church of Jesus, especially Jacob, the leader of the Jerusalem assembly and who presided over the council, since he was a brother of Jesus and was also well-known for his strictness as to the observance of the law of Moses, so giving special weight to his support for Gentile freedom from that law. These men publicly displayed their goodwill and friendship towards us, acknowledging that we were all working in partnership together as a mutual alliance, and one that Barnabas and I were equally glad to be part of. So we agreed to continue working as before in our two different spheres with equal apostolic authority. Having said this, it is always my custom wherever I go to first proclaim the Gospel to the Jews in that place, and also, Peter on occasions preaches to the Gentiles.

only, that we should keep on remembering the poor, which very thing I have made a diligent and eager effort to do.

As part of the agreement we were to continue to care for the poor, which care we had demonstrated to them by bringing financial help to the Jerusalem believers at the onset of one of the frequent famines that occur in Judaea. These believers in Jerusalem are also in a near permanent state of chronic poverty due to the ill-will and persecution they undergo at the hands of unsaved Jews, so they are in need of continuous help with regard to the necessities of life, which ministry we are keen to continue in.

But when Cephas came to Antioch, to his face I opposed him, because he stood condemned.

There then arose the question of whether saved Jews are still bound to the law of Moses. The eating of certain foods according to the law was not only a matter of diet, to promote the physical well-being of the Jews, but was also a way of keeping Jews a separate people from the Gentiles since they could never eat together, which practice could not continue within the Church of Jesus where we are all one in Him. This legislation was set aside at the Cross, as God had made clear to Peter in a vision. So when Peter came to Antioch, he participated in our meals where Jews and Gentiles ate together. But when Jacob's representatives from Jerusalem arrived, they challenged Peter, saying that he was going against legislation, and convinced him to stop eating with Gentiles, which then caused other Jews in the assembly to follow him in this, so creating a division. I resisted Peter, which shows again my not being in submission to the Jerusalem apostles so as to follow orders from them, and also shows my apostolic authority which gave me the right to stand openly against them in matters of wrong conduct i.e. I again demonstrated my independence as an apostle and my willingness to maintain my position as an apostle when coming under attack. I had to protect the Gentile Christians at Antioch who were indignant at Peter's behaviour and the effect it was having in causing them to be considered unclean once again, so I could not keep silent. I had to face Peter, my equal in rank and in the Gospel ministry, now as being his superior in character and courage.

For before certain from James came, with the Gentiles it was his habit to eat meals. But when they came he began gradually to draw himself back, and began slowly to effect a final separation, fearing those of the circumcision.

Jacob sent these men to Antioch, to whose requests Peter obsequiously bowed. Jacob held the view that Jewish Christians should still obey the law of Moses. He caused me to lapse at a later stage, convincing me to take upon myself a Jewish vow in order to show the Jerusalem Jews that I was still a strict Jew, but which then led to them trying to kill me, and for which I was arrested and later sent to Rome. On this occasion it was Peter who was caused to lapse when Jacob insisted that Jewish and Gentile Christians should not eat together or have close fellowship together, which Peter had been doing, in that he had eaten and worshipped in Gentile homes. Peter formed a strategy to draw back, due to his fear of offending Jacob's emissaries, these being important men, so he trimmed his sails to the sudden change of wind that came from Jerusalem, to come to a safe place, away from contention with them. Finally he even stopped eating with

Gentiles in our gatherings at the church meeting place. Peter had somewhat of a reputation for this kind of fickle behaviour, having previously displayed a tendency to quickly withdraw from a newly discovered truth or from a bold declaration of his faith.

And the rest of the Jews also played the hypocrite jointly with him, so that even Barnabas was swept along with their hypocrisy.

So the entire group of believers was split into a Jewish branch and a Gentile branch. The Jews, by their misconduct, covered up a better knowledge of how Christian unity should operate, changing their behaviour, but not their belief, due to a fear of those who had come from Jerusalem. Worst of all, Barnabas acted the same way. His defection from the Gentile cause was far more serious than Peter's vacillating, given his record in saving Gentiles and in representing Gentile believers to the Jerusalem council and in being a champion of Gentile liberty in Jesus. This betrayal of his contributed to my parting company with Barnabas shortly afterwards.

But when I saw that they were not pursuing a straight-forward course in relation to the truth of the gospel, I said to Cephas in the presence of everybody, If you, being a Jew, habitually are living after the manner of the Gentiles, and not after that of the Jews, how is it that you are compelling the Gentiles to live after the Jewish manner?

When I observed their wavering and insincerity to the truth, imitating Peter's warping of it and misrepresenting it, I rebuked him in front of them all, since all had been led astray by him. I told him, "Genuinely, aside from pretence, you were happy to live as a Gentile, especially given the vision you previously had, but now you are in effect compelling Gentiles to follow the Jewish law with respect to eating, since them choosing not to do so would cause a split in the assembly between Jew and Gentile". I could not allow this to happen, given my calling to administer unity in the Church. It had been agreed at the council that there should be a division of territories in the preaching of the Gospel i.e. a preaching to Jews and a preaching to Gentiles, but to create such a division within the Church was out of the question and not to be permitted. The council had not decided what to do when there was a difference between Jewish and Gentile believers with respect to keeping the law of Moses, such as was happening here. I insisted that in such an instance, the Jews were not obligated to keep the law.

As for us, we are Jews by nature, and not sinners of Gentile origin;

I reminded Peter and the Jewish Christians, "We have a common Jewish origin, none of us being looked-down upon Gentiles nor even Gentile converts to Judaism, and, as such, we have special privileges".

and knowing that a man is not justified by law works but only through faith in Christ Jesus, we also placed our trust in Christ Jesus, in order that we might be justified by faith in Christ and not by law works, because by law works there shall no flesh be justified.

I continued, "We Jews believe that obedience to God's laws is required for divine approval, disobedience subjecting us to divine condemnation. So this divine approval is a matter of debt which God owes to the one who obeys, on the basis of their works. This concept is not actually taught in the Word with reference to man's salvation, but has its origin in the thoughts of man, and which view I held to strongly when I was a Pharisee. Despite our Jewish privileges, not one of us can be declared righteous by virtue of our obedience to the law of Moses. But faith, being an acceptance of that which accredits itself as true and a trust in the person concerning whom the facts are presented, which faith we all have, in Jesus alone, brings divine approval. God justifies a believing sinner by taking away his guilt and its penalty, Jesus having borne both for us on the Cross. And God imputes His righteousness, being Jesus Himself, to us, in which state we stand guiltless and uncondemned for time and eternity, positively righteous in the sight of the eternal laws of God".

But if, as is the case, while seeking to be justified in Christ, we [Jews] ourselves also were found to be sinners, is Christ therefore a promoter of sin? Away with the thought;

I went on, "Since we, as Christian Jews, seek to be justified in Jesus by grace, we show ourselves to be sinners, just like the Gentiles, admitting that there is no justification by works. Being justified by Jesus awakens our consciousness of sin and compels us to put ourselves on the plane of the Gentile i.e. we are forced to admit that we are also sinners and that the law of Moses has failed us as an agent that justifies us. The Judaizers argue that since in Jesus causing us to abandon the law as a justifying agency, we have therefore put ourselves in the place of the lawless Gentile, whom they call a sinner and a dog, and that since violation of the law is a sin, so then is an abandonment of the law, meaning, in their view, that Jesus promotes sin. What a senseless line of reasoning".

for if the things I tear down, these again I build up, I exhibit myself as a transgressor;

To make my case with regards this issue of eating I then said, "If I were to declare the law valid again, having previously abandoned it in favour of Jesus, I would be a transgressor in that I would be disregarding the ethical spirit and true meaning and purpose of the law as embodied in Jesus. This is the truth, rather than that it is a sin to abandon the law in favour of grace. And if I were to declare valid again that which I had abandoned, I admit my guilt in that abandoning. Your declaring of Jewish food rituals to be valid again, having previously set them aside, is in error, since you are obeying the letter of the law, which you knew had been set aside by God, and ignoring the spirit of the law; that the law was a temporary measure for the time of the Old Testament, to be done away with at the Cross".

for, as for myself, I through the intermediate agency of the law died to the law, in order that I might live with respect to God.

I told them my own strongly held position; "With respect to obedience to divine law as a means of acceptance with God, that principle I have died to. I am not dead to law, being neither a law to myself nor lawless, since I still hold to the principles of love and justice et cetera, being both eternal and principles that exist permanently in God's character and in His government. It is the legal statutes that I have died to. I no longer have a relation to them and they have no further claim upon me, nor any control over me. My attempt to fulfil the requirements of the law of Moses as a means of salvation taught me of my own inability to meet its demands, and of its inability to make me righteous but rather condemn me. It made me a sinner and punished me for being one. So I abandoned it as a means of justification and accepted salvation in Jesus Who sets me free and gives me wings to fly. Jesus lived under the law, fully obeyed that law, assumed the guilt and penalty which humanity incurred by having violated the law, and in dying under the law satisfied its requirements, so passing out of the realm where law in its legalistic aspect had control over Him. Since we believers were identified with Jesus in His death and in His resurrection, we with Him have also passed out of that same realm of legalism. Subjection to the law as a means of acceptance with God, in reality prevents one from living a life of unreserved devotion to Him i.e. legalism comes between the soul and God. So I died to the law that I might live to God".

With Christ I have been crucified, and it is no longer I who live, but there lives in me Christ. And that life which now I live in the sphere of the flesh, by faith I live it, which faith is in the Son of God who loved me and gave himself on my behalf.

And I continued, "In my act of believing I identified with Jesus at the Cross, and the spiritual benefits that have come to me from this identification with Him are present realities with me now. By dying with Him I died to the law, since He died under its penalty and bore it for me, releasing me from its hold on me, its demands on me being satisfied by Him. In being crucified with Jesus, I died to self; the self-righteous Pharisee in me died, what I had done up to that time passed away, and my old self and my old life were buried, so that the dominating control of my sinful nature, inherited from Adam, had its power over me broken. My old self died, but my new self, as an apostle of Jesus, lives. I no longer lead a self-centred life, but a Christ-centred one. My new life is a Person, Jesus, living in me, Jesus being manifested in my life through the ministry of the Holy Spirit. I no longer attempt to draw near to God in my own righteousness. Now Jesus, the Person within me, lives out His life in me. Rather than attempting to live my life in obedience to a set of rules, I yield to the indwelling Holy Spirit and cooperate with Him to produce a life pleasing to God, energised by His life residing in me and by His regenerating work".

I do not thwart the efficacy of the grace of God. For if through law comes righteousness, then Christ died to no purpose.

I concluded my argument by saying, "I do nothing that would nullify what God has laid down, so as to make void what has been presented and established by Him. Adding law-works to faith in Jesus' sacrifice as the ground of justification with God, undoes the ability of the free gift to bring about God's salvation as procured by Jesus at the Cross, by trying to somehow earn it. For such a person, who depends in the least upon good works as a means of acceptance with God, there is no salvation. If it were possible to be saved by good works, Jesus died without a cause and needlessly".

O, unreflecting Galatians, who bewitched you, before whose eyes Jesus Christ was placarded publicly as the crucified One?

I am surprised and indignant at your current state. Galatia is supposedly a province of high education, whose people are intellectual, wise, and insightful, having thrown off the shackles and benumbing influences of your local customs and magic and superstitions, rather having an appreciation of the better things. How is it then, that on the issue of faith in Jesus your intellect appears to be impotent, dead even, and you show yourselves to be unwise? You are failing to use your powers of perception, so failing in the first characteristic of what it means to be a Galatian. Has the 'evil eye' from your superstitious culture with its mysterious power infatuated you? It was publicly announced by me that Jesus was crucified, raised, and ascended for you, He Who is alive and Whose glorified body still bears the marks of His suffering for you, and Who is the living Saviour by virtue of His atoning work on the Cross. This should have been enough to hold your attention and to keep your eyes from wandering to the enticements of the Judaizers.

This only am I desiring to learn from you. By means of law works did you receive the Spirit or by means of the message which proclaims faith?

I only need to ask you one thing in order to show you your error; how did the Holy Spirit enter you? Was it through your putting your trust in Jesus because you heard my message of grace where one receives salvation by faith? Or was it because you obeyed the law?

Are you so unreflecting? Having begun by means of the Spirit, now are you being brought to spiritual maturity by the flesh?

And as to the working of the Spirit in you, are you so irrational? Can you go from dependence on Him to begin with, to growing in Him by self-effort? Can you complete the work which He started? Can the combined power of your natural body, soul, and spirit, controlled only by your totally depraved nature, be as effective as the morally transforming, regenerating power of the Holy Spirit in you? So why are you beginning to abandon your position of grace and put yourselves in the sphere of law and legalism, not trusting the Spirit to sanctify you, but depending upon your own effort? How foolish to think that you can bring yourselves into a state of spiritual maturity in your Christian lives. That is the work of the Spirit. Only He can do that for you.

So many things did you suffer in vain? If indeed they really were in vain?

You suffered persecution when you received Jesus as Saviour. Do not allow these sufferings to have been for nothing by now turning your backs on grace and putting yourselves under the Judaizers' legalistic system. This would be such an unreasoning shift that I am, for my part, unwilling to believe that you will continue in your current direction.

Therefore, the One who is constantly supplying the Spirit to you in bountiful measure, and constantly working miracles among you, by means of law works is He doing these things, or by means of the message which proclaims faith?

And what of the manifestations of the Spirit; His special, supernatural gifts, and the miracle-working power of His that you see in evidence amongst you? Is this power supply to be generated by your good works in future? Or by your faith and your continued dependence on Him? Do the Judaizers have such evidence? You have the evidence, the Spirit still working among you, proving that grace and not law is the way of salvation and life in the Spirit.

Just as Abraham believed God, and his act of faith was credited to him, resulting in his righteousness.

Looking at the example of Abraham we see that he was saved by faith and not by works. The Judaizers wrongly teach that natural descendants of circumcised Abraham, being his circumcised children, were accepted with God, meaning only the circumcised can be saved, and making circumcision a prerequisite of salvation. Their error is in failing to distinguish between the Jewish national covenant God made with Abraham to do with His chosen people being used as a channel to bring salvation to the earth, of which circumcision was the sign, and the salvation which would come through a descendant of Abraham, being the Messiah, namely Jesus. Circumcision was thus a mark of separation on the Jew, isolating him in the midst of Gentile nations, in order that God might use the nation of Israel for His own purposes. It had nothing to do with the Jew accepting salvation. Indeed Abraham was declared righteous before he was circumcised. The Holy Spirit is the mark of separation on the believing Christian, affirming his salvation. Abraham's faith was placed to his account and put on deposit for him, computed as to its value and evaluated as righteousness, not that his act of faith was looked upon as an action deserving of reward i.e. not a good work being rewarded by the bestowal of righteousness. Rather he cast off all dependence on good works as a means of finding favour with God and accepted God's way of bestowing salvation, which faith God answered by giving him that salvation. Righteousness is to do with one's relation to God and one's walk before Him, and shows itself in behaviour conformable to and corresponding with God, so being of value before Him. It is the state commanded by Him and which stands the test of His judgement, being in-line with the sum-total of all that He commands. God Himself is the standard of righteousness. We are the righteousness of God in Jesus by faith, our state of believing called forth by our divine acquittal, He having removed our guilt and the penalty incurred and having bestowed His righteousness on us. This is what God did for Abraham when he believed Him. This cannot be earned by our own good works, as the Judaizers would lead you to believe.

You perceive, therefore, that those who are of faith, these are sons of Abraham.

Thus the faith exercised by Abraham is declared to be the fundamental condition of acceptance with God. Since faith for salvation was the way that Abraham was justified, it follows that those who exercise like faith are his true followers, and ethically his sons.

And the scripture, forseeing that on a basis of faith God justifies the Gentiles, announced the good news beforehand to Abraham, namely, All the Gentiles shall be blessed in you.

So it is through like faith that the Gentiles become Abraham's spiritual children. The Judaizers say that all nations must be circumcised in order to be incorporated in Abraham's descendents and so blessed, but what did the Scripture foresee? God, foreseeing that He would justify the Gentiles by faith, announced to Abraham, before he was circumcised, the Gospel message, that some day the Saviour would arise out of his nation of Israel and that the Gentiles would be saved through Him, as Abraham himself was saved, by faith. Thus Abraham rejoiced to see the coming of that day. He became the pattern to all who would follow, of how a sinner, Jew or Gentile, must appropriate salvation. This rule of action God operates for all time, that the condition on which any person was to be justified was faith, and this was announced to Abraham before he was circumcised, which means that circumcision has nothing to do with the acceptance of salvation, and never has done.

So that those who are believing ones are being blessed in company with believing Abraham.

Believing ones are those blessed with salvation, not those who depend upon good works. Abraham was an educated, wealthy, sophisticated citizen of the world, living in a state of culture and opulence that we can only dream of. With all of this, and in spite of it, he saw that much of life is taken upon faith, including the way of salvation. We who exercise faith like him share with him in the same salvation which he received from God.

For as many as are of the works of the law are under curse, for it stands written, Cursed is every one who is not remaining constantly in all things which stand written in the book of the law in order to do them.

By putting themselves under the law of Moses, rather than their being blessed, men put themselves under a curse. The Judaizers claim that a knowledge of the law entitles them to eternal life and to the blessings which were attached to the sons of Abraham. And Israel, also having ignored the righteousness of God, Jesus, similarly attempted to establish its own righteousness by obeying the law of Moses, but rather than being justified by the law it inevitably led to the curse of the broken law, for no man can keep it. The curse is not merely suffering the wrath of God in eternal banishment from His presence with everlasting sorrow and misery, but is also in the present state of alienation from Him, caused by a violation of his law. The law is a prescribed domain in which one either remains, as we do by faith in Jesus, or out of which one goes.

But that in a sphere of law no one is being justified in the sight of God is clear, because, The righteous man shall live by means of faith.

The man who does not continue in the domain of the law of Moses is under the curse. The man who attempts to remain in the domain of the law by obeying it will fail in his objective, since this remaining is only possible by faith. Obedience to the law cannot pay for sin. Only blood poured out in death can pay for sin since death is the wages of sin. When we believe we are declared righteous, on the basis that Jesus met the requirements of the law which we broke and Himself became our righteousness. Only by believing are we approved by God and given new, divine life, and we then have a new experience of living in relationship to God, that of being accepted in the Beloved.

And the law is not of faith; but the one who has done them shall live in them.

When it comes to justification, the principles of law and of faith are mutually exclusive with no overlap at all, and they are opposed to each other. The righteousness of the law, being a perfect obedience to it, no sinful human can do, but a sinless perfect being could. Under law it is futile for any sinner to work out a righteousness which God could approve. Under grace a believing sinner can accept, as a gift, a righteousness which God has approved, namely Jesus Himself.

Christ delivered us by the payment of ransom from the curse of the law by becoming a curse in behalf of us, because it stands written, Accursed is everyone who is suspended upon a tree,

We were bought like slaves out of the market place. We were thus set free from the law, which had us imprisoned and under sentence of death, that we might be the bondslaves of Jesus for time and eternity, never to be put up for sale again. The law of Moses made no allowance for human sin and frailty, and the curse, which came upon anything less than perfect obedience to the law, involved the wrath of a righteous God and brought condemnation upon the offender. So we Jews were in a hopeless state, helpless to redeem ourselves and helpless to satisfy the demands of the law so as to find acceptance with God. Only through Jesus' sacrifice could a holy God bestow mercy on the basis of justice satisfied. We Jews were under the curse of the law, where the Gentiles were held responsible under the all-inclusive principles of right conduct that exist permanently in God's character and in His dealings with humanity, and so were also lost and guilty. For our Jewish nation Jesus came above us but under the curse, so between us and the curse. He took the penalty that hung over us and took us out from under the curse, having become a curse above us, as a substitutionary sacrifice. So was the law of Moses fulfilled for the Jewish nation. Israel, having been under the curse, but now redeemed by Jesus from the curse, the blessing of Abraham, being justification by faith, which in the plan of God was to flow through Israel to the Gentiles, was now at liberty to flow out from Israel to the Gentiles. The law, having satisfied its demands upon Jesus, thrust Him out of the boundaries of its legal jurisdiction. We who are identified with Him in His death when He paid our penalty, are likewise cast out with Him, therefore no longer under curse.

in order that to the Gentiles the blessing of Abraham might come in Jesus Christ, to the end that the promise of the Spirit we [Jew and Gentile] might receive through faith.

Jesus becoming the curse has allowed the blessing of Abraham to flow to Jew and Gentile. The law of Moses, which was the barrier that separated Jew and Gentile, is done away with in Jesus. By its removal the Gentiles are put on a common level with the Jew, and thus united, both are now recipients of the Holy Spirit through faith.

Brethren, what I have to say is in accordance with common human practice. Even though it be a man's covenant, when it has finally been ratified, no man annuls it nor adds stipulations to it.

The covenant that God made with Abraham is still in force since even a human contract cannot be changed except by the mutual consent of both parties. The law of Moses could not modify the covenant since it was introduced centuries later, long after Abraham's death. My brothers in Galatia, I am trying to make this understandable to you by speaking in everyday terms. God obligated Himself to Abraham to do what He said He would i.e. that He would justify Abraham on the basis of his faith, by the atoning sacrifice which He Himself would one day offer, that of Jesus the Saviour. God later also gave the law, and He would not invalidate His covenant, since Abraham had died, by adding another specification to it, so making obedience to law coupled with faith as now the two prerequisites to salvation, since the matter of the covenant was a past, closed, established matter. The Judaizers tell you that they are only adding some harmless new conditions to the covenant of grace, but the character of these new conditions, good works, annuls the entire covenant, since any dependence on works necessitates an abandoning of faith. If anyone claims to be saved on the basis of works plus faith, they are still lost in sin.

Now to Abraham were made the promises, and to his Descendant. He does not say, And to the descendants, as in respect to many descendants, but in respect to one Descendant, and to your Descendant, who is Christ.

The promises were made to Abraham and his seed, Jesus, which then extends to and includes all who are saved by Jesus through their faith in Him. So this faith way of salvation existed before the law of Moses was given, continued through the time the law was in force, and still is in effect after the abolition of the law at the Cross. So the entrance of the law did not affect the covenant at all.

This now is what I mean. A covenant previously established by God, the law which came after four hundred and thirty years does not render void with the result that the promise becomes inoperative,

The giving of the law to Moses all that time later was something new and different, which could not therefore be an element forming part of the previous promise. God was saving men on the basis of faith without works since the time of Adam, two thousand five hundred years before the law was given. The law was in force from Moses to Jesus, for a period of only fifteen hundred years, now ended, since at the Cross it was abolished. The Judaizers attempt not only to retain the law for the Jews, but try to impose it upon the Gentiles, to whom the law was never given in the first place. Since a human covenant cannot be changed or rendered void by any subsequent action, how much more so God's covenant with Abraham, since God is more certainly true to His promise than man.

for if the inheritance is from law [as a method of divine dealing], no longer is it from promise [as a method of divine dealing]. But to Abraham, through the intermediate instrumentality of promise, God has in grace freely bestowed it.

If the law of Moses affects the promise at all, it renders it null and void, since the law cannot be added to the promise without destroying it. Salvation must rest either upon the promise or upon the law. The Judaizers claim that salvation rests upon both the promise and the law, but since the law had no effect on the promise, it follows that if the inheritance is based on obedience to the law then it is not on the basis of promise. God gave the inheritance to Abraham on the basis of promise, so law and promise are two opposing principles i.e. you cannot appeal to both. This promised inheritance God gave to Abraham, and to any who put their faith in Jesus, as a free gift, given out of the spontaneity of His heart, with no strings attached, not upon terms of mutual agreement, but as a voluntary act of His, He expecting no pay for it. Such is the difference between law and grace, since law is a mutual agreement where God obligates Himself to give salvation to anyone who earns it by obedience to the law. God's past act of giving an inheritance based on a promise to Abraham, has present results in us who come to Him now by faith.

What is then the significance of the law? For the sake of transgressions it was added until there should come the Descendant to whom the promise was made, having been promulgated by angels through the instrumentality of the hand of a mediator.

So why was the law of Moses given, since no one can be saved by it, but rather all stand condemned? It was given to produce transgressions, being steps taken into forbidden territory through deviations from a right course of action, violating the rights of others and going beyond one's own legal limitations. So the law showed sin not to be merely a following of evil impulses, but also a violation of explicit law, thus revealing the exceeding sinfulness of sin to the human race i.e. it shone a light so as to reveal man's overstepping from right into wrong, causing man to fear God's wrath and to strengthen his weak moral sense by educating his conscience so as to make it more sensitive to sin, in particular with respect to the law's "You shall" and "You shall not". So the law set the stamp of positive transgression upon already existing sin, not so as to give a knowledge of sin as sin, but to show that it was a violation of God's commandments. The law was placed in a supplementary position to the covenant of grace, therefore subordinate to it, its purpose to show men their need of grace and their need of a Saviour Who, in infinite grace, now offers them a salvation, free, in answer to faith. The law was brought in alongside the promise until the seed of Abraham should come, to whom the promise was made. Grace has flowed full and free from the time of Adam until now, even while the law was in force, and it will continue to flow until sin is done away with completely, being the only way in which God saves sinners. The law was given by intermediaries; angels and Moses, while the people stood far off, the promise was spoken directly and intimately by God to His friend Abraham. The law says, "Stand off", grace says, "Come near". The law does not have a direct and positive relation to the divine plan of salvation, as does the promise, and it was of only transitory significance, where the promise has an eternal value and meaning.

Now, the mediator is not a go-between representing the interests of one individual, but God is one individual.

This means of giving shows the superiority of the promise over the law. A mediator stands in the midst of two parties, therefore the law of Moses is a contract between two; God gives through Moses and man is obliged to obey, with blessings for obedience and punishments for disobedience. But the promise of free grace is not a contract between two parties, since He acts alone and directly when He promises salvation to anyone who will receive it by the outstretched hand of faith. Grace is unconditional, with no good works to be done to merit acceptance with Him. God acts without a mediator in respect to the promise of grace, therefore grace is superior to law, the dignity of the law being inferior to that of the promise.

Is therefore the law against the promises of God? God forbid. For if a law had been given which was able to impart life, righteousness in that case would have been from the law.

There is no conflict between the law of Moses and the promises since each has a distinct function. The law is a ministry of condemnation, the promises a ministry of salvation. The law judges a person on the basis of obedience or disobedience, the promises judge a person on the basis of faith. The law was not intended to express God's attitude towards man, since His attitude is one of grace, neither is the law the basis of God's judgement of man. A sinner who rejects Jesus goes to a lost eternity not because he has broken God's laws, since his sin has now been paid for, but because he rejects God's grace in Jesus. The law reveals the sinner's legal standing so condemns him since it cannot justify him, as the Judaizers claim that it can. To speak again in everyday terms; if a son disobeys his father's command, the father calls the son's attention to his disobeyed command and pronounces his son guilty, using this guilty sentence to bring his son to see his misdemeanour in its true light, causing the son to become repentant, so putting himself in a position where his father can forgive him, at which point the father assures his son of his forgiveness, so there is no conflict between the father's commands and the father's grace, it is just that they operate in different spheres. So is a man's seeing his transgression of God's will, the first step in his act of repentance and faith, which faith is answered by God with the gift of eternal life. Law cannot give eternal life, rather it demands of the sinner the death penalty; spiritual and physical death. The law will not accept good works in lieu of the death penalty, only Jesus' blood could satisfy the righteous demands of the broken law. So salvation is by grace, since Jesus, God the Son, took the sinner's place on the Cross and offers salvation to everyone who believes on Him.

But the scripture shut up all under sin in order that the promise on the ground of faith in Jesus Christ might be given to those who believe.

Everyone who does not keep the law of Moses is cursed, confined as by a jailer, being shut up in sin as in a prison. Being so confined by the law, the intention is that the convicted one might then turn to Jesus for salvation.

But before the aforementioned faith came, under the law we were constantly being guarded, being shut up with a view to the faith about to be revealed.

In this Age of Grace we now have faith in Jesus, looking back to the Cross, whereas Abraham's like faith looked forward prophetically to the Cross. The law of Moses, with a view to Jesus' coming and men then exercising their faith in Him, kept men under lock and key, holding them in custody, so that they might escape neither their consciousness of sins nor their liability to punishment, shutting them up to one avenue of escape; faith in Jesus. Those thus imprisoned who looked forward, in faith, to the day when a Saviour would pay for their sins, were saved by Jesus' blood, though it had not yet been shed, just as surely as we are now saved, who have acknowledged Jesus' death for us. Now that the sacrifice has been made, the law has been abolished.

So that the law became our guardian until Christ, in order that on the grounds of faith, we might be justified;

Like a slave employed by a family to have charge over their young son, watching over him and his behaviour, taking him to school, and morally supervising him, so the law of Moses was given the role of a temporary and inferior guardian of Israel, with its commands and prohibitions keeping the nation in a condition of dependence and restraint, it continually revealing to the Jewish people their sin as a positive transgression of itself.

but this faith having come, no longer are we under the guardian,

Now that Jesus has offered us faith in Him as the way of salvation, there is no longer any role for the law of Moses.

for all of you are God's sons through faith in Christ Jesus,

So my brothers, Jews and Gentiles alike, the separating wall of the law of Moses having been broken down at the Cross, you have now become mature children of God, of full age and no longer under a guardian, in Jesus.

for as many as were introduced into union with Christ, put on Christ.

You became 'in Jesus' when you put your faith in Him as Saviour, the Holy Spirit placing you into living union with Him. Now you have clothed yourselves with His strength, righteousness, glory, and salvation, and are in relationship with Him, He being in you and you being made like Him, and you have been brought into one family and one nature with Him.

There is neither Jew nor Greek, there is neither slave nor free, there is neither male nor female. For you are all one in Christ Jesus.

There is a unity as believers in our common life that transcends and overcomes any differences between us due to race, status, or gender. All our hearts now beat as one, the pulsating life of Jesus being our motivating power. His mind guides us all, His life is lived by us all, as produced by the Holy Spirit in the various circumstances and relations of each of our individual experiences.

And since you are Christ's, then are you Abraham's descendants, heirs according to the promise.

The Judaizers teach that by obeying the law of Moses you become the seed of Abraham, but, as I have shown you, it is by faith in Christ that this privilege comes to you. Abraham is the spiritual father of all who put their faith in Jesus, whether circumcised or uncircumcised, so that salvation has been made available to all, both Jew and Gentile, by God. Physical kinship to Abraham does not lead to salvation, being the false Jewish notion. Rather we, by belonging to Jesus, Abraham's promised Seed, are Abraham's posterity, since we now share Jesus' state and so are Abraham's seed, and thus saved.

Now I say, that as long as the heir is in his minority, he does not differ one bit from a slave, even though he is owner of all, but is under guardians and stewards until the time previously fixed by his father.

The person under the law of Moses is treated as immature, intellectually and morally, a child unable as yet to speak and needing to be restrained. In this way was Israel treated, as a minor, with no more rights than a slave, able to do nothing without the sanction of a guardian with respect to his person and his property. God, when giving the law, also determined the fixed time at which its stewardship over Israel would end, namely when Jesus satisfied its demands on the Cross.

In like manner, we also, when we were in our minority, were in a permanent state of servitude under the rudimentary first principles of mankind.

All of us, Jew and Gentile, were immature ones, just on the first, most basic step of moral progress in unsaved humanity, whether that be the performing of the symbolic ceremonies and legalisms of Judaism, or in the ritual observances of pagan religions.

But when there came the fullness of the time, God sent off His Son, woman-born, made subject to law,

In due course, the moment came which completed the period of time designated by God that should elapse before the coming of the Son of God in incarnation. So He sent forth His Son to represent Himself, sent out from His presence to this dark world, with a commission and the credentials to make the way for man's salvation. The time chosen for His coming had been announced to Daniel after the edict of the Medes and Persians to rebuild the temple in Jerusalem, four hundred and eighty-three years previously. But all was now in place. Now the law of Moses had fully served its purpose, showing the world that the most highly favoured nation, Israel, was, despite all of God's blessings and mercy, totally depraved, and so giving the Gentiles a picture of their own totally depraved heart. Now this law, with its ten commandments, social rules, and sacrifices could be done away with as a legal system, to be superseded by the Gospel of Grace centring faith in this God-sent Saviour. Now was there a time of world peace, with the Roman roads making travel for missionaries easy, and with the universal Greek language making speedy propagation of the Gospel possible. So was the stage set for the greatest event in human history; the incarnation, sacrificial death, and bodily resurrection of God the Son. His was a virgin birth, being Eve's Seed, and His life was lived in perfect obedience under the law of Moses and within the Jewish legal economy.

in order that He might deliver those under law to the end that we might be placed as adult sons.

His purpose in sending the Son was that He might buy from the market all who were slaves to law, whether that law was written on their hearts or in an external legalistic system. Jesus died under law and was raised to a realm where law as a legalistic system does not exist. He died so that we who have faith in Him might be delivered and raised with Him into that same realm where law does not operate. So, under grace we are no longer immature, but have become adult sons, adopted by the Father, and placed into His family. Now we are treated like adults under grace, where before we were treated like servants and minors under law.

And because you are sons, God sent forth the Spirit of His Son into your hearts crying, Abba [namely], my Father.

Since you are His children, God sent the Holy Spirit to live in your hearts, placing you as adult sons of God by releasing you from your position as minors under the law, and giving you a consciousness of the affectionate, fond, filial relationship that now exists; yourselves living as His sons and He as your Father, no longer your Judge. The joy you feel in knowing Him as Father is earnest and intense, and the Spirit cries out from within you that yes, He is indeed your Father.

So that no longer are you a slave but a son, and since you are a son, you are also an heir through God.

Your possession of the Spirit proves that you are adult sons of God. Each of you is no longer a slave but now a son. So you are heirs of God with an inheritance, but not due to any good works of yours, but due only to the grace of God. Only in freedom from the law of Moses can you obtain the blessing of Abraham, which blessing the Judaizers tell you is only obtainable through circumcision. I exhort you then to retain your status of adult sons under grace, rather than go back to the position of a minor and a slave under law.

But at that time, in fact, not knowing God, you were in a slave's bondage to the gods which are not gods by nature.

Back then you were slaves to demonic deities, which are real but not god-like, as I have told you before in person, and you were in bondage under a system of legalism.

But now having come to know God, indeed, rather having become known by God, how is it possible that you are turning back again to the weak and beggarly rudimentary principles to which you are again bent on being in bondage?

You owe your personal knowledge of God to Him, your escape from idolatry and from bondage to the law of Moses effected by His choosing to come to know you in a saving way. So how is it possible, having been rescued, that you would want to return to bondage or to slavery to demons? Surely you can see the absurdity of this? Only the Gospel of Grace has divine power and richness. If you proceed in your current direction and intent, you will return to your initial state of poverty, having no spiritual blessings, and return to being lost and without hope, with only condemnation to look forward to. Although the Jews, in the law of Moses, had a spiritual element to their practice that was truly divine, as opposed to the Gentiles' demon-inspired soul-destroying promptings, both Jews and Gentiles had a similar ritualistic element to their religion. This is even more the case for the Jews now that Jesus has come, absorbing the spiritual aspect of the law of Moses into Christianity, and leaving a mere mass of lifeless ordinances, so making Judaism similar to any other ritualistic system. Both Jews and Gentiles among you then, were under restraint, held by rituals that multiplied your transgressions and convicted you of sin, but which rituals were also preparing you both for your liberty of manhood in Jesus. Having been so liberated, do you really want to return to your former captivity?

Days you are scrupulously and religiously observing, and months, and seasons, and years.

You have already begun to carefully follow the calendar of the law of Moses with respect to festivals and fasts, the Judaizers having convinced you to do so, knowing that these observances would not seem repulsive to you, and so would be a way to gain a foothold with you with a view to you subsequently adopting circumcision and finally the whole law. The strictness with which you are observing these prescribed events shows how you are falling back from grace into formal, lifeless, legalistic ritual. Sabbaths, New Moon festivals, Passover, the monthly and annual feasts, and Jubilee years, all these were but a shadow of events to come and whose purpose has now been fully served, the law now having been abolished by Jesus' atoning sacrifice.

I am afraid about you lest perhaps in vain I have laboured to the point of exhaustion for you.

I suspect that what I fear has already happened and that you have abandoned grace. I am anxious for your spiritual welfare, following the work I did in evangelizing you.

Become as I am, because I also became as you were, brethren; I am beseeching you. You had done me no wrong.

Become like me in being free of the law of Moses, as I became as you are, a Gentile, by forgoing my advantages as a Jew. I lived like you, giving up my time-honoured Jewish customs. I abandoned all for you, so do not abandon me. When I arrived in Galatia you besought me to preach the Gospel message freely to you after the Jews had expelled me, so now I appeal to you to maintain the freedom of that same Gospel.

But you know that because of an infirmity of the flesh I preached the gospel to you on the occasion of my first visit.

It was because of a sudden attack of ophthalmia that I was forced to stay with you when I was first in Galatia, as it had been my intention not to evangelize your territory but to go on to another place. You saw the repulsive progress of the illness, but were tenderly sympathetic towards me. Rather than spurning me, a Jew and a stranger, you welcomed me with open arms and my Gospel message with open hearts. You knew that I was only detained with you due to this chronic illness and was in reality headed for Asia Minor and Greece, but you cared for me like one of your own.

And the test to which you were subjected and which was in my flesh, you did not loathe nor utterly despise, but as a messenger of God you received me, as Christ Jesus.

Yes you did not spit me out or reject me or my message, but rather received me as an angel of God, even Jesus Himself. Do you remember how, in your excitement following the healing of the lame man, you claimed that I had come from Heaven, and you declared me to be Hermes and Barnabas Zeus come down in human form? Looking back, I am sure that you can thank God with joy that we were not in fact mere Greek gods of Olympus, but messengers of the living God Who made Heaven and earth.

Where is therefore your spiritually prosperous state? For I bear witness to you that if it had been possible, you would have dug out your own eyes and given them to me.

Back then you were wealthy in your self-denial and your self-sacrificial love for me. What has happened to that rich, true love of yours?

So then I have become your enemy because I am telling you the truth?

But now I am your enemy and you are hostile towards me. I told you the truth about the Judaizers and spoke plainly against them when I last visited you, warning you of the impending danger of you listening to their teaching. And that which I warned you about has now turned out to be true. Is this a reason to hate me; that I sincerely and truthfully spoke to you?

They are zealously paying you court, but not honestly, desiring to isolate you in order that you might be paying court to them.

I have always been true with you in what I say, but these are talking dishonestly to you, just to try and win you over. They seek to separate you from the Gospel of Grace so that you would then need to come to them for guidance and fellowship to do with matters of the soul.

But it is good to be zealously courted in a good thing at all times, and not only when I am present with you, my born ones, concerning whom I am again striving with intense effort and anguish until Christ be outwardly expressed in you.

I have sought after you persistently, not so that you attach yourselves to me, but that I might join you to Jesus. And you had warm feelings towards me when I was with you. How I wish these feelings of yours towards me would continue. I am glad if others court you while I am absent from you, as long as their courting is done in a right spirit and in connection with the truth of the Gospel of Grace. I love you deeply, my children. You are saved and Jesus resides in your hearts, so let His beauty show in your lives as it used to, since now it shows only a little, if at all. By coming under the law of Moses, you have substituted self-effort to produce a Christ-like life, for your previous dependence on the Holy Spirit to do this. You need to once again recognise the Holy Spirit and return to depending upon Him to minister Jesus to and through you in a full measure.

Moreover, I was wishing that I were present with you at this very moment and could thus change my tone, because I am perplexed about you.

I regret the severity of my language when I last visited you and warned you about the Judaizers. I long to be with you so that I may speak the truth to you more tenderly and affectionately. And I would rather speak with you than send you a message by this letter. Currently I am at a loss about you, not knowing which way to turn, not knowing how to deal with you nor how to find an entrance into your hearts, my mind being full of doubts and fears about you so that I am tossed to and fro.

Be telling me, you that are bent upon being under law, are you not hearing the law?

You are on the point of adopting law and upholding its authority over you, seemingly unaware of the full significance and alarming consequences of your doing this.

For it stands written, Abraham had two sons, one from the maidservant and one from the freewoman.

Your desire to be under law is not in harmony with Scripture and here is the Scripture.

But, on the one hand, the son of the maidservant was one born in the ordinary course of nature. On the other hand, the son of the freewoman was one born through the promise,

Ishmael was born after the flesh by natural generation. Isaac was born according to promise through the miraculous interposition of God, when the parents were too old to have children. Ishmael's descendants do not then belong to the covenant people, Israel. Isaac's descendants are those that have the promises. Whereas the two had one father, Abraham, they had different mothers.

which class of things is allegorical. For these are two covenants, one from Mount Sinai, begetting bondage, which is as to its nature classed as Hagar.

This illustration proves that the law is superseded by grace. The law of Moses was given at Mount Sinai, identified here with Hagar, Ishmael's mother. This covenant places its children in a condition of bondage.

Now this Hagar is Mount Sinai in Arabia, and corresponds to the Jerusalem which now is, for she is in bondage with her children.

Sinai's Arabic name resembles Hagar. Sinai corresponds to Jerusalem by virtue of it being the centre of the apostate observance of Judaism, whose legalistic followers are in bondage to law.

But the Jerusalem which is above is free, which is our Mother.

The heavenly Jerusalem represents Sarah, Isaac's mother, and corresponds to the faith way of salvation, in contrast to the earthly Jerusalem which represents legalistic Judaism.

For it stands written, Rejoice, barren woman who does not bear. Break forth and cry, you who do not travail, because more are the children of the desolate than of the one who has a husband.

Sarah, who was childless until old age, has given birth according to the promise, by the grace of God which emanates from the heavenly Jerusalem, and whose children will be its everlasting citizens.

And, as for you, brethren, after the manner of Isaac are you children of promise.

You Galatians are not like Ishmael, born to a slave by natural means, but like Isaac, born to a free woman according to the promise, born miraculously, and born of the Holy Spirit. You now stand before God not on the basis of physical descent from Abraham, but on the basis of the promise made to Abraham, which promise applies to all who have like faith to him.

But just as then, he who was born according to the flesh was constantly persecuting him who was born according to the Spirit, so also now.

As Ishmael persecuted Isaac, so the Judaizers are persecuting me and all who will not forsake grace for law.

But what does the scripture say? Throw out the maidservant and her son. For the son of the maidservant shall by no means inherit with the son of the freewoman.

The rejection of Ishmael points to a rejection of the children of Abraham after the flesh, in favour of those who become children of Abraham by faith. The law must disappear with the arrival of the Gospel, the two cannot co-exist. Thus has Judaism now been dealt a death blow, though the Judaizers misguidedly still cling to the law of Moses with a frenzied, jealous affection, and purpose to influence and infect the Gentile assemblies that I have founded, seeking to undermine my authority and to endanger my life.

Therefore, brethren, we are children, not of a maidservant, but of the freewoman.

So we believers are not a community in bondage to legal statutes, but members of the community whose relation to God is that of sons, and who do not have a spirit of bondage but the Spirit of sonship. So let me continue now to some practical teaching, emphasising the ministry of the Spirit, under Whose control I exhort you to put yourselves once more.

For this aforementioned freedom Christ set you free. Keep on standing firm therefore and stop being subject again to a yoke of bondage.

Jesus died on the Cross to give you the advantage of freedom from the law of Moses, no longer bound in your actions by a set of guardian's rules, but old enough to act alone in your maturity in Him by the power of the Holy Spirit. Do not therefore, as adults, put yourselves under rules made for children. Live in dependence on the Holy Spirit, your hearts having now been occupied with Jesus as your Lord, and guided also by the ethics that emerge from my teaching and that of the other apostles, so that you do what is right because it is right, and in order to please your Lord, and to show your love for Him, not because you are commanded to by the law. Remain in this freedom and don't become entangled again.

Behold, I, Paul, am saying to you that if you persist in being circumcised, Christ will be advantageous to you in not even one thing,

You are on the verge of being circumcised. Realise that this will not benefit you in any way in your growth in the Christian life. Rather, doing so will put you under the law of Moses and deprive you of the indwelling ministry of the Holy Spirit, which ministry is made possible through Jesus' death and resurrection, and which ministry is not provided for under law.

and I solemnly affirm again to every man who receives circumcision, that he is under obligation to do the whole law.

If you are circumcised you will also take on the burden of the entire legalistic system, which consequence the Judaizers have not made clear to you in their offering you participation in the blessings of the Abrahamic covenant with Israel. I protest to you in the strongest terms not to be circumcised. Do not be bound to the law of Moses. You are free in Jesus, firstly free from the condemnation of those who disobey the law, secondly free from the law as a means of justification, and thirdly free from the obligation to render obedience to its statutes. In this Age of Grace you are obligated to either obey all of it, or, through belief in Jesus, none of it. So do not submit to a rule of your own choosing, for example to keep the Sabbath, the seventh day, rather than the first day of the week, the Lord's day. How can you distinguish which rules are for Christians and which others are purely Jewish in application? The ministry of the Holy Spirit takes the place of and is in advance of the whole of the economy of Moses. Whatever is of value for the Church in the legal enactments of that previous code, is found in the passages of the letters from me and from the other apostles where we exhort you as to your conduct. The Old Testament was superseded by the New, which is specially designed for the Church, and can only be referenced now in view of the facts that firstly, it is specially adapted to the needs of Israel and for the time before the Cross, and secondly, its legal enactments to do with general principles of conduct that are universal and eternal in their application must never be treated as legally binding upon a believer but simply as ethics to guide their conduct.

You are without effect from Christ, such of you as in the sphere of the law are seeking your justification. You have lost your hold upon [sanctifying] grace.

If you look to the law of Moses for your justification, your union with Jesus has been broken, and being no longer joined intimately with Him, you cannot grow, since your relation to Him is now ineffective and you are no longer able to please Him and no longer derive any spiritual benefit from Him. To live under law is to have fallen from grace, being the grace for daily living that is ministered to you by the Holy Spirit. You still have His grace for justification, which you received when you accepted Jesus as your Lord, being a judicial act of God, and that transaction was closed and permanent at the moment you believed and as such He still holds on to you. Rather it is grace for sanctification, being a life long process in your Christian life that you have lost your hold on. Lack of progress in sanctification does not mean that you are no longer saved. If that were the case salvation would depend on works and not on grace anymore.

For, as for us, through the agency of the Spirit, on the ground of faith, a hoped-for righteousness we are eagerly awaiting,

We believers yearn intensely for the presence of an experimental righteousness as our faith is expressed in love in our lives, being a consequence of our yielding ourselves to the Holy Spirit. We are already declared righteous with respect to salvation through our putting our faith in Jesus, which was a matter between Father and Son in making us in right relation to the laws of God. This hope of righteousness with respect to our conduct will not come to fruition if we depend on our own efforts in attempting to obey the law of Moses as the Judaizers do.

for in Christ Jesus neither circumcision is of any power nor uncircumcision, but faith coming to effective expression through love.

Being joined to Jesus by faith, in that life-giving union which was initiated when the Holy Spirit placed us into Jesus, is the thing that is of power to effect a transformation in the life of the justified believer. This faith in Jesus issues in love in a believer's life, that love produced by the Holy Spirit. Whether one is circumcised or not circumcised has no power for anything in one's life.

You were running well. Who cut in on you and thus hindered you from obeying the truth?

You were conducting yourselves bravely, honourably and becomingly. But someone has broken into your race, impeding you and slowing your progress. Those Judaizers have robbed your lives of the fragrance of Jesus and of the enabling power for service given you by the Holy Spirit.

This persuasion is not from the One who calls you.

It is not Jesus, your Redeemer, Who has persuaded you to desert Him. It is not the Father, Who called you into salvation and freedom in Christ, Who is now turning you from grace to enslaving practices, so making you hostile to Him. It is not the Holy Spirit, Who is truth, Who is now teaching you false doctrine.

A little yeast is permeating the whole lump.

This insidious, evil teaching of the Judaizers is slowly beginning to corrupt the life of your groups, endangering them, and, unrebuked, it will spread throughout all of your assemblies so as to control them.

As for myself, I have come to a settled persuasion in the Lord with respect to you, namely, that you will take no other view than this. But the one who troubles you shall bear his judgement, whoever he is.

But I at least, have confidence in you, based on my confidence in Jesus, that you will also take the view that the Judaizers' teaching is not from God but is from an evil source, and that their doctrine is therefore false. Anyone who would so disturb your faith will have to carry the judgement of God, which is a grievous burden.

And I, brethren, if I am still preaching circumcision, why am I in spite of this fact still being persecuted? Then the stumbling block of the Cross has been done away.

They claim that I still teach circumcision. So why then am I being persecuted? I am persecuted because of my teaching of anti-legalism. Before I was saved by faith and was a Pharisee, yes, I did preach the necessity of circumcision. But after putting my faith in Jesus, I made a clean break with legalism, and that before commencing my ministry. The Cross is only an offence to the Jews because from it flows the teaching that believers in Jesus are free from the law of Moses, which teaching they regard as blasphemy. The Cross sets aside the entire economy of Moses and offers salvation by grace through faith alone, without the factor of works to merit acceptance with God, not that that system ever taught that a sinner was accepted on the basis of good works. The Cross would hold no offence to the Jews if circumcision was still a prerequisite to salvation.

I would that they who are upsetting you would even have themselves mutilated.

These men are driving peace and order out of your assemblies. I wish that they would not stop at circumcision, but would emasculate themselves, like your priests of Cybele do in their heathen self-devotion to their god. This act might be an even more powerful help to the Judaizers in gaining their salvation!

For, as for you, upon the basis of freedom you were called, brethren. Only do not turn your liberty into a base of operations for the evil nature, but through love keep on constantly serving one another,

So you have freedom in Jesus, but now that the restraint of legalistic statutes has been thrown off, be wary that you do not allow this lack of restraint to lead you into indulging your sinful desires, but rather to live freely within Christian ethics. Since you now have the divine nature, you hate sin and love the right, and have both the desire and the power to keep from sinning and to do God's will. The indwelling Holy Spirit exercises a stricter supervision over you than the law of Moses ever did, and His power to restrain is far more effective than the law's ever was, and He gives you the desire and power to refuse the wrong and choose the right which the law was never able to do. Now you are under the control of a Person rather than a system of legal enactments. Legalistic teachers in the Church are not helping God, though they think they are, to control this world, by imposing law on grace. They teach thus because they are ignorant of and do not recognise the ministry of the Holy Spirit. Human flesh does still need restraint, the flesh still being with the believer though its controlling power has been broken, but this restraining is a work of the Spirit, and not through obedience to law, as that just incites to evil. Acquaintance with the ministry of the indwelling Holy Spirit is far more productive of victory over sin than the imposition of the law, and His controlling ministry is the secret of holy living. Your liberty is not to be used as a springboard from which to take off with the intention of sinning.

Serving one another in the self-sacrificial love of the Spirit is the antidote to this abuse of your freedom, along with willingly serving God in love and gladness. This attitude of serving subordinates all selfish desires to love and annihilates self, which death to self means defeat for sin, since sin's essence is self-will and self-gratification. Death to self then is the secret to victory over the totally depraved nature, whose power over the believer was broken when God saved him, whenever that nature attempts to induce you to use your liberty as a pretext to sin. The Spirit will restrain evil in the world through the Church, until He goes to Heaven taking the Church with Him at the Rapture.

for the whole law in one utterance stands fully obeyed, namely, in this, Love your neighbour as you do yourself.

So you are free from bondage to the law of Moses, and by loving self-sacrificially you please God since, in this one attitude, love, you meet His divine principles and standards i.e. those that exist permanently in the being of God and represent those things that go to make up right conduct on the part of man. Being released from an obligation to obey legal statutes, all that is required to fully obey God's law, being an expression of His will, is included in love, which in turn fulfils all that the law of Moses would require of you were it still in force. Walking in love will cause the believer to incidentally obey the law without him ever obeying it as a system of statutes. Now, under the law of love, there is an ethical and spiritual dynamic produced in the heart of the yielded believer by the Holy Spirit, giving them the desire and power to live a life in which the dominating principle is love. God's love is far more efficient at putting sin out of life than the legalisers think the dictates of the law of Moses ever were.

But if, as is the case, you are biting and devouring one another, take heed lest you be consumed by one another.

The Judaizers have caused much strife amongst you so that you are fighting with each other like animals in a deadly struggle, which partisan hatred amongst you will result in actions that lead to mutual injury and to eventually destroy the organic community life of your assemblies.

But I say, Through the instrumentality of the Spirit habitually order your manner of life, and you will in no wise execute the passionate desire of the evil nature,

The absence of the law's restraining you does not mean that you will now fall into sin, as those who oppose my teaching claim. It is true that your evil nature has not been eradicated, but its power over you has been broken and you need not obey it anymore. It is there, constantly attempting to control you, as it did before salvation wrought its work in your being, but by following the Spirit's leading, you will never never act on the impulses of your fallen nature, but will be able to resist and conquer them. You must learn to say "No" to sin by the power of the Holy Spirit, so that you cooperate with Him in His work of sanctifying your life, since He is always there to give you victory over that nature of yours as you trust Him to do that. You must choose to yield to Him rather than to obey your evil nature. So continue to govern your lives by the inward impulses of the Holy Spirit, subjecting yourselves to Him as He ministers to your spiritual needs.

for the evil nature constantly has a strong desire to suppress the Spirit, and the Spirit constantly has a strong desire to suppress the evil nature. And these are entrenched in an attitude of mutual opposition to one another so that you may not do the things that you desire to do.

Your evil nature and the Spirit are antagonistic towards each other. When your flesh presses hard on you with its evil behests, the Holy Spirit, Who is there to oppose the flesh, will give you victory over it so that you will not sin. When the Spirit places a course of conduct on your heart, your flesh opposes the Spirit in an effort to prevent you from obeying the Spirit. The choice of which course of action you take lies with you. You must develop the habit of keeping your eyes fixed on Jesus and of maintaining your trust in the Holy Spirit. The more you say "No" to sin, the easier it will be, until it becomes a habit. The more you say "Yes" to Jesus, the easier it will be, until it becomes a habit. If you obey your evil nature it is because you choose to, but the Holy Spirit has given you a new nature, the divine nature, so that its sweet influences are constantly permeating the activities of your will as you keep yourself yielded to the Spirit, allowing Him to keep on suppressing the activities of your evil nature and any control which it might attempt to exert over you.

But if you are being led by the Spirit you are not under law.

You Galatians are still trying to live Christian lives but you are going about it the wrong way, so you are failing. The entrance of the law of Moses and with it a required dependence upon self-effort to obey that law, has undone all that you were previously doing in following the instructions given to you by me from the beginning. God has installed in you the spiritual machinery that allows the Spirit to minister inwardly to you, but you have thrown a spanner of self-dependence into His mechanical setup in you, rendering it ineffective. The right way to live is in being free from statutes and from the sinful nature, a faith way, with a dependence on the Spirit. So be led by the Spirit. Then you will not live your lives on the principle of legalism, since being led by the Spirit and attempting to obey the law are methods of living that are diametrically opposed to one another. The flesh and the law are closely allied, in that the law provokes the flesh to more sin, so both, in this alliance, should be renounced. The law finds nothing to condemn in the life of a Spirit-led believer, since every wrong desire of their evil nature is suppressed by the Spirit, so that they fulfil the law. Such is the blessed moral freedom of the Spirit-led believer, the law having no power to censure, condemn or punish.

Now the works of the evil nature are well known, works of such a nature as, for example, fornication, uncleanness, wantonness,

Love would never have anything to do with these fleshly acts, and they are not things which you are now free to do in your liberty from law. You are able to decide if in doing any of these things you are being led by the Holy Spirit or by your flesh; things that are impure though pleasing to the senses, things prompted by lawless insolence with a contempt for public opinion, things characterised by living with no restraints but rather daring to do whatever imagination and wanton petulance may suggest, things that shamelessly outrage public decency.

idolatry, witchcraft, enmities, strife, jealousy, angers, self-seekings, divisions, factions,

Worship of images, sorcery and magic arts, things done in hostility, contention and quarrelling, envying of another's possessions, outbursts of anger, things done out of selfishness, dissensions and discord, following beliefs that cause separation and lead to heresy.

envyings, drunkenness, carousings, and the things of such a nature which are like these things, respecting which things I am telling you beforehand even as I told you in advance, that those who are in the habit of practicing things of that nature shall not inherit the kingdom of God.

And nocturnal riotous half-drunken revelries. Those who practice these and similar things, to the extent that they characterise them, their fleshly actions being a true indication of their nature, shall not inherit anything from God.

But the fruit of the Spirit is love, joy, peace, longsuffering, kindness, goodness, faithfulness, meekness, self-control. Against such things as these there is no law.

Rather, use your freedom from law to live lives motivated by divine love. In contrast to the works of the flesh and in direct opposition to them, the fruit of the Spirit-led life is a well-rounded complete Christian life with all these elements present in unity; self-sacrificial love that puts others' interests ahead of one's own, spiritual joy, heart peace and tranquillity of mind at being bound together with God through the blood of Jesus, steadfastness of soul and patient endurance under provocation without anger or thought of revenge, a gentle benign nature, being ruled by and aiming at all that is good, a continuing loyalty to Jesus and the believers, a mild and gentle disposition, having a mastery of one's own desires and impulses. A life comprising these qualities fully meets the demands of God's laws.

And they who belong to Christ Jesus crucified the evil nature with its dispositions and cravings once for all.

When we put our faith in Jesus as Saviour, we crucified our old nature with its affections and lusts, in that we received the actualised benefits of our identification with Him in His death on the Cross, these benefits only being potential at the time He was crucified. In particular, the breaking of the power of the sinful nature over our lives was procured by Jesus at the Cross, but as we now yield to the Spirit, that victory over the sinful nature is made actual and operative in our lives, the Spirit now also ministering the freedom from that nature's control in His producing His fruit in our lives. Beyond this initial putting to death of the sinful nature by Jesus, we then decide to count ourselves as having died to that nature by continually saying, "No" to sin, "No" to the evil innate forces resident in our evil nature, and "No" to those forces that reach out from that nature trying to find expression in the gratification of its evil desires.

In view of the fact that we are being sustained in spiritual life by the Spirit, by means of the Spirit let us go on ordering our conduct.

Since we have a new life principle operating in our beings, let us now walk by the Spirit, in a right and straight path, under the guidance, impulses and energy of the divine life that is resident in us. If we will to live the highest type of Christian life, the grace of God will make that possible for us. So desire to live a Christ-like life, depend on the Holy Spirit to enable that life, and step out on faith and live that life. This will bring all the infinite resources of grace to your aid, and all the activities of the Spirit will be put in operation on your behalf.

Let us stop becoming vain-glorious, provoking one another, envying one another.

Let us stop pretending that we have a rightful claim to a position of honour when this is not the case. Rather let us seek God's glory. Those of you who believe it right to live with no restraint at all, do not be proud of this 'liberty' nor dare the other more scrupulous of you to do things which the law of Moses forbids, insinuating that they are afraid to do so, and provoking them to then do things that they believe to be wrong. On the other hand the scrupulous of you are tempted to regard this 'liberty' as something to be desired, and envy those their so-called freedom, wishing you had similar feelings as them about their freedom. The strong Christians among you are those who are still living Spirit-controlled lives and who should bear the infirmities of these weak ones.

Brethren, if, however, a man be overtaken in a sin, as for you who are the spiritual ones, be restoring such a one in a spirit of meekness, taking heed to yourself lest you also be tempted.

Those of you who are being led astray by the Judaizers have found that sin is creeping into your lives, since attempting to obey the law of Moses brings sin into your life as your evil nature is aroused to active rebellion by the very presence of the law. You seem surprised by this since you were not conscious of harbouring any sinful desire. This is the result of not knowing or acknowledging the delivering power of the Holy Spirit. You need to depend on Him and not on self-effort to obey the ethics I taught you or the legal enactments of the law. You have made yourselves an easy prey to the Tempter of men's souls and he is wreaking havoc amongst you. You have found that you are overtaken by a sin before being aware that you have done wrong. You are lapsing rather than walking straight, doing wrong because you are not availing yourselves of the God-appointed method of living the Christian life, even though you wholeheartedly desire to do what is right. You lapsed because you were helpless to prevent it, which helplessness was self-imposed since I had taught you how I had previously failed as a Christian when living under law but subsequently found the way of victory, which Spirit-led way of victory you have turned your backs on with the resulting failure you now experience. You who are still living Spirit-led lives, I ask that you restore your brothers who have abandoned this way and are following the way of the Judaizers, to restore them to their former good condition, bringing them into line. They have wandered off the right road of grace and are stumbling in the quagmire of self-dependence and legalism. You need to restore them into the grace way of living the Christian life, to repair the damage caused by the Judaizers, and to equip them to go on living their lives in the right way. You also need to help them in now judging their sins and confessing them and putting them away, so restoring them to their previous communion with Jesus, which communion has been interrupted by the entrance of sin into their lives. Do this restoring work with a gentle spirit, and keeping a sharp watch upon yourselves in case you are also attracted by the Judaizers' teaching and fall into sin yourselves.

One another's burdens be constantly bearing, and thus you will fully satisfy the requirements of the law of the Christ.

You should feel a responsibility for one another's spiritual welfare, especially when the other has sinned. So you Spirit-dominated ones should feel the responsibility of rescuing your brothers who have put themselves under legalism, to take them out of abject slavery to the law of Moses and into dependence once more on the Spirit, also in helping them to go to Jesus with a confession of their sins committed while living under law. Be willing to do this restoring work, in a helpful and sympathetic way, though it may involve some unpleasantness and heartache for you. In doing this you will fulfil the law of love.

For if anyone thinks himself to be something when he is nothing, he is deceiving himself.

To do this restoring work, you will need not to think more highly of yourselves than you do of those you are restoring. Any hint of superior feelings on your part will mean that you are not fulfilling the law of love and have a false understanding as to your true status in the Christian experience.

But his own work let each one put to the test and thus approve, and then with respect to himself alone will he have a ground for glorying, and not with respect to the other one [with whom he had compared himself],

If you do feel superior to any of your brothers, you are merely comparing yourselves with someone that you believe to be inferior to yourself, which judgement is only correct in your own eyes. He who tests his own status in isolation from anyone else bases his appraisal on an absolute rather than a relative foundation i.e. on himself alone. What in your own character and life merits approval that you might truly congratulate yourself upon?

for each shall bear his own private burden.

You should bear the burdens of others. Since each of us has a burden of our own, how can anyone claim superiority when we are all in the same situation? i.e. we each have a susceptibility to certain sins to which we all have succumbed. So we should each take the responsibility of bearing our own burden as our responsibility towards God and man, and not focus our attention purely on the failings of others. If we recognise our own failings we will have no inclination to compare ourselves with others.

Moreover, let the one who is being taught the Word constantly be holding fellowship with the one who is teaching in all good things.

You who have received oral instruction in the Word of God, should share in the blessing of grace with your former teachers, they being true teachers of the Word, which blessing they are currently enjoying. Make common cause with them in everything that is morally good and which promotes salvation by faith alone. The breach that has occurred between you and them cannot but have interfered with your moral and spiritual life. You are to work in common with your teachers, including me, so as to promote the spiritual life of the assemblies, ending the hindrance to their growth that has been caused by the disruption of your abandoning of grace. I am not in any way saying that you should support your teachers financially. I am talking here about moral and spiritual support and not looking for any financial gain, as the Judaizers often accuse me of doing, being one of their favourite lines of attack against me.

Stop leading yourselves astray. God is not being outwitted and evaded. For whatever a man is in the habit of sowing, this also will he reap;

It is of the utmost importance who you fellowship with, whether that be with your former teachers who taught you the truth, or with the Judaizers who are teaching you error. By not making this a matter of importance, you are deceiving yourselves as to the consequences of your choice in this matter. You cannot ignore or ridicule God, turning your nose up at Him, saying one thing but acting in a contrary way, making your words pleasant and respectful but then betraying hidden ill-will and contempt in cynical gestures and indirect expressions that are disrespectful. If you sow your actions of works, in alliance with the Judaizers, you will reap disaster in your lives, and chastening from the hand of God, since you are spurning His way of grace and dependence on Him.

because the one who sows with a view to his own evil nature, from his evil nature as a source shall reap corruption. But the one who sows with a view to the Spirit, from the Spirit as a source shall reap life eternal.

By following the teachings of the Judaizers, you are catering to the desires of your evil nature, since they make no demand for the necessity of regeneration nor of faith in an atoning sacrifice that paid for sin, but rather stress a salvation-by-works religion which glorifies man, not God, and which allows you to go on in your sin while seeking to buy the favour of

God by your so-called good works. This only leads to corruption in your lives, as you can already see is happening. But by choosing your course of conduct in accordance with the desires of the Holy Spirit, you will reap the blessings of God's gift to you of eternal life.

Let us not slacken our exertions by reason of the weariness that comes with prolonged effort in habitually doing that which is good. For in a season which in its character is appropriate, we shall reap if we do not become enfeebled through exhaustion and faint.

Do not be overcome by the ever-present battle with temptations that are presented to you by your evil nature, nor relax your effort in maintaining the Spirit's control over you, for if you continue in Spirit-given victory and in active participation in His purposes, you will gather a harvest, at the time of His choosing.

So then, in like manner, let us be having opportunity, let us be working that which is good to all, but especially to those of the household of the Faith.

So let us have a permanent season for doing good, as led by the Spirit and in His energy that is the product of His work in us, always alert for occasions when we may be a blessing to others, especially our fellow believers, and making that endeavour a labour into which we put much energy.

You see with what large letters I am writing to you with my own hand.

See how I have written all of this letter myself, in singly-formed inch-high letters, rather than it being one of my usual dictated letters which are written for me in small joined-together letters, but to which I then add my own personally-written greeting at the end. One reason I have done this is so as to authenticate this letter since I know of one letter, to the Thessalonian assembly and which said that the Tribulation had already started, that claimed to be from me in that it had a large forged signature of my name at the end, but which was written by someone else. You know my writing and the largeness of it from the time you nursed me, since which time ophthalmia has rendered me almost totally blind. But my main purpose in writing this all myself is that I wanted this letter to be as personal as possible, as if I was actually there with you. See the effort I have put into writing this, aiming to appeal to your tender hearts, hoping that it might lead you to remember your previous gracious treatment of me and not now forsake me, your suffering, self-sacrificing teacher.

As many as desire to make a good outward appearance in the sphere of the flesh, these are trying to compel you to receive circumcision, their only motive being that they might not be persecuted by reason of the cross of Christ,

The Judaizers wish to remain in good standing with the Jewish community, who have rejected Jesus as being their Messiah and the One Who takes away sin, but they cannot do so as long as the Church, of which they are a part, proclaims grace in place of the law of Moses. By teaching the Church to accept salvation by works, beginning with feast observances and circumcision, they seek to bring an end to the persecution of the Church by the Jews. Whilst this is the human motive for their infiltration, the core of the attack, below the outward appearance, is one of spiritual motive, being an attempt by Satan to destroy the Church.

for not even those who are circumcised are themselves keeping the law, but they desire you to be circumcised in order that in your flesh they may glory.

The Judaizers do not keep all of the law of Moses, but are just seeking to gain favour with the Jews by demonstrating their zeal for it, in deceitfully coercing the Gentiles in the Church to put themselves under its obligations, requirements, and statutes.

For, as for me, far be it from me to be glorying except in the cross of our Lord Jesus Christ, through whom to me the world stands crucified and I to the world.

I do not boast in the flesh in any way, but only in Jesus' atoning death on the Cross. I nailed all my worldly reasons for boasting to His Cross; my Jewish ancestry, my Pharisaic traditions, my zeal for the law. To all these things I am now dead, separated from them by His Cross, so that they no longer have any appeal to me or any influence on me.

For neither circumcision is anything, nor uncircumcision, but a new creation.

Circumcision is of no benefit to the Jew. Uncircumcision is of no benefit to the Gentile. It is the Cross of Jesus that has the power to make of the believing Jew and of the believing Gentile a new man, which results in a radical transformation of character.

And as many as by this rule are ordering their conduct, peace be upon them, and mercy, even upon the Israel of God.

Those who follow the principle of the Cross and all that goes with it in the New Testament economy, ordering their lives by the Holy Spirit's control, it is they who are the chosen ones and who make up the true Israel of God, not the Jews who have the name of Israel but are only children of Abraham after the flesh.

Henceforth, let no man furnish me trouble, for I bear branded the marks of the Lord Jesus in my body. The grace of our Lord Jesus Christ be with your spirit, brethren. Amen.

The marks of Jesus' ownership of me are on my body. So do I bear His Name as my Master and Commander. This burden of pain and suffering that I bear is from stoning and beatings that I endured at the hands of my enemies, all for the sake of Jesus and the Gospel of Grace. My beloved Galatians, do not add more sufferings to the suffering I have already borne by now rejecting His grace to you and so creating spiritual division in your assemblies which will greatly harm the cause of Christ. I, your teacher in grace, commend to you His grace, so that you might live freely as children of the Father, remaining in union with Jesus by the power of the Spirit Who is in you. That is my heartfelt desire.

From Paul to Rome

Paul, a bondslave by nature belonging to Christ Jesus, an ambassador by divine summons, permanently separated to God's good news

I write to you under my Gentile name that was given to me by my parents in addition to my Jewish name of Saul, which name I have now discarded, given my calling as the apostle to the Gentiles. I was born a slave of sin at my physical birth, but now, having had the cords that bound me to Satan rent asunder by my identification in Jesus' death on the Cross, and having been born anew by my faith in Jesus as Saviour, I am His slave and proud to be so, a slave to the King of kings, living only to please His interests, my will swallowed up in His, bound to Him by cords of love, and bound to Him eternally since He will never die and since He is my new divine life so that now I live in Him. He has called me to the office of apostle in His service, to represent Him in preaching the Gospel, He having given me the credentials, namely miracles, and the responsibility of carrying out His orders, and I diligently exercise the authority this office confers on me. God has separated me from all mankind for my apostleship, being the one thing that I do. The good news I bring is not the earthly everyday kind that is linked to the homage of Caesar, but is God's eternal good news of peace for the good of all men, and I have been separated out by Him to declare it to the Roman world i.e. it is good news that is God-like and not to do with the state religion of Caesar worship, being diametrically opposed to that religion and to the political atmosphere of Rome.

which He promised aforetime through the intermediate agency of His prophets in holy writings concerning His Son, who came from the ancestral line of David so far as His humanity is concerned, who was demonstrated in the sphere of power as Son of God so far as His divine essence was concerned by the resurrection of the dead,

What is this good news? It is news that was promised by the writers of the Old Testament, so is not in principle a new thing, and not a subversion of the economy of Moses, but rather the fulfilment of hopes which God Himself inspired. This good news is concerning His Son, He being the chosen object of divine love and being God's instrument for accomplishing the salvation of His people. The Son is He Who, though deity, has now entered into a new condition, that of humanity, when He put Himself under human limitations, and so comprising within His Person two natures, that of deity and that of humanity, and appointed as the Son of God among men by His resurrection. He was born like other men with respect to His earthly descent, in humiliation, and He was declared with respect to His divine essence i.e. Who He truly was, by His resurrection, in power, that men might be convicted and saved. He lived His earthly life according to the flesh, He was raised from the dead according to His spirit of holiness, this holiness being the seat of the divine nature that He possesses. In His resurrection is made possible the resurrection of all who assume His righteousness by faith.

Jesus Christ our Lord; through whom we received grace and apostleship in order that there may be obedience to the Faith among all the Gentiles in behalf of His name, among whom you also are divinely summoned ones belonging to Jesus Christ, to all who are in Rome, God's loved ones, divinely summoned saints. Grace to you and peace from God our Father and our Lord Jesus Christ.

I received salvation by faith, being God's grace to me. I was then given the office of an apostle, my commission being to bring about an obedience to the Christian Faith among the Gentiles. I am to do this for the sake of Jesus and in recognition of all that He is in His Person, comprising His majesty, glory, power, holiness, and righteousness, my endeavour being a service of love. You believers in Rome are the called of Jesus, called to be His and now belonging to Him, since you have heard and obeyed the Gospel. Now you are set apart by the Holy Spirit to live a life of separation; separated from sin to holiness, and from Satan to God, out of the first Adam and into the last Adam, namely Jesus. I pray that grace will be yours, the grace that is for daily living as ministered to you by the Holy Spirit, and that peace will be yours, being a state of Christian tranquility in your hearts.

First, I am constantly thanking my God through Jesus Christ concerning all of you because your faith is constantly being spread abroad in the whole world;

I am so delighted with you that I am always giving thanks through Jesus, through Whom salvation came to you, for the lives that you are living as believers. You shine in that city where all that is vile and abominable flows and is indeed encouraged, like beacons of purity in a dark place, so being living witnesses to the divine source of your faith. Your faith is spoken of throughout the empire, your assembly being like a city set high on a hill, prominently looking down onto the world.

for my witness is God, to whom I render sacred service in my spirit in the good news concerning His Son, how unceasingly I make mention of you always at my prayers, making supplication if somehow now at last I may be prospered in the will of God to come to you, for I long to see you in order that I may impart some spiritual gift to you resulting in your being stabilised, that is, moreover, that I may be strengthened by you through the mutual faith which is both yours and mine.

God has seen and knows how consistent and incessant is my making requests to Him for you, He Whom I worship in spirit, so He is my sole Witness to you who I have never seen in person, of my love for you, and which testimony I offer as proof of my affection for you. I am so eager to visit you, that if possible, already, after so long a time, I may be blessed to be with you there, so that I may minister to you in the Spirit, imparting to you His gifts so as to establish your character and service, which strengthening by the Spirit I also have need of along with you. And I know that you will bless me by your faith, comforting and strengthening me.

Moreover, I do not desire you to be ignorant, brethren, that often I proposed to myself to come to you, but I was prevented up to this time, in order that I might procure some fruit also among you even as also among the rest of the Gentiles.

Please be assured that it has long been my determined purpose to come to you, but until now I have been hindered from doing so. My desire is to carefully obtain some reward amongst you Gentiles.

Both to Greeks and to those who do not possess Greek culture, both to wise and unwise, I am debtor in such a manner that to the extent of my ability I am eager to proclaim the good news also to you who are in Rome.

I am personally and morally obliged to all, regardless of nation or culture, counting all as being my creditors, owing my life and my person in virtue of the grace bestowed on me in Jesus, and of the office which I received from Him. I owe the civilised and the rude, the good and the immoral. To all, I, for my part, stand in readiness to declare the Gospel of Grace, as I also stand ready to declare it to you.

For I am not ashamed of the good news. For God's power it is, resulting in salvation to everyone who believes, to Jew first and also to Gentile, for God's righteousness in it is revealed on the principle of faith to faith, even as it stands written, And the one who is just, on the principle of faith shall live.

I stand ready since I am not deterred by the contempt in which the Gospel is held, nor by the prospect of my own humiliation as its preacher. Rome may well be a city where visible human military power is honoured due to the brutal dominance of the empire which it maintains, but my good news is to do with the infinite energy and power of God leading to man's salvation for all who will accept it, being a sweet message of mercy and grace which works invisibly in the heart of the sinner elected to salvation before the foundation of the universe. The message speaks of God's righteousness, being His measure of what is right and ordered, and of His standards and how they result in behaviour that is conformable to Him i.e. in behaviour which is of value before Him, being a different standard of behaviour to that which the world considers righteous. He Himself is the goal and standard of righteousness, being that holiness in which His nature manifests itself. This righteousness is bestowed by God on the one who believes, so that the state of the justified one is solely due to God, and meaning that they then have a righteousness which God declares to be righteous i.e. God's very own righteousness, in which the believer will stand, in right relation to Him forever. Previously we were kept out of God's presence by three aspects of righteousness, as symbolised by the three curtains of the temple court, being the righteousness which God is, the righteousness which He demands of anyone who would be in right relation to Him, and the righteousness which He bestows in answer to faith. Having now obtained access into the Holy of Holies through Jesus' blood sacrifice and having entered in, those same three curtains now keep us in His presence forever. The sinner's guilt was borne in that atoning sacrifice on the Cross, and a positive righteousness, Jesus Himself, is now given to him in grace. Since Jesus is God's Righteousness, the same righteousness that damns a sinner for eternity for rejecting Jesus, saves and keeps saved for eternity the one who accepts Jesus i.e. one can only become righteous by accepting God's righteousness, namely Jesus. The means by which righteousness is given is by faith i.e. through faith in God's grace in the atoning death of Jesus, thus allowing God to bestow His righteousness on the believer. The means by which righteousness is received is also by faith, and not by works nor by looking to anything of man's merits, but recognising one's own unworthiness, helplessness, and need of redemption. This is not a new concept, it being found in the prophetic writing of Habakkuk; by faith is there life. The source of the new life in Jesus is faith, and faith is the means by which we receive righteousness and life in Him.

For there is revealed God's wrath from heaven upon every lack of reverence and upon every unrighteousness of men who in unrighteousness are holding down the truth.

God's righteousness is the only thing that can deliver from God's wrath. God could not love good unless He hated evil, the two attitudes being inseparably linked i.e. He must do both or neither. The righteous must feel anger at sin since God abhors and hates sin. Sinful men lack reverence toward God, and repress the truth that there is a supreme Being Who created the universe, a Creator with divine attributes, to Whom worship and obedience are due. They reject this truth, and, refusing to acknowledge the moral implications of this, they go on in their sin.

Because that which is knowable concerning God is plainly evident in them, for God made it clear to them; for the things concerning Him which are invisible since the creation of the universe are clearly seen, being understood by means of the things that are made, namely, His eternal power and divine Being, resulting in their being without a defence.

There is a universal, instinctive knowledge within men of God as the Creator. This knowledge obligated men to glorify God, but this they did not do, and they are without excuse since God, through the light of the created universe, clearly revealed Himself as Creator and God to the human race i.e. He made His invisible attributes visible to men in the material universe in order that men might know something of Him through seeing His works. Men, understanding that every effect has a cause, were forced to conclude that there must be a Being of eternal power to create such a tremendous effect as the universe, and that this Being must be the Deity Who should be worshipped and obeyed, but this truth they senselessly and sinfully denied.

Because, knowing God, not as God did they glorify Him, nor were they grateful, but they became futile in their reasonings, and their stupid heart was darkened. Asserting themselves to be wise, they became fools and exchanged the glory of the incorruptible God for a likeness of an image of corruptible man and of birds and of quadrupeds and of snakes.

Failure to glorify the Creator God led to men being ungrateful for His gifts of food, clothing, and shelter, and for the gift of life itself. Nature reveals God to be great and good but men chose to be blind to this. Instead they were led by their dark imaginations and proud deliberations into a lack of intelligence and understanding. They claimed to be learned and cultivated, but their words and thoughts were moronic, foolish and silly, their arguments being drivel. They chose to glorify man-made idols in ever descending depravity; in Greece the idols are of men, in Egypt beasts and snakes, similarly in Rome, as you well know.

On which account God delivered them over in the passionate cravings of their hearts to bestial profligacy which had for its purpose the dishonouring of their bodies among themselves;

Since men chose to give up God and worship the creature, God could do nothing but give men into the control of the sinful things that they preferred to Him, since He would not violate man's will and force him to do something he did not want to do, and when men persisted in following their totally depraved natures He gave them free rein, so that men became vilely immoral. God not only permitted this depravity, He judicially delivered man over to uncleanness i.e. as sin gave birth to more sin, and darkness of mind descended ever deeper into darkness, so grace gave place to judgement. This divine wrath hardened men's hearts and hurried them on to yet greater degrees of depravity, so that they participated in more than mere overindulgent sensual behaviour in the satisfaction of natural lust, but performed impure physical acts, with their sinful desires operating unrestrained in their hearts.

who were of such a character that they exchanged the truth of God for a lie and worshipped and rendered religious service to the creation rather than to the Creator who is to be eulogised forever. Amen.

Men totally rejected acknowledging God, passing Him by completely, and instead gave their complete service to created things. They performed the acts that you would expect of those who dared to reject God's truth and whose character was to always embrace falsehood. They praised creation but never spoke well of the Creator, as they should have done.

Because of this God gave them over to dishonourable passions, for even their females exchanged their natural use for that which is against nature.

The passions that men allowed to control them brought on them a diseased heart condition out of which the lusts spring, causing them to put an incorrect estimate upon the sacredness, dignity, and purity of the physical body and thus to use it in a way which dishonoured it. Females perversely participated in doing things that are against nature's laws with respect to the sexual use of their bodies,

And likewise also the males, having put aside the natural use of the females, burned themselves out in their lustful appetite toward one another, males with males carrying to its ultimate conclusion that which is shameful, receiving in themselves that retribution which was a necessity in the nature of the case because of their deviation from the norm.

Males became inflamed with lust in all its rage, their deeds an eager, all-out endeavour to satisfy the appetites and desires of their totally depraved natures, doing things disfiguring, unseemly, and immodest, in their nakedness. Divine law ordained the necessary evil consequences of their so violating the laws of nature, so that they were paid back the natural result of their sin, paying the price for their wandering from the standards laid down for the sexual use of human bodies.

And even as after putting God to the test for the purpose of approving Him should He meet their specifications, and finding that He did not, they disapproved of holding Him in their full and precise knowledge, God gave them up to a mind that would not meet the test for that which a mind was meant, to practice those things which were not becoming or fitting;

Men found that God was not to their liking, that He didn't match their expectations and desires, so they refused to give Him worship and desired to know nothing of Him. God was put on trial by the human race, and, because it then rejected Him, God gave it a 'trialess' mind, being a mind which cannot stand trial and one incapable of functioning as a mind with respect to the things of salvation i.e. men disapproved the true God and would have none of Him so in turn He gave them up to a disapproved mind, a mind which is no mind, a mind in which the divine distinctions of right and wrong are confused and lost so that God's condemnation cannot but fall on it at the last. Not only reason but also conscience was perverted, meaning that the last deep of evil had been reached and that men were left in the darkness, without God, and willing participants in whatever their unrestrained animal impulses led them to do.

being filled with every unrighteousness, pernicious evil, avarice, malice, full of envy, murder, wrangling, guile, malicious craftiness; secret slanderers, backbiters; hateful to God, insolent, haughty; swaggerers, inventors of evil things; disobedient to parents, stupid, faithless, without natural affection, merciless; such are those who, knowing the judgement of God that these who practice such things are worthy of death, not only habitually do the same things but also take pleasure in those who practice them.

Having disapproved of holding God in their knowledge, as a consequence, men were completely filled with sins like these, as is still the case now, to the exclusion of the normal bonds of love between parents and children and between husband and wife.

Therefore, you are without a defence, O man, everyone who judges, for in that in which you are judging another, yourself you are condemning, for you who judge practice the same things.

And now I speak to the Jews, which people pronounce all Gentiles to be born in sin and under condemnation. Yes you have more knowledge of God than the Gentiles, but you are condemned by the same principle; that you do evil in spite of better knowledge. You also sin against light, though your sins are different to theirs. You cannot talk yourselves off from this same charge of failing to live up to the light that you have, so you cannot judge or even criticise the Gentiles, or form a derogatory appraisal of their character so as to condemn them.

But we know that the judgement of God is according to truth against those who practice such things.

The contents of God's judgement against you are in accordance with the facts, though you may seek to cover over them due to your nation's privileges in its standing with God.

And do you reason thus, O man, who judges those who practice such things, and are doing the same things, that as for you, you will escape the judgement of God?

Have you deliberated the matter and calculated, you the Jew, that your privilege of birth in itself ensures your entrance into God's Kingdom? From your attitude this would seem to be your conviction, yet you forget that you, of all men, since having a special revelation of God in being part of His chosen nation, should the least have fallen into the error of neglecting His will. You, more than any of the Gentile nations, knew His will, so should have rigorously obeyed it.

Or, the wealth of His kindness and forbearance and longsuffering are you treating with contempt, being ignorant that the goodness of God is leading you to repentance?

Do you despise God's patience with you, looking down your nose at His compassion as being unnecessary? I would say that you do. This holding back of His wrath was a temporary truce with you with a view to Jesus coming to deal with your sins. But if there is now no change of heart on your part along with an obedience to Him, His judgement will be held back no longer. Your believing that His delaying His judgement against you is due to His approving of your behaviour, rather than of His giving you time to change your heart so as to acknowledge your sins, shows a contempt of His goodness towards you. And if you claim you did not know that your behaviour was worthy of judgement, your very ignorance is contempt.

But according to your obstinate and unrepentant heart you are storing up for yourself wrath in the day of wrath and revelation of the righteous judgement of God

So, in your stubbornness, you are heaping up and storing away wrath that will fall on you once God's patient withholding of it comes to an end, on that day when His righteous judgement against Jews and Gentiles is revealed.

who recompenses each according to his works, to those on the one hand who by steadfastness of a good work seek glory and honour and incorruptibility, life eternal; but to those on the other hand who out of a factious spirit are both also non-persuadable with respect to the truth and persuadable with respect to unrighteousness, wrath and anger. Tribulation and anguish upon every soul of man who works out to a finish the evil, both upon the soul of a Jew first and also upon the soul of a Gentile, but glory and honour and peace to everyone who works out to a finish that which is good, both to a Jew first and also to a Gentile.

In governing the world, God judges according to each man's works, punishing the evil and rewarding the righteous. I will go on to show that no one can be justified before God by works of law. So I am not saying here that works can in some measure justify one before God, nor that faith in Jesus is a good work, but I am just describing the overriding principle of divine justice with respect to good and evil by which everyone will be paid their due. It is commendable to patiently continue walking with God, subjecting oneself to Him and remaining under His discipline, suppressing one's own natural attitude of rebellion with a view to spending eternity with Him. It is not commendable to be disobedient and obstinate, withholding one's belief in, and compliance to, God's way of righteousness. For the latter awaits God's anger, and an eternity of extreme affliction, distress, pressure and oppression, picture it as in being confined to a narrow constrained place of dire calamity. For the former awaits an eternal state of joy and freedom, picture it as in being brought into a large room.

For there is not partiality in the presence of God. For as many as without law sinned, without law shall also perish. And as many as in the sphere of law sinned, through law shall be condemned.

God does not look at your face when judging you, but at your heart. You Jews shall not be treated as favourites of Heaven, but shall be regarded as first in responsibility, since you had the law of Moses to live by, given to you by God, and it stands as your judge. All sinners, whether Jew or Gentile, will be condemned and will perish.

For not those who are instructed in the law are righteous in the presence of God but those who are doers of the law shall be justified.

It is not enough just to hear the law of Moses read, however often that be, or to be one whose business is hearing. Familiarity with it is not a substitute for doing it.

For whenever Gentiles, who do not have law, do habitually by nature the things of the law, these not having law, are a law to themselves, they being such that they show the work of the law written in their hearts, their conscience bearing joint-witness and their reasonings in the meanwhile accusing or also excusing one another in the day when God judges the hidden things of men according to my gospel through Jesus Christ.

A Gentile, even though not under a divine written law, nevertheless is not absolutely without a knowledge of God's will, so can still by nature do things that are required by the law of Moses, being a law to himself. The presence of this inner law can be seen in his conduct which indicates that there is a law written on his heart, in his conscience which joins its testimony to his conduct, and in his thoughts that bear witness to a law at work in him inasmuch as they accuse or, at times, defend him. There will be a day of judgement when those under the law of Moses shall be judged by it, and the Gentiles shall be judged according to the unwritten law in their hearts. But all will be judged according to the standard of the Gospel that I preach.

Now, assuming, as for you, that you bear the name of Jew, and have a blind and mechanical reliance on the law, and boast in God, and have an experiential knowledge of His will, and after having put to the test for the purpose of approving the things that differ, and having found that they meet your specifications, you put your approval upon them, being instructed in a formal way in the law, you have persuaded yourself and have come to a settled conviction that you are a guide to the blind, a light of those in darkness, a corrector of those who are without reflection or intelligence, a teacher of the immature, having the rough sketch of the experiential knowledge of the truth in the law.

You who are called a Jew, are of the nation that was set apart from the Gentile nations, and you boast in God as the covenant God of Israel, meaning that you, as opposed to the Gentiles, were chosen by Him. You are always keen to test what is truth and what are just the philosophical speculations of men, as you are being taught and instructed systematically out of the law of Moses in the synagogue. So much so that you have persuaded yourself and now believe beyond a doubt that you are the perfect guide to the blind and untaught. This was indeed God's intention; that the Jews were meant by God to be guides of the Gentiles and to lead them to salvation, but instead, you have become conceited and arrogant, looking down on the Gentiles as being inferior to yourselves due to their lack of knowledge of God. You think of the Gentiles as senseless, stupid, and foolish, calling them dogs. This was not God's motive for giving you the law. The law was given so as to be in charge of you, as a slave is guardian to an immature son, and you, similar to the young child not fully understanding his position relative to the slave, only have a rough idea of the law's true purpose, seeing just an outline but not the substance of it.

Therefore, you who are constantly teaching another, are you not teaching yourself? You who are constantly preaching a person should not be stealing, are you stealing? You who are constantly saying that a person should not be committing adultery, are you committing adultery? You who are turning away constantly from idolatry as from a stench, are you robbing temples? You who are making your boast in the law, through your transgression of the law are you dishonouring God? For the Name of God because of you is reviled among the Gentiles, even as it stands written.

You who are guides, do you need to guide yourselves? Do you ever miss the mark? Do you ever overstep a line? Are you ever disobedient to a voice? Do you ever fall when you should have stood? Are you ever ignorant of what you should know? Do you ever diminish what you should have rendered in full? Do you ever fail to observe the law? Have you ever fallen short of the law's demands? Have you ever gone where you knew you should not go? Have you ever spoken contemptuously about God or about sacred things?

For, indeed, circumcision is profitable if you are making a practice of law, but if, on the other hand, you are a transgressor of law, you circumcision has become uncircumcision.

For any observance required by the law of Moses, for example the seal of the covenant, circumcision, doing what the law says to do gives you an assurance that you belong to the race which was the heir of God's promises. This is indeed an advantage. But if the inheriting of the promises has any moral conditions attached to it, which I will in due course show that it has, then the advantage of circumcision, or any other law observance, lapses, until these conditions are fulfilled. As you have to admit, you have not fulfilled any such conditions, since you have broken and transgressed the law. Therefore you are in a state of being uncircumcised as far as law observance is concerned.

Therefore, if the uncircumcision habitually guards the righteous requirements of the law, will not his uncircumcision be credited to his account for circumcision?

So if an uncircumcised Gentile carefully maintains the just requirements of the law of Moses, he will be accounted as circumcised, since he has done what circumcised Jews pledged to do, and he will be treated as if in the Jew's position.

And the uncircumcision which by nature is fulfilling the law will judge you who with the advantage of the letter and of circumcision are a transgressor of law.

The Jew is a law-transgressor in spite of the fact that he possesses a written revelation of God's will and bears the seal of the covenant on his body. In these he has firstly an outward standard, the law of Moses, which does not vary with his moral condition, and secondly an outward pledge, in circumcision, that he belongs to the people of God, to encourage him when he is tempted. So in both these respects he has an immense advantage over the Gentile, yet both are neutralised by his being a law-transgressor.

For, not he who is so in an outward fashion is a Jew, nor even that which is in an outward fashion in flesh is circumcision. But he who is so in the sphere of the inner man is a Jew, and circumcision is of the heart, in the sphere of the spirit, not in the sphere of the letter, concerning whom the praise is not from men but from God.

So that which constitutes the Jew in the true sense of the term and which gives the name 'Jew' its proper content and dignity, is not anything outward and visible, but something inward and spiritual, and this concept also applies to true circumcision. The inward Jew is the one who lives up to his covenant relation to God, and it is this inner observance that is needed for anyone who would call themself a Jew. What is inward and concealed is the man's soul-life, his spirit. It is one's behaviour in one's spirit, rather than in the realm of outward meticulous law observance, that counts. The outward observances and behaviour gain recognition and praise from other law-observers, which human acclaim the Jews love, and which tends to religious vanity. Rather, the religious behaviour in the spirit, in the God-conscious inner life, where practices are seen and praised by God alone, should be the focus of service to God.

What pre-eminence or advantage is there therefore which the Jew possesses? Or, what profit is there in circumcision?

So is the Jew reduced to a position of entire equality with the Gentile? Jesus said, "Salvation is of the Jews". The Jews do indeed have an advantage, their unbelief possibly even acting as a foil to God's faithfulness and thus setting it in more glorious relief, but these advantages do not exempt the Jew from liability to judgement, since God's character as righteous Judge of the world must be maintained, meaning all are treated the same with respect to judgement.

Much every way, for, first of all, because they were entrusted with the divine utterances of God.

The surplus of the Jew is much from every angle. The chief of the advantages is that God made him the depository of the contents of a revelation which He authored, comprising the Old Testament.

Well then – if, as is the case, certain ones did not exercise faith? Their unbelief will not render the faithfulness of God ineffectual, will it? Let no one ever think such a thing. Let God be found veracious and every man a liar, even as it stands written, To the end that you may be acknowledged righteous in your words, and may come out victor when brought to trial.

So, how stands the case? The Jews were without faith, so did this render God's faithfulness inefficient? May it never come to pass. When God's justice is put on trial, let Him be found to be righteous by His creatures who judge Him, so that His justice prevails and gains the case.

But in view of the fact that our unrighteousness establishes by proof God's righteousness, what shall we say? God is not unrighteous who inflicts wrath, is He? I am using a mode of speech drawn from human affairs. Away with the thought. Otherwise, how will it be possible for God to judge the world? Moreover, assuming that the truth of God by means of my lie became the more conspicuous, resulting in His glory, why then yet am I also being judged as a sinner? And not, as we were slanderously reported and even as certain are saying that we are saying, Let us do the evil things in order that there might come the good things; whose judgement is just.

Human sin is a foil which shows and establishes God's righteousness so that it is seen all the more clearly by its very contrast to sin. God is right to bring His anger to bear on sin, it is His holy wrath. I mention a phrase of men's reasoning now, though it is unworthy of the subject; "Is God unjust Who inflicts wrath?" It is only in condescension to human weakness that I transfer to Him language which is customary for men to employ when referring to human relationships. Similarly I could ask, "If, as a Jew, my moral falsehood and my unfaithfulness to the claims of conscience and of God, especially in relation to Him proffering salvation through Jesus, highlight His truth and lead to His being glorified, why, as a favoured Jew, am I judged?" But I preach justification by faith in Jesus and not by works, which message the Jews twist and wrongly testify that I teach 'do evil that good may come'.

What then? Are we better? Not in any way, for we previously brought a charge against both Jews and Gentiles that all are under sin;

How then are we to understand the situation? Do we Jews excel and surpass the Gentiles? Not at all, since we have no advantage in escaping divine condemnation.

as it stands written, There is not a righteous person, not even one. There is not the one who understands; there is not the one who seeks out God. All turned aside; all to a man became useless. There is not the one who habitually does goodness; there is not as much as one.

It is written in the Old Testament and the truth still stands; no one determinedly searches after God, but all have deviated from the right way and become unprofitable, all have gone bad and become sour like milk, not one is morally good and living a life of perfect integrity and kindness.

Their throat is a grave that stands open. With their tongues they continually were deceiving. Asp's poison is under their lips; whose mouth is full of imprecations and bitterness; their feet are swift to pour out blood. Destruction and misery are in their paths. The road of peace they did not know. There is not a fear of God before their eyes.

The words of all men stink with the stench of a newly opened grave. With smooth tongues they have spoken deceit, and they persevere in their hypocrisy. Their speech is poison. Wherever they go, you can trace them by the ruin and distress they leave behind, as they tread continually in paths of violence.

But we know absolutely that whatever things the law says, it says to those within the sphere of the law, in order that every mouth may be closed up and the whole world may become liable to pay penalty to God. Wherefore, out of works of law there shall not be justified any flesh in His sight, for through law is a full knowledge of sin.

The law of Moses applies to all those who are legally within its jurisdiction. It provides overwhelming evidence against the accused so that the mouths of all who are under its judgement are stopped up and silent. God is the injured party, His rights having been infringed, so that all under the law must pay penalty to Him. And Gentiles are within the jurisdiction of divine law that is written in the heart, so both Jews and Gentiles are judged on their moral deeds, with both outer acts and inner choices and states under scrutiny. So there is no man who can be brought into a right state as related to God by his moral deeds. Law merely acquaints the sinner with sin. No law has the power to give life, hence there are no works of law by which men can be justified. The law's purpose is simply to show men how sinful they are and to bring them down to this point of realisation, but it is not for the law to lift them up again.

But now, apart from law, God's righteousness has been openly shown as in view, having witness borne to it by the law and the prophets; indeed, God's righteousness through faith in Jesus Christ to all who believe, for there is not a distinction, for all sinned and are falling short of the glory of God;

But as for non-dependence on the law of Moses, as for living without the law, as for living in a different sphere from the one in which the law says, "Do this and live" yet offers no assistance, how much better a word the Gospel brings; that God removes the guilt and penalty of sin from a sinner who places his faith in Jesus as Saviour and bestows upon him a positive righteousness, namely Jesus, in Whom the believer stands as a righteous person before God's law for time and eternity. This is all made possible by and based upon the satisfaction which Jesus offered on the Cross as a complete payment of the penalty imposed by the law because of human infractions of that law, thus satisfying God's justice, maintaining His government, and making possible the bestowal of mercy upon the basis of justice satisfied, being a legal standing that neither changes nor affects the character of the person, instead that character being changed by the work of the Holy Spirit in progressive sanctification. In Jesus God's righteousness has been manifested and made visible, attested to by the law itself and by the prophets of the Old Testament. By faith in Jesus is God's righteousness given to all who believe. Such is the Gospel. Everyone needs this divine plan of salvation since humanity does nothing except commit sin, always missing the mark, and ever failing to obey the law. All men right now come short and fail to reach the goal, having been left trailing behind in the race of justification by works.

being justified gratuitously by His grace through the redemption which is in Christ Jesus, whom God placed before the eyes of all as an expiatory satisfaction through faith in His blood for a proof of His righteousness in view of the pretermission of the sins previously committed, this pretermission being in the sphere of the forbearance of God, also for a proof of His righteousness at the present season, with a view to His being just and the justifier of the one whose faith is in Jesus.

There was no just cause demanding that we be justified. Rather, God freely favoured us, who hated Him, out of the spontaneous generosity of His heart without any expectation of return and with no strings attached, being an act of pure grace. We who receive this grace then turn from sin to serve the living God and live a holy life, since grace includes not only the bestowal of His righteousness, but also the inward transformation consisting of the power of indwelling sin broken and the divine nature implanted, which liberates the believer from the compelling power of sin and makes him hate sin, love holiness, and gives him the power to obey the Word of God. Jesus paid the price to thus set us free from sin and free to live a life pleasing to God in the power of the Holy Spirit, with His precious blood shed on the Cross. Jesus was made public, on view to all, unlike the ark of the covenant which was veiled and approached only by the high priest. Jesus' sacrifice was not to appease an angry god and buy his love, as you see happening all around you in Rome, but to reconcile us to God in the act of getting rid of the sin which has come between us and which creates a necessary alienation, interposing an inevitable obstacle to fellowship between God and man. Jesus' blood shed in sacrifice makes the place of the law's judgement into a place of God's mercy, since His blood comes between the violated law of Moses and the violators, satisfying the just requirements of God's holy law which mankind broke and paying the penalty for man, thus removing that which had separated between a holy God and sinful man, namely sin, its guilt and penalty. The benefits of Jesus' sacrifice are available to all who will put their faith in that shed blood's ability to save. God's righteousness was demonstrated and proved in the remission of sins committed before the Cross, that is, before they were actually paid for, in His forbearance i.e. in the past He passed those sins by for the time being, leaving it open in the future either entirely to remit or to adequately punish them, as may seem good to Him. Thus God saved believing sinners without their having their sins paid for, and bestowed mercy without having justice satisfied, which would appear to make God condone sin, which appearance had to be set right in human thinking, though it was always right in God's eyes as He looked forward to the satisfaction of the broken law at the Cross of Jesus, being an eternal fact in the reckoning of God. The Cross thus demonstrated that when He declared a believing sinner righteous, He all the time maintained His righteousness. So Jesus' atoning sacrifice on the Cross was both just and merciful; in that sin was paid for, not condoned, in that the believing sinner is saved by the mercy of God, and also by the righteousness of God, his sins having been paid for whilst God's justice has been maintained. God is just, and the One Who justifies the believing sinner.

Where then is the glorying? It was once for all excluded. Through what kind of a law? Of the aforementioned works? Not at all, but through the law of faith, for our reasoned conclusion is that a man is justified by faith apart from works of law.

So the Jews cannot glory, proclaiming their own goodness by virtue of ceremonial observances. This was excluded by the coming in of the revelation of righteousness by faith. What nature of law excludes the law of Moses? Is it a law of works? No, it is a law of faith, not that there are two laws in operation with one being better than the other, but that there is one divine law of possessing salvation, the quality of which is such that now, instead of prescribing the Jew's works to be performed, it prescribes faith and belief.

Or, of Jews only is He God? Is He not also of Gentiles? Yes, also of Gentiles, assuming that there is one God who will justify the circumcision out of a source of faith and the uncircumcision through the intermediary instrumentality of faith. Then are we making law of none effect through this aforementioned faith? Let not such a thing be considered. Certainly, we are establishing law.

Faith does not make God's law of no effect. Rather faith establishes the law in its rightful place. By faith law is set upon a secure footing and for the first time it gets its rights. My task, and that of the other apostles, is to prove that faith in Jesus satisfies the law of Moses, so making the way of salvation available to all, since Jesus came to fulfil the law and the prophets, not to destroy them. I shall now go on to show how saints living under the Old Testament, in particular Abraham, were justified by faith, which way of salvation is still the divine order, being now more secure than ever under the Gospel I preach. I shall also show that the just demands of the law are fulfilled in those who believe in Jesus as Saviour, and in those believers only, through faith in Him.

What then shall we say that Abraham our forefather found with reference to the flesh? For, assuming that Abraham was justified out of a source of works, he has ground for boasting, but not when facing God. For what does the scripture say? Now Abraham believed God, and it was put to his account, resulting in righteousness.

So then, looking at the example of Abraham, was he justified by any of his own efforts, he who is the spiritual father of all believers? Was he saved through his works, as the Jews seek to do, or through his faith? Abraham was saved by believing, not in the act of believing itself as being a righteous work, but in his faith in God to perform His promise, which faith introduced him into the blessing promised by God i.e. Abraham placed himself in an attitude of trust in, and acceptance of, God's blessings that made it possible for God to bestow righteousness upon him. Like a drowning man, he proffered his hand to his rescuer, so there was nothing of merit in him stretching out his hand in order to be saved, it just being the medium by which he was saved. So, in faith, we reach out to God for salvation and He grasps our hand in His own to lift us out of the mire of sin and to place us upon the Rock which is Jesus. For Abraham, God put to his account, and placed on deposit for him, and credited to him, righteousness. The actual payment had not at this time been made, nor had the actual bestowal of righteousness been consummated, since Jesus had not yet paid the penalty for man's sin nor yet been raised from the dead, but now that Jesus has been resurrected, Old Testament saints share with New Testament believers in possessing Jesus as the Righteousness in which they stand, so are considered guiltless and righteous for time and for eternity.

Now, for the one who works with a definite result in view [his wages], the remuneration is not put down on his account as an undeserved, gratuitous gift, but as a legally contracted debt. But in the case of the one who does not work with a definite result in view [salvation] but who places his trust upon the One who justifies the person who is destitute of reverential awe towards God, there is put to his account his faith, resulting in righteousness,

A workman works in order to earn wages, being his merited reward, so that he who they work for is in debt to them and is legally obliged to pay them. The workman can thank his employer but he is not legally obligated to do so. If we earned salvation by good works, God would be indebted to man and legally obligated to save him, so it would not be a favour which God would do for man, and man would not need to thank God or glorify Him for saving him. But if a sinner rejects performing good works as the means of his earning salvation, and instead puts his trust in the God Who justifies the ungodly and impious person, that act of faith is put down to his account as the efficient medium through which God bestows righteous standing upon that person. Every sinner who has not trusted Jesus for salvation falls into this category of being ungodly and impious, so is lost, but God justifies any such who will put their faith in Jesus as Saviour i.e. all can be saved by faith in Him.

even as David also speaks of the spiritual prosperity of the man to whose account God puts righteousness apart from works: Spiritually prosperous are those whose lawlessnesses were put away and whose sins were covered. Spiritually prosperous is the man to whose account the Lord does not in any case put sin.

David adds his agreement that blessed indeed is he to whom God imputes righteousness not on the basis of any good works on their part, and whose violations of the law of Moses are put away in a judicial sense, as was done at the Cross.

Therefore, does this spiritual prosperity come upon the circumcised one or the uncircumcised one, for we say, There was put to Abraham's account his faith, resulting in righteousness? How then was it put to his account, at the time when he was circumcised or at the time when he was uncircumcised? Not in circumcision but in uncircumcision. And he received the attesting sign of circumcision as a seal of the righteous character of the faith which he had in his uncircumcision, resulting in his being the father of all who believe while in the state of uncircumcision, in order that there may be put to their account the righteousness; and the father of circumcision to these who are not of the circumcision only but to those who walk in the footsteps of the faith of our father Abraham when he was in uncircumcision.

Circumcision was the seal of God, stamping Abraham's faith as a faith which resulted in the bestowal of righteousness. Is then the bestowal of righteous standing before God connected with observing ordinances, or is it entirely apart from such things? Looking at Abraham we see that he was declared righteous in answer to his faith some fourteen years before he was circumcised, so his being made righteous was indeed nothing to do with any works of his.

For not through law was the promise made to Abraham or to his offspring that he should be the heir of the world, but through a righteousness which pertains to faith. For, assuming that those who are of the law are heirs, the aforementioned faith has been voided with the result that it is permanently invalidated, and the aforementioned promise has been rendered inoperative with the result that it is in a state of permanent inoperation. For the law results in divine wrath. Now, where there is not law, neither is there transgression.

The Jewish conception of the universal dominion of Messiah's theocracy, as prefigured by the nation's inheritance of Canaan, is now raised to apply to Jesus' reign as the King of all kings. This promise that Abraham was to be heir of the world was not made to one under law, but to one justified by faith. And this promise was not affected in any way by the appearance of the law of Moses, and remains unaffected now that the law has been fulfilled in Jesus.

On account of this it is by faith, in order that it might be by grace, to the end that the promise might be something realised by all the offspring, not by that which is of the law only, but also by that which is of the faith of Abraham who is father of all of us; even as it stands written, A father of many nations I have established you permanently, before Him whom he believed, before God who makes alive those who are dead and calls the things that are not in existence as being in existence;

Since the only thing the law can do is condemn, the inheritance is by necessity of faith. Eternal life is dispensed by God through faith, as appropriated when the sinner believes, so that it is by God's grace that all are saved, both Jew and Gentile. Abraham was saved before the law of Moses was instituted, so he is the spiritual father of both Jew and Gentile in that both are saved exactly like he was, by pure faith, with no necessity for works as a preliminary requirement to salvation.

who, being beyond hope, upon the basis of hope believed, in order that he might become father of many nations, according to that which has been spoken with finality, In this manner will your offspring be.

Abraham's faith was contrary to any hope that natural events could offer, rather his faith rested on the hope that God could do what nature could not; he was past hope so he trusted in hope, he was beyond human hope but, in spite of this, he rested his faith on hope in God, and in God's promise to him that he, despite being childless in his extreme old age, would have descendants as numerous as the night sky stars.

And not being weak with respect to his faith, he attentively considered his own body permanently dead, he being about one hundred years old, also the deadness of Sarah's womb. Moreover, in view of the promise of God, he did not vacillate in the sphere of unbelief between two mutually exclusive expectations but was strengthened with respect to his faith, having given glory to God, and was fully persuaded that what He had promised with finality He was able also to do; wherefore also it was put down in his account, resulting in righteousness.

Abraham fixed his eyes and his mind upon his natural situation, staring his obstacles right in the face; that his body had ceased to function with respect to producing a child and would never function again, and that Sarah's womb was similarly dead. The door was absolutely and forever closed so far as his having offspring was concerned. Nevertheless he believed God and did not waver between that belief and any unbelief with respect to his difficulty and the ability of God to meet it. It was a mental struggle but he was not divided in his mind by unbelief. Rather his faith was strengthened in God that He would meet his impossible difficulty with a miracle. It was not that his faith was strengthened so that his physical powers again became equal to bringing children into the world, rather that Isaac was the result of a biological miracle performed by God in answer to Abraham's faith, so that all the glory would be to God.

Now, it was not written for his sake alone, namely, that it was put to his account, but also for our sakes, to whose account it is to be put, to ours who place our faith upon the One who raised Jesus our Lord out from among the dead, who was delivered up because of our transgressions and was raised because of our justification.

The object of the Christian's faith is the same as that of Abraham's; God that gives life to the dead. While for Abraham, more generally, it was in God Who can do what man cannot, for us, specifically, it is in God Who raised Jesus. Our spiritual attitude toward God is the same as Abraham's, but God is revealed to us, and offered to our faith, in a character by which Abraham did not yet know Him. We have seen Jesus delivered up for our offences to the justice that required the payment of the penalty for human sin, and we have seen Jesus raised from the dead as the means of, and to accomplish the fact of, our justification, so we can conceive of God's omnipotence not as mere unqualified power, as Abraham did, but as power, no less than infinite, engaged in the work of man's salvation from sin. So we see His omnipotence exhibited as redeeming power, and in this omnipotence we, like Abraham, believe. Jesus' work was finished on the Cross, but we also know Him as the Risen One Who, though He died, now lives and has the virtue of His atoning death ever in Him, and as such evoked in us the faith by which we were justified, He being the only One, through faith in Whom, sinful men, who have all deviated from the right path and turned aside, could ever be justified.

Having therefore been justified by faith, peace we are having with God through our Lord Jesus Christ,

So far I have proved man's need for the righteousness of God, and shown how that righteousness comes and how it is appropriated, and used the example of Abraham and the testimony of David to show that salvation by faith alone does not upset but rather establishes the spiritual order revealed in the Old Testament. Now I would like to write extensively on the intense happiness of the justified and especially on their assurance of God's love and future blessedness. Since we are saved neither by works nor by ordinances nor by law obedience, but by faith, we have peace with God; now justified before Him, having a legal standing in Jesus to be in His presence, this being our permanent condition, which condition all believers enjoy. Jesus concluded peace through His blood shed on the Cross, binding us together again to God where we had previously been separated from Him by sin. Now we face God and stand in His presence, guiltless and uncondemned and righteous in a righteousness which God accepts, namely Jesus. Now we are forever joined to God in Jesus.

through whom also our entrée we have as a permanent possession into this unmerited favour in which we have been placed permanently, and rejoice upon the basis of hope of the glory of God.

Now Jesus brings us into the Father's presence and introduces us to Him, since we have been made acceptable in Jesus in that we are cleansed by His blood and robed in His righteousness. Thus have we been put into a friendly relation to the Father and are assured that He is favourably disposed towards us. Grace has brought us into this safe haven of full favour with God. Here we stand permanently, with the hope also of participating in the glory of Heaven.

And not only this, but we also are exulting in our tribulations, knowing that this tribulation produces endurance, and this endurance, approvedness, and this approvedness, hope. And this hope does not disappoint, because the love of God has been poured out in our hearts and still floods them through the agency of the Holy Spirit who was given to us.

In the supernatural grace supplied by the Holy Spirit I glory because of the afflictions, pressure, and distress that are the natural outcome of leading a Christian life, since they have a beneficial effect on my life in Him. I remain under these difficulties so as to learn the lesson they are sent to teach, rather than attempting to get out from under them in order to be relieved of their pressure I let them do their work of generating and achieving patience, steadfastness, and constancy in me, so that the difficulties do not cause me to swerve from my deliberate purpose, but instead I remain loyal to faith and piety. Having withstood each test I stand approved by God, which produces and increases hope in me as I experience what He can do, indeed what He does do for me, amid the tribulations of this life, animating into new vigour the hope with which the life of faith begins. This hope does not deceive since it rests upon my assurance of the love of God to me, as evidenced in His support of me. His Spirit, Whom I received at my conversion, also assures me of God's love, which divine love was poured in at first, and which He ever still pours into me, so that my heart is always overflowing with it.

For when we were yet without strength, in a strategic season Christ instead of and in behalf of those who do not have reverence for God and are devoid of piety died; for, very rarely in behalf of one of those individuals who is legally exact and precise in his observance of the customs and rules of the society in which he lives will anyone die, yet perhaps in behalf of the one who is generous in heart, always doing good to others, a person would even dare to die. But God is constantly proving His own love to us, because while we were yet sinners, Christ in behalf of us died.

We can see how great this love of His toward us is; when we were powerless for good He died instead of us, in our place. Jesus died in behalf of us to take our penalty, His death being in our interest. God chose the particular point of time for this action, it having been announced to Daniel some four hundred and eighty years previously, as determined by the human circumstances; firstly the law of Moses had fully served its purpose so that its commandments and sacrifices could be done away with as a legal system and be superseded by the Gospel of Grace based on faith in this God-sent Saviour, secondly it was a time of world peace with the Roman roads making travel for missionaries easy, and thirdly the universal Greek language made speedy propagation of the Gospel possible. From human experience, if there was a call to die in exchange for another's life, this might only be done, if ever, for a good, benevolent, kind man, one who does what he ought and gives to everyone his due, being innocent and excellent in honour, and being one for whom that person has an affection. How greatly is the utmost love of man surpassed by the love of God as shown in His own love towards us. This love is now continuously established, in that the death of Jesus remains as its most striking manifestation. No man would give his life willingly for an enemy who is hostile towards him, but Jesus died as an act of His love for those who are at enmity with Him and who bitterly hate Him.

Much more therefore, having been justified now by His blood, we shall be saved through Him from the wrath. For though, while being enemies, we were reconciled to God through the death of His Son, much more, having been reconciled, we shall be saved by the life He possesses. And not only so, but we also rejoice in God through our Lord Jesus Christ, through whom now we received the reconciliation.

Since Jesus died for us when we were unlovely, unlovable, rebellious against Him, and antagonistic to His divine nature in our sin, how much more will He save us from future wrath, our now being as lovely as He is in the sight of the Father. By His atoning sacrifice on the Cross, Jesus exchanged the relation of hostile parties into a relation of peace by firstly, God moving toward man in the Person and work of Jesus with a view to breaking down man's hostility by commending God's love and holiness to him and by convincing him of the enormity and the consequence of sin, secondly a corresponding moving on man's part toward God in yielding to the appeal of Jesus' self-sacrificing love and laying aside his enmity and renouncing his sin and turning to God in faith and obedience, thirdly a consequent change of character in man in that his sin is put away and forgiven and cleansed causing a revolution in all his dispositions and principles, and fourthly a corresponding change of relation on God's part since the thing which alone rendered Him hostile to man has been removed so that He can now receive man into fellowship and let loose upon him all His fatherly love and grace. Thus there is complete reconciliation. Jesus said, "Because I live, also you shall live", and in His resurrection power He is able to save us completely and to the end, in that He sanctifies us progressively by the work of the Holy Spirit in us, and in that He will glorify our bodies at the Rapture. So we have a triumphant confidence and joyful hope in God.

Wherefore, as through the intermediate agency of one man the aforementioned sin entered the world, and through this sin, death; and thus into and throughout all mankind death entered, because all sinned. For until law, sin was in the world, but sin is not put to one's account, there being no law. But death reigned as king from Adam to Moses, even over those who did not sin in the likeness of the transgression of Adam, who is a type of the One who is to come.

Sin and death come to us from the First Adam, and righteousness and life from the Second Adam, Jesus. Sin originated with the angel Lucifer, who in rebelling against God contracted a sinful nature. Adam, in his disobedience to God, was the channel through which sin entered the human race. Through sin, death came to humanity, both physical and spiritual, affecting everyone i.e. death affects all since all sinned. I can demonstrate that all sinned as follows; when Adam, the federal head of the human race, sinned, constituting him a sinner, all human beings participated in his sin, bringing death upon all i.e. we are sinners not because we have committed acts of sin, but because Adam sinned. I can demonstrate that we inherit Adam's sin as follows; sin was in the world before the law of Moses came, but it was not yet put to men's accounts since there was no law to transgress, but still death reigned over all, and since death comes by means of sin and since none of those after Adam were accounted to have sinned, they must have died due to Adam's sin i.e. they sinned in him their federal head. Adam was a type of Jesus in that he exercised a pre-eminent influence on the human race, though his influence was destructive, where Jesus' was saving.

But not as the transgression, thus also is the gratuitous favour. For since by the transgression of the one the many died, much more the grace of God and the gratuitous gift by grace which is of the one Man, Jesus Christ, to the many will abound.

Adam's original sin was a violation of the known will of God, which resulted in death to all. Jesus' obedience results in the gracious gift of eternal life being made available to all, though none merit it. As believers we have a much more certain basis of belief in what is gained through Jesus, given the character of God Who we know as Father, than in the certainties of sin and death that came through Adam.

And not as through one who sinned, was the gift, for the judgement, on the one hand, was out of one transgression as a source, resulting in condemnation. But the gratuitous gift, on the other hand, was out of many transgressions as a source, resulting in justification.

From the source of one sin, that of Adam, God's judgement fell, resulting in the condemnation of all. From the source of many transgressions, as an occasion for the display of God's grace, the free gift of salvation came, resulting in justification for all who would put their faith in Jesus.

For in view of the fact that by means of the transgression of the one death reigned as king through that one, much more those who receive the abundance of grace and of the gift of righteousness, in life will reign as kings through the One, Jesus Christ.

The effect of Jesus cannot fall behind that of Adam, so if death reigned before, there must now be a reign of life.

So then, therefore, as through one act of transgression, to all men there resulted condemnation, thus also through one act of righteousness, to all men there resulted a righteous standing that had to do with life.

Jesus' purpose was to perform the righteous act of satisfying the demands of the law of Moses which mankind broke. Then could God declare men free from guilt and acceptable to Him, and bestow a righteousness upon man which is connected with the impartation of spiritual life, this righteousness being a purely legal matter and a standing that neither imparts life nor changes character, but which righteousness is accompanied by the life that God is, which life is imparted to the sinner when he believes.

For just as through the disobedience of the one man the many were constituted sinners, thus also through the obedience of the One, the many will be constituted righteous.

Adam's disobedience was due to his inattentive, careless hearing of God, failing to listen when God was speaking. How often in Old Testament times was Israel's disobedience described as a refusing to hear? Obedience on the other hand stems from a willing listening to authority. Jesus came to the Father in answer to His call so as to then do the Father's will. The Father's will for the Son was the Cross. Now all who believe in Jesus are changed so as to be approved by God, in a judicial act of His.

Moreover, law entered in alongside in order that the transgression might be augmented. But where the sin was augmented, the grace superabounded with more added to that,

So what as to the office of the law? It came in with sin, created as a subordinate accessory to sin since not having the decisive significance in history which the objective power of sin has. It was taken up into the divine plan and was made an occasion and opportunity for the abounding of grace in the opening of the new way of justification and life, now that sin was present. The law stood between Adam and Jesus, its place in the divine arrangement such that it did not frustrate the end contemplated in the work of Jesus, but rather furthered it. The law, on encountering the flesh, evoked its natural antagonism to God and so stimulated men into disobedience. As the sum total of evil grew, made up of repeated acts of disobedience to the law, the need of redemption and the sense of that need were intensified.

in order that just as the aforementioned sin reigned as king in the sphere of death, thus also the aforementioned grace might reign as king through righteousness, resulting in eternal life through Jesus Christ our Lord.

Sin reigned as absolute monarch in man's being, resulting in the totally depraved nature of the unsaved person, and exercised in his death. Grace is supplied superabundantly in order that it might reign, resulting in the righteous nature of the believer, and exercised in eternal life, this gracious offer being made possible through Jesus' work on the Cross.

What then shall we say? Shall we habitually sustain an attitude of dependence upon, yieldedness to, and cordiality with the sinful nature in order that grace may abound?

When I talked about sin reigning as king, I was not talking about individual acts of sin, but the evil sinful nature which is still resident in the believer, which results in his acts of sin. I now turn to addressing the God-ordained method whereby a believer can live a victorious life over sin. I am repeatedly asked two questions about grace by the legalists, who do not themselves understand grace. In answer to the first question I will show the mechanical impossibility of a Christian continuing to live a life of habitual sin. In answer to the second I will show that for a Christian, having changed masters to now serve Jesus, it is not his nature to sin. In answering both these questions I need to explain to you the machinery and the mechanics of the Spirit-filled life, in particular the inner workings of this setup that God brings into being when He saves a sinner, breaks the power of indwelling sin, and implants the divine nature. So in answering these two questions about grace, I am not talking about what kind of life the believer should live, but by what method, or how, he should live that life. The first line of questioning by the legalists is this; since I say that where sin abounds grace is in superabundance with more on top, am I saying that God is willing to forgive a person's sins as often as he commits them? And when I answer "Yes" to this, they go on; am I therefore saying that it is acceptable for Christians to keep on habitually sinning in order that God may have an opportunity to forgive us and thus display His grace? This is the first question. So the issue is, shall we continue in the sinful nature, being at home and comfortable with its presence in us, and yielded to it so as to have the habit of following its promptings, as we used to before we were saved?

May such a thing never occur. How is it possible for us, such persons as we are, who have been separated once for all from the sinful nature, any longer to live in its grip?

For a Christian to sustain the same relationship with indwelling sin as before God saved him is a mechanical impossibility. We are dead to sin, so how can we live any longer in it? How could a born-again child of God do such a thing? It is against our new divine nature to habitually yield to the evil nature. There are two things that result from God's performing His major surgical operation in the inner being of every sinner He saves, which prevent this from being the case. The first result is the breaking of the power of indwelling sin, so that the believer is rendered dead to the sinful nature i.e. separated from it, as physical death is separation of a person from his body and spiritual death is separation of a person from God. God used His surgical knife to cut the believing sinner loose from his evil nature, being a permanent, thorough, once for all act, never to be repeated. This act occurred potentially in the mind and purpose of God when the believing sinner, having been elected to salvation before the universe was created, was identified with Jesus in His death on the Cross, and occurred actually the moment the sinner placed his faith in Jesus as Saviour. The sinful nature is not taken out of the believer, but remains in his inner being, though he is separated from it, so dead to it. Though we believers still sin, God has now so constituted us that we need not do so. The divine nature He imparted to us gives the believer a hatred of sin and a love for righteousness. Also the Holy Spirit has been caused to take up His permanent residence in the believer to aid him in his battle against sin and in his effort to live a Christian life. So how is it possible for us to live in sin any longer? We now have absolute dominion over the sinful nature in our inner being, it being a dethroned monarch. Now Jesus is on the throne of the believer's heart, and stays on the throne so long as the believer keeps yielded to the Spirit and rejects the promptings of the sinful nature. When the believer does sin, the sinful nature dethrones Jesus in his heart, which choice of the believer creates a guilty conscience in him and also grieves the indwelling Holy Spirit. You could think of this separation of the sinful nature from the believer as being like a millstone which, when disconnected from its water-driven mechanism, ceases to grind the corn as its source of power has been cut off. Disconnecting the believer from the sinful nature means that he ceases to function as a sinner, since the source of power to operate as a sinner has been cut off. Reconnect the sinful nature, as a believer can choose to do, and he sins again. But he is under no compulsion to put himself back into the control of the sinful nature again, nor can he do it habitually, nor frequently, since God has so adjusted things in the believer's life that, whilst being free to choose which nature he obeys, whether the divine or the sinful, yet the greater number of his choices are Godward. Thus is it a mechanical impossibility for a believer to habitually sustain the same relationship to the sinful nature which he sustained before he was saved.

Do you not know that all we who were placed in Christ Jesus, in His death were placed? We therefore were entombed with Him through this being placed in His death, in order that in the same manner as there was raised up Christ out from among those who are dead through the glory of the Father, thus also we by means of a new life imparted may order our behaviour.

The separating from the sinful nature was brought about by God's act of placing the believing sinner into Jesus so that that person would share His death on the Cross, which identification with Him in His death changed the believer's condition and brought about the separation of the believer from the sinful nature i.e. he died to it. The believing sinner is introduced into vital union with Jesus in order that the believer might have the power of the sinful nature broken and the divine nature implanted through his identification with Him in His death, burial, and resurrection, thus altering the condition and relationship of that sinner, with regard to his previous state and environment, by bringing him into a new environment, namely the Kingdom of God. In sharing His death we come into the benefits of that identification with Him, namely, being separated from the sinful nature as part of the salvation He gives us when we believe. We were placed in a new environment, Jesus, in Whom we have righteousness and life, where previously we came under condemnation, and our condition is changed from that of a sinner to that of a saint. We were also placed into Jesus that we might share in His resurrection and thus have divine life imparted to us, so having a new quality of life. This is the second result of God's operating on the inner being of every believer He saves; that he can walk in newness of life, being life that is divine, so having a new source of ethical and spiritual energy, which then enables him to order his behaviour in accordance with Christian conduct, as led by the Spirit. So we are both disengaged from the sinful nature and have the divine nature imparted to us, giving us the desire and the power to do God's will. The Christian's will has been made absolutely free where before it was not, with respect to choosing between good and evil, having been enslaved to the sinful nature. Now it is our responsibility, being poised between two natures, to reject the sinful and to obey the divine. When it becomes a habit to constantly say "No" to the sinful nature and to constantly say "Yes" to the divine nature, then the victorious life has been reached. So the Christian who is living under grace is not compelled to sin and does not want to sin, so he should not sin.

For in view of the fact that we are those who have become permanently united with Him with respect to the likeness of His death, certainly also we shall be those who as a logical result have become permanently united with Him with respect to the likeness of His resurrection, knowing this experientially, that our old [unregenerate] self was crucified once for all with Him in order that the physical body [heretofore] dominated by the sinful nature might be rendered inoperative [in that respect], with the result that no longer are we rendering a slave's habitual obedience to the sinful nature, for the one who died once for all stands in the position of a permanent relationship of freedom from the sinful nature.

What I have just said is so important that I feel the need to reiterate it. We are now united with Jesus, growing up together with Him in a living, vital union. We were united with Him in a death on the Cross, His death being to save us from the guilt, penalty, and power of sin, our death being one which we in justice should have died as a result of that sin, but which in the grace of God was borne as to its guilt and penalty by His Son Jesus. As Jesus now lives a new life where His human spirit is in prominence as opposed to His human soul, so we believers, in our new condition, now order our behaviour in the power of a new life imparted, namely the resurrection life of Jesus i.e. as His resurrection life is being lived in a new sphere to that which He lived when He was on earth when his soul life had prominence, so is the believer's life new in quality compared to that which he lived when he was a sinner. As I said before, the power of the sinful nature over us is now broken. The person the believer was before he was saved, when he was under the power of the sinful nature, was totally depraved, unregenerate, and lacking the life of God. That person was crucified with Jesus in order that his physical body might be rendered inactive, that it might be caused to cease. So now we should not serve sin, since we have been disengaged from the sinful nature, as brought about by God. The sinful nature controls the body of the sinner, but when we believed in Jesus, God disconnected the sinful nature from the body so that the believer's body is now inoperative so far as any control which that nature might have over the believer is concerned. My exhortation to you then is; maintain the relationship of disconnection which God has brought about between you and the indwelling sinful nature. Your divine nature and the witness of a grieved Holy Spirit together prevent any possibility of your taking advantage of divine grace. Since Jesus' death on the Cross brought complete separation from your sinful nature, God setting you free permanently from it when you put your faith in Jesus as your Saviour, take on your responsibility and maintain that freedom from your sinful nature moment by moment.

Now, in view of the fact that we died once for all with Christ, we believe that we shall also live by means of Him, knowing that Christ, having been raised up from among those who are dead, no longer dies. Death over Him no longer exercises lordship. For the death He died, He died with respect to our sinful nature once for all. But the life He lives, He lives with respect to God.

And also let me reiterate that since we died off with Jesus, we assuredly believe that we will also live with respect to Him i.e. the believer's new life imparted to him at the moment of believing is Jesus Himself, and we will live by means of Him, the believer deriving his spiritual life from Him. I am not speaking here about the believer's fellowship with Jesus here or in eternity, but that since Jesus died once for all and since He defeated death He will live forever, so if we derive our spiritual life from Him, we will be sustained in spiritual life for time and eternity, Jesus being our life.

Thus, also, as for you, you be constantly counting upon the fact that, on the one hand, you are those who have been separated from the sinful nature, and, on the other, that you are living ones with respect to God in Christ Jesus. Stop therefore allowing the sinful nature to reign as king in your mortal body with a view to obeying it [the body] in its passionate cravings. Moreover, stop putting your members at the disposal of the sinful nature as weapons of unrighteousness, but by a once-for-all act and at once, put yourselves at the disposal of God as those who are actively alive out from among the dead, and put your members as weapons of righteousness at the disposal of God, for [then] the sinful nature will not exercise lordship over you, for you are not under law but under grace.

Let me now show you another aspect to the method whereby we obtain victory over sin. I have already described the inner spiritual machinery God has installed in us by which we live our Christian lives. You need to adjust yourselves properly to this inner change if you are to avoid living a mediocre Christian life, but rather to expect the best results from it. Firstly you need to reckon yourself dead to sin, and secondly you need to reckon yourself alive to God. In your efforts to live a life in accordance with the Word you need to take into account that you have been disengaged from the sinful nature, so are dead to sin and can say "No" to that nature now. Also you need to take into account that you are alive to God, that the divine nature has been imparted to you, giving you the desire and the power to regulate your life in accordance with the Word. It is God Who constituted these states, your reckoning them did not make them so, but your reckoning them allows for a better operation of God's spiritual machinery in you so as to bring beneficial results and leading to a fruitful Christian life. Act in such a way that shows that you know that the power of the sinful nature over you is broken and that you no longer have to obey it, but can rather turn your back on it and do what is right. But if you do not count upon the fact that the divine nature is implanted in your inner being, you will only live life as best you can, mostly in the energy of your own strength, resulting in a mediocre Christian experience. If rather, you count upon the fact that you possess the divine nature, you will cease from your own struggles at living a Christian life and avail yourself of the life of God that is in you. When you count upon the fact that the power of the sinful nature over you is broken, you will stop allowing it to rule you, aided by the urging and empowering of the Holy Spirit in you. Guard against the sinful nature, this unseen enemy, by keeping watch over the actions of the members of your body; what your eyes look at, what your ears listen to, what your mind thinks about, what your hands do, where your feet carry you. Knowing that this nature's power over you is broken, you will also stop yielding up your bodily members to the disposal of that nature. These are weapons to be used in the Christian warfare against evil, and not for participating in unrighteous deeds. So, now, dedicate yourselves to God as a once-for-all dedication never needing to be repeated, but from now on continuously in evidence, moment by moment, throughout your life in devoted service to Him. The sinful nature will not rule you since you are now living under grace, no longer attempting to obey the law by your own effort, but as a saved person who has been subject to the surgical operation in which the power of the sinful nature has been broken and the divine nature implanted. This then is my answer to the legalists who claim that living under grace means that Christians can keep on habitually sinning.

What then? Shall we sin occasionally, because we are not under law but under grace? Away with the thought.

The second line of questioning by the legalists is this; since I say that grace makes it impossible for the believer to sin habitually like he did before he was saved, am I saying that believers can live a life of planned, occasional sin, since they are no longer under the uncompromising rule of law, but now under the lenient sceptre of grace? This is the second question. They do not know grace. Law is indeed uncompromising but grace is never lenient, it being far stricter than the law ever could be, and being a far greater deterrent of evil than the law ever was. The Holy Spirit indwelling us takes notice of the slightest sin and convicts us of it, where the law could act only generally, and then only when our conscience cooperated with it. And grace not only forgives, it also teaches. Under grace there is a new propelling and compelling deterrent to sin; divine love, produced in our being by the Spirit, which causes us to hate sin and obey the Word of God.

Do you not know that to whom you put yourselves at the disposal of as slaves resulting in obedience, slaves you are to whom you render habitual obedience, whether slaves of the sinful nature resulting in death, or obedient slaves [of Christ] resulting in righteousness?

The answer to this question is found in the believer's change of master. Before salvation you were an abject slave of Satan, but since you were saved you are now a slave of Jesus. You have changed masters because you have a new nature, the divine, and the evil nature which compelled you to serve Satan has had its power over you broken. You do now sin at times, but you do not provide in your life's plan for occasional acts of sin, as you now hate sin and endeavour to keep it out of your life. In the event that you do commit an act of sin, you deal with it in confession to your new Master, Jesus, putting it out of your life and receiving the cleansing that His blood offers. We were born into slavery to Satan, having inherited a totally depraved nature from Adam. Now, having been born again by the act of regeneration through the Holy Spirit, we are given a new, divine nature, which nature gives us the desire and power to do God's will. So have we changed masters from Satan to Jesus. Now you do not want to live even a life of planned occasional sin because firstly you do not have to, and secondly because you do not desire to do so. Before salvation your will was swallowed up in the will of Satan, but since you have been saved your will is swallowed up in the sweet will of God, so that you do not desire to live a life of planned occasional sin. Your identification with Jesus in His death broke the bands which bound you to Satan. Now you are bound to Jesus as His bondslave in bands so strong that only death can break them, so these bands are unbreakable since Jesus is your life and Jesus will never die again, meaning you are bound to Him forever. The only way you could live a life of planned occasional sin is to become the slave again of the evil nature and Satan, but this is impossible as you are now forever Jesus' slave. Before salvation you served Satan to the disregard of your own best interests because you were compelled to do so, for which service you got sin and death, sorrow and suffering. Now, as a believer, with your own will and accord you serve Jesus with an abandon, seeking only that Jesus is glorified. A person who so disregards himself for the sake of Jesus does not want to live a life of planned occasional sin.

But God be thanked, that [whereas] you were slaves of the evil nature, you obeyed out from the heart as a source a type of teaching into which you were handed over.

In salvation God constituted you inwardly so that you would react to the doctrines of grace in your new divine nature in such a way as to receive and obey them i.e. you were delivered into the teachings of grace in the sense that you were so constituted in salvation that you would obey them, making you now a slave of righteousness.

And having been set free once for all from the sinful nature, you were constituted slaves to righteousness.

Having been set free from your old evil bondage, you were legally established as a slave of righteousness.

I am using an illustration drawn from human affairs because of the frailties of your humanity. For just as you placed your members as slaves at the disposal of uncleanness and lawlessness resulting in lawlessness, thus now place your members as slaves at the disposal of righteousness resulting in holiness. For, when you were slaves of the sinful nature, you were those who were free with respect to righteousness.

I apologise for using the illustration of a slave, but I was forced to do so in order to make clear my reasoning to you.

Therefore, what fruit were you having then, upon the basis of which things now you are ashamed? For the consummation of these things is death. But now, having been set free from the sinful nature and having been made bondslaves of God, you are having your fruit resulting in holiness, and the consummation, life eternal. For the subsistence pay which the sinful nature doles out is death. But the free gift of God is life eternal in Christ Jesus our Lord.

As soldiers are not paid with money but rather corn, meat, fruits, and salt, being their rations, so in this battle that we are engaged in between Satan's hosts of wickedness and the people of God, Satan's rations, that he pays his slaves with, is death. As believers and slaves of Jesus, your reward is to live with Him forever in the Father's presence.

Or, are you ignorant, brethren, for I am speaking to those who have an experiential knowledge of law, that the law exercises lordship over the individual as long as he lives?

By the death that we died in Jesus we are freed from the law, the law getting its power from man's sinful nature, by which it perpetually stimulates sin. Those who live under law are obligated to obey it, but the law gives neither the desire nor the power to obey its precepts, but rather brings out sin all the more since its very presence incites rebellion in the totally depraved nature of the individual. Believers are not under law anymore. A believer who puts himself under law fails to avail himself of the resources of grace and so is a defeated Christian, since the law incites him to more sin, not that the law is responsible for this, rather the sinful nature, which nature can only be conquered when the believer cries, "Who shall deliver me?" and looks away from himself and his own efforts and looks to Jesus. The law is for the living. Once you die you have passed out of the realm where the law has jurisdiction over you. Unsaved people are alive to the law, but when a believing sinner has been identified with Jesus in His death, burial, and resurrection, he has passed out of the realm where the law holds sway, now being a saved individual.

For the woman subject to a husband is permanently bound by law to her husband during his lifetime. But if her husband dies she is released from the law of her husband. So then, while her husband is living, an adulteress she will be called if she is married to another man. But if her husband is dead, she is free from the law, so that she is not an adulteress, though being married to another man.

There is no release for a wife from her husband except by his death. When he dies she also dies, so far as the marriage relation is concerned i.e. her relationship to the marriage, and the husband, has died. Similarly we believers are made dead to the law, killed in respect of our marriage relation to the law.

So that, my brethren, as for you, you also were put to death with reference to the law through the intermediate agency of the body of Christ, resulting in your being married to another, to the One who was raised up from among the dead, in order that we might bear fruit to God.

We were made dead to the law and sin, that death being an ethical one in fellowship with Jesus' violent death. Our marriage relation to the law was killed through the body of Jesus, His death being the atoning sacrifice for us.

For when we were in the sphere of the sinful nature, the impulses of the sins which were through the law were operative in our members, resulting in the production of fruit with respect to death.

Previously the emotions of sin were stirred to activity by the law so that they operated in our bodily members, resulting in the production of diseased, decaying fruit.

But now we were discharged from the law, having died to that in which we were constantly being held down, insomuch that we are rendering habitually a slave's obedience in a sphere new in quality, that of the Spirit, and not in a sphere outworn as to usefulness, in a sphere of that which was put in writing.

By our death with Jesus on the Cross we were discharged from the law, so not under law anymore nor subject to it. But the sinful nature in us has not died. In fact it is more alive than ever, being the point through which Satan seeks to obtain control over us, though its power in us has been broken. Having been discharged from the law, it is the natural consequence that we are now obedient to the Spirit and the fact is that we do so live in this new obedience. We serve Jesus in the power of the Holy Spirit, under a new energy and control, not in the oldness of attempting to obey the law of Moses anymore, it being marred through age and now useless since it was set aside at the Cross.

What therefore shall we say? The law, is it sin? Away with the thought. Certainly I did not come into an experiential knowledge of sin except through the instrumentality of law, for I had not known evil desire except that the law kept on saying, You shall not desire evil.

If we as believers put ourselves under law, we will not avail ourselves of the resources of grace and so be defeated Christians, which experience I had before I came to know that the power of the sinful nature over me had been broken. I will go on to tell you of my Christian experience while I attempted to live a Christian life under law. Since it is the law that incites my sinful nature into activity, causing me to desire what is forbidden, does that mean that the law is sinful? Never. Rather it was through the law that I came to know sin in my experience, in that I found myself to be in conflict with a prohibitive law, so the law, since it shows me the sin in my life, must be holy.

But the sinful nature, using the commandment as a fulcrum, brought about in me every kind of evil craving. For without law, the sinful nature was dead.

The law is not sinful, but sin found occasion in the law, making it a base of operations and a starting place from which to work, the law furnishing sin with the material and the ground for launching an assault in the energy of the evil principle. Without the incitement produced by the law, the sinful nature was relatively dormant, but the sinful nature used the law like a stick by which to pry itself loose from its relative inactivity into activity.

But I was alive without law aforetime. But the commandment having come, the sinful nature regained its strength and vigour, and I died.

Prior to me coming face to face with the law of God I was alive and flourished without the law, being a period of childlike innocence. But then the law showed me the exceeding sinfulness of sin and incited in me a rebellion against it. When the commandment 'Do not have evil desire' came to me in all its implications, my evil nature, that was previously almost dead, came to life. At this point I ceased to live and flourish as before and fell into a state of unhappiness.

And the commandment which was to life, this I found to be to death; for the sinful nature, using the commandment as a fulcrum, beguiled me and through it killed me.

This very commandment, the aim of which was life, I found, to my surprise, led to death. I had expected my Christian life under law to result in a testimony and experience that would be a living one, I being alive with the life of God, and this accomplished through my attempt at law-obedience. But I found that mere effort at obeying an outside law resulted in defeat. The law, using my sinful nature as a stick, brought out sin all the more, putting me in a condition of death.

So that the law is holy, and the commandment holy, and righteous, and good.

The law and the commandment are a revelation of God Himself, and they are just in their requirements which correspond to His holiness, and they produce good effects at the last.

Therefore, that which is good, to me did it become death? Away with the thought. But the sinful nature, in order that it might become evident that it is sin, through that which is good [the commandment] brought about death in me, in order that the sinful nature [its impulses and working] through the intermediate agency of the commandment may become exceedingly sinful.

Can what is good produce evil? Never. It was sin, not the commandment, which became death to me. And this was the divine purpose in sending the commandment; that sin might appear as sin, in its true colours. It is sin that turns God's intended blessing into a curse, but then our eyes are opened to sin and we desire deliverance from it all the more.

For we know that the law is spiritual. But as for myself, I am fleshly [being dominated by the sinful nature], permanently sold under the sinful nature. For that which I do, I do not understand. For that which I desire, this I do not practice. But that which I hate, this I am doing.

How dismal a state it is to be carnal; to be saved, but not to have found deliverance from the power of sin in the fullness of the Spirit, so still being more or less under the control of the sinful nature. This was my condition in that, though having been liberated from my sinful nature, I was nevertheless still under its control, due to my living under law instead of under grace. I was sold and sin owned me as its slave. I did not understand my experience as a Christian since the good thing I did not do, but the thing I hated I did, even though I desired to do good and I hated sin. I was attempting to do in my own strength that which can only be accomplished in the supernatural power of the Holy Spirit.

In view of the fact then that what I do not desire, this I do, I am in agreement with the law that it is good. And since the case stands thus, no longer is it I who do it, but the sinful nature which indwells me; for I know positively that there does not dwell in me, that is, in my flesh, good; for the being desirous is constantly with me; but the doing of the good, not; for that which I desire, good, I do not; but that which I do not desire, evil, this I practice. But in view of the fact that that which I do not desire, this I do, no longer is it I who do it, but the sinful nature which indwells me does it.

I agreed with law in my desire of what I wanted not to do, which proved my acceptance of God's law as being good. And in my doing evil against my will, my will agreed with the moral beauty of the law, that it is good. Logically then, it was no longer I that was doing the evil i.e. my proper personality and moral self-consciousness had approved the law and had developed vague desires for something better, rather it was the sinful nature, which has its abode in me, that did the evil. To be saved from the sinful nature one must at the same time own it and disown it i.e. I acknowledge that, as a creature of flesh and apart from any relation to or affinity with God and His Spirit, there dwells no good in me, yet now, the Spirit's presence in me enables me to have complete victory over this nature. The divine nature in me constantly desired to do God's will, but the ability and power to do it was not always with me, since I was depending on my own efforts to do God's will, rather than relying on the Spirit's power within me.

I find therefore the law, that to me, always desirous of doing the good, to me, the evil is always present. For I rejoice in the law of God according to the inward man. But I see a different kind of a law in my members, waging war against the law of my mind, making me a prisoner of war to the law of the sinful nature which is in my members.

The sinful nature, the law in my bodily members, warred against the law of my mind, so that when I desired to do good, my sinful nature asserted itself against the doing of that good, though I delighted in the law in my ethical personality, that personality being the side of me that is akin to God and the point of attachment, so to speak, for the regenerating Holy Spirit. So the law of my inward man, as exhibited in my mind, was practically identical with the law of God, yet the law of my flesh, as exhibited in my members, asserted itself and made war on my good desires. Two authorities were at work in me, both saying 'Do this', and the higher authority succumbed to the lower, the lower authority prevailing and leading me captive to the law of sin in my members so that I was made obedient to it, doing those things that my sinful nature urged and instructed me to do.

Wretched man, I. Who shall deliver me out of the body of this death? Thanks be to God, through Jesus Christ our Lord. Therefore, I myself with my mind serve the law of God but with my flesh the law of sin.

Through exhaustion at my law-keeping efforts I wailed in anguish at my failure to do good and cried for help. I had been ignorant of the delivering power of the Holy Spirit, about which I now have much to say, and which I will go on to describe to you. The moment I cried, "Who will help me?" I found the path to victory, since I called upon a Person for help. The Spirit delivered me from this existence of death where my sinful nature was in ascendancy, since though I desired victory over it, I was still dominated by it. I needed to be delivered from this bondage to the law of sin into moral freedom where my body would no longer serve as the seat of this shameful state of living death. I needed deliverance from my condition of defeat, which condition my residence in my physical body made a possibility, and which condition my lack of spiritual knowledge up to that moment resulted in. Deliverance came through Jesus, through faith in Him, for which I thank God. The law is holy, though it holds a relation to sin in that it gives life to it due to man's natural aversion to the commandment. In me, even though I had been delivered by Jesus, the conflict between the law and sin continued, and still does, which would have resulted in an unceasing life of death for me were not a glorious deliverance effected. Without this deliverance, the flesh, even in the spiritual man, is essentially subject to the law of sin, and carries him its own way and commands his allegiance to the economy of sin. Such was my condition before I found the way of deliverance and victory through Jesus. So it is not that the law is sin that resulted in my sinning, since the law is not sin, it is that I threw the spanner of self-dependence into God's mechanics in my inner being, which stopped the machinery working, and prevented victory and the production of fruit in my Christian life.

Therefore, now, there is not even one bit of condemnation to those who are in Christ Jesus,

I shall now describe the victorious state into which Jesus has delivered us, being the triumph of the Spirit over the flesh. Though this victory is incomplete while we are here on earth, nevertheless it is not an inconsiderable one, and after this life on earth, the victory will indeed be complete and glorious. So we need have no reason to fear, but all reason to hope, for nothing can sever us from God's love in Christ Jesus. Although our flesh is still subject to the law of sin, because of our position in Jesus where we are liberated from the compelling power of the sinful nature and made a partaker of the divine nature, we shall not come into condemnation, but rather to glory with Jesus, this divine nature being a new inner condition which produces in every believer a life which has for its motive obedience to His commandments, and which divine nature ensures that there is no cause for condemnation in us.

for the law of the Spirit, that of the life in Christ Jesus, freed you once for all from the law of the sinful nature and of death. For that which is an impossibility for the law, because it was weak through the sinful nature, God having sent His Son in likeness of flesh of sin, and concerning sin, condemned sin in the sinful nature, in order that the righteous requirement of the law may be brought to completion in us who, not as dominated by the sinful nature are ordering our behaviour but as dominated by the Spirit.

The Holy Spirit exercises a regulative control over the life of the believer in the form of the energy He gives to him both to desire and to do God's will, this energy coming from the life that God is, which life is in the believer, given him by reason of his position in Jesus. This life which is in Jesus freed me from the regulative principle of sin and death i.e. from the sinful nature, at the moment I put my faith in Jesus and was saved. Since I am freed from the law of sin and death so that I now serve another Master, all claim of sin on me is at an end and I am acquitted and suffer no condemnation. The Spirit which brings the believer the life which is in Jesus, brings with it also the divine law for the believer's life, but this law is able to give life, unlike the written law, and hence righteousness comes by it, it proving more than a match for the authority exercised over man by the forces of sin and death. God condemned sin in the flesh, expressed in His sending His Son in our nature, Jesus being really human and conformed in appearance to the flesh whose characteristic is sin, yet He being sinless, His sinless life lived in our human nature so condemning our sinful lives and our unholiness and leaving us without excuse and without hope. But this condemnation Jesus took upon Himself by His death on the Cross. Jesus' death exhibits God's condemnation of sin in the flesh, and by this condemnation sin was executed, in that God pronounced the doom of sin and brought its claims and authority over man to an end, deposing and dethroning it from its dominion. God did this in order that the righteousness of the law might be fulfilled and find its full accomplishment in us, in our sanctification, which is the ultimate end of our being saved by Him through His grace.

For those who are habitually dominated by the sinful nature put their minds on the things of the sinful nature, but those who are habitually dominated by the Spirit put their minds on the things of the Spirit. For to have the mind dominated by the sinful nature is death, but to have the mind dominated by the Spirit is life and peace; because the mind dominated by the sinful nature is hostile to God, for it does not marshall itself under the command of the law of God, neither is it able to. Moreover, those who are in the sphere of the sinful nature are not able to please God.

The unsaved person is habitually dominated by his indwelling sinful nature, and habitually puts his mind on those things that his sinful nature always has welling up within itself, namely the things of sin, his mind being possessed by, controlled by, and dominated by, his sinful nature, which is marshalled under the command of Satan, and as such he is unable to please God, since the flesh cannot submit itself to God, it being in a state of permanent revolt against Him. Such is the unsaved person, dead in trespasses and sins and separated from God and His life, so dead to Him, and on his way to a final and everlasting state of death in eternity, headed to death since he is at enmity against God, the Fountain of Life. But the believer is bound to God and His life, so is at peace with Him, possessing the life that God is, and having a mind possessed by, controlled by, and dominated by, the Holy Spirit.

But, as for you, you are not in the sphere of the sinful nature but in the sphere of the Spirit, provided that the Spirit of God is in residence in you. But, assuming that a person does not have Christ's Spirit, this one does not belong to Him.

But you, assuming that the Spirit dwells in you actively and is living in you having made His home in you, are not under the control of the sinful nature. You have been taken out from the realm of the sinful nature and put into the realm of the Spirit. God has done this by breaking the power of the sinful nature over you and imparting to you the divine nature so that it is present in you, thus enabling the Spirit's ministry in you, Whose purpose is to give you victory over sin and to produce His own fruit in you. So the saved person is not in the grip of the sinful nature, but under the control of the Holy Spirit, to the degree that the believer yields himself to Him. The unsaved person does not have the Spirit of Jesus, so does not belong to Him, but the moment he puts his faith in Jesus he becomes the possession of Jesus, and so must possess the Holy Spirit as an indweller at that same moment.

But, assuming that Christ is in you, on the one hand the body is dead on account of sin, but on the other hand the [human] spirit is alive on account of righteousness.

Adam's sin brought both spiritual and physical death to all men. As believers, our bodies are dead in the sense that they have death in them because of sin, but our spirits, being that part of us that is conscious of God, are made alive and energised by the Holy Spirit with divine life, righteous in quality, enabling us to worship God now and forever in spirit.

And assuming that the Spirit of the One who raised up Jesus out from among the dead is in residence in you, He who raised from among the dead Christ Jesus, will also make alive your mortal bodies through the agency of the Spirit who is resident in you.

As Jesus was raised to life physically, so will your bodies be raised out from among the dead at the Rapture by the Spirit Who is in you.

So then, brethren, we are those under obligation, not to the sinful nature to live habitually under the dominion of the sinful nature. For, assuming that you are living habitually under the dominion of the sinful nature, you are on the way to dying. But, assuming that by the Spirit you are habitually putting to death the deeds of the body, you will live.

Since we believers are no longer in the realm of the sinful nature, its power over us having been broken, and since we are in the realm of the Spirit, we are under no obligation to again live as those dominated by the sinful nature. Those still living such sin-dominated lives are unsaved, and so on their way to final death. But the one who is yielded to the Spirit, putting the actions inspired by his sinful nature to death through the aid of the Spirit, will live, he being a saved person.

For as many as are being constantly led by God's Spirit, these are sons of God. For you did not receive a spirit of slavery again with resulting fear, but you received the Spirit who places you as adult sons, by whom we cry out with deep emotion, Abba, [namely] Father. The Spirit himself is constantly bearing joint-testimony with our [human] spirit that we are God's children, and since children, also heirs; on the one hand, heirs of God, on the other, joint-heirs with Christ, provided that we are suffering with Him in order that we also may be glorified together,

When we received Jesus as Saviour we did not receive with Him an attitude of fear, so we no longer shrink from God as we did when living under the law of sin and death, since now we have been adopted, and His

Spirit in us assures us of our new filial relation to God. The Spirit places all born-again children of God as adult sons before God, in a legal standing and in relation to Him. Having been so adopted by God we have been chosen to be His heirs, entitled to the possession of His property, His status, and His rights, one with Him, as you see happening in Roman society. Now the Holy Spirit enables us to call God, Father, the Spirit bearing testimony to this fact, and our spirit, as energised by Him, then bearing joint-testimony with Him to our adoption. This testimony is separate from any inferences or conclusions of ours, and is no mere indefinite feeling, but rather an absolute conviction arising out of the Spirit's presence and work in us, His direct testimony similarly forming the basis of all our conviction respecting Jesus and His work. Those who share Jesus' sufferings now will share His glory hereafter. In order to share His glory hereafter, it is necessary to begin by sharing His sufferings here.

for I have come to a reasoned conclusion that the sufferings of the present season are of no weight in comparison to the glory which is about to be revealed upon us.

I have calculated the cost of following Jesus and have arrived at the conclusion that the present sufferings that we endure are nothing when compared with the glory that will be revealed in us when we return with Jesus in His second Advent, since then we will be included in His radiance and reflect His glory.

For the concentrated and undivided expectation of the creation is assiduously and patiently awaiting the revelation of the sons of God; for the creation was subjected to futility, not voluntarily, but on account of the One who put it under subjection upon the basis of the hope that the creation itself also will be delivered from the bondage of corruption into the liberty of the glory of the children of God.

Creation is watching, with head erect and outstretched, in suspense, not looking elsewhere, but patiently focused on the coming glorification of the saints, that it might be released from under its curse. Creation is the natural ally of our souls, being neither inert nor unspiritual, and its hopes being linked with ours. Creation was originally perfect and was brought forth to glorify God, but the curse led to a perishing, dying creation that cannot perfectly glorify Him. Adam's sin was the direct and special cause of this interference to creation's purpose. The punishment for man's sin fell also on the whole realm that was intended originally for his dominion. But the sentence on man was not hopeless, so creation will share in his hope as it shared in his doom. When the curse is removed from man at the revealing of the sons of God, it will also pass from creation, in anticipation of which creation sighs, as she possesses in her unmerited suffering a sort of intuitive feeling of her future deliverance.

For we know that the whole creation groans and travails together up to this moment, and not only, but we ourselves also who have the first-fruit of the Spirit, we ourselves also are groaning within ourselves, assiduously and patiently waiting the full realization of our adult sonship at the time of the redemption of our body.

The whole of creation in all its elements longs for its freedom from the curse. Though we have been adopted by God and, as led by the Spirit, are sons of God, only when our mortal bodies have been made immortal, the corruptible having put on the incorruptible, will we possess all that this sonship involves. For this moment we wait and sigh, the inextinguishable hope for which is born of the Spirit indwelling us, guaranteeing its fulfilment.

For we were saved in the sphere of hope. But hope that has been seen is not hope, for that which a person sees, why does he hope for it? But if that which we do not see, we hope for, through patience we expectantly wait for it.

We are waiting for adoption, though we currently enjoy sonship, since salvation is essentially related to the future. We wait for adoption since we were saved in hope, hope being an essential characteristic of our salvation. Since we hope for salvation, we do not yet see it, otherwise it would not be a hope but an observable fact. We do not see all that the Gospel held out to us, but it is nevertheless the object of our Christian hope. It is as true and sure as the love of God which, in Jesus, reconciled us to Himself and gave us the Spirit of adoption, and therefore we wait for our salvation in patience.

And in like manner also the Spirit lends us a helping hand with reference to our weakness, for the particular thing that we should pray for according to what is necessary in the nature of the case, we do not know with an absolute knowledge; but the Spirit himself comes to our rescue by interceding with unutterable groanings. Moreover, He who is constantly searching our hearts knows what is the mind of the Spirit because, according to God, He continually makes intercession on behalf of the saints.

The Spirit helps us with the load that we are carrying, coming to our aid in our spiritual problems and difficulties, allowing us to work out our own problems and overcome our own difficulties but with His assistance. We need His power when we are weak in prayer. We know what the general objects of prayer are, but not the specific, detailed objects in any given emergency or situation i.e. we do not know the particular what to pray for. We know the end, the perfecting of salvation, which is common to all prayers, but not what is necessary according to the need of the moment, at each crisis of need, in order to enable us to attain this end. When we are thus weak and in trouble, and cannot state in fit language as we ought our desire in prayer, but can only disclose it by inarticulate sighings, God receives our prayer since it comes from a soul full of the Holy Spirit. The Spirit knows our wants better than we do and Himself pleads on our behalf in our prayers, raising us to higher and holier desires than we can express in words. God knows what is the mind of the Spirit i.e. the Father, Who searches the hearts of His children, understands the intent and inclination of our unutterable prayers, unutterable because we do not know the particular things we should pray for in the circumstance, for He knows the mind of the Spirit Who is praying for us and in our stead in our prayers. The Holy Spirit prays according to the plan of God for our lives, He being our source of power and the Operator of God's machinery in our inner being, according to the dynamics of the Spirit-filled life.

And we know with an absolute knowledge that for those who are loving God, all things are working together resulting in good, for those who are divinely-summoned ones according to His purpose.

We are beloved by God and are thus secure from harm. All things work for our good, since we love Him Who works all things, and because He Who works all things has loved and chosen us and carried us through the successive steps of our spiritual life. He called us in His everlasting purpose whereby before the foundations of the world were laid, He had decreed by His secret counsel to deliver from curse and damnation those whom He chose in Jesus out of mankind, being all those who would put their faith in Jesus, and to bring them by Jesus to everlasting salvation. It is God Who makes all things work together in our lives for ultimate good. I accept fully the free agency of men, but behind it all and through it all runs God's sovereignty in His dealings with us, and on its gracious side.

Because, those whom He foreordained He also marked out beforehand as those who were to be conformed to the derived image of His Son, with the result that He is firstborn among many brethren. Moreover, those whom He thus marked out beforehand, these He also summoned. And those whom He summoned, these He also justified. Moreover, those whom He justified, these He also glorified.

Let me explain the five steps of how this calling of believers out from their lost estate came about. Firstly God eternally appointed men to salvation; the Triune God in council convened, the purpose of which was to select out from the three Persons of the Godhead the Lamb for sacrifice Who would pay the penalty for man's sin. The counsel was that the Son of God was to die on the Cross, this being the successful conclusion to their deliberations and being a fixed and unchangeable outcome. Secondly God determined that those who would put their faith in Jesus be conformed to the image of His Son and be placed as adult sons of His, this conforming and placing being the special limitations put upon believers provided within the scope of the salvation which they were to receive, and being the effective carrying out of God's will in the case of those appointed to salvation. This conforming to the image of Jesus in the inner heart life is the work of the Holy Spirit in the process called sanctification, which begins the moment the sinner is saved and which continues throughout eternity, the believer always approaching Jesus' likeness but never equalling it, since the finite can never equal infinity, but nevertheless resulting in a change of the believer's outward expression so that it ever more reflects the beauty of Jesus. The believer inherits Jesus' image when he is born again, though it is initially indistinct, but it becomes progressively clearer and more distinct as he grows in the Christian life. The purpose of this sanctifying is that Jesus might be the firstborn among many brethren, pre-eminent among those who are, by adoption through Him, sons of God, He being shown, acknowledged, and glorified by His brethren as the Son of God, and as their elder Brother and Head. Thirdly these so conformed to the image of Jesus, God called, being the effecting in time of His eternal appointing of them. The setting-apart work of the Spirit is His pre-salvation work of bringing the sinner who is appointed to salvation to the place where he puts his faith in Jesus as Saviour, being the effectual call of God. Fourthly those God called into salvation He justified, taking away the guilt and penalty of their sins and bestowing upon them His righteousness, Jesus Himself, in Whom the believer stands forever innocent, uncondemned, and righteous in point of law. Fifthly those God justified He glorified, to be effected at the Rapture when the believer's body will be transformed into a body like the resurrection body of Jesus, so that not only are believers acquitted of sin but also clothed with glory. Though this is a future event, justification and the new life of holiness in the Spirit are inseparable experiences, so I speak in faith that this glorifying has already been consummated, as it is complete and certain in the divine counsels.

What then shall we say to these things? In view of the fact that God is on our behalf, who could be against us? Indeed, He who His own Son did not spare, but on behalf of us all delivered Him up, how is it possible that He shall not with Him in grace give us all things?

So what should we say given the eternal victorious purpose of God's love in us who believe? Given this love of His for His children how could He allow any to do us harm? We derive our faith in this from His eternal efforts to redeem and rescue us. He has done so much already that He is certain to continue, since the Father's very own precious Son, infinitely dear to Him, He gave for us, so all the good that flows from that Gift, why would He withhold it?

Who shall bring a charge against God's chosen-out ones? God, the One who justifies? Who is the one who condemns? Christ Jesus, the One who died, yes, rather, who has been raised, who is on the right hand of God, who also is constantly interceding on our behalf?

Will God accuse the ones He justifies, being those who He has paid the penalty for? He cannot do both. We now stand in Jesus, He being our righteousness, as uncondemned and unchargeable as He is, so how could we again be accused and brought under condemnation? Can Jesus, Who is always making our case before the Father, at the same time condemn us? He cannot do both. Our faith rests on Jesus risen from the dead, triumphant, glorified, and infinite.

Who shall separate us from the love of Christ? Shall tribulation or distress or persecution or famine or nakedness or peril or sword? Even as it stands written, For your sake we are being put to death all the day long. We were accounted as sheep destined for slaughter. But in these things, all of them, we are coming off constantly with more than the victory through the One who loved us. For I have come through a process of persuasion to the settled conclusion that neither death nor life, nor angels, nor principalities, nor things present, nor things about to come, nor powers, nor height, nor depth, nor any other created thing will be able to separate us from the love of God which is in Christ Jesus our Lord.

The love of Jesus to us is permanent and unchanging so that whatever the adverse circumstances, nothing can affect it. Moreover this love enables us to obtain a surpassing victory over all such adversities, so that we have a holy arrogance of victory in His might. Indeed these trials actually give us a more intimate and thrilling experience of His love to us. And none, including Satan and his demonic forces, can separate us from His love.

Truth I speak in Christ. I am not lying, my conscience bearing joint-testimony with me in the Holy Spirit that I have a consuming grief, a great one, and intense anguish in my heart without a let-up. For I could wish that I myself were accursed from Christ on behalf of my brethren, my kindred according to the flesh,

I have, in this letter, declared the Gospel in its fullness and freeness, as the power of God to salvation to everyone who believes. I now turn, with great sadness, to consider the people to whom the promises of old were made, being my nation of Israel, but who have now rejected this Gospel. The Abrahamic covenant promised Israel an area of land in which to live, and the Davidic covenant promised to Israel an eternal dynasty of kings the last of whom would be an eternal Person, but neither of these have been fulfilled since these covenants were designed for a spiritual people, whereas Israel have currently renounced their religious beliefs. I am neither hostile nor indifferent to the Jews, rather longing that they would accept my message and turn to Jesus. I mourn for them and am continually tormented in pain at their refusal to do so. If I could I would offer my salvation and be eternally cut off from Jesus myself in order to save them, but it is not possible since I cannot be separated from Jesus' love nor condemned by Him. To save Israel is a work of the Holy Spirit, and Israel will be saved at the second Advent of Jesus when it will be brought back, in sovereign grace, saved and restored to its land under its covenanted King, Jesus.

who in character are Israelites, who are possessors of the position of a son having been placed as such, and of the glory, and of the covenants, and to whom was given the law, and who are possessors of the sacred service and the promises, of whom are the fathers, and out from whom is the Christ according to the flesh, the One who is above all, God eulogized forever. Amen.

Consider the greatness of my people and their unique place of privilege in God's providence, and the splendour of the inheritance and of the hopes which they now forfeit by their unbelief. They are members of a theocracy having God Himself as their sovereign, partakers of the theocratic privileges and glorious vocation of the nation of Israel, and heirs of the promises of God, but their renouncing of these has denied them their inheritance. The nation was known as a son of God in the Old Testament. The glory of Yahweh, the Shekinah, led them out of Egypt and rested over the Mercy Seat in the Holy of Holies, being the visible manifestation of God's presence with His Chosen People. God made covenants with Israel, being something He never did with the Gentile nations, because that nation was to be used as a channel to bring salvation to the human race. The law of Moses was given exclusively to Israel, and never pertained to the Gentiles. Service was offered by them to God in the tabernacle, offerings and priesthood. And promises were made to them about their coming

Messiah. Abraham, Isaac, and Jacob were the fathers of the nation, who were each called by God, but whose sons forfeited everything. Supremely the Messiah, Jesus, according to the flesh, came out of Israel, though as far as His deity is concerned He is over all, God, the One praised forever.

But the case is not such as this, that the word of God is fallen powerless; for not all who are out of Israel, these are Israel, nor because they are offspring of Abraham are all children, but: In Isaac an offspring shall be named for you.

But Israel's failings in the past and at present in no way mean that the Word of God has come to nought and is of no effect. For not all that are physically Israel by descent are spiritually Israel, being the true Israel, the people of God. Being a physical descendant of Abraham does not ensure a place in the family of God. The promise to Abraham was that from Isaac, the child born of a promise, would his true descendants come, which descendants by faith would inherit the promises made to Abraham by God.

That is, not the children of the flesh, these are children of God, but the children of the promise are counted for offspring; for the word of promise is this, According to this season I will come and there will be to Sarah a son.

The Old Testament saying amounts to this; it is not the earthly descendants of Abraham, the 'children of God', but rather the children of the promise who are counted as Abraham's children, being those who are saved by their faith. The promise was; when the season revives again next year, then will the son of the promise be born.

And not only, but also Rebecca, conceiving by one, Isaac, our father. For not yet having been born nor having practiced any good or evil, in order that the purpose of God dominated by an act of selecting out may abide, not out of a source of works, but out of the source of the One who calls, it was said to her, The older shall serve the younger; even as it stands written, Jacob I loved, but Esau I hated.

And there is not only an example of the election of a son of Abraham by one woman and a rejection of his son by another woman, but also of the election and the rejection of the twin children of the same woman, hence only the divine disposal constitutes the true and valid succession, and not the physical descent. God selected out those whom He had determined so to do after deliberating on His own course of conduct. Jacob and Esau were both legitimate sons of Isaac, but Jacob, the younger of the two, was made heir of the promises, while Esau, the elder, was rejected. And this choosing, done by God in His sovereign freedom, was spoken to their mother before they were even born, so before either of them had achieved anything good or evil. So claims as of right, made against God, are futile, whether they are based on descent or on works, since He acts in entire disregard of them. God's purpose to save men and make them heirs of His Kingdom, which purpose is characterised by election or choosing, is not determined at all by consideration of such claims as the Jews put forward i.e. that they are physical descendants of Abraham. In choosing Jacob over Esau, by loving Jacob and loving Esau less, God's promise has not broken down, though many of Abraham's children have no part in its fulfilment in Jesus, but this just shows that there has always been a distinction among the descendants of the patriarchs, between those who can merely boast of a physical connection to them, and those who are the Israel of God, this distinction being entirely within God's sovereignty i.e. not of man's works, but of Him Who effectually calls men. So no Jew can say that God is bound to honour him due to his birth within the nation of Israel nor due to his legal works in obeying the law of Moses, and neither can he say that because his claims are disallowed so that he gets no part in the inheritance of God's people, that God's Word has become of no effect.

What shall we say then? There is not unrighteousness with God, is there? Away with the thought. For to Moses He says; I will have mercy upon whomever I will have mercy, and I will have compassion on whomever I will have compassion. Therefore, then, it [this being the recipient of God's mercy] is not of the one who desires nor even runs, but of the One who is merciful, God.

God responds to manifestations of human wretchedness and to man's inner feelings which result in sighs and tears. He determines those who should be the objects of His mercy and compassion, as here, in response to Moses' request in prayer of "Forgive everyone". It is not though that God is saying I will have mercy on whoever I desire to have mercy, rather, I will have mercy on anyone, whoever he is, that I will show mercy to in the future. His mercy is not obtained by working for it, since God is laid under no obligation by a human will or a human work, rather His mercy is dependant upon His sovereign will alone.

For the scripture says to Pharaoh, For this same purpose I raised you up, in order that I may demonstrate in you my power, and in order that there may be published everywhere my Name in all the earth. Therefore, then, upon whom He desires, He shows mercy; and whom He desires to harden, He hardens.

The Scriptures tirelessly speak, continuing to speak to us now, here concerning a man who does not and cannot receive mercy. God allowed Pharaoh, an avowed, implacable adversary of God, to appear, and brought him forward on the stage of events, the purpose being to give an example of divine intervention, which to this day is still realised as it is read and recounted throughout the world, and being the explanation of Pharaoh's very being, he being foolhardy and with an infatuated insensibility to danger. God did not arbitrarily and directly force upon Pharaoh an obstinate and stubborn resistance to Himself. God not only does not solicit a sinner to do evil, but He also does not cause man to do evil. When man does wrong, that wrong comes from his own totally depraved nature, that nature being the source of Pharaoh's stubborn rebellion against God. When God is said to harden Pharaoh's heart, it is that He, by demanding the release of Israel, confronted him with a demand which he did not wish to meet. Pharaoh was incorrigible and God simply used him as He found him to demonstrate His power to the human race, being, in the last analysis, an act of mercy to the larger number, while also an act of perfect justice toward Pharaoh since God's demands were just.

Then you will say to me, Why does He still persist in finding fault? For, with respect to His counsel, who has taken a permanent stand against it? O man, nay, surely, as for you, who are you who contradicts God? The mouldable material shall not say to the one who moulds it, Why did you make me thus, shall it? Or, does not the potter possess authority over the clay, out of the same lump to make, on the one hand, an instrument which is for honourable purposes and, on the other hand, one which is for dishonourable uses?

A man may resist God's will but cannot maintain his resistance, since who can resist Him? The answer to this question, no finite mind can reason out or understand since it involves the sovereignty of God and the free moral agency of man. You cannot interpret all human life through the will of God alone. If Moses and Pharaoh are to be explained by reference to that will i.e. explained in precisely the same way, then the difference between them disappears, and any moral interpretation of the world is annulled by the religious one, and if God is equally behind the most opposite moral phenomena, how could He find fault, since none can withstand His resolve? To attempt to understand the relation between the human will and the divine seems to lead to the opposition of one law to another, which mere human intelligence has not yet succeeded in transcending. If God is absolute, this makes moral life unintelligible, but explaining moral life by ascribing to man a freedom over against God reduces the universe to anarchy. I will attempt to show an intermediate standpoint; that God does not act arbitrarily in a freedom uncontrolled by moral law, and that man in his moral freedom should not act irresponsibly. In all of this I am trying to understand the painful situation that has arisen due to the acts of Israel with respect to the will of God for it. The Jews, by their stand against the Gospel, reply in a spirit of contention to an answer which God has already given. Men need to be reminded that they are thus speaking against God Himself, so should not adopt this tone toward Him. God created us with a human nature with its moral possibilities, before the assigning of any definite, individual, moral stamp, so as to be implements used by Him for His special purposes. Thus incorrigible Pharaoh was used to demonstrate His power, while meek Moses was used to demonstrate His grace, but both were used to His glory.

But if, as is the case, God desiring to demonstrate His wrath and to make known His power, endured with much long-suffering instruments of wrath fitted for destruction, and in order that He might make known the wealth of His glory upon instruments of mercy which were previously prepared for glory, even us whom He called, not only from among Jews but also from among Gentiles.

God did not have a determined purpose to show His wrath, but restrained Himself to His spontaneous will, growing out of His holy character i.e. though His holy will would lead Him to show His wrath, yet He withheld it and patiently endured the acts of those that led them to fall under His wrath, so making themselves ripe for destruction. Human sin reciprocates the divine judgment, to which men in turn harden or become blind, every development of sin being a network of human offences and divine judgments. God's endurance is also that He might bring into glory those whom He had previously prepared for this. So the image of the potter and the clay is not the last word of the Christian revelation. If it were, it would be a bitter mockery of the legitimate desires of a soul aspiring toward its God. But it is neither the last word nor the only word, nor has it any immediate observable bearing on the development of our lives, since we see bright glimpses of something beyond. We are living souls, not dead clay, and there is a power both within and without our beings by which, as by an all-powerful alchemy, mean clay vessels can be transmuted into gold vessels.

As also in Hosea He says, I will call those, not my people, my people, and those, not beloved, beloved. And it shall come to be that in the place where it was said to them, Not my people are you, there they shall be called sons of the living God.

Gentiles, as well as Jews, are within the scope of God's mercy. In Jesus they are now adopted and beloved, so that God receives as His people those who were formerly not His people. We see this in the history of Israel when it was announced that they would be taken back following His previous rejection of the nation, and now this is taking place with regard to the Gentiles i.e. in Israel's being favourably received back by God, was the prophetic mirror in which He foreshadowed, on a small scale, His future dealings with mankind.

And Isaiah cries in anguish concerning Israel, If the number of the sons of Israel be as the sand of the sea, the remnant will be saved. For the Lord will execute His word upon the earth, finishing and cutting it short. And even as Isaiah said before, Except the Lord of Sabaoth had left us offspring, we would in that case have become even as Sodom and been made like Gomorrah.

Isaiah the prophet earnestly screamed over Israel's rejection of God, and called out to the faithful few who are elected to salvation by the sovereign grace of God, being those which are left of the nation that has otherwise abandoned Him. The Jews cannot then quarrel with the situation in which they find themselves, when it reflects so exactly the Word of God.

What then shall we say? That Gentiles, the ones who do not earnestly endeavour to acquire righteousness, appropriated righteousness, in fact, a righteousness which is out of a source of faith. But Israel, earnestly endeavouring to acquire a law of righteousness, did not measure up to the law. Because of what? Because, not out of a source of faith but even as out of a source of works they sought to acquire it. They stumbled up against the stone which is a stumbling stone, even as it stands written, Behold, I place in Sion a stone, a stumbling stone, and a rock of offence. And the one who places his faith upon Him will not be put to shame.

So the Jews have no claim as of right to salvation, their whole history as recorded in the Scriptures exhibiting God acting on quite a different principle. I will now show that it was owing to their guilt that they were rejected, since they followed and persisted in following a path on which salvation was not to be found, and they are inexcusable in doing so, since God has now made His way of salvation plain and accessible to all. The Jews pursued righteousness, but in the wrong way, since they did so by works. Righteousness is the main concept on which my Gospel rests and it is what the Jews contend with me about i.e. what it is and how it is to be attained. They do not understand how Gentiles can be right with God when this has never been the Gentiles' main interest. And they object to the idea that righteousness can be acquired by faith, that it can be found by those not in quest of it, righteousness being brought and offered to men, and faith being the simple act by which it is appropriated. Israel knew they possessed the law of Moses by which, through careful observance, righteousness would be obtained, and they aimed incessantly at bringing their conduct up to the standard of the law, but were never able to achieve the law's purpose, it always remaining out of their reach, so that their legal religion proved a failure. They needed faith in the coming Messiah, but when that One appeared, the One Whom they had so long invoked in all their prayers, He proved to be an obstacle in their previously clear path, upon which Stone they were broken. And they stumbled at the offence of the Cross, not because of the humility suffered there by this 'Messiah', but that His sacrifice summoned them to begin their religious life, from the very beginning, at the foot of this crucified Saviour, and with the sense upon their hearts of an infinite debt to Him which none of their works could ever repay. Such was their offence that they could not bring themselves to put their faith in Him. So the Gentiles, who did not pursue righteousness, appropriated it by faith, while Israel, who did pursue righteousness, failed to reach it.

Brethren, the consuming desire of my heart and my supplication to God on behalf of them is with a view to their salvation.

My beloved Gentile brothers, the longing of my heart, and the need for which I beg God, is that my countrymen may find their salvation by faith in Jesus. Then will my heart rest in perfect satisfaction.

For I bear testimony to them that a zeal for God they have, but not according to a full and accurate knowledge. For, being ignorant of the righteousness of God and seeking to set up their own private righteousness, to the righteousness of God they have not subjected themselves. For the termination of the law is Christ for righteousness to everyone who believes.

Having been a Pharisee myself, I know something of the Jews' zeal for God, emanating from a partial, insufficient knowledge, which because insufficient, leads them astray with regards to the method by which salvation can be appropriated. They claim that their opposing my lawless Gospel shows their zeal for the divinely-given rule of life, and that their opposing the crucified Messiah shows their zeal for the divinely-given promises, so claiming that they are honouring God by refusing to accept the Gospel. They pride themselves in their endeavour to be righteous, so pursuing it to their own glory and not to God's. They baulk at feeling obligated to God and thanking Him for His free gift of righteousness, namely Jesus, as this would mean discarding all their dependence on self and self-effort for salvation, but rather submitting their hearts to Jesus as Saviour and Lord. Jesus is the termination at which law as a means of attaining righteousness ceases to be. The moment one sees Jesus and understands what He is and what He has done, one feels that legal religion is a thing of the past, now obsolete, and that the way to righteousness is not by the observance of statutes, even though given by God Himself, rather that it is by faith and by the abandonment of one's soul to the redeeming judgement and mercy of God in Jesus.

For Moses writes that the man who does the righteousness which is of the law shall live in its sphere. But the righteousness which is out of a source of faith speaks in this manner, Do not say in your heart, Who shall ascend into heaven? This, in its implications, is to bring Christ down. Or, Who shall descend into the abyss? This, in its implications, is to bring Christ up from among those who are dead. But what does it say? Near you the word is, in your mouth and in your heart. This is the word of the Faith which we are proclaiming.

To keep the law of God and live by doing so was the natural aim and hope of a true Israelite, but not as being a mere collection of statutes, rather as a revelation of God's character and will, and he who sought to keep it did so in conscious dependence on God Whose grace was shown above all other things by His gift of such a revelation. But the legalists try to obey all the statutes of the law, which way of keeping the law is an impossibility. Moses understood and taught that obedience to legal requirements of conduct would never give that person a righteous standing in point of law before a holy God. Only faith in the coming Sacrifice for sin that God Himself would offer could give that person such a standing. The sacrifices of the Old Testament were just symbolic of, and prefiguring, the sacrifice of Jesus, which would atone for all of man's sin. Moses taught that for a saved Jew, being one who looked for salvation by faith alone, obedience to the statutes would result in a righteous character, but that it was his having faith in the coming Sacrifice for sin which would result in his righteous standing before God. Moses never taught that anyone would receive eternal life by reason of his obedience to the law. Eternal life is a gift, in both Old and New Testaments, and is never earned. The one who has eternal life lives in the realm of the commandments when he obeys them, his activities and interests being within their scope. Echoing Moses I say, let not anyone who sighs for deliverance from his own sinfulness suppose that the accomplishment of some impossible task is required of him in order to enjoy the blessings of the Gospel, nor that the personal presence of the Messiah is necessary to ensure his salvation. Jesus needs not to be brought down from Heaven nor up from Hades, the world of the dead, to impart forgiveness and holiness, since Jesus' incarnation and resurrection are facts, He having descended to the earth and having risen from the dead. The Christian message contains no impossibilities. I do not offer the

Gospel knowing that any are powerless to fulfil it, rather I tell everyone that Jesus' Word is so near that he can speak it with his mouth and meditate on it with his heart. The Gospel is graciously adapted to the necessity of the very weakest and most sinful of God's creatures. Such is my message; that faith in Jesus as Saviour is the appropriating method of obtaining salvation.

If you confess with your mouth Jesus as Lord and believe in your heart that God raised Him from among the dead, you will be saved. For with the heart faith is exercised resulting in righteousness, and with the mouth confession is made resulting in salvation.

Let me now elaborate and explain what I meant when I said, 'the word is in your mouth and in your heart'. You need to agree with all that the Scripture says about the Person of Jesus; by name 'Yahweh saves' and that He is deity. So by declaring Jesus as Lord, you speak your heart-belief in His deity, incarnation, atoning sacrifice, and bodily resurrection. This demands that the Jew really trust Jesus, else this would be blasphemous, and that the Gentile cease worshipping Caesar as his lord. Also your believing and thinking about Jesus need to be similarly guided by the Holy Spirit. To be saved you must attain righteousness, and this depends on having faith in your heart, which faith, leading to salvation, must confess itself. A heart believing unto righteousness and a mouth making confession unto salvation are not two different things, but two sides of the same thing i.e. when faith comes forth from its silence to announce itself and to proclaim the glory and grace of Jesus, its voice is confession.

For the scripture says, Everyone who believes on Him shall not be put to shame. For there is not a distinction between Jew and Greek. For the same Lord is over all, constantly rich toward all those who call upon Him. For whoever shall call upon the Name of the Lord shall be saved.

Isaiah, in agreement, says that none who call upon the Lord shall be repulsed. So none who put their faith in Jesus as Lord will be repulsed, or defeated, or disappointed. I am not ashamed of the Gospel since I am not afraid that it will not work, rather I believe in its power to save all, whether Jew or Gentile.

How is it possible then that they shall call upon the One in whom they did not believe? Moreover, how is it possible that they will believe on the One concerning whom they did not hear? And how is it possible that they shall hear without one who proclaims? And how is it possible that they shall make a proclamation except they be sent on a mission? Even as it stands written, How beautiful are the feet of those who bring good tidings of good things.

Since everyone who invokes the Name of the Lord shall be saved, the conditions of such an invocation must be put within the reach of everyone, both Jew and Gentile, so that there is no excuse for disobedience on the part of any. May the feet of those bringing the Gospel message be swift and vigorous, hastening in their scaling obstructing mountains, in their appearance and descent from mountains symbolising the earnestly-desired, winged movement and appearance of the Gospel itself at Jesus' baptism.

But not all lent an obedient ear to the good news. For Isaiah says, Lord, who believed our message? So then, faith is out of the source of that which is heard, and that which is heard [the message] is through the agency of the Word concerning Christ.

In spite of this universal preaching, there has not been a universal surrender to the Gospel, particularly among the Jews, but this lack of acceptance is referred to in Isaiah's prophecy, so I am not dismayed. I know that as the Gospel is preached in the power of the Holy Spirit, that the Spirit will engender faith in the message in the hearts of those elected to salvation, being the message about Jesus.

But I say, did they not hear? Most certainly. Into all the earth their sound went out, and into the extremities of the inhabited earth, their words.

The process of convicting the Jews is now under way and they have indeed heard the Gospel message. As easily as the revelation of God is seen in nature all around us, so easily can they hear the Gospel, since it has now been preached in all the areas where the Jews are scattered throughout the Roman Empire.

But I say, Israel did not fail to know, did it? First Moses says, I will provoke you to jealousy by those who are no people, and by a foolish people I will provoke you to anger. Moreover, Isaiah breaks out boldly and says, I was found by those who are not seeking me. I was made manifest to those who are not inquiring about me.

Did Israel not understand? Above all nations they ought to have understood a message from God. Israel did know about the Messiah and about salvation for all people, but in its bigotry claimed it had a monopoly on salvation, despite what had been prophesied by Moses and Isaiah about the salvation of the Gentiles. And Isaiah also prophesied Israel's opposition to salvation for all. By giving salvation to the Gentiles, a desire for the same salvation should have been aroused in Israel, since their condition is akin to that of the Gentiles i.e. seeing God's treatment of those who were a no-people, those being outside of His heritage, they could have deduced that God would also take the initiative in showing His unmerited goodness and mercy to them as well, they being faithless Jews who had made no appeal to Him nor ever sought Him, so forfeiting their place among the people of God. The calling of the Gentiles should have led Israel, out of jealousy if nothing else, to vie with these outsiders in welcoming the righteousness that comes by faith.

But to Israel He says, The whole day I stretched out my hands to a non-persuasible and cantankerous people.

God's arms were outstretched all day long, for a thousand years, incessantly pleading love to Israel, which Israel through all its history consistently despised, not for want of knowledge or intelligence, but through wilful and stubborn disobedience, in opposition to God and refusing to have anything to do with Him, which explains the exclusion of Israel, for the present, from the Kingdom of Jesus and all its blessings.

I say then, God did not repudiate His people, did He? Far be the thought, for as for myself, I also am an Israelite, the offspring of Abraham, of the tribe of Benjamin.

I struggle with the perplexing fact that the Jews do not receive the Gospel while the Gentiles do. But I will endeavour now to show how in the sovereign providence of God, even the sin of Israel is made to contribute to the working out of a universal purpose of redemption in which Israel also shares, in accordance with the inviolable promise of God. Has God cast away the nation of Israel, His chosen people? Definitely not. If that were true, I myself, being a true Israelite by physical descent, would be excluded from God's Kingdom. There is a remnant of Jews, even at this present time, according to the election of grace. And the part of Israel which is for a time hardened, shall ultimately come in, and so all Israel shall be saved. So shall God's covenant with that nation be fulfilled to them, as a nation, not by the gathering in of individual Jews, or of all the Jews individually, into the Church, but by the national restoration of the Jews as a Christian believing nation.

God did not repudiate His people whom He foreordained. Or, do you not know absolutely in the case of Elijah what the scripture says, how he pleads to God against Israel? Lord, your prophets they killed. Your altars they demolished. And as for myself, I was left alone, and they are seeking my life. But what does the divine answer say to him? I reserved for myself seven thousand men who are of such a character that they did not bow the knee to Baal.

God, in His own eternal decree before the world, selected Israel and appointed it as the chosen nation, to be His own, the depository of His law, the vehicle of the theocracy, from its first unveiling to its completion in Jesus' future Kingdom. Given these reasons for His choosing the nation, it is impossible that He would reject them now. God foreknew the nation; Israel stood before God's eyes from eternity as His people, and in the immutableness of the sovereign love with which He made it His, lies the impossibility of its rejection by Him. Look at Elijah and how similar his complaint is to one I could make now. I too am lonely and persecuted, and Israel seems to have abandoned God or been abandoned by Him, but I understand God's way and His faithfulness better than to lose heart. God's reply to Elijah when He says that He has reserved a remnant for Himself, shows that He did not, and does not now, cast off His people. The seven thousand were Israel to Him, those who remained faithful to Him, who He would not let go of, but rather keep as His own private possession.

Therefore, thus also at this present season a remnant according to a choice of grace has come into being. But since it is by grace, no longer is it out of a source of works. Otherwise no longer is grace, grace.

At this strategic time, marked by the inclusion of the Gentile together with the Jew in the one Body of Jesus, despite Israel's abandoning of God there is a remnant in the nation, saved in the sovereign grace of God, being those who are left of Israel. This remnant is chosen for salvation by God in His grace and spontaneous overflowing love, since they do not deserve that gift, rather the appropriate and deserved punishment for sins committed. So this remnant is now part of the great host of the saved. All salvation is by grace to the exclusion of all human work. Grace and work must be kept distinct from one another, any attempt to mix them destroying the meaning of each.

What then? That which Israel is constantly seeking, this it did not obtain. But those chosen out obtained it. And the rest were hardened, even as it stands written, God gave them a spirit of insensibility, eyes for the purpose of not seeing, and ears for the purpose of not hearing, until this day. Even David says, Let their table become for a snare and a trap, and a stumbling block and a just retribution to them. Let their eyes be darkened in order that they may not see and in order that they may always bow down their back.

The Jews' eyes are covered with a thick skin and their hearts are dull, and they have a spirit of slumber rendering their souls lethargic so that they are not affected at all by the offer of salvation through the Messiah. They feast in wicked security, having a presumptuous confidence in the law. A just retribution awaits them, bringing peril, loss, and destruction, and, as captives, having to bear back-breaking burdens. All of Israel not in the remnant, though chosen to salvation by grace, is hardened in its insensibility to the Gospel, with sightless spiritual eyes and deaf ears. Israel is hardened since it continually rejected God and His Word, and the more it did so, the harder its heart became, and light rejected blinds. In addition to this natural hardening of the heart, there was God's judicial action of hardening, as a just judgment on Israel's sin of rejection i.e. they would not obey God, and then, in God's reaction against their sin, they could not obey.

I say then, Surely, they did not stumble so as to fall, did they? Away with the thought. But through the instrumentality of their fall salvation has come to the Gentiles with a view to provoking them [Israel] to jealousy.

The rest of Israel, aside from the remnant, has not fallen to their irredeemable destruction. Their falling though has been the occasion for the Gentiles to be offered salvation by faith in Jesus. Wherever I go I preach the Gospel first to the Jews, and only when they have rejected it do I then preach to the Gentiles.

But since their fall is the enrichment of the world, and their defeat and loss the enrichment of the Gentiles, how much more their fullness?

The fall and spiritual defeat and diminishing of the nation of Israel in its loss of the blessings that accompany salvation, due to their rejection of the Messiah and the salvation offered to them, and to their consequent temporary rejection by God, has been to the benefit of the Gentiles. And how much more to their benefit when Israel receives its Messiah at His second Advent, since Israel will then be complete in its return to God and its salvation. Then will Jesus reign in Jerusalem for a thousand years in universal righteousness, peace, and prosperity, that the residue of men and the Gentiles might seek after the Lord.

But to you I am speaking, the Gentiles. Inasmuch then, as for myself, as I am an apostle of the Gentiles, I do my ministry honour, if by any means, possibly, I may provoke to jealousy those who are my flesh, and save some of them.

So I labour the more so among you Gentiles, that I might provoke my own people to also seek salvation in Jesus. I faithfully and fully discharge my duties to you Gentiles, but I feel it necessary to show the relevance, in such circumstances, of bestowing so much attention on the condition and prospect of the Jews i.e. the more successful my mission to you, the greater the prospect of provoking my fellow countrymen to jealousy so that some of them might be saved.

For, in view of the fact that their repudiation results in the world's reconciliation, what will the receiving of them result in if not in life from among the dead?

Since God has substituted the Church for the nation of Israel as a means of bringing the good news of salvation to the world with a view to bringing Israel back into fellowship with Himself and service in the Millennium, the Gentiles have now arisen as the heralds of salvation through their acceptance of the Gospel message, and the unsaved are thus reconciled to God in that their attitude of unbelief and hatred is turned to one of trust and love. When Jesus returns to the Mount of Olives, Israel will be saved by the sovereign grace of God, out from a spiritually dead state and from among those who remain spiritually dead.

Now, in view of the fact that the firstfruit is holy, also the lump, and since the root is holy, also the branches.

Since Abraham was justified by faith and so made holy i.e. set apart for God, thus was the whole body of the people of Israel that seek to be justified by faith, being Abraham's descendants in this respect, set apart for God, as a chosen nation through which salvation could be produced and channelled to the rest of the human race. The holiness by call and destination of Israel, as represented by Abraham, implies its future restoration. And since Abraham was made holy, thus are the Gentiles that are justified by faith and therefore also his descendants in this respect, included in God's holy people, the Church.

Now, since certain of the branches were broken off, and you, being a wild olive, were grafted in among them and became joint-partaker with them of the root of the fatness of the olive, stop boasting against the branches. But, assuming that you are boasting, you are not sustaining the root, but the root you.

Israel, having abandoned God, was set aside by God temporarily as the channel through which He would work, so broken off from the olive tree of those who are the true people of God. The Gentiles were then grafted into the olive tree, made possible by God breaking down the separating wall between Jew and Gentile at the Cross, by the abolishing of the economy of Moses, so allowing the inclusion of the Gentile with the Jew in one Body, the Church, by faith in Jesus. The tree is kept alive by the root, Abraham, from which the natural and grafted-in branches draw their life. The life-force and the blessing are received by the Gentile through the Jew, not the other way round, since the spiritual plan moves from the Abrahamic covenant downward, and from the nation of Israel outward. Thus the inferior is inserted into the good stock, a process which naturally speaking would never succeed. It is only in the Kingdom of Grace that a process thus contrary to nature can be successful, magnifying the mercy shown to the Gentiles, that they were grafted into the Church, being brought into an artificially formed relationship with the nation they despised, and caused to flourish there and bring forth fruit unto eternal life.

You will say then, Branches were broken off in order that I might be grafted in. Well! Because of their unbelief they were broken off. But, as for you, by faith you stand. Stop having a superiority complex, but be fearing; for in view of the fact that God did not spare the branches which were according to nature, neither will He spare you.

There is no superiority to be boasted of in the Gentiles' new status. Rather be in fear of the God Who made it possible for you to be brought in, which was an act of His that you did nothing to merit. I am talking here about the nation of Israel and the Gentiles, as two distinctive parts of the human race, not of an individual Gentile boasting and possibly losing his salvation through glorying against the Jew. The Jews have been more securely invested in the Kingdom than the Gentiles, being native branches on the tree of God's people, yet the unbelieving Jews were cut off from the tree. Similarly, unsaved Gentiles are in danger of being cut off from the place where God might use them.

Behold therefore God's benevolent kindness and His severity; on the one hand, upon those who fell, severity, and, on the other hand, upon you, God's benevolent kindness, upon the condition that you continue to remain in and abide by His benevolent kindness. Otherwise, also you will be cut out.

God can be long-suffering and kind, and He can be abrupt and rough. You need to remain indebted to God's goodness, and to it alone, for your current right standing with Him. This excludes presumption and all such temper as is betrayed in taking an attitude of superiority over the Jews. The Jews lost their standing because they came to believe that it was permanent and unassailable, and independent of moral conditions, and if the Gentiles make the same mistake, they will incur the same doom. Those parts of the visible organised church that are not truly in the Body of Christ i.e. those parts which fail to function as the means through which God works for the salvation of sinners, will be set aside and cut out from the main trunk of the tree at the Rapture, in favour of Israel which will then be restored as the final channel through which God will work to bring the good news of salvation to the human race. You Gentiles therefore, maintain a friendship and companionship towards the Jew and towards the benevolent kindness of God in including you in the salvation offered to the Jew by faith in Jesus.

And, moreover, those also, if they do not remain in unbelief, will be grafted in, for God is able to again graft them in.

It is not impossible to put the unbelieving Jews right, since even in the case of the most hardened rejecter of the Gospel we cannot limit either the resources of God's power or the possibilities of change in a self-conscious, self-determining creature. So we can never say that anyone's unbelief is final, or that their becoming a believer is impossible. If the Jews give up their unbelief they will be incorporated again in the true people of God, since, though this is a difficult thing, with God nothing is impossible, and this is indeed exactly what will take place at Jesus' second Advent; Israel as a nation will, in the sovereign grace of God, be regenerated and filled with the Spirit, to become again the channel through which God will operate, for a thousand years, to bring salvation to a Christ-rejecting world. So I do not despair for the future of Israel.

For, as for you, in view of the fact that you were cut out of the olive tree which is wild by nature, and contrary to nature were grafted into the good olive tree, how much more will these who are according to nature be grafted into their own olive tree. For I do not desire you to be ignorant, brethren, concerning this mystery, in order that you may not be wise in yourselves, that hardening in part has come to Israel until the fullness of the Gentiles has come in.

This mystery of this time of the Gentiles was a hidden purpose in the counsel of God which has now been revealed and is understood by the believer. The time of the Gentiles is until the completion of the Body of Christ, being made up of Jews and Gentiles saved from Pentecost to the Rapture. Then the hardening of Israel will end, and at Jesus' second Advent, Israel will be saved.

And thus all Israel shall be saved, even as it stands written, There shall come out of Sion the Deliverer, and shall turn ungodliness from Jacob.

And this to them is the covenant from me when I shall take away their sins.

In the Jews' jealousy, as they see the Gentiles in their fullness peopling the Kingdom, shall all Israel be saved, meaning each member of the nation living at the time of Jesus' second Advent. This individual cleansing from sin will be followed by a national restoration to the Messianic Kingdom, with Jesus reigning on the throne of David in Jerusalem as King of kings and Lord of lords for a thousand years.

On the one hand, with reference to the gospel they are enemies for your sakes; on the other hand, with reference to the selected-out ones they are beloved ones for the fathers' sake; for the gifts in grace and the calling of God are with respect to a change of mind irrevocable.

In view of Israel's rejection of the Gospel, God counts Israel as an enemy. But His attitude towards Israel with reference to the elect remnant in that nation is that those whom He counts as enemies of His by reason of their rejection of the Gospel, are beloved ones, for the sake of the fathers of Israel, for example Abraham, with whom He made an everlasting covenant. The covenants and promises to Israel and its position of sonship, along with its calling to embrace salvation in the Messianic Kingdom of God, these things can never be withdrawn, since God will never change His mind about Israel's God-ordained mission and destiny.

For, even as you formerly disbelieved God, yet now have been made recipients of mercy through the occasion of the unbelief of these, thus also these now have disbelieved in order that through the occasion of the mercy which is yours, they themselves also might now become the recipients of mercy, for God included all within the state of unbelief in order that He might have mercy upon all.

God confined both Jew and Gentile within the scope of one kind of guilt, that of unbelief, of stubbornly withholding belief and obedience. The mercy you Gentiles presently enjoy following your past unbelief, and the mercy the Jews are determined to enjoy in the future following their present unbelief, not only correspond to each other, but are interwoven with each other, being parts of a system which God controls and in which every element conditions and is conditioned by all the rest i.e. there is a divine necessity pervading and controlling all the freedom of men, a divine purpose mastering all the random activity of human wills; God shut all up into disobedience that He might have mercy upon them all, and Jew and Gentile alike have been made to feel the need of grace by being so shut up. The sin of the Jews and Gentiles to whom I preach the Gospel does not lie outside of the control or the redeeming purpose of God, but sin is not ordained by Him with a view to redemption i.e. He subordinates sin to His purpose but it is not a subordinate element in His purpose.

O the depth of the wealth and wisdom and knowledge of God. How unsearchable are His judgments, and how untraceable the paths He takes; for whoever knew the Lord's mind? or who became His counsellor? or who has previously given to Him and it will be recompensed to him? Because out from Him and through Him and for Him are all things. To Him be the glory forever. Amen.

I have reached the summit of my thoughts on God's elective grace and goodness which have indeed carried me to the heights, so that I can turn and pause and contemplate God's wisdom and knowledge; depths are at my feet, but waves of light illuminate them, and there spreads all around an immense horizon that I can see. I am unable to describe these depths with human reason and in words, since His ways cannot be tracked out. All glory be to God.

I therefore beg of you, please, brethren, through the instrumentality of the aforementioned mercies of God, by a once-for-all presentation to place your bodies at the disposal of God, a sacrifice, a living one, a holy one, well-pleasing, your rational, sacred service, [rational, in that this service is performed by the exercise of the mind].

I have so far written about the doctrines of condemnation, justification, sanctification, and glorification, and have explained to Israel why the Abrahamic and Davidic covenants have not been fulfilled. Now I want to go on and exhort you all to live a life in conformity with your God-given exalted position and in view also of the God-given ability which you now have to live such a life, which exhortation to a holy life is reasonable since based in doctrine, and since I have informed you as to the resources of grace that you possess with which to obey my exhortations. So, since we are justified persons, righteous in our standing before God, we are under obligation to live a righteous life, and in view of the fact that we are the objects of the Holy Spirit's work of sanctification, we are to live those lives in the spiritual energy that He supplies, since we are not yet glorified but rather are looking forward to the Rapture, and so we purify our lives now. Bring your physical bodies to Jesus as a sacrifice that is alive, in contrast to the slain offerings presented by priests, for example let your eyes look on no evil, let your tongue utter nothing base, let your hands work no sin, and actively exert yourselves for good; giving alms, blessing them that curse you, ever listening and attentive to the Spirit Who is in you so that you are pure and free from sin as your Father is infinitely pure and without any trace of sin. So the sacrifice of your putting your physical body at His disposal is holy, holy in the sense of it being set apart for His use, and holy in the sense of it being used for pure and righteous purposes and free from sinful practices. This sacrifice is well approved, eminently satisfactory, and extraordinarily pleasing as you so serve God, in that you give your very selves rather than you just bring an external offering i.e. this sacrifice is spiritual rather than just being an outward practice that is symbolic of a spiritual truth.

And stop assuming an outward expression that does not come from within you and is not representative of what you are in your inner being but is patterned after this age; but change your outward expression to one that comes from within and is representative of your inner being, by the renewing of your mind, resulting in your putting to the test what is the will of God, the good and well-pleasing and complete will, and having found that it meets specifications, place your approval upon it.

Stop now from performing outward actions that do not represent your inner heart life, and do not continue to masquerade in the clothing of this world; its mannerisms, speech expressions, styles, and habits, so that you hide Jesus Who is living in your heart, these worldly traits being an opaque covering through which the Holy Spirit cannot radiate Jesus' beauty. You are living in the world's atmosphere with its current thoughts, opinions, maxims, speculations, hopes, impulses, aims, and aspirations all around you all the time, being a real and effective power that you constantly inhale and exhale, so do not conform to this atmosphere with the result that the modernism of your appearance nullifies the fundamentalism of your doctrine. Rather be transfigured, so that your inner glory is visible to the world. You change your outward expression from the one you had before you were saved by the gradual conforming of your mind and mental processes more and more to that of the new spiritual world into which you have been introduced and in which you now live and move, the divine image having been created in you, to the end that you are renewed and renovated and completely changed for the better so that you can now be fellow-workers with God. This conforming is accomplished through the ministry of the indwelling Holy Spirit Who, when definitely and intelligently and habitually yielded to, puts sin out of your life and produces His own fruit in you. Then you can put your life to an approval test; that it conforms to the Word of God, as you obey the Word and feel the perfect, finished, Word saturating and controlling your life, and so pass that test.

For I am saying through the grace which is given me, to everyone who is among you, not to be thinking more highly of himself, above that which the necessities in the nature of the case impose upon him to be thinking, but to be thinking with a view to a sensible appraisal of himself according as to each one God divided a measure of faith.

We, as members of the Church, have a duty to avoid self-exaltation, rather we have a call to mutual service, in the measure of the gift bestowed on each of us, since humility is the immediate effect of self-surrender to God. I speak through the grace given to me, to put wisdom and love at the service of the Church. We need to see each other as God sees us, with the spiritual insight that He measures out of to each of us, whether that be to a greater or a lesser degree, and always in humility, since none of us has anything that he has not received from God. We ought not to be high-minded above that which we ought to be minded, but to be so minded as to be sober-minded. We appraise fairly the gifts God has given us, as governed by the measure of spiritual insight God gives to each of us which degree of insight qualifies us for our office, whether that be prophet, teacher, or minister et cetera, and we glorify Him for their bestowal and their exercise through dependence upon the Holy Spirit. We must never, in mock humility, make light of anyone or of anyone's gift. With faith we receive the power of discernment as to the actual limitations of our gifts, so that we can accurately determine the character, nature, and extent of our powers and not think too highly of ourselves.

For even as in one body we have many members but all the members do not have the same function, thus we, the many, are one body in Christ, and members severally one of another.

There are many differing modes of action given to us individual members of the Body, but under the Spirit's guidance we all act as one.

Having therefore gifts differing according to the grace given us, whether that of prophecy, prophesy according to the proportion of faith; or serving, exercise that gift within the sphere of service; or teaching, within the sphere of teaching; or he who exhorts, within the sphere of exhortation; the one who distributes of his earthly possessions, in the sphere of an unostentatious simplicity; the one who is placed in a position of authority, with intense eagerness and effort; the one who shows mercy, with a joyous abandon.

There are some extraordinary powers distinguishing certain Christians and enabling them to serve the Church, the reception of which gifts is due to the power of divine grace operating in their souls by the Holy Spirit. Prophecy, being the inspired delivery of warning, exhortation, instruction, judging, and making manifest the secrets of the heart, should be done according to the strength, clearness, and fervour of the faith bestowed on that person, the character and mode of their speaking being conformed to the rules and limits of their individual degree of spiritual insight. He who renders service, comprising acts of the practical nature rather than utterances or miracle-working, should do so in the realm in which God has placed him and for which He gave him that gift. He who teaches should aim to increase others' understanding, and he who exhorts to strengthen the wills and hearts of others. Each of these people should stay within the circle of service for which the Holy Spirit has fitted him, and not invade another field of service for which he is not fitted. He who gives should do so in sincerity and mental honesty and with a liberal and open heart, as God Himself gives. He who is placed in front to a position of superintendence should do his best in that role, performing it with diligence, taking care, and being determined in his actions and words. He who shows kindness should be ever ready to minister in a spirit of amiable grace with joy, bringing sunlight into the sick-room and into the heart of the afflicted.

Love, let it be without hypocrisy. Look with loathing and horror upon that which is pernicious. Stick fast to that which is good. In the sphere of brotherly love have a family affection for one another, vying with one another in showing honour; with respect to zeal, not lazy; fervent in the sphere of the Spirit, serving the Lord; rejoicing in the sphere of hope; patient in tribulation; with respect to prayer, persevering in it continually; with respect to the needs of the saints, being a sharer with them, eager for opportunities to show hospitality.

Let your love be sincere and genuine, not just impersonating what a loving person would do. Develop a hatred of evil and express this by withdrawing from it, rather cleave to the good and cement yourselves to that. Have a brotherly, natural, kind affection for one another, since you are all one family, and show respect among yourselves since, being one family, you value each other, each of you seeking to give a lead in being readier than the others in the showing of honour to your brothers for God's gifts in them. Do not hesitate, each of you, to be diligent in your Christian vocation, but rather, as led by the Spirit, be burning hot and on fire for Him as you fulfil your office. When earthly prospects are dark, rejoice in the hope that Jesus will send deliverance and that, in the meantime, He will take care of you in your afflictions. In each pressing, oppressive, distressing event, remain under the test in a God-honouring manner, not seeking to escape it, but eager to learn the lessons it was sent to teach, persevering in it bravely and calmly. Give constant attention to prayer, being devoted to it and unremitting in it, and in continual readiness for the spiritual battle as a soldier is for war. Share each other's needs, partnering with them as if their needs were your own. Develop a fondness for being hospitable to guests and strangers with respect to food, clothing, and shelter, and seek opportunities to do so, since many Christians are currently banished and persecuted on account of their testimony to Jesus.

Be constantly blessing those who are constantly persecuting you; be blessing and stop cursing. Be rejoicing with those who are rejoicing, and be weeping with those who are weeping; having the same mind towards one another, not setting your mind upon lofty things, but associating yourselves with lowly things and lowly people. Stop being those who are wise in their own opinion,

Always speak well of your persecutors, responding to their mistreatment of you with kindness and love because of your testimony to Jesus, and stop calling down divine curses upon them. Be united among yourselves, in your thinking, attitudes and desires, having a common and well-understood feeling of mutual allowance and kindness i.e. possessing a unanimity of love. Avoid things which would destroy this unanimity, such as being carried away by conceitedly believing that you are superior to others in your thinking. Rather have a lowliness of mind and a humble opinion of yourself, leading you to lament as you perceive your own moral littleness and guilt. This will lead you to appreciate those who are considered of little worth by the world and to be drawn into sympathy with them so that you yield yourself to fellowship with them, even guided by them in determining your own conduct. Thus are the most ignorant and least influential in the Church given prominence as equally valued members, since all are equal in the sight of God. There should be no spiritual aristocracy in the Church. Love requires that we each put our own judgments into the common stock of thinking and estimate each other's views as impartially as our own, with the result that we have the same mind, one toward another.

requiting to no one evil in exchange for evil, taking thought in advance with regard to things that are seemly in the sight of all men. If it is possible so far as it depends upon you, with all men be living at peace.

When evil is done to you by anyone do not return evil to them, as a person of the world would do, rather think beforehand as to how to express outwardly your inward goodness, being an honest expression of Jesus Who is in you, you being His representative as a child of God. If others will allow it, live peaceably among men, but never disturb the peace yourselves, since we are bringing a message of peace.

Do not be avenging yourselves, beloved ones, but give place at once to the wrath, for it stands written, To me belongs punishment, I will repay, says the Lord. But, if your enemy is hungry, be feeding him. If he thirsts, be giving him to drink, for doing this, you will heap burning coals of fire upon his head. Stop being overcome by the evil, but be overcoming the evil by means of the good.

Do not vindicate your rights or take the law into your own hands when you have been wronged, but leave room for God's wrath, otherwise you will be taking His proper work out of His hands. The idea is not that we abandon the offender to God's vengeance, but that we leave the righting of wrong to Him Who is the maintainer of moral order in the world. Acts of kindness done to our enemies may soften their heart and lead them on to repentance, as when one helps a neighbour by giving him live coals by which he can keep his hearth fire going, being essential for cooking and warmth, which he then carries home on his head in a container. Also you, in supplying your enemy's basic food and drink needs, can overcome evil with good.

Let every soul put himself habitually in subjection to authorities who hold position over them, for there is not an authority except that ordained by God. Moreover, the existing authorities stand permanently ordained by God.

As well as our mutual responsibilities and duties within the Body of Jesus, we also have obligations to the human government under which we live. I particularly mention this for the Jewish members of your assembly, since many Jews hold to the Old Testament teaching that to acknowledge a Gentile ruler is sinful, but law and its representatives are of God and as such are entitled to all honour and obedience from Christians. Human government is a divine institution brought into being by God for the regulation of human affairs, though the incumbents of government offices are not always ordained by Him. If civil powers command you to violate God's commands, you must obey God before man. Similarly if you are required to disobey the common laws of humanity, obedience is due to the higher and more general law rather than to a lower unjust or unreasonable law, as decided by the wisdom granted you by God

So that the one who sets himself in array against the authority, against the ordinance of God has set himself, with the result that he is in a permanent position of antagonism against the ordinance. And those who resist shall receive for themselves judgment.

Do not withstand what has been instituted by God, otherwise you may receive a judicial sentence from the magistrate, which judgment is in the form of punishment from God through His minister, the civil power.

For the rulers are not a terror to the good work but to the evil. Now, do you desire not to be afraid of the authority? Keep on doing the good, and you will have commendation from him, for he is God's servant to you for good. But if you are habitually doing that which is evil, be fearing, for not in vain is he wearing the sword, for he is God's servant, an executor of wrath upon the one who practices the evil.

Recognise the divine right of the state to bring judgment on those who do wrong, and know that the judge has the power and the authority to inflict loss of life on offenders.

On which account there is a necessity for putting one's self in subjection, not only because of wrath, but also because of conscience, for because of this you pay taxes; for God's public servants they are, continually giving their attention to this very thing. Deliver to all the debts due them to the one collecting the tax, the tax; to the one collecting the custom, the custom; to the one to whom the fear is due, the fear; to the one to whom the honour is due, the honour.

We need to submit for two reasons; to avoid the external wrath of God, and to satisfy our inner conscience, which, apart from the consequences of disobedience, recognises the divine right and function of the authority and so freely submits to it. We are obliged to pay taxes so should do so conscientiously, since in putting ourselves in subjection to the authorities that is one of our responsibilities i.e. to pay for these rulers as they discharge their divinely ordained service. Pay all your debts and duties, giving from your store of resources.

Stop owing even one person even one thing, except to be loving one another; for the one who is loving another, has fulfilled the law.

Do not continue to owe anyone anything. Pay your debts. The only debt you are allowed is that of divine self-sacrificial love to others, as produced in your heart by the Holy Spirit, as a debt to God's love for you. This debt increases more, the more it is paid, because the practice of love makes the principle of love deeper and more active i.e. the more you love the more you feel the need to love.

For this, You shall not commit adultery, you shall not kill, you shall not steal, you shall not covet, and if there is any commandment of a different nature, in this word it is summed up, in this, You shall love your neighbour as yourself. The aforementioned love does not work evil to a neighbour. Therefore, love is the fulfilling of law.

The statutes of the law of Moses can be summed up and condensed into one word; love, being the divine love produced by the Holy Spirit and which is self-sacrificial in nature. Of course, love is an inspiration rather than a restraint, and transcends law as embodied in merely negative commandments, but since the law exists in this form, I express its relation to love in this way.

And this, knowing the strategic season, that it is an hour now for you to awake out of sleep, for now our salvation is nearer to us than when we believed. The night has long been on its way, and the day has arrived. Therefore, let us at once and once for all put off the works of the darkness, and let us at once and once for all clothe ourselves with the weapons of the light.

It is important that you comply with these exhortations of mine since the Rapture is imminent, when you will stand before the Judgement Seat of Jesus. This current time has a critical place in the working out of God's designs, so do not live a lethargic non-aggressive, lazy Christian life any longer, but rather live a Spirit-controlled life, since our glorification draws ever nearer when our salvation will be completed.

In the same manner as in the day let us order our behaviour in a seemly fashion, not in carousals and drunkenness, not in sexual intercourse and dissolute abandon, not in strife and jealousy. But clothe yourselves with the Lord Jesus Christ and stop making provision for the sinful nature with a view to a passionate craving.

Live in such a way that you give an honest impression of yourselves to the world, given your high station in life as children of the Most High God. Do not indulge in riotous half-drunken processions in honour of the gods or in drinking parties that lead to unbridled lust and shameless excesses. Rather clothe your souls with the moral disposition and habits of Jesus. If you have even the slightest interest in the sinful nature it will result in your neglecting the spiritual part of your life and lead to sin. We are under no obligation to obey the sinful nature so should not provide for it in any part of our lives.

Now, to the one who is weak with respect to his faith, be giving a cordial welcome, not with a view to a critical analysis of his inward reasonings.

Some among you are weak in respect of faith, not fully appreciating what your Christianity means, in particular not seeing that he who has committed himself to Jesus is set free from all law, except that which is involved in its responsibility to Jesus, and that salvation is of faith from first to last. Hence the weak one has a conscience fettered by scruples in regard to customs dating from pre-Christian days, for example the use of wine and flesh, the religious observance of certain days, and the practice of severe self-discipline. When you are joined by such a one who has doubts concerning which is the correct way of conduct in these matters, do not pass sentence on his doubts or censure him in any way, rather welcome him into the fellowship of the Church unreservedly, and not for the purpose of judging him or of seeking to rule his mind with your own i.e. receive him in the same way that God graciously accepts men. I desire that the weak among you will become strong.

One, on the one hand, has confidence that he may eat all things; but the one, on the other hand, who is weak, constantly eats vegetables. The one who eats, let him not be treating with contempt the one who does not eat; and the one who does not eat, let him not be criticising the one who eats, for God received him.

The strong among you have faith to eat all things, while the weak one's faith limits him to being a vegetarian, which scruple is a product of an inadequate understanding of God's Word and an over-sensitised conscience which is relatively unenlightened. You strong one, do not treat such a weak one as nothing and as one who is to be mocked. Neither is the weak one to be severely critical of, nor to bully, the strong one. Both these attitudes are a form of spiritual pride. When both the strong and the weak believed on Jesus, God accepted all, and He still does accept all.

As for you, who are you who are judging another's household slave? To his own personal master he stands or falls. Indeed, he shall be made to stand, for the Lord has power to make him stand.

You weak one, with love I say to you, do not allow your scrupulousness to lead you to tyrannise another about his conduct. The strong in faith must answer to the Lord and not to you, and he shall indeed be preserved in the integrity of his Christian character by Him. This criticising by the scrupulous is one of the perils in the wake of our liberty in Jesus, but I am confident that, through the grace and power of Jesus, this freedom we have in Him will prove a triumphant moral success.

For, on the one hand, there is he who judges a day above another day. On the other hand, there is he who subjects every day to a scrutiny. Let each one in his own mind be fully assured.

Some of you weak ones abstain from flesh and wine only on certain days, observing a fast, while others of you observe certain feasts and eat what you would ordinarily abstain from. Nothing in the Christian life is statutory or legalistic, not even the observance of the first day of the week, rather we observe practices only as maintained by faith. Let each pursue his own course in these matters, whether that be as in a narrow canal or as in a spacious lake.

The one who has formed a judgment regarding the day, with reference to the Lord he judges it. And the one who eats, with reference to the Lord he eats, for he gives thanks to God. And the one who does not eat, with reference to the Lord does not eat, and he gives thanks to God.

Both weak and strong have the same end in view, namely the interest of the Lord. Thanksgiving to God consecrates every meal, whether it be given by the one who eats only vegetables or by the one who eats all, and shows that both are acting to the glory of God and therefore that the Lord's interest is safe. A Christian measures what each day stands for and thus what is his appropriate conduct in it, as conditioned by his estimation of Jesus and what is fitting behaviour with reference to Him. So is a Christian's stand on any certain thing controlled or conditioned by the measure in which he knows Jesus.

For no one lives with reference to himself, and no one with reference to himself dies. For, whether we are living, with reference to the Lord we are living. Whether we are dying, with reference to the Lord we are dying. Therefore, whether we are living or whether we are dying, we belong to the Lord; for to this end Christ both died and lived, in order that He might exercise lordship over both dead ones and living ones.

This practice of following or not following observances is part of the larger truth that our whole life belongs to Jesus. We no longer live to ourselves, but with His interests constantly in mind i.e. everything we do is to be done in relation to Jesus. Similarly we do not choose either the time or means of our dying, but this occurs as and when He wills, so that even by our death we glorify Him. So did Jesus' own death glorify the Father, and the Father then glorified Him by giving Him the Name above all names so that He is now proclaimed as Lord over all, both the living and the dead.

But as for you, why are you judging your brother? Or, as for you also, why are you treating your brother with contempt? For we all shall stand before the judgment seat of God. For it stands written, As I live, says the Lord, every knee shall bow to me, and every tongue shall confess to God. Therefore, then, each one of us shall give an account concerning himself to God.

You weak one, why do you judge your Christian brother in his freedom, since we all have a common responsibility to Jesus? You strong one, why do you despise your brother just because he is scrupulous? These attitudes you hold are to be shunned since they are sinful. We all stand at one bar since God is the universal Judge, and it is He alone Who will reward us according to our lives lived for Him.

Therefore, no longer let us be judging one another. But be judging this rather, not to place a stumbling block before your brother, or a snare in which he may be entrapped.

So let us not have a habit of criticising one another. Rather let us develop ways of conduct that do not offend our brothers so that we do not cause them to stumble or fall or to be drawn into error or sin.

For I know with an absolute knowledge and stand persuaded in the Lord Jesus that not even one thing is unhallowed in itself except it be to the one who reasons it out to be unhallowed. To that one it is unhallowed.

On this matter I am not ignorant and I have no doubt, having gone through a process of reasoning which is now complete so that I am permanently persuaded, and not merely in my own reasoning but in the Lord; when it comes to diet and the observance of days there is nothing in the world that is essentially unclean or unholy in the sense that it is opposed to the ritualistic worship and ceremonial service of God. So I am siding with the strong since I have no scruples about meats or drinks or days and am convinced beyond sway that all things can be consecrated and Christianised by Christian use. But to the weak in faith these things cannot be brought into relation to God in their judgment since their imperfect conscience will not allow them to do so. As it is a matter of their conscience, the strong should respect them, even though it is an unenlightened view that they hold.

For, if because of food your brother is made to grieve, no longer are you conducting yourself according to love. Stop ruining by your food that one on behalf of whom Christ died.

If any of you strong ones goes ahead and eats something that goes against your weak brother's scruples, you will cause him uneasiness and distress, since you are doing something which his conscience cannot approve. This is a violation of the law of Jesus since you have ceased to walk in love, which is the supreme Christian rule. He might even be cajoled by your overbearing attitude into doing what his conscience disapproves of, which would be to his ruin, which ruin you would be a party to in your selfish flouting of your Christian liberty.

Therefore, stop allowing your good to be spoken of in a reproachful and evil manner; for the kingdom of God is not eating and drinking, but righteousness and peace and joy in the sphere of the Holy Spirit; for the one who in this serves the Christ is well pleasing to God, and because having met the specifications is approved by men.

You strong ones stop being inconsiderate in the way you exercise your freedom in Jesus, otherwise, in your lack of love, you will give a bad name to that freedom which was won by Him, and the way of living under grace will be reviled. The Kingdom, being the heavenly sphere of life in which God's Word and Spirit govern and whose organ on earth is the Church, is not about following a morality to do with meat and drink. Rather it is about brotherly self-sacrificial love and unity, with a prevalence of concord in the Church, as produced by the Holy Spirit in the hearts of those who welcome Him there as a guest. Jesus can be served whether eating or abstaining, but He cannot be served where there is an indifference to righteousness, peace, and joy. So be Jesus' slaves in these good characteristics and you will be approved.

Accordingly, therefore, the things of peace let us be eagerly and earnestly seeking after, and the things which edify, which edification is with a view to the edification of one another.

Pursue those things then that lead to unity and common growth, in Christian wisdom, affection, grace, virtue, holiness, and blessedness, as you relate to each other.

Stop on account of food ruining the work of God. All things indeed are pure. But it is evil to the man who eats so as to be a stumbling block. It is good not to eat flesh, nor to drink wine, nor even anything by which your bother stumbles.

Stop tearing down the work of God for the sake of food by spoiling your weak brother's Christian character and testimony. The principle of you strong ones is that nothing is unclean, with which I concur, but this is not to be what rules your Christian conduct. The principle is true, but we must act on it with love i.e. to know that all things are clean does not settle what you have to do in any given case. Your duty is defined as you look with love at your weak brother and consider the effect of your conduct on them, so that you realise that while all meat is clean, not all eating of it is.

As for you, the faith which you have, be having to yourself in the sight of God. Spiritually prosperous is the one who does not judge himself in that which he has tested with a view to approving it should it meet specifications and, having found that it does, has placed his approval upon it. But the one who doubts, if he eats, stands condemned because not by faith did he eat. Moreover, everything which is not of faith is sin.

You strong one, your enlightened faith is not in danger of losing its value if you do not always act on it, rather your fullest freedom must be balanced by your fullest sense of responsibility to God. You are rightly happy that you have no scruples to trouble your conscience, but do not risk injuring your brother's conscience for the sake of exercising this spiritual freedom which you are happy to possess. The weak one is not clear in his own mind if it is permissible to do as you do, and since he is not certain, if he follows you and eats while in that state of mind, his conscience pronounces against him after he has eaten, and he has become inconsistent with his own morality and is potentially being led into a chaotic moral life.

As for us, then, the strong ones, we have a moral obligation to be bearing the infirmities of those who are not strong, and not to be pleasing ourselves. Each one of us, let him be pleasing his neighbour with a view to his good, resulting in his edification. For even the Christ did not please himself, but even as it stands written, The reproaches of those who reproached you fell upon me.

So strong ones, we are bound by duty to bear with the mental weakness of others, foregoing what we know is right since they consider it to be wrong, curtailing our own freedom for the sake of not offending them, so denying ourselves something that is legitimately ours, which therefore becomes a burden to us. As I said before, do not shelter your own self-pleasing or wilfulness under the disguise of following a Christian principle, since the overriding principle, which has no qualification, is love. Instead, you can be pleased that by denying yourself you have removed a source of temptation to them and so made their attempt to live a life pleasing to God easier. Take for your example Jesus; He was pleased to leave Heaven and all His heavenly rights and freedoms and to live an earthly life within human limitations, and to be made sin on the Cross and to endure the loss of fellowship with the Father, in order to bear the penalty for sin for us who were weak and helpless.

For whatever things were written aforetime with a view to our learning were written, in order that through the patience and through the encouragement arising from the scriptures we might be having hope.

The Old Testament was written to teach us and therefore has abiding value. Through the comfort wrought by the Scriptures we have our hope, being our Christian hope and our hope of the glory of God, and we have that comfort that enables us to maintain a brave and cheerful spirit amid all the sufferings and reproaches of life, as His Word consoles, exhorts, admonishes, aids, and encourages us.

Now, the God of the patience and the encouragement give to you to be thinking the same thing among one another according to Christ Jesus, in order that with one mind and one mouth you may keep on glorifying the God and Father of our Lord Jesus Christ. Wherefore, be receiving one another even as also the Christ received us, with a view to the glory of God.

I pray for harmony among you, that your moral judgements and temper may all be determined by Jesus, so that you can then glorify God in unity, as one in Him. When you so glorify God, all the troubles over food and drink and eating and abstaining will be transcended as you grow together into Him. God received you who were formerly estranged from Him, reuniting you to Himself by the blessings of the Gospel. If Jesus so received both the weak and the strong among you, thus are you bound to receive each other.

For I am saying, Christ has become a servant to the circumcision on behalf of God's truth, resulting in the confirmation of the promises to the fathers and [resulting] in the Gentiles, on behalf of His mercy, glorifying God; even as it stands written, Because of this I will openly confess to you among the Gentiles and in your Name sing.

Jesus became One Who served the circumcised, namely the Jews, in fulfilment of the Messianic promises to Israel. But this was a means to an end, the end being that the Gentiles might be reached through Israel and so glorify God for His mercy. So you Gentiles must not be contemptuous of the scruples or weaknesses of the Jews, especially such as arise out of their association with the old covenant. Nor should you Jews be critical of the freedom of the Gentiles, which has its vindication in the free grace of God, since Jesus gives thanks to God among the Gentiles when they give thanks to God through Him.

And again He says, Rejoice, Gentiles, with His people. And again, Be extolling, all you Gentiles, the Lord. And let all the people extol Him. And again Isaiah says, There shall be a sprout out of the root of Jesse, even the One who arises to be a ruler of the Gentiles. Upon Him will the Gentiles place their hope.

From the lowest place, the root, the banner of Jesus' rule rises highest, so as to be seen throughout the world, even by the remotest of nations.

Now the God of the hope fill you with every joy and hope in the sphere of believing, resulting in your super-abounding in the sphere of the hope by the power of the Holy Spirit.

You place your hope in the God Who gives us the hope which we have in Jesus. In your believing and putting your faith in Jesus He imparts to you His joy and peace, which joy and peace flow from His acceptance of you. The more joy and peace you have the more you abound in the Christian hope in the power of the Holy Spirit, which abounding is the end to which I pray for you believers in Rome.

But I have reached a settled conviction, my brethren, even I myself, concerning you, that you yourselves also are full of goodness, having been filled completely full of every knowledge with the result that you are in an abiding state of fullness, able also to be admonishing one another.

I in no way deem you to be defective in either love or intelligence, but believe rather that you, who I have never ministered to, are full of goodness, in that you have self-sacrificial love for one another which bears the infirmities of the weaker brother, and in that you possess Christian knowledge in its entirety.

The more boldly indeed I write to you in some measure as recalling to your mind again because of the grace which was given to me from God, resulting in my being a servant of Christ Jesus in holy things to the Gentiles, exercising a sacred ministry in the good news of God in order that the offering of the Gentiles might be well pleasing, having been sanctified by the Holy Spirit.

See how I have written, not too boldly, but nevertheless more boldly because you are full of goodness. And in some of my writing I have been especially plain. I minister the Gospel as a priestly duty, being of no less value and sacredness than the ministry of the Old Testament priesthood. The priestly function which I perform is to preach the Gospel to the Gentiles and the offering which I present to God is the Gentile Church.

I have therefore my glorifying in Christ Jesus with reference to the things which pertain to God. For I will not dare to be speaking concerning anything of the things which Christ did not bring about through my agency resulting in the obedience of the Gentiles, by word and deed, by the power of attesting miracles and miracles of an extraordinary character, by the power of the Holy Spirit: so that from Jerusalem and the environs of Illyricum I have fulfilled my commission of preaching the good news of the Christ. Indeed, in this manner I have been actuated by considerations of honour to be ambitious to announce the glad tidings not where Christ was named, in order that I would not be building upon a foundation belonging to another; but as it stands written, They shall see, those to whom there was not made an announcement concerning Him, and those who have not heard, they shall understand.

So Jesus glorifies me in relation to my priestly service to Him. All other boasting I decline, but I boast only in what He has wrought through me i.e. He working in me to make the Gentiles obedient to the Gospel, as part of which commission I have written now to you. The miracles that I perform by the Holy Spirit prove that my message is from Jesus and is authenticated by Him, and the miracles draw the attention of my hearers by impressing themselves upon their memories. I have fully preached the Gospel in every particular and in every region up to Illyricum, so that I have carried on my work of preaching to a successful termination in that in all areas where Christianity was not established I have brought to them my Gospel message.

Wherefore, I also have been continually hindered by the many things in coming to you. But now no longer having opportunity in these parts, and having a passionate desire to come to you these many years, whenever I journey into Spain I am hoping to see you as I journey through, and by you to be furnished with the necessities of travel to that place, if first in part I may be fully satisfied with your fellowship.

My preaching in those regions, and many other hindrances, kept me from coming to you. But now there is no longer a demand for me here, so I am free to come to Rome and have my desire of seeing you fulfilled. I hope that you will be able to satisfy my travel needs and that also I may be partly satiated with your company, only partly since I would wish to remain with you much longer than I anticipate being able to, as I pass through Rome on this occasion.

But now I am going on my journey to Jerusalem, ministering to the saints. For it was the good pleasure of Macedonia and Achaia to make up a certain benefaction jointly contributed for the poor of the saints which are in Jerusalem; for it was their good pleasure, and their debtors they are. For in view of the fact that the Gentiles were fellow-partakers of their spiritual things, they are under moral obligation to minister to them in the sphere of things needed for the sustenance of the body, considering this material ministry as a sacred service.

I am now about to travel to Jerusalem, to bring financial aid to the believers there, and also to bring about a better understanding between Gentiles and Jews in the Church at large. The contribution I am taking was given spontaneously and cordially, the Gentiles here making the necessities of the believers in Jerusalem their own, so sharing of what they had with them, given that they owe a debt to the Jerusalem Jews since they are now also partaking of the spiritual blessings of salvation, which salvation is of the Jews.

Then, having brought this to a successful termination and having secured to them this fruit, I will come through you into Spain. And I know positively that when coming to you, in the fullness of the blessing of Christ I will come.

So I am anxious to quickly complete this project of the collection of money for the Jerusalem poor, this money being a gracious result of the reception of the Gospel by the Gentiles, which I deem to be a spiritual fruit to be credited to their account.

But I beg of you, please, brethren, through our Lord Jesus Christ and through the love which is of the Spirit, contend vigorously with me in your prayers on my behalf to God, in order that I may be delivered from those who are non-persuasible in Judaea, and that my service which is for Jerusalem may become well pleasing to the saints, in order that in joy, having come to you through God's will, I may rest and refresh myself with you. Now, the God of the peace be with you all. Amen.

You are able to sympathise with me in all that I have to encounter in my service of Jesus since we both bow to His Name. In view of what Jesus means to you and me, and in view of the love of the Spirit in all our hearts, pray for my safety and success in Jerusalem where both the stiff-necked, obstinate Jews, and also many Christian Jews, regard me as being false to the nation and to the law of Moses. As you pray for me you are sharing and contending along with me as a team of athletes would, in opposing with me the hosts of wickedness that I will encounter. Even though well-meaning brethren may warn me against setting foot in Jerusalem for fear of the Jews, yet will I do so since I am prepared to be bound and to die there. Pray that the financial gift I am bringing might be warmly welcomed by the Jerusalem believers as a pledge of brotherly love, and not be seen by them as a bribe on my part, attempting to seek their condoning of my opposition to the law and their acceptance and acknowledgment of my upstart Gentile assemblies in the Kingdom of God. Pray also that in the end I may enjoy a time of rest with you prior to travelling to Spain.

Now, I recommend to you, Phoebe, our sister, who is a deaconess of the assembly which is at Cenchrea, to the end that you take her to yourselves in the Lord in a manner which is fitting to the saints, and that you stand by her in whatever business she may have need of you, for verily, she herself became a benefactress of many, and of me myself.

I can vouch for Phoebe, who brought this letter to you on the long and dangerous journey from Corinth to Rome, as to her servant role in the assembly near here at Cenchrea. As a widow she takes care of the sick and the poor out of her own resources, ministers to those in prison, and exercises a general supervision over female members of the assembly. I ask that you receive her fully as a sister in Jesus, with a welcoming that weighs as much as the position you hold in God's family. She has business to attend to in Rome in which I ask that you stand with her and assist her.

Greet Prisca and Aquila, my fellow-workers in Christ Jesus, who are such that on behalf of my life they laid down their necks, to whom I not only give thanks, but also all the assemblies of the Gentiles. Also, greet the assembly which meets in their home. Greet Epaenetus, my well-beloved, who is the first-fruit of Asia with reference to Christ.

Greet Prisca and her husband Aquila who helped me greatly here in Corinth while we lived and worked and preached together, and who risked their very lives for me. And greet all those who meet in their house of prayer, and also Epaenetus.

Greet Marian who is such as to have laboured with wearisome effort to the point of exhaustion on your behalf with reference to many things. Greet Andronicus and Junia, my fellow countrymen and my fellow prisoners who are of excellent reputation among the apostles, who also came in Christ before I did. Greet Amplias, my beloved in the Lord. Greet Urbane, our fellow helper in Christ, and Stachys, my beloved.

Greet these fellow countrymen and fellow captives in war, some of whom were saved before I was, all of whom are still in Jesus, being now eternally secure.

Greet Apelles, the one who, having been put to the test and having been found to meet the test, is approved in Christ. Greet those belonging to Aristobulus. Greet Herodion, my fellow countryman. Greet those belonging to Narcissus, those who are in the Lord. Greet Tryphena and Tryphosa, those who laboured to the point of exhaustion in the Lord. Greet Persis, the beloved who was such that she laboured to the point of exhaustion with reference to many things in the Lord. Greet Rufus, the one selected out in the Lord, and his mother and mine. Greet Asyncritus, Philegon, Hermas, Patrobas, Hermes, and the brethren with them. Greet Philologus, and Julia, Nereus and his sister, and Olympas, and all the saints with them. Greet one another with a holy kiss. There greet you all the churches of Christ.

Greet all of these, the household, slaves of Aristobulus, Herodion of the Herod family, the slaves of Narcissus the wealthy secretary to Caesar Claudias, the slaves Tryphena, Tryphosa, and Philologus, and Rufus the son of Simon of Cyrene and his mother who also ministered maternally to me. Greet and kiss one another as is customary among the Jews, not being the ordinary greeting of affection or friendship, men kissing men, women kissing women.

Now, I beg of you, please, brethren, be keeping a watchful eye ever open for those who are causing the divisions and the scandals which are contrary to the teaching that you learned, and be turning away from them. For they are such as are not rendering service as bondslaves to our Lord Christ, but to their own stomachs; and with smooth and plausible address, which simulates goodness, and with polished eulogies, are leading astray the hearts of the innocent; for your obedience has come to the ears of all. Because of you, therefore, I am rejoicing. But I desire you to be wise ones with reference to that which is good, and pure ones with reference to that which is evil. And the God of the peace will trample Satan under your feet soon. The grace of our Lord Jesus be with you.

Keep an eye on, so as to avoid, the false teachers. These have not yet appeared in Rome or begun their work there, but I have seen this danger in other places. You have already heard of the divisions and offences that they stir up, and of their methods of leading people into error or sin as they seek to create a moral prejudice against the Gospel so as to prevent people from accepting it, and of their causing dissension within the Church. Turn away from such teachers and shun them, they being those who serve their own base interests, having a self-seeking spirit, and who beguile their hearers with their fine, polished language. But you, rather than being false and rather than misleading people are obedient, and your obedience is what is being talked about everywhere. So I rejoice over you. But make sure that your moral intelligence is not impaired in the least by any dealings with evil. In this way, by keeping your thinking pure, you will instinctively repel any seductive but erroneous teaching. There are no divisions in God so there should be none in His Church. Divisions are Satan's work, and the suppression of them by the God of peace is a victory over Satan which victory will come speedily, so be patient and loyal to Jesus in the meantime. When divisions are bound together again the result is peace.

There greet you Timothy, my co-worker, and Lucius, and Jason, and Sosipater, my countrymen. As for myself, I, Tertius, greet you in the Lord, the one who is putting this letter in writing. There greets you Gaius, my host and host of the whole assembly. There greet you Erastus, the manager of the city, and Quartus, the brother.

Timothy, my young understudy greets you. Tertius, your fellow believer, greets you in his own words, being the one to whom I dictated the rest of this letter that you are reading due to my almost total blindness. Gaius greets you, he who hosts all believers who come to Corinth.

Now, to the One who is of power to establish you according to my gospel, even the proclamation concerning Jesus Christ, according to the uncovering of the mystery which during eternal times has been kept in silence but now has been made known through prophetic writings according to the mandate of the eternal God, having been made known with a view to the obedience to the Faith among all nations, to God alone wise, through Jesus Christ, to Him [God alone wise] be the glory for ever and ever. Amen.

I long to impart some spiritual gift to you so as to make you stable and to strengthen you, but only Jesus has the ability to do this. But when my Gospel is achieved among you, you will be settled and confirmed in Christianity. I say my Gospel since it was given to me directly by Jesus and I was not taught it by any man, and also since it has something characteristic of me about it, being my sense of the absolute freeness of salvation in that we are justified by faith alone, apart from any works of law, and my resolve that it is absolutely universal, being for everyone who would submit to it and believe. I proclaim Jesus in accordance with the revealing of the mystery that was given to me by Jesus Himself; that God's plan of redemption embraces the whole world of sinners. This secret which has now been made known was kept hidden from the eternal ages before creation. The Old Testament prophets alluded to it, prophets to whom I constantly refer in my preaching, so in that sense the mystery was made known through them. But the significance of their prophecies only came to light through the knowledge of Jesus, which revelation was given to me by Him, the One Who is without beginning and without end, eternally God. It was by God's command that the mystery and secret that had been kept for so long was made known. Glory be to Him.

From Paul to Timothy

Paul, an ambassador of Christ Jesus by command of God our Saviour and Christ Jesus our hope, to Timothy, my genuine child in the Faith. [Sanctifying] grace, mercy, [tranquilizing] peace, from God our Father and Christ Jesus our Lord.

I write as an apostle of Jesus, the Anointed One of God, being He Who saves, Who paid the price for our sins by pouring out His blood on the Cross, thus satisfying justice so that we no longer face the penalty of death, He having died on our behalf. I am an apostle, appointed by, and under the orders of, God and Jesus Who are equally deity. Jesus is not only our Saviour through His work on the Cross, by which we believers are made righteous, He is also our hope for the future; that we shall be like Him. I write to you Timothy, though this letter is also to be read in the assemblies committed to your charge, you whom I gave birth to in winning you to a saving faith in Jesus. I introduced you to His grace, grace that loved us and saved us by sending Jesus while we hated Him, and which grace makes us more like Jesus by the work of the Holy Spirit in our lives as we yield to Him. I introduced you also to His mercy to us, mercy in offering us His free gift of forgiveness while we were helpless and in misery in our sins, so as to remove them from us, which mercy was made way for by His grace, and which mercy I bid you be mindful of as you administer the assemblies. Now are we bound together again to God, so at peace with Him. Dear Timothy, when the sanctifying grace and the remedial mercy of God are operative in your life and ministry, then that pleasant, satisfying feeling of tranquility, comfort, and well-being will be secured in you.

Just as I begged you to continue on in Ephesus when I was going into Macedonia in order that you might charge certain ones not to be teaching things contrary to sound doctrine, nor to be giving assent to fables and useless genealogies which are of such a character as to provide occasion for exhaustive investigations rather than a [knowledge of the] administration of the things by which God has provided for and prepared salvation, which salvation must be embraced by faith.

I am writing to you so as to provide you with a written memorandum of what I previously instructed you in verbally, especially in respect to dealing with speculations that sap the vitality of the Gospel whose root is sincerity and love. We were together in Ephesus at the time and I had to plead with you to remain there in an apostolic role after I left. As I told you then, be watchful of doctrines which are touted as being Christian, but which are actually diametrically opposed to the Gospel. And do not tolerate rumours and stories which are just the talk of men, whether supplements to the law or allegorical interpretations of it, or Jewish stories of miracles, or fabrications of rabbis. These can be in the form of allegorical interpretations of genealogies, or of Old Testament genealogies adorned with fables, or in using genealogical registers in order to foster the religious and national pride of the Jews against the Gentiles or in order to ascertain the descent of the Messiah. There is nothing to be gained by any of these. You need rather to focus on the operation of God's salvation in the lives of the believers in those assemblies which are under your charge i.e. concentrate on the faith within which their salvation operates.

Now, the objective which is the aim of the aforementioned charge is divine and self-sacrificial love out of a heart which is pure, and a conscience which is good, and a faith which is not assumed but real, from which things certain having deviated, have turned off into talk which is futile, desiring to be law teachers, though they neither understand the things they are saying nor what kind of things they are concerning which they speak so confidently.

If you do thus concentrate on the faith, you will exercise a careful stewardship of the Gospel message and preach it in such a way that sinners will be saved. God works through this message to produce love in the believer, and a simple, perfect conscience, leading to a sense of well-being and contentment as they genuinely accept the message into their heart. Some have turned aside from the Gospel in a serious doctrinal wrench from the truth. Their talk is vain and useless and what they teach is without merit, though they speak assuredly and confidently as they interpret the law of Moses in error.

But we know that the law is good if a person uses it properly, knowing this, that law is not enacted for a law-abiding person, but for lawless ones and for unruly ones, for those who are destitute of reverential awe towards God and for sinners, for unholy ones and for those who are irreligious, for those who ill-treat fathers and ill-treat mothers, for manslayers, for whoremongers, for sodomites, for slave dealers and kidnapers, for liars, for perjurers, and if, as is the case, there is anything of a different nature which is opposed to sound teaching, according to the good news of the glory of the blessed God with which I was entrusted.

There is a true use of the law, as against the use to which these false teachers put the law. The law is good and is seen to be good when used correctly. It does not convict the morally upright, but is for those who recognise no law or who refuse to submit themselves to law. These make themselves accessible to evil influences, living in common, secular, unhallowed territory. They have no natural affection for their parents. They are inflamed with lust leading to an all-out endeavour to satisfy the appetites and desires of their totally depraved natures, doing things unseemly and immodest, in their nakedness violating the laws of nature and wandering from the standards laid down for the sexual use of human bodies. They unjustly reduce free men to slavery and steal the slaves of others in order to sell them themselves, so exploiting men and women for their own selfish ends. They do anything that is opposed to healthy, wholesome teaching in which is found true freedom, but rather live as slaves to sin. They live in darkness, but in the Gospel is found the glory of God, being a blessed state to which we who obey the Gospel may attain.

I am constantly grateful to the One who endued me with the necessary strength, Christ Jesus our Lord, because He deemed me trustworthy, having placed me in service, though I was the very one who heretofore was a reviler and a persecutor and an insolent, destructive person. But I was shown mercy because, being ignorant, I acted in unbelief. Moreover, the grace of our Lord superabounded together with faith and love which is in Christ Jesus.

I am always thankful that this Gospel was entrusted to me, and that Jesus clothes me with strength in order to proclaim this good news of salvation. He considered me faithful, having weighed the facts and having deliberately and carefully judged me, concluding that my fiery, intense zeal as a Pharisee, as exhibited in my insolent and contemptuous persecution of Jesus and the Church, would render me a fiery, intense, zealous servant and proclaimer of the Gospel when saving grace was operating in me, and so He put me into the ministry. His grace to me was to grant me an opportunity to serve Him Whom I had injured, He having overflowing mercy on my wanton and outrageous acts of sinful disbelief.

Trustworthy is the word and worthy of unqualified acceptance, that Christ Jesus came into the world to save sinners, of whom I in contradistinction to anyone else am foremost. Moreover, on this account I was shown mercy, in order that in me first Jesus Christ might demonstrate all the long-suffering [which He has] as an example to those who were to be believing on Him for life eternal. Now, to the King of the Ages, the incorruptible, invisible, unique God, be honour and glory forever and ever. Amen.

My experience of Jesus' dealings with me in His saving of me is not unique, but His longsuffering will never undergo a more severe test than it did in my case, so no sinner need ever despair of being beyond salvation since without any doubt I am the chief of sinners. Could I be saved? Was I worth saving? Yes indeed, and Jesus had a special object in view in extending to me His mercy; that I might be the representative instance of God's utmost longsuffering in withholding His anger toward such a high-handed transgressor i.e. an example, in my conversion, that the same grace which I had obtained would not be wanting also to any who should hereafter believe. Glory to the One Who is not liable to corruption or decay, but Who always has been and always will be, Who is eternally King and forever worthy of all veneration and reverence.

This charge I am entrusting to you, son Timothy, in accordance with the prophetic intimations which were made long ago concerning you, to the effect that in their sphere you are to wage the good warfare, holding faith and a good conscience, which [latter] certain having thrust from themselves concerning the Faith, have suffered shipwreck, among whom are Hymenaeus and Alexander, whom I have delivered over to Satan in order that they may be taught not to be blaspheming.

Dear Timothy, I commit now this charge to you, in accordance with prophetic indications which I formerly received concerning you; that you boldly proclaim the Gospel according to these prophecies and that you contend in the power of your prophesied and designated spiritual gifting. You will need to battle against those who have, with wilful violence against conscience, abandoned Christianity. These, whom I have named here I have excommunicated from the Church and cast back into the world which is under Satan's power, with a view to their being reformed, after having suffered a while at his hands.

I exhort therefore, first of all, that petitions be made continually for personal needs, prayers, intercessions, giving of thanks on behalf of all men, on behalf of kings and all those holding high positions, in order that a quiet and peaceful life we may be leading in every godliness and becoming deportment.

The most important part of my exhortation to you concerns the universal scope of public prayer. Pray for your own needs as related to the government under which you live. Your approach to God should be free and familiar as you make prayers a factor in your relation to your secular rulers. Then, by keeping aloof from political agitations, you will have no outward disturbance and be free from governmental persecutions, since you will be deemed by the ruling authorities to be noble and honest, so inviting reverence from them.

This is good and acceptable in the sight of our Saviour God who desires that all men be saved and come to a precise and experiential knowledge of the truth, for there is one God, and one mediator between God and men, a Man, Jesus Christ,

Praying for all men is good, being approved by our natural conscience and also being in accordance with the revealed will of God. Human government is a divinely appointed institution, yet you are in no way to acknowledge Caesar as saviour. He indeed holds mankind together under the great Roman power, providing peace, order, prosperity, and protection, thus ruling over men's temporal affairs and acknowledged as one of their gods and as being their lord. Rather Jesus is our Saviour, God, the One Who alone is to be worshipped, Who saves our souls from sin, exercising a spiritual control over our lives. Caesar has a right to rule over the temporal aspects of our lives, but is not to be worshipped or submitted to as the highest ruler. God loves our lost race and has a determined desire for the salvation of all sinners, that all men might know the truth and might know Him, though He will not force men to accept His free offer of justification in Jesus. Jesus is the one and only Saviour, He being of the unity of the Godhead. The oneness of God means that it is possible for all men to be saved, since there are not many gods exercising conflicting willpower toward men but only One. One Godhead stands over against one humanity, and the Infinite and the finite can enter into relations with each other since they are linked by a mediator, Jesus, Who is both God and human. It is only because deity is also a Man that Jesus can be an adequate Mediator, Whose sympathy with and understanding of both parties is clearly identifiable to and easily recognisable by both God and mankind. So He can intervene in order to restore peace and friendship between God and man in making a compact and in ratifying a covenant. Jesus interposed Himself by His sacrificial death and made possible the restoration of the harmony between God and man which had been broken by sin.

who gave himself as a ransom on behalf of all, the testimony of which is to be given in strategic seasons having a unique character of their own, to which [testimony] I was appointed an official herald and an ambassador; I am speaking truth, I am not lying; a teacher of Gentiles in faith and truth.

Jesus' death was a spontaneous and voluntary sacrifice on His part, He having cooperated in the eternal counsels and purpose of the Father as regards the salvation of man in His pre-Incarnation existence, being the sacrifice of His lifetime in His whole humiliation and self-emptying in leaving Heaven to come to earth and live as a human. He gave His life in substitution for us when we were slaves to sin and held captive by the law, which payment of His the law was satisfied with; that He become the curse instead of us. This exchange of His life for ours was not merely an exchange of things equal in value, His life being of infinite more worth than ours, so the exchange was of benefit to us. His act of self-sacrifice is timeless, though was apprehended by us in time, and testimony to which is for this particular period of history, from the Holy Spirit's descent at Pentecost until the end of the Millennium, this period being God's unique, particular season for the proclamation of the Gospel based on the historic work of Jesus on the Cross. The Gospel was preached all through Old Testament times, but upon the basis of a prophetic work of salvation which was yet to be wrought out on the Cross. I was appointed to convey this Gospel message from God to men by Jesus, having been commissioned by Him and given His credentials so as to be His representative. I tell people exactly what He bids me to proclaim, nothing more nothing less, so I am not on the defensive, though suffering constant opposition wherever I declare God's message of grace. I always speak openly and welcome investigation of my teaching by others. I preach with a sincere faith in the Gospel and always give a truthful representation of the Gospel which I believe.

I desire, therefore, that the men [definite article before "men" and distinctive word for a male individual designating the man as leader and in authority in the church] be praying in every place, lifting up holy hands without anger or sceptical criticism.

Let the men, rather than the women, be leading these public prayers wherever Christian assemblies congregate, raising your hands as part of your experience of life in Jesus, having no irritation towards men or criticism of the character and behaviour of those being prayed for, but rather confidence towards God without any scepticism as to His character and dealings.

Likewise, I desire that women be adorning themselves in apparel that is fitting [to their sex and to their position as Christians], having along with this, modesty and sober-mindedness; not with braided hair, or gold, or pearls, or very costly garments, but with that which is fitting for a woman professing godliness, adorning themselves by means of good works.

In these public gatherings let the women present themselves in harmonious order. This orderliness must govern not merely their external appearance, for example the articles of clothing worn, but also their appearance with respect to their Christian character and testimony i.e. a woman's appearance must be consistent with her status of being a child of God, being one of modesty and humility, and being of one who is at His command, able to express their free will, yet exercising self-control in the energy of the Holy Spirit. A woman is to depend for her adornment on a Christian character and on good works done through the Spirit. Then will her apparel be in keeping with her Christian character.

Let a woman be learning in silence with every subjection. Moreover, I do not permit a woman to be a teacher [in an official position exercising authority over the man in matters of Church doctrine or discipline], neither to exercise authority over a man, but to be in silence,

Let not the women disturb the public gatherings by asking their husbands questions about what is being preached, since quiet needs to be maintained in the assemblies, though women can take an active part in the work of the Church, each in her own office. When it comes to matters of doctrine and interpretation, I do not allow a woman to have authority in this office of God-called and God-equipped teacher.

for Adam first was moulded, then Eve, and Adam was not deceived, but the woman, having been completely hoodwinked, has fallen into transgression. Yet she shall be saved [in the sense of sanctifying, salutary influences in her spiritual life through the pains of childbirth] in her childbearing if they continue in faith and love and holiness accompanied by sober-mindedness.

The reason for the relative positions of men and women in the Church is found in the original order of creation and in the fall of man. Man was made first and it was the woman who was cheated and beguiled and thoroughly deceived by Satan, the penalty for which transgression was to have greatly increased sorrow in bringing forth children, but which sentence has proved to be a blessing in that in undergoing these pains she finds her salvation. For both men and women, in discharging their normal and natural duties, as far as their individual efforts can contribute to it, each work out their salvation. Without these duties they would be caused to deteriorate instead of making progress in character in the adjusting of themselves each to their own circumstances and surroundings. So the stumbling block of sorrow in childbirth is made into a stepping-stone that expresses a woman's necessity, duty, privilege, and dignity. Common-sense then points to women's primary function as being that of childbearing, rather than that of public teaching or the direction of affairs with respect to correct or false teaching. So let the husband and wife each take on their own roles within the marriage relation in love and purity and mutual submission.

This is a trustworthy word. If a certain one is seeking the office of an overseer, he passionately desires a good work.

Having given you directions about public prayer, let me now take up the matter of Church organisation. Firstly the role of those who exercise spiritual oversight and care over the assembly. Their role is similar to that of a supervisor of building construction. This person is to direct the spiritual life of the local assembly. So those who stretch themselves and reach out to take on this office are seeking something that is beneficial to all.

It is necessary in the nature of the case, therefore, that the overseer be irreproachable, a one-wife kind of a man [that is, married only once], calm, dispassionate and circumspect, sober-minded, one whose life is in accord with the position he holds and which is an adornment to it, hospitable, a skilled teacher,

The overseer needs to be someone who cannot be laid hold upon by others so as to criticise i.e. of a spotless character with nothing in their life that could cast reproach on the cause of Jesus, his conduct furnishing no grounds for accusation. He should be a man who loves only one woman as his wife and who is not to marry again should she die, since in his position he is more open to criticism, requiring that he must hold up a high ideal. This regulation is made given the present circumstances in which we live, but in future, when circumstances change, and if the Christian life enters another totally different phase, this may not still apply. The overseer should be wise and cautious, serious, earnest, and dignified. He should also be fond of offering hospitality to strangers and guests since, due to Roman persecutions, Christians are being banished and persecuted and rendered homeless. Travelling preachers and teachers should also be received and cared for by the overseer. He must also be glad to open his house for gatherings of the local assembly. And he should be skilled and willing in the duty of instructing believers and of refuting critics who contradict and oppose the Faith.

not addicted to wine, not pugnacious but sweetly reasonable, being satisfied with less than his due, not contentious, not a lover of money,

The overseer, in the partaking of wine, as is common with meals, must not drink of it so freely as to become intoxicated, petulant, and quarrelsome, leading him to be one who is ready to strike another. In his attitude when contentions arise, he should be more just than strict justice would be, not asserting his own legal rights lest these be pushed into moral wrongs i.e. not being unduly rigorous in making a determined stand for his own just due. He should not be one who fights or one who is fond of silver.

presiding over his own household in a beautiful manner, holding children within the sphere of implicit obedience, doing so with the strictest regard to propriety. Indeed, if a person does not know how to preside over his own household, how is it possible that he take care of God's assembly?

The overseer must be one who can manage his own private household, as a superior army officer arranges his soldiers in battalions in military order. He should thus be treated with respect and dignity by all in his own house, as he should also be by those in the house of God.

[He must] not [be] a new convert, lest having his mind blinded by pride, he fall into the judgment of the devil.

If he is like a newly planted palm tree, he may smoulder with conceit in his thinking, so assuming a beclouded, stupid state of mind as the result of this pride. Then he will be in a similar state to Satan who was condemned by God for rebellion against Him, which sin was motivated by pride.

Moreover, it is a necessity in the nature of the case for him also to be having an excellent testimony from those on the outside, lest he fall into reproach and into the snare of the devil.

Finally the overseer should be well thought of by the non-Christian world in the midst of which you live, since if they see something blameworthy in him and the consensus of their opinion is unfavourable to him then, no matter how well thought of he may be by the assembly, he will bring discredit on the Church. When the world is in antagonism to us Christians, we cannot safely assume that we are absolutely in the right and that the world is wholly wrong, and to so defy public opinion in a superior spirit is to be caught in the devil's schemes i.e. if the world condemns a certain course of action on our part, we can never suppose that the action is therefore right and that the world's verdict may be safely set aside.

Deacons, in like manner [should] be grave and dignified, not double-tongued, not addicted to much wine, not greedy of gain, holding the mystery of the Faith in a pure conscience.

Moving on from overseers of the spiritual welfare of the assembly, the role of the deacon is to manage your temporal welfare. He is to be genuine in his speech, saying what he means and making the same representation to different people on any given issue, also speaking with the same tone whether conversing with a superior or a subordinate. He must not have a base and disgraceful gain-greedy way, making the acquisition of money his prime object, rather than the glory of God. He must be especially wary of this temptation since he ministers the finances of the assembly so must not misappropriate funds in any way so as to supplement his own wages. By the illumination of the Holy Spirit the deacon should understand the truth of the mystery of the divine Christian system of revelation in a sincere conscience, so as not to fall away from the Faith as one would if they had just an intellectual attitude towards this mystery, resulting in doubt, questioning, wordy strife, moral laxity, and despair. An intellect, however powerful and active, if joined with an impure conscience, cannot solve but only aggravates the mystery, whereas a pure and loyal conscience and a frank acceptance of imposed duty along with mystery puts one in the best attitude for attaining whatever solution of the mystery is possible.

And these moreover are to be first put to the test for the purpose of being approved, and then approved if they meet the specifications; then let them be serving as deacons, provided they are unaccused.

Deacons, as well as overseers, must be proved before being appointed, being judged suitable and of fulfilling their role's specifications, in the general judgment of the assembly.

Women, likewise [should be] grave and dignified, not slanderers, calm, dispassionate, and circumspect, faithful in all things.

Women deacons should similarly have a dignity which invites the reverence of others. They should not accuse or defame others, but rather, like the overseer, be calm, dispassionate and circumspect, and true to the trust imposed in them.

Let the deacons be one-wife sort of men [that is, married only once], ruling their children and their own households in a commendable way, for those who have ministered in the office of a deacon in a commendable manner acquire a good standing for themselves and much confidence in the sphere of faith which is in Christ Jesus.

Like the overseer, the deacon should be a man who loves only one woman as his wife and who is not to marry again should she die, and be one who can manage his own private household. He who does well as a deacon due to his character and abilities will be esteemed by the assembly and may be promoted to overseer, and in themselves will become more assured in their speech and attitude, both in the assembly and elsewhere, and more bold in their faith in Jesus.

These things to you I am writing, hoping to come to you quickly, but if I delay, in order that you may know how it is necessary in the nature of the case for ~~me~~ men to be conducting themselves in God's house which is of such a nature as to be the living God's assembly, a pillar and support of the truth.

I am writing these instructions to you Timothy concerning the officers of the assemblies under your charge with respect to their duties and qualifications, and concerning matters of Church discipline, so that you know how the members under your authority should conduct themselves.

And confessedly, great is the mystery of godliness; who [Christ Jesus] was made visible in the sphere of flesh [His humanity], vindicated in the sphere of spirit [as to His deity], seen by angels, proclaimed among the nations, believed on in the world, taken up in glory.

We agree with the greatness of the mystery which invites our respect and reverence towards God, as revealed to us believers. This mystery is Jesus, revealed in the Gospel as the Saviour from ungodliness, as the norm and inspiration of godliness, and as the divine life in man, causing us who believe to live to God as He did and as He still does. God does not have a physical body so is therefore invisible, but in the Incarnation, the invisible Jesus became visible as He took upon Himself a physical body as the Man Christ Jesus. He was endorsed and proved in the Spirit as to what He was in His pre-incarnate state, as pure spirit, Deity, in the form of God, being the express image of God's substance. During Jesus' life on earth, His humanity was clearly seen, but His deity was usually hidden under the cloak of His humanity, and only occasionally were there moments when His deity was seen, as on the Mount of Transfiguration when the Father's voice from Heaven said, "This is My Son, the dearly Beloved Chosen One, in Whom I take pleasure. Be constantly hearing Him". His deity was also seen in His exalted and spotless character, in His works of love and power, and in His words of authority. All these proved and endorsed Him for what He was; God manifest in human flesh. Jesus was seen by angels; at His Incarnation, in His temptation, in His agony before His crucifixion, at His resurrection, and at His ascension. The Gospel is preached in the whole world and Jesus is believed on everywhere. He was taken up into glory with attendant heavenly pomp and majesty, being received out of the sight of the disciples by the cloud of God's Shekinah Glory.

But the Spirit says expressly that in the last strategic, epochal periods of time some will depart from the Faith, giving heed to spirits that lead one into error, and to teachings of demons, doing this through the hypocrisy of liars, branded in their own conscience, forbidding to marry, commanding abstinence from foods, which things God created for those to receive with thanksgiving who are believers and who have a precise and experiential knowledge of the truth;

Beware of false teachings now and in the future which will cause some to fall away from the truth, these being misled by evil spirits whose role is to actuate human agents who then speak lies, lies to do with living a life of false and severe self-discipline, forbidding certain foods and only allowing marriage under stringent regulations as a necessity for preserving the race. Those who are thus seduced by these teachings and led astray have their conscience seared with the marks of Satan. The false teachers are deceivers who act deliberately, against conscience, wearing a form of godliness and contradicting their profession by their crooked conduct. But to those who believe and know the truth, all foods were created to be partaken of.

because every created thing of God is good, and not even one thing is to be rejected if it is received with thanksgiving, for it is consecrated through God's word and through prayer.

Whatever food that we give thanks for and acknowledge as being a gift from God, is sanctified and thus made holy by prayer, so can be partaken of as nourishing the life of God's service.

Constantly reminding the brethren of these things, you will be a good servant of Christ Jesus, continually nourishing yourself by means of the words of the Faith and of the good teaching which you have closely followed.

Gently suggest these things to the members of the assemblies of which you are the superintendent, they having the same Father as you, thus rendering Jesus a service by setting yourself against these errors. Constantly feed on the Word of God with its good teachings, which you have always carefully attended to.

But unhallowed and old wives' fictions be shunning. On the other hand, be exercising yourself with a view to piety toward God. For the aforementioned bodily exercise is of some small profit, but the aforementioned piety toward God is profitable with respect to all things, holding a promise of this present life and of that about to come.

Reject and avoid all the false inventions and myths of the Jewish teachers and those who claim to have mystical knowledge. Exercise your spirit as you would your body in the gymnasium, building up your mind, will, and emotions so as to excel in godliness, as opposed to those false teachers whose discipline of their body is their teaching's only practical expression. A pious discipline of the body is good in that it can lead to physical health, but a pure practice of abstinence does not lead to an advance in holiness of life. Discipline and exercise of the spirit, which leads to godliness, involves a promise for this life as it reflects the heavenly life, being shaped and controlled by it and bearing its impression i.e. godliness has promise for the present life because it has promise of the life which is to come. Only the life which is in Jesus is life indeed.

This is a trustworthy word and worthy of every acceptance, for with a view to this we are labouring to the point of exhaustion; yes, we are putting forth great efforts against opposition, because we have set our hope permanently upon the living God who is the Saviour of all men, especially of believers. These things be constantly commanding and teaching.

Piety toward God is indeed profitable in all things. And for this truth we strenuously and painfully labour, as athletes engaged in the games, and suffer agony and reproach, since we have a settled hope in Jesus, being the One Who is the deliverer of the human race and the true Saviour of the world, which title Caesar falsely claims, to all who believe in the salvation that He provided at the Cross, and which salvation is for all who will put their faith in Him.

Stop allowing anyone contemptuously to be pushing you aside because of your youth, but keep on becoming an example of the believers, in word, in behaviour, in divine and self-sacrificial love, in faith, in purity.

Timothy, you are younger than many of the Ephesians that you pastor, and being around forty years of age you are a relatively young man to have attained the role of superintendent and overseer. This leads others to actively despise you and treat you with contempt. You need to stop allowing this. Assert the dignity of your office even though men may think you too young to hold it and let no one push you aside as a boy. Rather continue to pattern the Christian life as an example to be imitated by others; in your teaching and verbal instructions, in a superabundance of the love that is produced in your heart by the Holy Spirit as you yield to Him, and in moral purity in your actions and motives.

While I am coming, keep concentrating on the public reading [of the Word], on exhortation, and on teaching.

Continue giving your attention to the Scriptures, reading them in the worship meetings of the assemblies, using them to teach and instruct, and then to exhort and appeal to the believers' moral sense and to their intellect.

Do not keep on neglecting the spiritual enduement which is in you, which was given to you through prophecy in connection with the imposition of the hands of the body of elders.

For the purpose of teaching and exhortation there was given you a special inward endowment directly imparted to you by the Holy Spirit. This gift was given you in accordance with prophetic intimations given to me by the Spirit as to your selection for the ministerial office which you now hold, which prophecies were repeated at your ceremony of ordination when the elders of the assemblies laid their hands on you, identifying you with them in the common work of the ministry of the Word, embracing you as one of them and one with them. While you are good at heart Timothy, you are rather shy and lacking in confidence and need me to occasionally prod you, so I say to you now, 'Stop neglecting this gift that is in you'.

Be diligently attending to these things; be constantly engrossed in them, in order that your progress may be evident to all.

So I say again, carefully practice the reading of the Word and teaching and exhortation, being constant in them, throwing yourself wholly into your ministry. Stick to your task so that you blaze a way forward, making a pioneer advance for the Gospel.

Keep on paying careful attention to yourself and to the teaching. Constantly stay by them, for in doing this you will both save yourself and those who hear you [from the false doctrines of demons].

Fasten your attention on yourself and then on your teaching, since personality goes before teaching. For the third time I say to you, continue in reading the Word and in teaching and exhortation. In doing this you and your hearers will be protected from the false teachings of abstinence, and not become entangled in these heresies.

Do not upbraid an elderly man, but entreat him gently as a father, younger men as brothers, older women as mothers, younger women as sisters, with the strictest regard to purity.

Respect those in the assemblies who are advanced in years and of an approved character, who have a respected and trusted standing, and who have long been members of the Church. Do not treat them harshly or chastise them with words, rather plead with them to please submit to you.

Be constantly showing filial reverence and respect to widows who are truly widows.

Honour and value the widows, and for those who have been but once married and who have no relatives, ensure that they have financial support. In return for their maintenance encourage them to care for orphans and for the sick and for prisoners.

But, as is the case, if a certain widow has children or grandchildren, let them be learning first to show filial reverence and respect to their own household, and to discharge their obligation relative to a recompense to their forbears, for this is acceptable in the sight of God.

Widows who do have relatives should be supported by their own family, since this is their natural duty in acting reverently in their own private household and repays a debt to their living ancestors, and which is also a service to God.

But the one who is a widow and has been left completely and permanently alone, has set her hope permanently on God, and continues constantly in petitions for her needs and in prayers night and day. But the one who lives luxuriously, lives while she is in the state of having died, with the result that she is dead. And these things constantly be commanding in order that they may be irreproachable.

But the widow who is truly alone I commend to the support of the assembly, especially the one who has always earnestly looked to her heavenly Father so that she has a settled and immovable trust in Him and continues to be devoted to Him. In contrast, the widow who lives in extravagance and wastefulness, giving herself to pleasure and leading a wanton life, though physically alive, is dead with respect to her Christian life.

But if, as is the case, a certain one does not anticipate the needs of his own and provide for them, and especially for those of his own household, he has denied the Faith and is worse than an unbeliever.

The one who does not foresee his family duties so as to be prepared and able to care for his own, practically denies his possession of faith in Jesus, since even unbelievers do such things from mere natural promptings. Rather his faith should perfect and strengthen his natural duties, since it includes the law of love, and since he has the supreme love of Jesus as an example.

Do not continue to allow a widow to be enrolled who is less than sixty years old; she must be a one-husband sort of woman [married only once], have testimony borne her in the matter of good works, if she reared children, if she showed hospitality to strangers, if she washed the saints' feet, if she succoured those who were hard pressed by circumstances, if she persevered in every good work.

You must now pick out only those widows who satisfy certain criteria as being those who are listed on the assembly's register of those who are to receive support. They should not have married more than once, be well thought of as to their conduct, those who received strangers hospitably, those who served the believers in washing their feet as they arrived for supper.

But younger widows refuse. For whenever they feel the impulses of sexual desire, thus becoming unruly with respect to Christ, they determine to marry, incurring [the reproachful] judgment [of their fellow Christians] because they have nullified their first faith.

Do not register young widows as their emotional desire to remarry withdraws them from serving Jesus in His Church, so setting themselves against Him. In their new married life they carry about with them a continuous reproach, since they initially pledged to devote themselves wholly to the service of Jesus and the Church after they became widows.

And at the same time they also learn to be idle, gadding about from house to house, and not only idle but tattlers, and those who pry into the private affairs of others, speaking the things which they ought not to speak.

The young widows also, as they visit from house to house as part of their Christian duties, are tempted by an insatiable curiosity on their part, resulting in their engaging in conversations involving idle accusations and empty charges, accusing others falsely with malicious words, and showing an interest in others' opinions so as to learn all manner of nonsense from those they meet.

Therefore, after mature consideration, I desire that the younger widows marry, be bearing children, be managing household affairs, affording not even one place of advantage from which the Adversary would be able to revile, for already certain ones have turned aside to Satan.

So, setting emotion aside, I have reasoned the matter out and have concluded that, since the whole world-position of the Church has altered considerably since its origin many years ago, that those young widows who cannot control their desires and emotions should remarry and lead responsible lives in a new household. This will prevent accusations from any who oppose and set themselves against Christianity.

If, as is the case, a certain person who is a believer has widows, let him be giving them assistance, and let not the assembly be burdened, in order that it may give assistance to those who are truly widows,

So I repeat, let only widows who have no other means of support be those who are registered with the assembly with respect to assistance, so that these may be best supported.

Let the elders that are ruling well be deemed deserving of double honour, especially those who are labouring with wearisome effort in the Word and in the teaching; for the scripture says, You should not muzzle an ox while he is treading out the corn, and, The worker is worthy of his pay.

Those elders who exhibit great capacity in wisdom in presiding over the assembly, and who teach in opposition to heresy to the point of exhaustion, let them also be financially rewarded for their services.

Against an elder do not receive a formal accusation before a tribunal, except it be upon the authority of two or three who bear testimony. Those [elders] who are sinning, in the presence of all be rebuking, in order that the rest may be having fear.

Only publicly oppose elders on the testimony of two or three believers. Those who are guilty, because of their public position, should receive a public rebuke as you wield the victorious arms of the truth so as to bring them to a conviction of their sin and ultimately to a confession, stating their agreement that they have indeed sinned. So, in seeing this, shall all the elders be led to be careful and pure in their own conduct.

I solemnly charge you in the presence of our God, even Christ Jesus, and the elect angels, that these things you are to guard without showing prejudice, doing not even one thing dominated by the spirit of partiality.

I call Jesus Who is the true God and Saviour and the heavenly angels as witnesses as I earnestly charge you; have moral courage and do not show any weakness through favouritism or through intimidation, but rather keep the law of love to all.

Be laying hands hastily on not even one [elder, that is, do not reinstate a sinning elder hastily], neither be a partner in others' sins. Exercise a watchful care over yourself with respect to your present purity.

If an elder sins, do not rush to again identify him with the assembly, rather wait until he has forsaken his sin, only then may he be restored to the fellowship. Be wary of the impulses of mere pity, since a hasty reconciliation tempts the offender to suppose that his offence cannot have been so very serious after all, smoothing the way to a repetition of the sin. I warn you that good-natured easy men cannot escape the responsibility for the disastrous consequences of their lax administration of the law, since in so doing they have a share in the sins of those who they have so encouraged to carry on sinning. And those leaders who give letters of recommendation too easily should fall under your apostolic condemnation. In all things maintain your honour and uprightness.

Be no longer an exclusive water-drinker, but be using a little wine for the sake of your stomach and your frequent illnesses.

Do not abstain from wine any longer as this will not enhance your purity, rather it imperils your own health. Drink wine for its medicinal purposes as proposed by the Greek physicians.

The sins of certain men are openly manifest to all eyes, going ahead to judgment; and in the case of certain individuals, they follow after.

The sins of some go before their perpetrator to the judgement-seat like heralds, proclaiming their sentence in advance, so that no judicial utterance is necessary in condemning them of these sins. The sins of others follow the offender to the bar of judgment and are first made openly manifest there.

Likewise, also the good works are openly manifest to all eyes, and those that are otherwise than manifest are not able to be hidden.

Similarly, works that are hidden now will come to light at the judgment-seat and be seen by all.

Let as many as are under the yoke as slaves consider their own absolute masters worthy of every respect in order that the Name of God and the teaching be not evil spoken of.

Slavery, in the current climate under the rule of Rome, is taken for granted. While the general ethics of Christianity do not allow such a thing, neither I nor the other apostles preach against it. Indeed some of you believers have slaves. In the case of believers who are slaves to unbelievers, their position being hard and disagreeable since they are owned absolutely by unloving masters who have uncontrolled power over them, I urge these to respect and honour their masters, given the position in society that these masters occupy, lest reproach be brought upon all that God is in His matchless Person i.e. since slavery is a common and accepted institution, it would hurt the cause of Christianity for believers who are slaves to rebel against their masters.

And those who have believing masters, let them not be despising them because they are brothers [in Christ], but rather be rendering them a slave's service because they are believers [Christians] and divinely loved ones [of God] who busy themselves in kindly service [to their slaves]. These things be constantly teaching and exhorting.

Those slaves who have believing masters are more conscious of their new freedom and of their equality in Jesus with their masters, but they should still carry out their duties faithfully. The believing master is in a difficult position since he is torn between the principles of a faith which he shares with his slave, and the laws of the state which he feels are not wholly wrong, and more so if the master is also a pastor of the assembly to which the slave belongs. The believing slaves are not to despise their believing masters for not liberating them, but are to do them service, and to serve them all the more since their masters are beloved by God, and since they are being kindly treated by them due to their masters loving them as brothers and appreciating the excellent service rendered to them.

If, as is the case, anyone is teaching things of a different nature and opposed to the things just mentioned, and does not give his assent to wholesome words, those of our Lord Jesus Christ, and to the teaching which is according to a godly piety, he is in a beclouded and stupid state of mind which is caused by pride, not doing any concentrated or reflective thinking in even one instance, but exercising a morbid curiosity about inquiries and quarrels about words, from which comes envy, strife, speech injurious to another's good name, malicious suspicions, protracted and wearying discussions of men corrupted in mind, and who have disinherited themselves of the truth, thinking that godly piety is a way of gain.

Others teach things that are diametrically opposed to my teaching and to what is right. These do not draw near to sound and healthy Christian teaching, being that which is free from clever but unsound reasoning and from the practice of arbitrary, unnatural restrictions, rather showing reverence and respect toward God. Their proud words raise a smoke and wrap their hearers in a mist, these teachers being devoid of a knowledge of facts and also unable to ponder the truth to any degree. They are sick in their minds, constantly questioning and debating, engaging in verbal disputes and continually causing friction. They once possessed the truth but they have, in their wandering from it and in their teaching of error, disinherited themselves, and so it has been taken away from them. Now they make religion to be a means of livelihood in that they teach that profession of Christianity is a way of material gain, suggesting to others, slaves for example, that belief in Jesus will improve their social position and worldly prospects, but this only results in their hearers becoming demoralised.

But godly piety associated with an inward self-sufficiency which is its natural accompaniment is great gain; for not even one thing did we bring into this world, because not even one thing are we able to take out. And having food and clothing, by these we shall be fortified sufficiently; but they that after giving the matter mature consideration desire to be wealthy, fall into temptation and a snare and many foolish and hurtful cravings which are of such a nature as to drown men in destruction and perdition; for a root of all the evils is the fondness for money, which certain ones, bending their every effort to grasp, have been led astray from the Faith and have pierced themselves through with many consuming griefs.

We believers are those who are independent of outward circumstances, being sufficient in Jesus alone, enabling us to maintain a spiritual equilibrium in the midst of both favourable circumstances and those which are adverse. Since we cannot take anything out of this world we did not therefore bring anything into the world, as that would require us to be separated from something we had before the creation of the world at our departure from the world. Therefore nothing the world can give is any addition to our self i.e. we are complete, though naked. Having food and clothing provided by God to protect our bodies, we are fortified against outward circumstances, and nothing of outward circumstances can injure our inner life. Some though have come to a reasoned desire to acquire riches in a planned way. This desire for riches leads to the temptation of finding any means by which to get more money than that which satisfies one's accustomed needs. It is not wrong to have an ambition to excel in some lawful department of human activity, which though it brings riches develops character, but it is wrong to have a single eye to the accumulation of money by any means.

But, as for you, O man of God, these things be constantly fleeing. But be as constantly eagerly seeking to acquire righteousness, godly piety, faith, divine and self-sacrificial love, steadfastness, gentleness.

But you Timothy, since you are a godly man, do not be like these others in any way, but always, as a habit, run from having a fondness for money, since this does more to discredit religion in the eyes of the world than does indulgence in many grosser vices. Rather, earnestly pursue morally correct behaviour and thinking, and that love which the Spirit produces in your yielded heart, along with patience, constancy, endurance, and loyalty to Jesus in the midst of the greatest trials and sufferings. Always maintain a mildness of disposition and a gentleness of spirit, accepting God's dealings with you as being good, without disputing with Him or resisting Him, which dealings also involve the insults and injuries of men as employed by God for the chastening and purifying of His children.

Be constantly engaging in the contest of the Faith, which contest is marked by its beauty of technique. Take possession of the eternal life into a participation of which you were called and concerning which you gave testimony to your agreement with the good profession [you made] in the presence of many witnesses.

I command you to be one who continuously fights as you take part in the Christian warfare against evil, and that you live a life pleasing to God. All around you is the atmosphere of the Greek games. See how intense are the struggles there, where boxers wear gloves of ox-hide with iron and lead sown into them and where losing wrestlers have their eyes gouged out. With these images in mind I tell you to be in earnest as you fight the fight of the Faith. Your fighting should be a beautiful thing to behold as you employ techniques inspired by the Holy Spirit to gain victory over sin and to live a life that pleases Jesus. In your fighting you will experience more of what this eternal life that you possess consists of, in your own life here and now. You were called into battle when you stated your agreement with the doctrines of Christianity at your baptism.

I am giving you a charge in the presence of God who is constantly preserving in life all things, and Christ Jesus, the One who in His testimony before Pontius Pilate made the good profession, preserve this commandment intact, unsullied, irreproachable, until the glorious manifestation of our Lord Jesus Christ, which [glorious manifestation] He will expose to the eyes in strategic seasons having a unique character all their own, the One who is the blessed and only Sovereign [the One having all power], the King of those who are reigning as kings, and Lord of those who are ruling as lords, who alone has immortality, dwelling in unapproachable light, whom not even one in the human race has seen nor even is able to see, to whom be honour and power forever. Amen.

There were human witnesses at your baptism, and I feel impelled to remind you that there are real, heavenly Witnesses of your ongoing conduct Whose real though unseen presence should be an encouragement as well as a check to you as you live out your Christian life. You are in the hands of One Whose protective power is universal and you have the example of One Who, as a Man, put that power to the test and was saved out of death, which example should stimulate you to similar moral courage. I command you now to be bold in fully and genuinely keeping my instruction that you oppose those who teach any other doctrine than that which you learned from me. You are shy by nature but you must develop a boldness in the Spirit Who enables you to do all that He bids you to do. Jesus will be glorified to all at His second Advent when He comes to reign for a thousand years, which appearing will be in God the Father's own personal time that is known only to Himself and which was foreordained by Him. He is the One Who is to be praised and Who has the power and ability to rule over all, blessed in His prosperity, being all that He is and possesses in His Person as deity, incapable of dying, and at home in unapproachable light i.e. wholly concealed by His dwelling, which is light.

To those who are wealthy in the present age, be giving a charge not to continue to be high-minded, neither to have their hope set upon the uncertainty of wealth, but upon God, the One who is constantly offering us all things in a rich manner to enjoy; to be doing good, to be wealthy in the sphere of good works, to be liberal, sharers with others, laying away for themselves a good foundation with a view to the future, in order that they may lay hold of that which is truly life.

We live in this present age, the now age, with all its mass of thoughts, opinions, speculations, hopes, impulses, aims, and aspirations, which atmosphere we continuously inhale. To those whose lives are subject to the spirit of the age, material wealth and possessions are believed to be the sum of all existence. Your responsibility Timothy is to charge them that they are not the lords of their own lives and that they should not be proud, nor put their trust in the things of this world. Rather they should look to God Who supplies true riches to those who believe in Jesus and who follow Him as their living example of love, which love expresses itself in Spirit-inspired acts of self-sacrificial kindness.

O, Timothy, that which was committed to you, guard, turning away from unhallowed and empty mouthings and oppositions of the falsely named knowledge, which [knowledge] certain ones announcing, missed the mark concerning the Faith. The grace be with all of you.

Guard as a sacred trust the deposit of truth I have delivered to you. Do not listen to vain babblings that are devoid of godliness. Avoid meeting or associating with those who claim to have superior knowledge, but which teaching of theirs is opposed to the Gospel, since they claim that it is by philosophic insight, rather than by faith, that humanity is to be regenerated. They say that faith is for the masses, for mere animal-men. They believe they can explain the work of creation and can account for the existence of evil. Their problem is how to develop the higher nature given the environment of matter which they say is essentially evil. These teachers place arguments against Christian doctrine and object to it. Shun and turn from all such teachers. May the free and undeserved grace of Jesus be with all who hear this letter read.

From Paul to Timothy again

Paul, an ambassador of Christ Jesus through the will of God, according to the promise of life which is in Christ Jesus, to Timothy, beloved child. [Sanctifying] grace, mercy, [tranquilizing] peace, from God the Father and Christ Jesus our Lord.

I write as an apostle of Jesus, the Anointed One of God, being He Who saves, Who paid the price for our sins by pouring out His blood on the Cross, thus satisfying justice so that we no longer face the penalty of death, He having died on our behalf. I am an apostle, commissioned as part of God's arrangements to this end, being one of the ways in which His will manifested itself, and according to His promise of life as it is offered in the Gospel, which Gospel speaks of Jesus as not only our Saviour through His work on the Cross by which we believers are made righteous, but also as our hope for the future; that we shall be like Him. I write to you Timothy, though this letter is also to be read in the assemblies committed to your charge, you whom I gave birth to in winning you to a saving faith in Jesus. I introduced you to His grace, grace that loved us and saved us by sending Jesus while we hated Him, and which grace makes us more like Jesus by the work of the Holy Spirit in our lives as we yield to Him. I introduced you also to His mercy to us, mercy in offering us His free gift of forgiveness while we were helpless and in misery in our sins, so as to remove them from us, which mercy was made way for by His grace, and which mercy I bid you be mindful of as you administer the assemblies. Now are we bound together again to God, so at peace with Him. Dear Timothy, when the sanctifying grace and the remedial mercy of God are operative in your life and ministry, then that pleasant, satisfying feeling of tranquility, comfort, and well-being will be secured in you.

I constantly have a spirit of thanksgiving to God, to whom I am rendering sacred service from the time of my forebears with a pure conscience, as unceasingly I have you in my mind in my petitions for needs, night and day, greatly longing to see you, remembering your tears, in order that I may be filled with joy, having been reminded of the unhypocritical faith which is in you, which is of such a nature as to have been at home first in your grandmother Lois and in your mother Eunice, and concerning which I have come to a settled persuasion is at home in you also; for which cause I am reminding you to keep constantly blazing the gift of God which is in you through the imposition of my hands, for God did not give to us a spirit of fearfulness but of power and of a divine and self-sacrificial love and of a sound mind.

I am continually having thanks to God, Who I serve as an inheritance from my forefathers' religious consciousness, and in which light of revelation I continue, though now this light is far brighter in the New Covenant than it was in the Old i.e. I am the result of generations of God-fearing people, so that my inborn, natural instincts are all towards the service of God, for which service God separated me from when I was still in my mother's womb. I remember your tears and those of all of the Ephesian assembly when I left there saying that none of you would ever see me again. I do have a strong desire to see you again Timothy, given the genuineness of your faith which influences you for good, in that it holds free sway over your life. Therefore I urge you to always give life to the fire that is in you, being that gift of the Holy Spirit which you received at your ordination, so that you may wisely and boldly administer the affairs of the assemblies under your charge. Your natural disposition of timidity and a certain lack of moral courage is prejudicial to your efficiency as a ruler of the assemblies. Rather, being assured of my constant thankfulness for you and of my prayers for your genuine, inborn faith, you need to exhibit a powerful force of character inspired by your divine appointment to the role, along with a love which is not soft, and an attitude of self-discipline which is opposed to all easy self-indulgence which issues in laxity of administration.

Therefore, do not begin to be ashamed of the testimony borne by our Lord, nor of me His prisoner, but be a partaker with me in my sufferings for the sake of the good news, [being a partaker of these sufferings] according to the power of God,

Maintain your confidence in Jesus' teachings as I do, even though I am a prisoner for His sake. Be a fellow partaker with Jesus and with me in our sufferings for the Gospel's sake and for the Church's sake, in the power of the Spirit, as you yield to Him.

the One who saved us and divinely summoned us in the sphere of a holy summons, not according to our works but according to His own private purpose and grace which [grace] was given us in Christ Jesus before the beginning of time,

This power that enables us to suffer hardship proceeds from Jesus' act of saving us. God effectually called us to salvation at a definite point of time and in response to which call we willingly accepted the salvation offered to us by God in Jesus. So God's calling of us should strengthen our faith with respect to the continuance of His gifts of power to us in the future, this faith that we have also having been given to us in the sovereign grace of God as part of our salvation. God's holy calling of us is not only the invitation to a holy life but also to the particular holy life which each of us who is called is expected to live, being in accordance with God's own purpose and grace, this call in no way being earned by us, so that God glorifies Himself in bestowing salvation and in the life of each person who receives that salvation. Salvation is a free gift with no strings attached. That is grace, since none of us deserve to be saved, but rather we deserve punishment for sins. This grace is given us in Christ Jesus, the gift of salvation being made possible through His death on the Cross by which He satisfied the just requirements of the law which sinners broke, thus making it possible for a righteous God to show mercy to us sinners on the basis of justice satisfied. This grace was decreed to us and bestowed on us by God before the world began, before the creation of the universe, even before eternal times, so prior to any past time conceivable by any human imagination.

but has now been made known through the appearing of our Saviour, Christ Jesus, since He not only made of none effect the death, but also brought to light life and incorruption through the good news, with reference to which good news I was appointed a herald and an ambassador and a teacher;

In Jesus' Incarnation and also in His future second Advent, and by His death on the Cross, death itself has been rendered inoperative and inactive. Though we taste death we do not look at it with any interest, it being on the periphery of our consciousness as we fix our attention on Jesus and the glories of Heaven, since we are now saved out of death by Him. In this has been revealed the hidden purpose of God; the forming of Jew and Gentile into one Body in Jesus. In the Gospel the offer of immortality comes to light and is made clear to all, which offer I proclaim in His Name, begging all people everywhere to receive His grace and mercy.

on which account I am also suffering these things. But I am not ashamed, for I know with an absolute knowledge the One in whom I have permanently placed my trust, and have come to a settled persuasion that He is of power to guard that which has been committed as a trust to me [his Christian service] with reference to that day.

I suffer because I am a herald and teacher of the Gospel. In spite of this I have not had my hopes disappointed nor am I defeated, since I am not afraid that the Gospel will not work, as it is the power of God to save all who believe. I know beyond any doubt, God in Himself being absolutely dependable in any circumstances, and I have a firmly settled faith in Him, which faith is immovable, that He is mighty and of power in Himself to do all that I trust Him to do. I know this since He keeps watch so as to defend the truth which He has deposited in me and to guard the responsibility of my preaching it, being that which He has commissioned me to do i.e. I am convinced that God is strong to enable me to be faithful to my apostolic calling which He entrusted to me, in spite of the sufferings which accompany it, until the day when I shall be summoned to render my final account at the Judgment Seat of Jesus, where my reward shall be determined with respect to the fulfilling of His call on my life.

Be holding fast the pattern of sound words which [words] from me personally you heard, in faith and love which is in Christ Jesus.

Continue within the outline of doctrine that I engraved upon your memory as I taught you in the Faith, so that you preach the same message as me. Use the same particular words I use so that the doctrinal statements of the truth remain accurate and are a norm for future teachers and preachers, which words I write down as led by the Spirit as He reveals truth to me. Maintain this adherence to my teaching according to the faith and love of Jesus.

That good thing which was committed in trust to you, guard through the Holy Spirit who indwells us.

The deposit of these beautiful words of truth which I entrusted to you, you are to keep safe and to defend, as opposed to those who defect from the Gospel. Uphold the truth in the power and ability of the Holy Spirit Who is at home in us who believe, as you yield to and cooperate with Him, allowing Him to be unrestricted in His sanctifying work in you.

You know this, that there turned away from me all those in Asia, of whom there are Phygellus and Hermogenes.

All the believers in Mysia, Lydia, Caria, and Phrygia have turned away from true doctrine and so from me also, being led astray by these two men.

The Lord grant mercy to the household of Onesiphorus, because he often refreshed me and was not ashamed of my handcuff, but when he was in Rome he sought me out with more than ordinary diligence, and found me.

Onesiphorus lost his life at the hands of Rome by reason of his visiting me in prison. Many times he brought me cooling comfort as I endured the ordeal of captivity in a Roman prison, manacled as I was to a soldier twenty-four hours a day, he not being deterred from the danger of visiting me as brought on by his being a friend of one who was a despised Christian and who was on trial for his life, but on the contrary he made an extraordinary effort to seek me out.

The Lord grant to him to find mercy in the presence of and from the Lord in that day. And in how many things he served me in Ephesus, you know by experience better [than I].

You, as the pastor of the Ephesian assembly, know even more than I do of his noble conduct in my service there too, for which I know he will be graciously rewarded by Jesus.

As for you, therefore, my child, be clothed with inward strength by the grace which is in Christ Jesus; and the things which you heard from me personally in the presence of many witnesses, these things commit as a trust to trustworthy men who are of such a character as to be capable of teaching others also.

Timothy, I am a little anxious for your future conduct in the Church. My dear son, be strong. Those things I spoke to you in person at your baptism and at your ordination, pass them on to those who you deem suitable successors to you as apostolic teachers, so as to maintain the direction of the Christian ministry.

Take your part with others in enduring hardships as a good soldier of Christ Jesus. No one when engaged in military service allows himself to become involved in civilian pursuits, in order that he may please the one who enlisted him as a soldier.

Endure hardships with me. I and other Christian workers suffer afflictions and so should you. Roman soldiers suffer in the service of Caesar, so why not you in the service of the King of kings? They focus on their military duties and do not get entangled in the occupations of civil life, so as to honour the one they are called to serve.

And if a person contends in the athletic games, he is not crowned as the victor unless he engages in the athletic contest according to the prescribed rules.

An athlete in the Greek games contends for a victor's wreath of laurel leaves, but will only receive this if he obeys the regulations governing the contest. During his ten months of training he engages in prescribed exercises and lives a strictly separated life from the ordinary legal pursuits of life, and is placed on a rigid diet. Should he break these training rules, he would be barred from engaging in the contest.

It is a necessity in the nature of the case that the tiller of the soil who labours with wearisome effort be the first to be partaking of the fruits.

And the fruit grower is the one who is the first to eat of his produce.

Be grasping the meaning of that which I am saying, for the Lord will give you understanding in all things.

Ponder the meaning of these three similes. If you cannot follow my argument, ask God for wisdom. In essence what I am saying is; firstly that you are to live a rugged, strenuous Christian life in which hardships as the result of serving Jesus are an expected thing, secondly that you are to live a life of rigid separation, not only with respect to evil things but also with respect to things that, while good in themselves, would interfere with the highest type of Christian service, and thirdly that in your efforts and labours in Jesus' service you have the right to derive financial support from this service so as to be able to give all of your time and strength to your work.

Be remembering Jesus Christ raised out from among the dead, from the ancestry of David according to my gospel [good news], in which sphere of action I am suffering hardship to the extent of bonds as a malefactor. But the word of God has not been bound, with the present result that it is not shackled. Because of this I am enduring all things for the sake of the selected-out ones [those sovereignly selected from mankind for salvation], in order that they themselves also may obtain salvation which is in Christ Jesus, together with everlasting glory.

Now plainly I show you, in a concrete example, that our suffering will be followed by glory. I have just laid stress on the certainty of reward for the servants of Jesus. Now recall His example, Jesus, the seed of David, the ideal soldier, athlete, and labourer, how He was raised from death to be crowned with everlasting glory and honour because of the suffering of death. Jesus' Incarnation and resurrection, being two truths that are especially imperilled and even denied by false teachers, are at the same time truths which, when believed and persisted in, will furnish you with the best grounds for steadfastness in your testimony to the Gospel and in your attachment to me in suffering for your faithfulness to them as I do. Jesus lived on earth, being deity manifested in human flesh, and was raised out from among the dead people to live forevermore while the rest of the dead stayed dead. Because of preaching the Gospel I suffer trouble and am treated as a criminal by Caesar Nero, but while I am imprisoned God is carrying on His work, and many have been and are now being saved through my ministry, which knowledge enables me to endure these afflictions, having the hope that more souls will in future be saved through me, and that my suffering here will also embolden those who, like me, were chosen by God and gifted with a view to the salvation of others.

Trustworthy is the word. For in view of the fact that we died with Him, we shall also live by means of Him. If we are persevering, we shall also reign as kings with Him. If we shall deny Him, that One also will deny us. If we are unfaithful, that One remains faithful, for to deny himself He is not able.

Faithful is the saying that those who are saved and endure suffering for the Gospel shall inherit eternal glories. We believers were identified with Jesus in His death and resurrection when He died on the Cross and was raised from the dead, therefore we shall live by means of Him, since He is our life, now and in the life to come. If we hold to our faith in Jesus despite undergoing trials we shall reign with Him in His Messianic Kingdom. If we do not acknowledge Him, He will not acknowledge us as His own. If we are untrue to Jesus in our Christian lives, He remains true to His nature and righteous character and requirements, according to which He cannot accept as faithful one who has proved untrue to Him, since to do so would be to deny Himself. As you know, some are now denying Him and are being unfaithful to Him.

These things constantly be reminding them, charging them in the presence of God not to be continually wrangling about empty and trifling matters, which results in not even one useful thing, since it ruins those who hear.

We are dealing with issues of life and death, so bring those whose earnest endeavour is to strive about words and issues that are of no real consequence, to a realisation of the relative unimportance of these things with respect to time and eternity, and warn them not to indulge in contentions that can destroy. We have been spoken to by the eternal Word so have been set free from a multitude of opinions.

Bend your every effort to present yourself to God, approved, a workman unashamed, expounding soundly the word of the truth.

Do your best, make haste, exert yourself with all diligence and hurry on and be eager to show yourself approved to God, being one who is of excellent quality in His service, so that when your work is inspected by Him you will not be made ashamed. As a stone mason cuts stones fair and straight so as to fit into their place in the building, so you, as a minister of the Gospel, present the truth rightly, not abridging it, not using it falsely so as to seduce people, not making it a matter of wordy strife, but treating it honestly and fully and in a straightforward manner.

But with reference to unhallowed and empty discussions, give them a wide berth, for they will progress to more impiety towards God, and their word will spread as does cancer, of whom are Hymenaeus and Philetus, the very ones who are of such a character as to have deviated from the truth, saying that the resurrection already has taken place, and are overthrowing the faith of certain ones.

In your efforts to present yourself to God as one who soundly teaches the Word, turn yourself away from vain, useless, and unholy babblings, avoiding and shunning them, since they yield nothing of benefit, being not merely empty of good but rather therefore filled with evil. These erroneous discussions will advance and grow, proceeding into ungodly teachings, their adherents showing a lack of respect for God, and left unopposed will spread like fire and will gnaw and eat away at others' faith, infecting others as gangrene spreads in the body, at last eating away at the bones.

However, the immovable foundation of God has stood and at present stands, having this seal, The Lord knows those who are His, and, Let those who name the Name of the Lord depart from every wickedness.

Nevertheless the Church has an ideal integrity, unaffected by those who only appear to belong to it, since it is firmly founded on divine knowledge, which foundation cannot be apprehended by man's intellect and by means of which the Church upholds the truth of God so that it withstands the assaults of error. The Church comprises men and women who have been sealed by God, marked so as to be recognised by Him as being His, which mark also serves as a reminder to believers that they are not their own and so are obligated to holiness of life i.e. this seal bears two complimentary aspects; that God has a superintending knowledge of His chosen, and that believers are each conscious of the relation in which they stand to God with its imperative call to holiness. To put it another way, there are two inscriptions on the foundation stone of the Church, one guaranteeing the security, the other the purity, of the Church, which two go together since the purity of the Church is indispensable to its security. So let us utter the Name of Jesus, acknowledging what that Name involves, as a confession of faith and allegiance.

Now, in a great house there are not only utensils of gold and of silver, but also of wood and of baked clay, also some which are highly prized and others which are treated with contempt. If, therefore, a person separate himself from these [the utensils held in contempt], he shall be a utensil highly prized, in a state of permanent separation, useful to the master, for every good work equipped.

I move on now from the Body of Jesus which is made up of believers only, to the visible organised Church on earth which is made up of saved and unsaved since unrighteous men steal into it. The foundation I spoke of indicates the inward, essential character of the Church, whereas the house I now speak of represents its visible, outward aspect. This mixed character of the organised Church points to its greatness. As in a great house whose furniture and equipment are of varying value, some items being treated with reverence and others with shame, so is the case with the men and women within the assemblies of God. To keep himself clean and useful to Jesus, a believer must separate himself from communion with the unrighteous ones. And you Timothy, continue in refusing to fellowship in the work of the ministry with any pastor who rejects Christian truths.

The passions of youth be constantly fleeing from, but be pursuing as constantly righteousness, faithfulness, divine and self-sacrificial love, peace, in company with those who are calling upon the Lord out of a pure heart.

Avoid the excessive desires of uncontrolled youth, since along with errors of the intellect, vices of the flesh are also harmful to you. Rather in your conduct be ever true and faithful to Jesus, all your actions motivated by the love that is produced in your heart by the Holy Spirit.

But stupid questionings, and questionings that come from an uninstructed and undisciplined mind be refusing, knowing that they constantly beget contentions.

Refuse to engage with those whose untrained mind is ever carried away with novel teachings and whose questions do not come from any trained habit of thinking, as to do so will only lead to quarrels and fighting.

And the Lord's bondslave must not in the nature of the case quarrel but be gentle to all, skilful in teaching, forbearing, in meekness correcting those who set themselves in opposition, if perchance God may grant them repentance resulting in a precise, experiential knowledge of the truth, and that they may return to soberness out of the snare of the devil, having been held captive by him, [returning to soberness so as to serve] the will of that One [God].

You Timothy, as a pastor, are a slave of Jesus. You must not wrangle or dispute with others, but maintain a mild and affable disposition. You must be patient with the ills and wrongs of believers when they err from right living, and you are to be just as tender and considerate of those who place themselves in opposition to you and to true doctrine in your seeking to correct them, since it is possible, however remotely, that they may recover themselves and awaken out of their drunken stupor, so that they might again serve Jesus.

This be constantly knowing, that in the last days difficult times will set in, for men shall be fond of themselves, fond of money, swaggerers, haughty, revilers, disobedient to parents, unthankful, unholy, without natural affection, implacable, slanderers, lacking self-control, savage, haters of that which is good, betrayers, headstrong, besotted with pride, fond of pleasure rather than having an affection for God, having a mere outward semblance of piety toward God but denying the power of the same. And these be constantly shunning.

Be keeping this in mind; before the Rapture there will be dangerous times that Christians will encounter. People in the world will be lovers of their own selves and of money, boasting and proud, refusing to enter into agreements, falsely accusing others, fierce, set against all that is just and pure and lovely, traitors, reckless, passionately pursuing evil, insolent, and with no love for God. They feign a respect for God but refuse to allow Him any access into their lives that they might be saved.

For of these are those who by means of insinuation slink into houses and take captive the minds of silly women who have been in times past heavily laden with sins, and who are at present heavily loaded down with them, who are under the impelling urge of variegated, passionate desires, ever learning and never able to come to a precise and experiential knowledge of the truth.

Out of these evil doers are certain ones who creep into houses by trickery and under false pretences, in order to bring under their control women who are easily deceived, as was Eve, due to their sin-laden conscience from which they seek the easiest method of relief. This relief is offered to them in the form of a false religion that satisfies their religious instinct but which fails to deal with the sin question and the true way of salvation. They listen to anyone who will teach them and so are caught and led by the instruction of itinerant religious quacks. These teachers sometimes endeavour to attain to the truth but are unsuccessful since they confine themselves to pursuing an intellectual understanding of the truth rather than submitting their hearts so as to receive it and resulting in their salvation.

Now, in the same manner as Jannes and Jambres set themselves against Moses, so also these set themselves against the truth, men corrupted in mind; after having been put to the test, disapproved concerning the Faith.

These false teachers, who are twisted in mind, show the same degree of hostility to the truth as did Pharaoh's magicians, and some of those in Ephesus do indeed practice magic, so are rejected with respect to Christianity.

But they shall make no further progress, for their insane folly shall become evident to all, as also their folly [namely, that of Jannes and Jambres] became evident.

These false teachers shall not advance in their activity since their teaching is senseless, being immoral in character and akin to madness. As Pharaoh's magicians were found lacking in their attempts to mimic the exhibitions of God's power through Moses, so will these teachers be undone as their doctrines prove to be without any merit or power.

But as for you, you were attracted as a disciple to me because of my teaching, conduct, purpose, faith, longsuffering, divine and self-sacrificial love, patience, persecutions, afflictions such as came to me in Antioch, in Iconium, in Lystra, what manner of persecutions I endured; and out of them all the Lord delivered me.

You, in distinction from others, cast in your lot with me, following me faithfully and conforming yourself to my example on account of my conduct.

And all indeed who desire to be living a life of piety towards God in Christ Jesus shall be persecuted.

All who are bent on living as Jesus' slave and are consistent in their service of Him must necessarily be always opposed by the world.

But pernicious men and impostors shall go on from bad to worse, leading astray and being led astray.

Those who actively oppose good and who chant spells so as to deceive, will increase and progress in their deceptions, but in deceiving others they impair their own sense of the distinction between truth and error, thus weakening their power of resistance to self-deceit and to the deceptive demands of others.

But, as for you, be remaining as you are in the things which you learned and have been assured of, knowing the persons from whom you personally learned them, and that from a very young child you know the sacred scriptures which are able to make you wise with respect to salvation through faith, that faith which is in Christ Jesus.

Stay true to what you heard from me and other ministers of the Gospel, and to what you learned from the Old Testament Scriptures which you were taught from the earliest years of your childhood, which Scriptures speak of salvation by faith in Jesus.

Every scripture is God-breathed, and is profitable for teaching, for conviction, for improvement, for training with respect to righteousness, in order that the man of God may be complete, fitted out for every good work.

Each separate passage of these Old Testament Scriptures is inspired of God, and can be used for instruction, for rebuking so as to bring to a conviction of sin and potentially to confession, for restoring to a right state of character, for the training and education of children in developing their minds and morals, for commanding and admonishing, and for the cultivating of adults' souls in correcting their mistakes and curbing their passions so as to increase the moral standards of their behaviour, that they might grow to comprise a harmonious combination of the different qualities and powers that mark out a mature believer.

I solemnly charge you as one who is living in the presence of our God, even Christ Jesus, the One who is on the point of judging the living and the dead, I solemnly charge you as not only living in His presence, but also by His appearing and His kingdom;

Hear my final charge, you Timothy, to whom I am now placing the responsibility for the care of all the assemblies and the leadership, in maintaining the Faith as delivered to me by Jesus against this background of erroneous teaching and departure from true doctrine, which departing will come to a head in the last days. I need to speak to you in strong terms since, though you have admirable moral and spiritual qualities, nevertheless you lack my dogged perseverance and moral courage, and I do so conscious that it is in the sight of Jesus our God that I so charge you, and that is also how I wish you to consider that this charge is made. Jesus will return soon and will judge, indeed He is already judging, both the Church and the nations. It is in light of His appearing so as to establish His Millennial Kingdom that I charge you as you take on the responsibilities that I have carried for many years, since I am expecting soon to be martyred.

make a public proclamation of the Word with such formality, gravity, and authority as must be heeded. Hold yourself in readiness for this proclamation when opportunity presents itself and when it does not; reprove so as to bring forth conviction and confession of guilt; rebuke sharply, severely, and with a suggestion of impending penalty. Pleadingly exhort, doing all this with that utmost self-restraint which does not hastily retaliate a wrong, and accompany this exhortation with the most painstaking instruction;

And this is my charge; I command you to announce the Word now and at once, in the manner of an Imperial Herald and spokesman of Caesar as he proclaims his commands which must be obeyed to public gatherings, but you more so in being an official herald of the One Who is the King of kings. Declare the Gospel with authority that demands respect and which commands the careful attention and proper reaction of those who listen. You are to preach the Gospel, nothing else, since this is the message given to you by your Sovereign Lord Jesus. You are to proclaim the Word when the time is favourable and also when the circumstances seem unfavourable, taking every chance you have to preach the Gospel. You are to deal with sin, both in the lives of your unsaved hearers and in the lives of the believers to whom you minister, and to do so boldly. As you do this you are to expect results, namely the salvation of the lost and the sanctification of the believers. Those who refuse to acknowledge their guilt rebuke, with, in some cases, a warning of impending penalty. Continue to rebuke sin even when there seems to be little hope of your hearers forsaking their failings, since you will have discharged your duty. It is the responsibility of your hearers to deal with the sin in their lives. You must mingle gentleness with severity in your preaching, entreating and urging acceptance of Jesus as Saviour. Bear with the obstinacy and perverseness of certain hearers and do not submit to a temptation to be angry with them, rather continue to present the truth with sound reasoning, founded on solid Christian doctrine, in a heart of Spirit-produced love.

for the time will come when they will not endure our wholesome doctrine in that they will hold themselves firmly against it, but, dominated by their own personal cravings, they, having ears that desire merely to be gratified, shall gather to themselves an accumulation of teachers. In fact, from the truth they shall also avert the ear, and [as a result] they shall receive a moral twist which will cause them to believe that which is fictitious.

You need to so proclaim the Word as there will come a defection from the Faith. Hold yourself firm against this. Those who set themselves against my Gospel are dominated by their own cravings, desiring personal gratification. Their hearers have itching ears and elect a multitude of teachers who tell them what they want to hear, not what they need to hear, and with an insatiable desire to be hearing the latest novel teaching. These teachers speak of the divinity of mankind, the relativity of truth, and the unproved hypotheses of science, rejecting the supernatural, rejecting the doctrine of total depravity and of Jesus' sacrificial atonement and of His resurrection, and of the need for new birth in Him. Rather they speak to man's pride, soothing his troubled conscience, and claiming to satisfy man's greedy, selfish desires. Their hearers not only turn their ears away from the truth, but see to it that their ears never come into contact with words of the truth, thus laying themselves open to every Satanic influence and so being easily turned aside to error i.e. their minds are wrenched out of place so that they have no freedom of thought, but have given themselves over to a delusion which incapacitates them for any independent thinking along religious lines which they might do for themselves.

But, as for you, you be constantly in a sober mood, calm, collected, wakeful, alert in all things. Endure hardships. Let your work [as a pastor] be evangelistic in character. Your work of ministering fully perform in every detail,

In view of this sad condition in the organised Church, I exhort you to do four things in connection with proclaiming the Gospel; firstly be self-restrained, rational, impartial, and cautious in all your dealings, secondly I command you to suffer any evils and troubles which come as a result of you clearly announcing the truth and of your standing against error, which persecutions may come from within the organised Church, thirdly be ever reaching out to lost souls as you teach and preach and have contact with others, and fourthly carry on your ministry through to the end, fully discharging the call on your life and shunning every temptation to laziness or neglect.

for, as for myself, my life's blood is already being poured out as a libation, and the strategic time of my departure is already present.

I am now ready to be offered and indeed am already being poured out as a sacrifice upon the service to Jesus of the believers that I have won, my sacrifice being less important than theirs, in that what I am now suffering is the beginning of the end. I have had a preliminary hearing before Nero and now expect a final hearing and then death by decapitation and the shedding of my blood, since I sense death standing by me here in this cold, damp dungeon. My work is over so my earthly life can now be taken from me as I strike my tent so as to journey heavenwards.

The desperate, straining, agonising contest marked by its beauty of technique, I like a wrestler have fought to the finish, and at present am resting in its victory. My race, I like a runner have finished, and at present am resting at the goal. The Faith committed to my care, I like a soldier have kept safely through everlasting vigilance, and have delivered it again to my Captain.

I can sum up my life in three similes; I have wrestled in the Christian warfare against evil, fighting my fight with sin to a finish so that I am resting in complete victory, and like a runner in the games I have crossed the finishing line, as my life's work is over, and the truth which Jesus deposited to me I have guarded, which work is now at an end, I having defended it against the attacks of the mystics and the Judaizers and the philosophers, and I have laid this preserved truth at Jesus' feet and am now awaiting my discharge from His earthly army.

Henceforth there is reserved for me the victor's laurel wreath of righteousness, which the Lord will award me on that day, the just Umpire [the umpire who is always fair and never makes a mistake], and not only to me but also to all those who have loved His appearing and as a result have their love fixed on it.

And as a winning athlete in the games looks up to the referee's stand, so do I look up for my eternal reward to the righteous Referee, Jesus. And all those who are longing for the Rapture with love for Jesus in their hearts, shall also receive their particular eternal reward from Him.

Do your best to come to me quickly,

I sit here alone in this dungeon and crave human fellowship and sympathy in my hour of trial, so make haste and exert every effort to visit me.

for Demas let me down, having set a high value upon this present age and thus has come to love it. And he set out for Thessalonica, Crescens for Galatia, Titus for Dalmatia. Luke alone is with me. Mark pick up and be bringing him with you, for he is profitable to me for ministering work. But Tychicus I sent off on a mission to Ephesus.

My associates who were carrying on the work in Rome have left. Demas who I trusted and who had proved dependable has deserted both the work and me since circumstances are now against me, preferring life in the world to Christian work. Crescens and Titus have set out on their own initiative to minister elsewhere, leaving just Luke of my fellow-labourers here with me, who continues to be my personal physician, sharing my hardships and privations and dangers. I sent Tychicus to take your place in Ephesus while you come here to Rome.

My cloak which I left behind at Troas in the care of Carpus, when you are coming, be carrying along, and my papyrus rolls, especially my parchments.

Bring my shepherd's cloak to me since it will keep out the cold and damp that I have to endure here. And bring my manuscripts that I might study while here and understand more of the hidden treasures in God's Word.

Alexander, the metal worker, showed me many instances of ill-treatment. The Lord shall pay him off in accordance with his evil works. And you also, with reference to him, be constantly guarding yourself, for he in an extraordinary manner set himself in opposition to our words.

Alexander, who makes silver shrines of the goddess Diana in Ephesus, has made it his mission to destroy me. Jesus will indeed punish his sin of opposition to Christianity, since evil will not always triumph over good. So you also, there in Ephesus itself, be ever wary of him, since your proclaiming of the Gospel interferes with his business.

During my self-defence at the preliminary trial, not even one person appeared in court, taking his stand at my side as a friend of mine, but all let me down. May it not be put to their account.

I defended myself before Nero, talking myself off from the charge brought against me, since there was no one with me so as to advise me or testify to my character. Those who I supposed would help me dared not appear in my defence, they having lived through Nero's last persecution which was so severe.

But the Lord took His stand at my side to render all the assistance I needed, and clothed me with strength, in order that through me the public proclamation might be heralded abroad in full measure, and that all the Gentiles might hear. And I was drawn to His side out of the lion's mouth.

But as God promises He never left me nor forsook me, rather making my needs His own and pouring His strength into me. So was the Gospel fully made known in Rome and to Caesar himself by me as I announced salvation through faith in Jesus at my trial. Thus I was saved from being humiliated at the hands of Satan since, had I not proclaimed the Gospel due to fear brought on by my having been let down by all of my earthly companions, he would have devoured me like a hungry lion.

The Lord will draw me to himself away from every pernicious work actively opposed to that which is good, and will keep me safe and sound for His kingdom, the heavenly one, to whom be the glory forever and forever. Amen. Greet Prisca and Aquila and the household of Onesiphorus. Erastus remained in Corinth, but Trophimus, being ill, I left behind in Miletus. Do your best to come before winter. There greet you Eubulus and Pudens and Linus and Claudia and all the brethren. The Lord be with your spirit. The grace be with you.

Failing to proclaim the Gospel publicly at my trial would have been an evil work on my part, but Jesus drew me to Himself out of harm's way and worked good through me, and He will continue to protect me from performing evil deeds. So I have faithfully preached the Gospel through all of my long life of hardships, trials, opposition, illness, heartache, and responsibility for the assemblies, all of these sufferings being the rule rather than the exception in my Christian experience. God's grace was sufficient for me throughout my service to Him, even right up to the end at my trial. I can now go to a martyr's death in triumph, having remained faithful to Jesus my Lord. May He similarly be with you always, ever upholding you in His grace.

From Peter

Peter, an ambassador of Jesus Christ, to those who have settled down alongside of a pagan population, sown as seed throughout Pontus, Galatia, Cappadocia, Asia, and Bithynia,

From Peter, as named by Jesus to indicate my firmness and strength of soul, in Aramaic Cephas, meaning a large detached fragment of rock, being a fragment of the massive living Rock that is Jesus seen in His deity. I am His representative, having been transformed from Simon, my birth name, into Peter, by the indwelling of the Holy Spirit at Pentecost, and armed with His credentials in the form of miracles, and on a mission; sent by Jesus to proclaim the good news of salvation by faith in Him. I write to you Christian Jews who I am not personally acquainted with, who have chosen to live among the Gentiles, outside of Palestine, and who providentially heard the Gospel declared by missionaries who fled Jerusalem due to persecution by the Jews there, and as a result put your faith in Jesus as Saviour. Consequently you yourselves have also become disseminators of the Gospel, since you now live as aliens in Satan's territory, that you might win those among whom you have been placed, from out of the world system to faith in Jesus.

chosen-out ones, this choice having been determined by the foreordination of God the Father, those chosen out to be recipients of the setting-apart work of the Spirit resulting in obedience [of faith] and [this resulting] in the sprinkling of the blood of Jesus Christ. [Sanctifying] grace to you, and [tranquilizing] peace be multiplied.

You were chosen out from mankind for God as an act of His sovereign grace, this choice being determined by His counsel and foreknowledge, He having interchanged opinions and mutually advised within the Godhead so as to come to a deliberative judgment, thus decreeing and appointing you to salvation. This resulting judgment of God was that Jesus was to be delivered into human hands to be crucified, on behalf of you who were chosen as part of the setting-apart work of the Spirit. So your salvation was enacted by the three Persons of the Godhead; the Father chose you out from among mankind to salvation, you were set apart by the Spirit from unbelief to the act of faith in Jesus, and you were cleansed from sin in Jesus' precious, sacrificial blood in answer to your becoming obedient to the Faith. Now that you believe, Jesus' grace enables you to daily follow Him in your Christian living as you yield to and depend on the Spirit, and as you so yield to Him you experience His peace in your heart.

Let the God and Father of our Lord Jesus Christ be eulogized, who impelled by His abundant mercy caused us to be born again so that we have a hope which is alive, this living hope having been made actual through the intermediate instrumentality of the resurrection of Jesus Christ out from among those who are dead,

Let us praise and speak well of the Father, the God of Israel as you were brought up to know Him, being also Father to the Saviour that He sent into the world, Jesus Christ, compelled by His merciful heart to make atonement Himself for sinners. To us who believe in Jesus, the Holy Spirit has imparted a new life, making us partakers of the divine nature and therefore children of God. Our hope in Jesus is actively alive, energising us and producing a Christian hopefulness and optimism in our hearts as we yield to the indwelling Holy Spirit. In this hope we expectantly look forward to the inheritance awaiting us in Heaven, and we experience blessing from God in this life, in view of our eternal blessedness in the next life. This hope is made possible by the resurrection of Jesus, in particular in our identification with Him in His resurrection, so that we are given new life in being born anew in Him into a heavenly inheritance. Jesus went to the part of Hades reserved for the righteous dead, but after three days was raised to life and left that place and reunited with His body glorified.

resulting in an inheritance, imperishable and undefiled, and that does not fade away, which inheritance has been laid up and is now kept guarded in safe deposit in heaven for you

As begotten children of the Father you become His heirs and joint heirs with His Son Jesus, and thus come into an inheritance, which inheritance is incorruptible since it belongs to the future life which you will share with God Himself, and which inheritance is now protected, reserved, and set aside for you.

who are constantly being kept guarded by the power of God through faith for a salvation ready to be revealed in a last season which is epochal and strategic in its significance.

You also are being garrisoned about by God's protecting care for you, an unchanging guard that is kept twenty-four hours a day, year in year out, until you arrive safe in Heaven. This protection is His response to your faith in Jesus as Saviour, which faith now rests in Him as your Preserver i.e. your faith lays hold of His preserving power, which power then strengthens your faith, so preserving you. You received your justification the moment you believed in Jesus' atoning, sacrificial death for you, you are receiving your sanctification, namely victory over sin and growth in the Christian life now, day by day, by the power and working of the Holy

Spirit in you, and you will experience salvation in the glorification of your bodies at the Rapture, when you are received by Jesus and taken to Glory.

In which last season you are to be constantly rejoicing with a joy that expresses itself in a triumphant exuberance, although for a little while at the present time if perchance there is need for it, you have been made sorrowful in the midst of many different kinds of testings

You will rejoice in exuberant triumph when you receive your glorified bodies at the Rapture, which joy will be made possible by your future glorified state and which joy is not possible now in your mortal bodies. Then you will be able to drink in and appreciate all the boundless joys of your Saviour Jesus' presence with you. This present life is little when compared to eternity, and though you experience shadows and heartache and trial now, your loving Father sees to it that you His children also have your days of sunshine even in this life. To those servants of Jesus whom He purposes to use in a larger, greater way, many trials are allowed to come, for the refining of His servant so as to make him more useful. And trials can also be for the purpose of purging sin so as to draw His servant into a closer walk with Him. Trials may come from God or, under His permissive will, from Satan, or may be the result of the believer's wrong doing, whereas temptations to do evil come from the world, the evil nature, or Satan, and these come in many forms, all of which bring sorrow.

in order that the approval of your faith, which faith was examined by testing for the purpose of being approved, that approval being much more precious than the approval of gold which perishes, even though that gold be approved by fire-testing, may be discovered after scrutiny to result in praise and glory and honour at the time of the revelation of Jesus Christ;

These trials of your faith are for your approving, resulting in your honour when Jesus appears and resounding to His praise, since your submissiveness to Him and your remaining faithful to Him in these trials demonstrates that the faith you have is a genuine God-given, Holy Spirit produced faith, which faith is to Jesus' glory when it has met the test and been approved. The fact that He finds your faith to be one which He can approve, is of far more value to Him and to His glory than the approved faith, since He has something to work with, being a faith that He knows can stand the testings and trials which may come to you. He is looking for faithful, dependable workers, not necessarily gifted, educated, cultured ones. In a similar way as to when gold is tested by fire, in which testing it has any impurities skimmed off until the goldsmith can see his face mirrored in the surface of the liquid gold showing that it is now pure, so does Jesus put you in the crucible of Christian suffering, in which process sin is gradually put out of your lives, you being thus purified from the waste matter of unbelief, and resulting in the reflection of Jesus' face in your character. Christlikeness is the Father's ideal for His children and Christian suffering is one of the most potent means to that end.

whom not having seen, you love because of His preciousness, in whom now not seeing yet believing you are to be rejoicing with an inexpressible and glorified joy upon the occasion of your receiving the promised consummation of your faith which is the [final] salvation of your souls.

Being converts of the apostles you did not see Jesus on earth during His time here while in His humiliation or during His post-resurrection ministry, yet you have a self-sacrificial love for Him, that love being a divine love which He Himself is, and this love for Him having been produced in you as part of your salvation. You know Him by the Holy Spirit Who is in you as He reveals Jesus' likeness to your spirit, so you will recognise Him in His glorified state. Your conception of Jesus is given to you by the Holy Spirit through the Word, and you can appreciate and love Jesus since you now have His nature. As you study the Word and subject yourselves to the Spirit you will see Jesus ever more clearly and vividly, and as you know Him better you will love Him better. You can have intimate, loving fellowship with Jesus as you allow the Holy Spirit control over your life, moment by moment. At the Rapture you will see Him face to face and rejoice with unspeakable joy as you receive both the salvation of your souls and deliverance from the presence of sin, in the glorification of your physical bodies.

Concerning which salvation prophets conducted an exhaustive inquiry and search, those who prophesied concerning the particular grace destined for you, searching as to what season or character of season the Spirit of Christ who was in them was making plain when He was testifying beforehand concerning the sufferings of Christ and the glories which would come after these sufferings; to whom it was revealed that not for themselves were they ministering these things which now have been reported to you through those who have announced the glad tidings to you by the Holy Spirit who was sent down on a commission from heaven, which things angels have a passionate desire to stoop way down and look into [like the cherubim above the mercy seat who gazed at the sprinkled blood and wondered at its meaning].

This salvation the Old Testament prophets investigated, as to the unique time or kind of time when this grace would appear, so as to throw light on the character of this particular and unique salvation, when one period of history would end and another begin. They searched the Scriptures for the event that the Holy Spirit was pointing to when He bore witness to the sacrificial death and the glory of Jesus, and it was revealed to them that this particular grace, which was destined for you in this age, was not for them but for those of this dispensation. This great event that ushered in a new order of things which they were looking for was Pentecost, the time when the Body of Jesus was formed; when the Gentiles would become fellow-heirs with the Jews, and of the same Body, and partakers with them of His promise in Christ by the Gospel. The prophets knew that the Gentiles were to be saved, but that the wall of separation so rigidly held in Old Testament times between Gentile and Jew was to be broken down at the Cross and that the two would become one Body, that was the mystery. Such is the Body of Christ, with Jesus as its living Head and its members being all believers of this Age of Grace which began at Pentecost and which closes with the Rapture. The angels bend down so as to look curiously and carefully into these things, peering into the mysteries of Church truth from beside it, being spectators of this salvation, this truth then being made known to them by means of the Church, it being their teacher. They watch in wonder at creatures once totally depraved, now living holy lives that glorify God. In the Church they catch the supreme view of God's love in that sinners are saved by His grace and raised to a seat in the heavenly places in Jesus, the intention of which grace was to make known to the heavenly principalities and powers, by means of the Church, the great and varied wisdom of God.

Wherefore, having put out of the way once for all everything that would impede the free action of your mind, be calm and collected in spirit, and set your hope perfectly, wholly, and unchangeably, without doubt and despondency, upon the grace that is being brought to you upon the occasion of the revelation of Jesus Christ;

In view of the fact that you are undergoing trials, yet in light of your heavenly inheritance that awaits you, be always ready and prepared in your mind, having permanently rid your thoughts of worry, fear, jealousy, hate, unforgiveness, and impurity, since these things, when harboured in the mind, prevent the Holy Spirit from using your mental faculties to their most efficient and so cause you to be stunted in your Christian growth and to impede your progress in your salvation. Thus, together with a Spirit-inspired Christian optimism, you should also have a carefree mind, living in a blessed mental state, as empowered by the Spirit, so as to be always ready and able to obey the exhortations which I will now charge you with. Firstly be restrained and self-controlled in your mind, enabling you to see things without the distortion of worry or fear et cetera. Secondly hope, with an assured expectation, in the grace that will be yours when Jesus is revealed since it is already on the way. It is as if you are at a meal and have eaten the first course of justification and are now enjoying the second course of sanctification, so that you are confident that the third course of glorification is next and will be brought to you as soon as you are ready for it, since it is on the menu.

as obedient children, not assuming an outward expression which does not come from your inner being [as a child of God] and is not representative of it, an expression patterned after that expression which you formerly had in the ignorance of your passionate desires,

As children of obedience to the Father, since you have inherited His nature, do not fashion yourselves after your former passions, since that would result in conduct that is not true to your new, divine nature. You have been saved out from the world, so do not continue to assume its habits, mannerisms, and behaviour, as this is not consistent with you being a regenerated child of God and rather hides Jesus Who should be seen in your life i.e. do not masquerade in the costume of the world.

but after the pattern of the One who called you, the Holy One, you yourselves also become holy persons in every kind of behaviour,

You have entered into a new state of being in your salvation, that of inward holiness, by virtue of the Holy Spirit residing in you. So let this inner holiness find expression in your outward lives. You have been set apart from sin to righteousness, now separated ones, saints.

because it has been written and is on record, You be holy individuals, because, as for myself, I am holy.

These words written by Moses are part of the eternal, unchanging Word of God; God, in contradistinction to anyone else, is holy.

And in view of the fact that you call on as Father Him who judges, not with a partiality based upon mere outward appearance, but with an impartiality in accordance with each individual's work, with a wholesome, serious caution order your behaviour during the time of your residence as a foreigner [a citizen of heaven living for the time being amongst the unsaved on this earth, which is foreign territory governed by the god of this world],

Since you are His children, near to Him, assured of His answering you, the objects of His special care and love, and that He does not take note of anyone's outward appearance or wealth or culture or social position or education or intellect, but rather sees your attitude and your service of Him in dependence on the Holy Spirit, in view of all this, conduct yourselves with a fear lest you dishonour Him, given that you are those who are living alongside people not of your kind, and that you are far from your heavenly home, living in a territory where the usurper Satan is reigning, and where the people are subject to him. You are being watched by them so you have a responsibility to bear a clear, ringing, genuine testimony to your Saviour by the kind of lives that you live; distrusting self, vigilant against temptation, not high-minded, and constantly aware of the sinful nature in you.

knowing as you do, that not by means of perishable things, little coins of silver and gold, were you set free once for all by the payment of ransom money, out of and away from your futile manner of life handed down from generation to generation,

You know intuitively that you were not bought out of slavery by means of mere pieces of metal. And the slavery from which you were freed was a bondage to your ineffectual attempts and unsuccessful effort to attain to the standards of God. That life was a fruitless one since it did not measure up to that for which human life was created i.e. to bring glory to Him, and being one that was continually passed down through heredity, teaching, example, and environment, you and your ancestors being born in sin and all having a totally depraved nature. From that life you were delivered.

but with costly blood, highly honoured, blood as of a lamb that is without blemish and spotless, the blood of Christ,

You were bought out of slavery to sin with the very blood of God, since deity became incarnate in humanity. For that reason, Jesus' shed blood is considered precious and highly honoured by the Father.

who indeed was foreordained before the foundation of the universe was laid, but was visibly manifested at the closing years of the times for your sake

In the councils of the triune God, Jesus was the Lamb marked out for sacrifice so as to be the Saviour of lost sinners, before even the foundations of the universe were thrown down into space by His words. You also were marked out to be recipients of this salvation that Jesus, having assumed a human body with all its limitations, procured at the Cross.

who through Him are believers in God, the One who raised Him out from among those who are dead and gave Him glory, so that your faith and hope might be in God.

You now believe in Jesus, He alone having been raised to life from among the dead who stay in death. And your belief is not a mere mental assent to His existence, but a heart faith in the God Who saves sinners in answer to their faith in the resurrected Jesus Who died for them so as to be their Saviour and Lord.

Having purified your souls by means of your obedience to the truth, resulting in not an assumed but a genuine affection and fondness for the brethren, an affection and fondness that springs from your hearts by reason of the pleasure you take in them; from the heart love each other with an intense reciprocal love that springs from your hearts because of your estimation of the preciousness of the brethren, and which is divinely self-sacrificial in its essence, having been begotten again not of perishable seed but of imperishable, through the word of God which lives and abides; for every kind of flesh is as grass, and its every kind of glory is as the flower of grass. The grass was caused to wither away, and the flower fell off, but the word of the Lord abides forever. And this is the Word which in the declaration of the good news was preached to you.

Since your souls were purified you have come to love your fellow Christians with an unfeigned love, where previously it was, in certain cases, hypocritical and insincere. Do not go back to your old associates who are still unsaved, nor look down on other believers due to their lower social standing, since either of these actions will cause you to love your fellow believers the less. Rather take pleasure in one another, liking them more than those in the world, since your fellow believers reflect the same characteristics in their personality as you, being also children of God, whereas those in the world no longer share your character. If you remain true to the Word, habitually and consistently obeying it, you will not prefer the company of your former sinful companions, but will share an unassuming heart-love for the believers, regarding all as of equal standing with you in the spiritual realm in Jesus, and also you will increasingly put sin out of your lives by the presence and power of the Spirit. Having this fondness for believers, develop also a Spirit-produced self-sacrificial love for one another, since you are all equally precious to God. This love is devoid of impatience, unkindness, envy, jealousy, boasting, pride, rudeness, selfishness, anger, falsehood, and slander, but rather bears up against all things, believing, hoping, and enduring, being a heavenly thing, glorifying Jesus, and most blessed in its results to you. So choose to submit to the Holy Spirit and to conduct yourselves in His love, and to be obedient to His eternal Word in the Gospel as was preached to you.

Wherefore, having put away once for all every wickedness and every craftiness, and hypocrisies and envies, and all slanderings,

Since a new divine life has been imparted to you, a new kind of experience is demanded of you, in that you put away, once for all, any sins that may be in your lives, separating yourselves from sin and allowing the Spirit to dominate the sinful nature in you. You need to cease from any kind of wickedness, and from pretence and deception. Rather your lives should be open and honest and easily read.

as newborn infants do, intensely yearn for the unadulterated spiritual milk in order that by it you may be nourished and make progress in [your] salvation

Since you have only recently begun your Christian life, like a newborn baby at its mother's breast, desire above all else to be fed with pure milk, with nothing added to it i.e. with the spiritual milk of the true Word of God whose only purpose is to nourish your soul so that you grow to maturity in Jesus. This hunger for the Word can only come when you put sin out of your lives, since sin in your life destroys your appetite for the Word, as does finding your satisfaction in the world. A spiritually healthy Christian is one who is hungry for the Word and for the desires of the Spirit, as he lives to serve Jesus.

in view of the fact that you tasted that the Lord is kind, loving, and benevolent;

You have tasted the Word of God and have found in it that the Lord is excellent.

toward whom we are constantly drawing near, himself in character a Living Stone, indeed by men repudiated after they had tested Him for the purpose of approving Him, in which investigation they found Him to be that which did not meet their specifications, but in the sight of God a chosen-out One and highly honoured and precious.

Now you enjoy an intimate association with God when you seek communion and fellowship with Him. Jesus was rejected by official Israel since He did not meet the requirements for its Messiah, He having lived in the midst of Israel for thirty-three years, though He is approved and dear to God.

And you yourselves also as living stones are being built up a spiritual house to be a priesthood that is holy, bringing up to God's altars spiritual sacrifices which are acceptable to God through the mediatorship of Jesus Christ.

You too are living stones since your life is in Jesus, and you are being built into His Body, the Church, of which He is the Head, so as to serve Him in offering spiritual sacrifices i.e. activities of the human spirit of man as energised by the Holy Spirit placed on the altars of your consecrated, dedicated hearts, which sacrifices God receives with pleasure. He was pleased with the animal sacrifices offered up in Old Testament times in that they spoke of Jesus, and He is pleased with your spiritual sacrifices now since He sees in them a reflection of Jesus.

Because of this it is contained in scripture, Behold, I lay in Zion a Stone, one chosen out, a Cornerstone, highly honoured and precious, and the one who rests his faith on Him shall positively not be disappointed.

Jesus, the Living Stone, our life, has become the Chief Cornerstone of the Church, being not only its Foundation but also the One Who holds the Church together. We who put our trust in Him shall not be put to shame nor defeated in this hope.

For you therefore who are believers is the honour and the preciousness [of the Living Stone], but to those who are disbelievers, the Stone which the builders repudiated after they had tested Him for the purpose of approving Him, finding Him to be that which did not meet their specifications, this Stone became a Head Cornerstone,

The preciousness of the Living Stone, Jesus, is for you who believe, but for unbelievers He is a stone of stumbling, since they refuse to allow Him to become precious to them. He was rejected by the builders of Israel, being the spiritual leaders of the nation, yet in grace God made Him a Head Cornerstone to them if they would later accept Him as such i.e. the door of mercy was not closed to them.

and an obstacle stone against which one cuts, and a rock which trips one, even to those who because they are non-persuasible, stumble up against the Word, to which [action of stumbling] they were indeed appointed.

To the unbelievers He is a loose stone in the path, which causes them to trip and cut themselves, and He is a ledge rising out of the ground as a trap set to make them stumble, He being a scandal to them. Their punishment for refusing to believe in Jesus and for being offended by Him, to which they were appointed, is to themselves be set aside in their unbelief.

But as for you, you are a race chosen out, king-priests, a set-apart nation, a people formed for [God's own] possession, in order that you might proclaim abroad the excellencies of the One who out of darkness called you into participation in His marvellous light, who at one time were not a people but now are God's people; who were not subjects of mercy, but now have become objects of mercy.

But you are now members of a God-chosen group which spans the generations, this Body having a common life and nature and descent, and in which you are kings and priests, as associated with our King and Priest, Jesus, you being set apart for His service and encircled and owned by Him in a unique, private, and personal way i.e. each of you is His unique possession. All of this is so that you might declare His excellent and gracious dealings with man and His glorious attributes that He has made known to you. And the result of your being so chosen is that you are now participants of the light that God is in His nature i.e. you are made creatures of His light by Him.

Divinely loved ones [loved by God], I beg of you, please, as aliens and those who have settled down alongside of pagan [unsaved] people should, be constantly holding yourselves back from the passionate cravings which are fleshly by nature [fleshly in that they come from the totally depraved nature], cravings of such a nature that, like an army carrying on a military campaign, they are waging war, hurling themselves down upon your soul;

You are dearly loved by the great God of the universe, He having bought you with His blood to be His children. And He, with love and humility and infinite condescension stoops to urge you, His handiwork, though He could command you; while you live amongst the unsaved, they being different from you, abstain from all fleshly lusts, since you have a testimony to maintain and a message to give. The power of your fallen nature over you was broken when you were saved, so continually put to death its sin-ward pull by the power of the Holy Spirit Who lives in you. By this means you will prevent yourselves doing the things that you used to do naturally, when you were unsaved and dominated by the totally depraved nature of man. You need to fight so as to maintain the purity of your soul.

holding your manner of life among the unsaved steadily beautiful in its goodness, in order that in the thing in which they defame you as those who do evil [namely, your Christianity], because of your works beautiful in their goodness which they are constantly, carefully, and attentively watching, they may glorify God in the day of His overseeing care.

Let your outward conduct strike the eyes of the unsaved among whom you live as being good. Behave in accordance with your inner cleansing and regeneration as a child of God, so as to give an honest testimony and picture of what you really are inwardly i.e. live in conformity to your profession of faith in Jesus. Since you are known as Christians and viewed carefully by the unsaved, you need to diverge from the things of the world and live a life of separation, since this is one of the most powerful means God has of convicting the world of its sin. The world does not like its sin being uncovered, hence the persecution which it directs against the separated believer. God attentively considers the unsaved, looking for the day when they will receive His mercy and grace so that He might, in these, visit them, and become the spiritual overseer of their souls, and on which day of their salvation, they will glorify Him because of the beautiful, separated Christlike lives of those believers that He used as one means of bringing them to Jesus, causing them to want the Saviour too.

Put yourselves in the attitude of submission to, thus giving yourselves to the implicit obedience of, every human regulation for the sake of the Lord, whether to a king as one who is supereminent, or to governors as those sent by him to inflict punishment upon those who do evil, and to give praise to those who do good;

As well as just obeying the ordinances of the human government under which you live, also have and maintain a heart-attitude that will always lead you to gladly submit to your earthly rulers. You are to do this because of your testimony to Jesus since He is a God of order.

for so is the will of God, that by doing good you might be reducing to silence the ignorance of men who are unreflecting and unintelligent; doing all this as those who have their liberty, and not as those who are holding their liberty as a cloak of wickedness, but as those who are God's bondmen. Pay honour to all, be loving the brotherhood, be fearing God, be paying honour to the king.

In doing good you will close the mouths of your enemies as with a muzzle. They lack understanding and speak without reasoning or reflection.

Household slaves, put yourselves in constant subjection with every fear in implicit obedience to your absolute lords and masters; not only to those who are good at heart and sweetly reasonable, satisfied with less than their due, but also to those who are against you;

Many of you are slaves, of whom most are working in the homes of the unsaved. Some of your masters are good and gentle, good at heart and good to you, being mild and indulgent and not unduly rigorous. Submit yourselves to such, and also to those who are unfair, surly, and hateful, they having their faces dead set against you since you are believers. Your purity, meekness, honesty, willingness to serve, and obedience is a powerful testimony for the Gospel and brings all in the houses where you work under conviction of sin. As I said before, when the world has its sin uncovered it directs persecution against the believer, so you may find that your holy conduct irritates your masters, causing them to react in an unpleasant way towards you, punishing you without provocation, though they will not sell you and buy an unsaved slave as you will serve them better. In this situation you are called to endure.

for this subjection to those who are against you is something which is beyond the ordinary course of what might be expected and is therefore commendable, namely, when a person because of the conscious sense of his relation to God bears up under pain, suffering unjustly.

Obedience to hostile masters and patience under any unjust punishment meted out by them is commendable, and in contrast to how an unsaved slave would be expected to react, since they would understandably show resentment at such ill treatment. You are to forgive these masters since God has forgiven you, and you have the example of Jesus to emulate, Who suffered unjustly at the hands of unbelievers. Also consider God's grace in that He stepped down from His judgment throne and in infinite love took upon Himself the guilt and penalty of human sin in order that He might satisfy the just requirements of His law which we disobeyed, making possible the righteous bestowal of His mercy on the basis of justice satisfied, a favour done out of the pure generosity of His heart for those who not only did not deserve to be saved but rather deserved divine wrath. This act of His at the Cross was surely beyond that which could be expected of Him, and therefore commendable, an act of such grace being foreign to the human heart.

For what sort of fame is it when you fall short of the mark and are pummelled with the fist, you endure this patiently? But when you are in the habit of doing good and then suffer constantly for it, and this you patiently endure, this is an unusual and not-to-be-expected action, and therefore commendable in the sight of God.

Suffering unjustly is to be praised and is of good report, since it is your Christlike living as used of the Holy Spirit that is convicting your masters of sin and causing them to become irate with you. Jesus Himself, as I remember only too well, was pummelled by the frenzied Jewish mob at His trial, such that His aspect was so marred from the form of man that His appearance was no longer human. Think of Him and how He reacted to those who mistreated Him, in meekness and with patience, which attitude was commendable in God's sight.

For to this very thing you were called [namely, to patient endurance in the case of unjust punishment], because Christ also suffered on your behalf, leaving behind for you a model to imitate, in order that by close application you might follow in His footprints;

God's divine call into salvation has, as an accompaniment to it, suffering for righteousness' sake, this suffering being the natural result of the believer's contact with the unsaved and their reaction towards Jesus as He is seen in the believer's life. Jesus paid the penalty of sin for lost sinners and thus He suffered for you. Now you are suffering for Him in that, by your patient endurance, you are bearing a powerful testimony to His saving grace. Think of when, as children, you would trace over written letters, slowly and with painstaking effort following the shapes of the letters of your teacher as you learned to write. So are you to plant your feet in the footprints left by Jesus in the realm of unjust suffering, and with painstaking effort to imitate Jesus in this and every other area of your personal lives, walking the same road that He walked.

who never in a single instance committed a sin, and in whose mouth, after careful scrutiny, there was found not even craftiness;

In all that He suffered Jesus did not sin, nor was there found any trickery in His words.

who when His heart was being wounded with an accursed sting, and when He was being made the object of harsh rebuke and biting, never retaliated, and who while suffering never threatened, but rather kept on delivering all into the keeping of the One who judges righteously;

Jesus' tender heart was wounded by totally depraved human nature. Continuous and worsening suffering at their increasingly insolent insults did not elicit from His lips any retaliatory words. Instead, having put the thought of any such words completely from His mind, He handed over His revilers and their revilings to His Father to take care of, in the midst of His suffering.

who himself carried up to the Cross our sins in His body and offered himself there as on an altar, doing this in order that we, having died with respect to our sins, might live with respect to righteousness, by means of whose bleeding stripe [the word "stripe" is in the singular here; a picture of our Lord's back after the scourging, one mass of raw, quivering flesh with no skin remaining, trickling with blood] you were healed,

Jesus, our High Priest and the Sacrifice, carried our sins as a burden of guilt up to the Cross. In this action Jesus broke the power of the sinful nature in the sinner when that sinner puts his faith in Jesus as Saviour. Jesus was first scourged by the Roman soldiers, and His back was so lashed that His veins were laid bare and His inner muscles, sinews and bowels were exposed. I remember seeing His flesh so dreadfully disfigured, and His face, unrecognisable, crowned with thorns. And on His bleeding, lacerated back was laid the Cross to which He was to be cruelly nailed. His blood heals our sin in that He, by one offering, put away sin forever. And through His shed blood, the Judge of the universe can offer mercy, resulting in our salvation and in there being peace between Himself and man, since justice has been satisfied at the Cross by Jesus' perfect sacrifice. And through His wounded and beaten body He obtained your healing and wholeness.

for you were as sheep that are going astray and are wandering about, but now have turned back to the Shepherd and [spiritual] Overseer of your souls.

Now, since you have received Jesus as your Saviour, He oversees your spiritual welfare, His all-seeing, loving eyes being always upon you, watching tenderly over you in order that He may nurture your spiritual growth and keep you from falling into temptations which the world, the flesh, and Satan are ever placing before you. So be ever mindful of His loving care over you and of your responsibility to always obey His Word and to continually yield to the Spirit Who is in you.

In like manner, wives, put yourselves in subjection to your own husbands with implicit obedience, in order that even though certain ones obstinately refuse to be persuaded by the Word and are therefore disobedient to it, they may through the manner of life of the wives without a word [from the wives] be gained,

Having addressed the conduct of household slaves with unsaved masters, now let me turn to wives with unsaved husbands. You seek to win your husbands to faith in Jesus but you are going about it the wrong way. Your husbands are obstinate and will not listen to reason, so your repeated giving them the Gospel is met with their stiff-necked resistance. So stop talking about it and just live a Christlike life before them. Your husbands won't be won to Jesus by your nagging, rather by your holy living. They now know the Gospel, so your Christian example will do the rest. Remain in the marriage and be submissive to your husbands, since incompatibility of religion does not justify the dissolution of a marriage, and your subjection to them will be a factor which God can use in winning your husbands.

having viewed attentively your pure manner of life which is accompanied by a reverential fear;

Your pure manner of life, coupled with your reverence and deference in obeying your husbands, will be used by Jesus to win your husbands to faith in Him.

let your adornment not be that adornment which is from without and merely external, namely, an elaborate gathering of the hair into knots, and a lavish display of gold ornaments, or the donning of apparel,

Do not depend upon worldly adornment that is immodest or gaudy or conspicuous to win your husbands to Jesus, hoping that this will please them and make them easier to influence, since your appearance will only appeal to their totally depraved nature so will actually nullify your Christian testimony. Your adornment should be such that is fitting and not diverse from your character i.e. not that of a person of the world. Do not adopt the practice of Roman women who are addicted to such ridiculous extravagance in the adornment of their hair that it is as if their whole reputation depends upon its appearance, it consisting of many tiers, making them appear as tall as a male warrior, and such that they will not touch their own heads lest they disturb it, and fear to sleep lest they spoil their coiffures unaware. The Holy Spirit does not use the styles of the world in winning lost souls to Jesus as He seeks to work through a believer. Ornate worldly displays only gratify the lust of the eyes and thus feed an appetite for sin. God seeks to glorify Himself in your personality and life since, now that you are reborn, you are made in His image, which image is the ideal medium through which He can reveal Himself. If that image is distorted or marred by artificiality, it becomes an imperfect medium and the beauty of Jesus is hidden under a veneer of worldliness. Similarly do not wear a lavish and conspicuous amount of jewellery, nor immodest clothing that attracts the eye to itself and to its wearer. Your business is to let Jesus be radiated from your life by the Holy Spirit, so do not masquerade in the behaviour and adornments of the world, since if you dress like the world and act like the world, the world will think you to be people of the world. Then when you come with the news of the Gospel, your message will fall on deaf ears.

but let that adornment be the hidden personality in the heart, imperishable in quality, the adornment of a meek and quiet disposition, which is in the sight of God very costly.

So you should depend upon an adornment that proceeds from your inner spiritual being and that is representative of your inner spiritual life. Your personality is made beautiful by the ministry of the Holy Spirit in glorifying Jesus and in manifesting Him in and through your life. As Jesus only once ever described Himself; as being meek and lowly in heart, so you too should have a meek and quiet spirit, which attitude is of great value to God. To depend on physical beauty or clothing in order to make a favourable impression on others, shows a realisation by that one that they lack those personal and spiritual qualities that make for a virile Christian character. It is a principle on which God operates that adornment should proceed from within. Consider God Himself, Who is clothed in light, which light was revealed to us when we saw Jesus transfigured on the mountaintop such that His face shone like the sun. Or consider Adam and Eve who lost their covering of glory when they fell into sin, leaving them ashamed and uncovered. And consider Jesus when He appeared to us after His resurrection, clothed with glory, so that we were afraid, thinking that we were seeing a spirit. At the Rapture our transformed bodies will shine with glory and have no need of clothing, as was the case when Adam was first created by God. For now, your chief adornment should be Jesus, as manifested in and through you by the Spirit. Having said all of this, I do not imply that you wives are to dress in austere and drab attire, since this would also make you conspicuous, rather that your apparel be neat and in good taste. True faith in Jesus is something joyful and expresses itself in colour while at the same time being appropriate. Pay careful attention to the appearance of your hair and to the jewellery and clothing that you wear, but guided by the principle that your chief adornment must be Jesus, so that everything about your physical appearance is in keeping with His sweetness, simplicity, and purity, and so that nothing attracts from Him i.e. you are to appear beautiful without detracting from His beauty, with a character of appearance that does not attract attention to yourself, being apparent but not obtrusive, so as to be in keeping with the sanctifying work of the Holy Spirit in your life. Then Jesus will be seen in your life and even your physical adornment will reflect Him, bringing glory to God.

For thus formerly also the holy women, the ones whose hope is directed to and rests in God, were accustomed to adorn themselves, putting themselves in subjection with implicit obedience to their own husbands,

Subjection to your husbands as a habit of life is another adornment of the Christian woman who is set apart from the world and whose hope rests in Jesus, nowadays just as much as in times of old.

as Sarah was in the habit of rendering obedience to Abraham, calling him lord, whose children [namely, Sarah's] you become if the whole course of your life is in the doing of good, and you are not being caused to fear by even one particle of terror.

The whole tenor of Sarah's life was one of obedience to her husband, and she honoured him with wifely courtesy in recognition of his authority over her. So let her become your mother in this respect, by your doing good as a habit of life, so that your unsaved husbands may not be aroused to anger by your behaviour and cause you to fear them.

Husbands, in like manner, let your home life with them be governed by the dictates of knowledge, they being the weaker instrument, the feminine, holding in reserve for them particular honour as to those who are also fellow-inheritors with you of the grace of life, and this, in order that no [Satanic] inroads be made into your prayers.

And you husbands, recognise with intelligence your marriage relation, deeming your wives which God has given to you as precious, treating them with honour, and having a special place in your hearts for them. You should each treat your wife with special deference, courtesy, respect, and kindness, realising that she is just as much an instrument of God as you are, to be used by Him to His glory in the same manner that you are. You are joint-heirs together of eternal life, Jesus having died for her as well as for you, and her soul is just as precious in the sight of God as yours is. I realise that in the society in which you live women are given a low place and are not held in high esteem nor given respect or reverence or honour, so in this matter, as in other things, you are to separate from the world's custom. If you fail to honour your wives, your united prayer times, as husband and wife, will be interrupted and reduced in their intended power.

Now, to come to a conclusion. Be all of you like-minded. Be sympathetic. Have a brotherly affection for one another. Be tender-hearted. Be humble-minded,

To conclude my exhortations to the various classes of you, be all of one mind in maintaining a unity of thought on both the major, important points of Christian doctrine and on your required conduct within the Body of believers. Have fellow-feelings with one another, whether they be of joy or of sorrow, avoiding all jealousy. Be brethren who are loving, being fond of each other, and affectionate. In this hard-hearted society in which you live, be full of pity as the love of God overflows out of your hearts to others. And always be courteous, having, each of you, a modest opinion of yourself.

not giving back evil in exchange for evil, or verbal abuse in exchange for verbal abuse, but instead, on the contrary, be constantly blessing, since for this very purpose you were called, that you might inherit a blessing. For he who desires to be loving life and to see good days, let him stop the natural tendency of his tongue from evil, and the natural tendency of his lips to the end that they speak no craftiness,

He who is loving life and wishes to continue to do so, let him refrain from his natural inclination to retaliate when spoken ill of or when verbally abused, but rather speak words that are always pleasant and reasonable, gracious and sweet and kind.

but let him rather at once and once for all turn away from evil and let him do good. Let him seek peace and pursue it,

Decide to always shun and avoid evil, bending aside from your path whenever you see evil approaching. Direct your steps towards peace and run down that road.

because the Lord's eyes are directed in a favourable attitude towards the righteous, and His ears are inclined unto their petitions, but the Lord's face is against those who practice evil things.

God looks favourably on you and His ears are into your prayers as He bends down to listen earnestly to you His child, eager to answer your requests and to come to your aid. So He is close to you, and there is no necessity for you to have to plead with Him in order for Him to answer, since you are guaranteed His favourable response, He being more desirous to answer you than you are to have your prayers answered.

And who is he that will do you evil if you become zealots of the good?

Seeing that God takes such good care of you, the righteous ones, who is he that will harm you? In the midst of your current persecution and suffering, as a result of your righteous lives and your earnest desire of good, together with God's care of you, your blessedness will be such as to override all the malice of your persecutors and make your suffering itself to be a joy.

But if even you should perchance suffer for the sake of righteousness, you are spiritually prosperous ones. Moreover, do not be affected with fear of them by the fear which they strive to inspire in you, neither become agitated,

If matters, in spite of this prophetic note of victory that no one can harm you, should lead to your actual suffering for righteousness' sake, still is your spiritual state one of prosperity, since Jesus pronounces that all who undergo such persecution are blessed with a great, eternal reward in the Kingdom of Heaven.

but set apart Christ as Lord in your hearts, always being those who are ready to present a verbal defence to everyone who asks you for a logical explanation concerning the hope which is in all of you, but doing this with meekness and a wholesome serious caution,

Dedicate your hearts to Jesus, as Yahweh, the Anointed One, your long-awaited Messiah, giving Him first place in your obedience of life, He being your Master and your Resource and Defender when persecution comes. Have your defence made ready for when charges are brought against you by your persecutors, so that you can talk the Gospel off from the charges preferred against it by presenting a verbal defence for it. But do so in a spirit of meekness and with fear in your hearts, following in the footsteps of Jesus, lest you offend Him through falling to temptation or pride, and ever wary of the deceitfulness of the human heart and of the insidiousness and inward, corrupt power of the sinful nature.

having a conscience unimpaired, in order that in the very thing in which they defame you, they may be put to shame, those who spitefully abuse, insult, and traduce your good behaviour which is in Christ;

In addition to meekness and fear you must also have a good conscience, so that your persecutors' misrepresentation of believers and of the Gospel will be shown to be wrong by the testimony of your life and your words. Maintain therefore behaviour that is in Jesus, in that He is the centre and circumference of all of your thoughts, words, and actions.

for it is better when doing good, if perchance it be the will of God that you be suffering, rather than when doing evil.

If you are called to suffer persecution for doing well, better that than to suffer for wrongdoing.

Because Christ also died once for all in relation to sins, a just One on behalf of unjust ones, in order that He might provide you with an entrée into the presence of God, having in fact been put to death with respect to the flesh [His human body], but made alive with respect to the spirit [His human spirit],

Let me now encourage you that blessing will always follow suffering for well-doing, as proved by Jesus' resurrection and consequent glorification in view of His suffering for sinful humanity. Your sufferings now are also in relation to sin, though yours are a natural consequence of your doing good, whereas He, being innocent, died in behalf of the guilty. He died in order to bring us to the Father, His sacrifice for us removing the barrier to accessing Him, and now He leads us into the Father's presence Himself, we being dressed in His righteousness, so that we can stand in a place of unlimited favour before the Father. Now let me address what happened on the Cross and what happened between then and His resurrection from the tomb. On the Cross, when Jesus prayed "My God, my God, why have you abandoned and deserted me, letting me down and leaving me helpless", His prayer was unanswered by the Father, His fellowship with Him having been broken since the sin of man was laid on Him so that He was made a curse for us. Throughout Jesus' ministry on earth, every word that He spoke, every miracle that He performed, and the sinless and wonderful life He lived, was done in dependence upon and in the energy of the Holy Spirit, so that He was able to offer Himself at the Cross without spot, to become the sacrifice that the Father would accept as an atonement for sin. But on the Cross, the Holy Spirit also abandoned Jesus just as surely as did the Father, withdrawing His sustaining presence while Jesus was suffering on the Cross. Thus the Holy Spirit ceased keeping alive in divine life the human spirit of Jesus, which spirit, though sinless, became dead, the life-giving power of the Holy Spirit having ceased to energise it. So in the day time of His sufferings, from the third hour until the sixth hour, and in the night season of His sufferings, from the sixth hour until the ninth hour, when a darkness came upon the whole land, His human spirit was devoid of the life-giving ministry of the Holy Spirit, and the Father would not hear Him. But then, sin having been paid for, so that the atonement was looked upon as complete, Jesus prayed that He might be raised from the dead, and the Holy Spirit returned to make alive again His human spirit, since that prayer could now be answered by Him, and fellowship between Jesus and the Father was restored. Then Jesus triumphantly shouted "It has been finished and stands complete! The price has been paid! Father, into Your hands I entrust my spirit", and He laid down His head, and His human body died on the Cross.

by which [human spirit] also having proceeded, He made a proclamation to the imprisoned spirits

Then Jesus, in His disembodied state, in His human spirit, journeyed to Tartarus, the place where the demons, the fallen angels, are kept bound in everlasting chains under darkness, and there He proclaimed to them His victory over Satan, resulting in their everlasting condemnation.

who were at one time rebels when the long-suffering of God waited out to the end in the days of Noah while the ark was being made ready; in which eight souls were brought safely through [the time of the deluge] by means of the intermediate agency of water,

The sin of these angels was committed just prior to the Flood, and they were not spared at that time, as neither was the pre-Flood world, except for Noah and his family. The angels' sin was, having abandoned the high Heaven and the holy eternal place, to have defiled themselves with women. They assumed bodies like that of human beings and then gave themselves over to fornication in going after flesh of another kind, so transgressing the limits of their own kind and invading the realm of another being. They sought after that which is unnatural in order to mingle two different orders of beings into one, one that was partly human, partly superhuman. This mingling, which resulted in giants with superhuman strength, being the men of ancient renown, warranted the almost total extermination of all who were upon the earth. Satan's plan in all of this was to defeat the divine plan of the Incarnation and substitutionary atonement of Jesus since, if he had succeeded, God would not have incarnated Himself in a race that was part angel and part man. The last Adam was to be God the Son come in a human incarnation so as to answer, in His humanity, to the humanity of the first Adam. Thus God, in completely exterminating the race and saving Noah and his family, prevented the spread of this unlawful mingling of angelic and human natures, so allowing the Incarnation to take place. This is what Jesus proclaimed to these fallen angels; that in His Incarnation and His sacrifice on the Cross, He had, despite their efforts, defeated the scheme of Satan to defeat His purpose i.e. it was a proclamation of His total victory. The waters of the Flood saved Noah and those in the Ark. What had become of the rest of the human race was drowned because they were not rightly related to the waters, whilst those in the Ark were saved because they were correctly adjusted to those same waters. Similarly the righteousness of God that banishes forever from His presence those who reject it because they refuse to place their faith in Jesus, saves and keeps saved forever those who accept God's righteousness at the hands of Him Who perfectly satisfied His just law which we broke, by stepping down from His judgment throne to take upon Himself our sin and penalty, thus satisfying His justice and making possible the righteous bestowal of His mercy. By faith in Jesus' blood we stand in a perfect righteousness, being Jesus Himself.

which [water] also as a counterpart now saves you, [namely] baptism; not a putting off of filth of flesh, but the witness of a good conscience toward God, through the resurrection of Jesus Christ who is at the right hand of God, having proceeded into heaven, there having been made subject to Him, angels, and authorities, and powers.

The waters of the Flood are a picture of the waters of baptism, which are a counterpart to your real salvation in Jesus. Similarly Old Testament sacrifices were counterparts to the reality of Jesus' sacrifice, the act of making them being just an outward testimony that the one so offering was placing his inward faith in the Lamb of God, of Whom these sacrifices were a type i.e. their faith leaped the centuries to the time when God would offer the Sacrifice that would pay for their current sin. Baptism is the outward testimony of the believer's inward faith by which, in answer, salvation is given to him. Baptism itself does not clean the soul nor regenerate the believer to new life, rather it is by being identified with Jesus in His resurrection that you are saved and made alive.

Therefore, in view of the fact that Christ suffered with respect to the flesh, you also yourselves put on as armour the same mind, because the one who has suffered with respect to the flesh has done with sin,

So now, I exhort you to arm yourselves with the heaviest spiritual armour and to take up your spiritual weapons, having the same mind that Jesus had regarding unjust punishment, as you endure persecution. The fact that you are being persecuted is an indication of the fact that you have ceased from sin, which ceasing antagonises the world against you. Since, in salvation, you have been released from sin's compelling power, you should react to unjust suffering as a saint would, rather than as a sinner would.

with a view to his no longer living the rest of his time while in his physical body in the sphere of the cravings of men, but in the sphere of the will of God.

The power of sin is broken in you so that you are no longer to live the rest of your earthly life in human lusts, but in obedience to God's purpose for you.

For adequate has been the time that is now past and done with for you to have carried to its ultimate conclusion the counsel of the pagans [the unsaved], conducting yourselves as you have done in disgusting sensualities, in cravings, in wine-guzzlings, in carousals, in drinking bouts, and in unlawful idolatries,

The time has passed by and is closed and fully accomplished for practicing the things that you used to do before you were saved. You died with Jesus and have been raised to newness of life, meaning that things that are not in accord with the Gospel have passed away for you, whether habits, associations, places, or amusements. All these things, being the desires of the world, are forbidden in the new life you are now living as a Christian. No longer do things that shock public decency, and reject all sinful desires. Stop participating in festivities where they consume an overflow of wine, being ecstatic and wild revelries, and stop engaging in practices that are such that, even given the sinful excesses of current customs, Roman law forbids.

in which they think it a thing alien to you that you do not run in a troop like a band of revellers with them in the same slough of dissoluteness, speaking evil of you,

The worldly sinners are mystified that you no longer join them in the same overflow of depravity that sinks them deep into moral degradation and spiritual dejection and from which they cannot free themselves, they living a totally abandoned, sensual, recklessly extravagant life, but rather that you now hate those things that you once loved, their power over you in your totally depraved nature having been broken, and that you now love the things that you once hated, according to your new divine nature.

who [namely, the unsaved] shall give an account to the One who is holding himself in readiness to judge the living and the dead.

These who so speak evil of you shall have to speak in their own defence before He Who judges all as to their righteousness and their deeds.

For, for this purpose also to those who are [now] dead was the good news preached, in order that they might be judged according to men with respect to their physical existence, but live according to God with respect to their spirit existence.

You are being persecuted for making Jesus the Lord of your lives, and you slaves are being unjustly punished because of your Christian testimony, so I have exhorted you as to how to now behave, and of the necessity of having Jesus' mind while you are suffering this disapproval for His Name. In light of all of this, be encouraged that those believers who have died, being they who believed the Gospel and consequently were judged by men in the form of persecution, that these who were indeed so judged by the world and who died as martyrs, that now, in Heaven, they live according to the Gospel with respect to their spirits, there serving Jesus in the future life. In a few moments I will write more about the glory of suffering for righteousness' sake.

But of all things the end has come near. Be of sound mind therefore, and be calm and collected in spirit with a view to [giving yourselves to] prayer;

Of all things the end is at hand. So be tranquil in spirit, since this is conducive to praying, and results in prayer. The believer whose mind is crowded with fears and worries, and whose heart is never at peace, will not do much praying.

before all things in order of importance, having fervent love among yourselves, because love hides a multitude of sins.

Extend each of you your love so that it reaches all the others of you, giving yourselves each for the benefit of the others self-sacrificially. This love is a prerequisite to all proper exercises of Christian duty, since courtesy and generosity alone, without a heart of love, are cold and harsh. Love makes all the other virtues what they should be. This love will not publish abroad others' failings, but will cover them up from the sight of others.

Show hospitality to one another without murmuring.

Be friendly to strangers since, due to persecution, or due to their travels in the service of Jesus, believers may come to you in need of food and shelter.

In whatever quality or quantity each one has received a gift, be ministering it among yourselves as good stewards of the variegated grace of God. If anyone speaks, as utterances of God let them be. If anyone ministers, let him minister as out of the strength which God supplies, in order that in all things God may be glorified through Jesus Christ, in whom there is the glory and the power forever and ever. Amen.

Responsibly and properly use the special spiritual enablements that were graciously given to you by Jesus so as to discharge the special duties to which He called you in the household of the assemblies. Thus shall Jesus be glorified in His Church.

Divinely loved ones [divinely loved by God], stop thinking that the smelting process which is [operating] among you and which has come to you for the purpose of testing [you], is a thing alien to you,

At this time, when you are suffering persecution, let me remind you that you are loved with all the love in God's heart. This suffering is a natural and expected thing in view of the world's hatred of Jesus and, therefore, of any who bear His Name and reflect Him in their life. And in this suffering your lives are being purified, as if by fire, so it is within His plan for you, in order to rid your lives of sin and to make you more like Jesus.

but insofar as you share in common with the sufferings of Christ, be rejoicing, in order that also at the time of the unveiling of His glory, you may rejoice exultingly.

In this suffering rather, you should rejoice, since you are partaking in Jesus' sufferings for righteousness' sake; sufferings which He endured prior to the Cross and sufferings which you now are also experiencing.

In view of the fact that you have cast in your teeth, as it were, revilings because of the Name of Christ, spiritually prosperous [are you], because the Spirit of the Glory, even the Spirit of God, is resting with refreshing power upon you.

You are being reproached because of your testimony to Jesus so you are blessed, since this is an indication of the spiritual prosperity of your lives i.e. the world does not persecute worldly, and so impoverished, Christians. This reproach is also an indication that the Holy Spirit is resting on you and refreshing you i.e. it is proof that He has taken over your battle with sin and is producing His own fruit in your lives and causing you to live lives which please God, toward which the world then hurls its venom and hate.

Now, let no one of you continue to be suffering [reproach] as a murderer or a thief or an evildoer or as a self-appointed overseer in other men's matters.

Stop now from behaving as you used to, in order that your sufferings are purely those which come as a result of your righteous living and not as a result of continuing to act in the sinful ways of your life before you were saved.

But if he suffer [reproach] as a Christian, let him not continue to be ashamed, but let him be glorifying God because of this name,

If though, you suffer, for honouring Jesus as Lord, He being the One Who will one day come back and take the government of the world upon His shoulder, rather than honouring Caesar as lord, he being the man who now exerts dominion over the world and who demands to be worshipped, do not be ashamed. The cost of lifting the Name of Jesus and of proclaiming Him to be above Caesar is to suffer in these bloody persecutions, in which I am prepared to die for my Lord, Jesus.

for the time is now, of the judgment beginning at the house of God. But if it start first with us, what shall be the end of those who are not obeying the good news of God?

The judgment of these short-term persecutions is a disciplinary one, designed to purify the lives of the believers in the Church. From this judgment, as a starting point, the judgement proceeds to those who reject Jesus, which judgment is eternal.

And if he who is righteous is with difficulty being saved, he that is impious and a sinner, where shall he appear?

Since it is necessary for God to purify the lives of believers by these drastic means, namely, persecution and suffering, what can be said as to the position of the unsaved in relation to Him? If the righteous need disciplinary judgments, how much more will the unrighteous merit the wrath of God, Whose offer of righteousness they have spurned and rejected.

Therefore, also let those who are suffering according to the will of God be constantly committing the safekeeping of their souls by a continuance in the doing of good to a faithful Creator.

So I encourage you who are undergoing persecutions, in view of the fact that these are allowed to come by God and are designed to purify your lives, that you have every reason to trust Him to take care of you through all of your sufferings.

Elders therefore who are among you, I exhort, I who am your fellow elder, and the one who saw the sufferings of the Christ and who has been retained as a witness to bear testimony concerning them, who also am a fellow partaker of the glory which is about to be unveiled;

I appeal to you elders, as one being similarly an elder, I therefore being equal in position within the Church to you, and as one who has been called to be an official witness by God to testify to Jesus' sufferings.

shepherd the flock of God which is among you, doing so not by reason of constraint put upon you, but willingly according to God; not in fondness for dishonest gain but freely,

Elders, tend, feed, guide, and guard those under your spiritual charge, pasturing and overseeing them. Do not commercialise your ministry.

nor yet as lording it in a high-handed manner over the portions of the flock assigned to you, but as becoming patterns for the flock.

Do not be autocratic in your behaviour as you discharge your God-ordained authority, but rather exercise your administration properly over the believers assigned to you by lot, so as to be an example to the entire flock in your pastoral conduct, modelling the life and ministry of the Chief Shepherd, Jesus.

And when the Chief Shepherd appears, you shall receive the victor's unfading crown of glory.

Unlike the leafy crowns given to victorious runners at the games or the garlands of flowers given to brides, your crown, given to you by your Shepherd, Jesus, will never fade, unto all eternity.

Likewise, younger ones, be in subjection to the elders.

You organised groups of youths within the assemblies I exhort each of you to be in obedience to the group of elders in your local assembly.

Moreover, all of you, clothe yourselves with humility toward one another, because God opposes himself to those who set themselves above others, but gives grace to those who are lowly.

All of you put on humility as a working virtue so as to make all the other virtues what they should be, since pride in a believer renders his otherwise good character to be of little or no value. Pride summons God's armies as He sets Himself in array against that proud believer. Rather follow Jesus' example of maintaining a lowly attitude towards others.

Permit yourselves therefore to be humbled under the mighty hand of God, in order that you He may exalt in an appropriate season,

The humbling process which God is using is the persecution and suffering through which you are now passing. I exhort you to react to this in a God-honouring way, being submissive to the disciplining which He is using in order to make you more humble. In accompaniment to this exhortation I comfort you with the hope that this humility that results from your submission is the prerequisite that God demands before He will exalt you to a high place of privilege and honour in His service, and in due time He will so exalt you.

having deposited with Him once for all the whole of your worry, because to Him it is a matter of concern respecting you.

The persecutions you are now suffering give you abundant opportunity to sin by worrying. So I exhort you, while you are being humbled, to cast all of your anxiety upon God i.e. resolve to cast once-for-all the whole of your future worries upon Him, so that when things occur that would otherwise worry you, you will not worry. Anxiety is in opposition to true humility before God, and unbelief is an exalting of self against Him, in depending on self and failing to trust Him. Since you are His great concern, why worry? He is more concerned about your welfare than you could possibly be. And since the humbling process has been allowed to come to you in His permissive will, and since He is using it to accomplish His purpose in your lives, He has it under control and has you in His care and concern, so again, why worry?

Be of a sober mind, be watchful. Your adversary who is a slanderer, namely, the devil, as a lion roaring in fierce hunger, is constantly walking about, always seeking someone to be devouring.

Be mentally self-controlled and stay awake, since your enemy Satan, who accuses, lies, and defames you, and who acts maliciously, insidiously, and with hostility against you, is always on the prowl.

Stand immovable against his onset, solid as a rock in your faith, knowing that the same kind of sufferings are being accomplished in your brotherhood which is in the world.

You cannot overcome the devil by taking the offensive against him, yet you can stand your ground in the face of his attacks by exercising your faith that depends on the strengthening and protecting power of God. So be courageous in battle and maintain a solid front and, as believers, keep close phalanx, standing together, heavily armed, as the Body of Jesus, as immovable as a tower, in the energy of the Spirit.

But the God of every grace, the One who summoned you in Christ with a view to His eternal glory, after you have suffered a little while, shall himself make you complete, shall establish you firmly, shall strengthen you, shall ground you as on a foundation. To Him let there be ascribed this power forever and forever. Amen.

God is the source of all spiritual comfort and help for every occasion. You freely decided to respond to His call on your life, as the Spirit enabled you. He called you to salvation, which is in Jesus alone, so that He may derive glory for Himself by virtue of your being saved. And He Who called you in His grace will supply all needed grace until you are ushered into the Glory. God's eternal glory is involved in His keeping a believer in salvation, thus you are eternally secure, through the power and work of your Saviour, Jesus. After this current time of persecution you will experience His power in building you up in your faith, adjusting you into right relationship and perfecting you, so as to be the more fruitful in your Christian life and the more useful in His service, there being no defect remaining in you, so that nothing may shake you and so that you may overcome every adverse force.

Through Silvanus, the faithful brother, which is my estimate of him, briefly I am writing to you, exhorting and testifying that this is the true grace of God, in which stand.

I finish this letter by my own hand, the rest having been dictated by me to Silvanus, who you know well and who brings this to you, and who I can recommend to you. In all that I have written, I beg of you to please be established.

The [church] in Babylon, chosen out with you, sends greetings; also Mark, my son. Greet one another with a kiss of love. Peace be with you all who are in Christ.

The assembly here on the Euphrates greets you. As is the custom after prayers, welcome each other with a kiss, men kissing men, women kissing women, so as to soften and level your relationships one with another. May the peace which only Jesus brings fill your hearts.

From Peter again

Simon Peter, a bondslave and an ambassador of Jesus Christ, to those who have been divinely allotted like precious faith with us by the equitable treatment of our God and Saviour, Jesus Christ.

From Peter, as named by Jesus to indicate my firmness and strength of soul, in Aramaic Cephas, meaning a large detached fragment of rock, being a fragment of the massive living Rock that is Jesus seen in His deity. I am His representative, having been transformed from Simon, my birth name, into Peter, by the indwelling of the Holy Spirit at Pentecost, and armed with His credentials in the form of miracles, and on a mission; sent by Jesus to proclaim the good news of salvation by faith in Him. I am now the most abject and servile type of slave to Jesus, having been born into servitude to Him at the time of my regeneration, and Who I now serve lovingly, willingly, and gladly, my will now being swallowed up in His sweet will, bound to Him until death, therefore for ever since He can never die and since my life is in Him, now disregarding my own interests, and serving Him with an abandon such that nothing matters about me so long as Jesus is glorified. He is deity and human, and He sacrificed Himself on behalf of humanity, coming to earth as the Incarnate and Anointed One. All who place their trust in Him exercise a faith that is given by God to those who are chosen out to salvation, and which faith is part of the salvation which is given the believer. You were chosen out from mankind for God as an act of His sovereign grace, this choice being determined by His counsel and foreknowledge, He having interchanged opinions and mutually advised within the Godhead so as to come to a deliberative judgment, thus decreeing and appointing you to salvation. This resulting judgment of God was that Jesus was to be delivered into human hands to be crucified, on behalf of you who were chosen as part of the setting-apart work of the Spirit. So your salvation was enacted by the three Persons of the Godhead; the Father chose you out from among mankind to salvation, you were set apart by the Spirit from unbelief to the act of faith in Jesus, and you were cleansed from sin in Jesus' precious, sacrificial blood in answer to your becoming obedient to the Faith. This heart-faith in Jesus as Saviour, while not given in the same measure to all is nevertheless of equal honour and of equal value to all those who receive it, admitting all believers to the same Christian privileges, it being priceless and of the highest honour. You Gentiles then have been given this faith by divine allotment, together with the Jews, through the righteousness of our God, Jesus, so that there is no partiality on His part.

[Sanctifying] grace to you and [tranquilizing] peace be multiplied in the sphere of and by the experiential knowledge [which the believer has] of God, even Jesus, our Lord.

Now that you believe, Jesus' grace enables you to daily follow Him in your Christian living as you yield to and depend on the Spirit, He bearing fruit through you. And as you so yield to Him you experience His peace in your heart. Your knowledge of God therefore stems from an intimate and personal relationship with Him by means of the ministry of the Holy Spirit, as well as by study of the Word, this knowledge of Him producing grace and peace, with the goal of your completely acquiring all truth yourself and of your unreserved acquiescence in His will.

Seeing that all things to us His divine power has generously given, the things which pertain to life and godliness, through the experiential knowledge [which the believer has] of the One who called us [into salvation] by means of His own glory and virtue,

And also, with respect to this grace and peace, consider God's inherent omnipotence through which He has bestowed in large-handed generosity and pure grace to you, all that is with reference to godliness, with no strings attached, and which things are now your permanent possession, this godliness being a reverence rightly paid and directed to God, Who is supremely worthy, in your conduct, conversation, sacrifice, and prayer. In this godliness we confess the one living and true God, our life corresponding to our knowledge of Him, and we seek a greater intensity of living in a deeper and more submissive communion with Jesus Himself, in order to experience absolute fullness of life, being the life which belongs to God, and which life He imparts to us, so transforming our inner being and thus our behaviour. Jesus called us in His own private, unique possession of glory, the attracting power of His beautiful life calling us to salvation, we beholding His glory in the evidences of the miraculous knowledge and power which He exhibited at the time of our call, His moral greatness overcoming any resistance on our part. The convincing power of our godly lives is of greater effect concerning the Person and work of Jesus than any scholarly discussions, in answering the contradicting of those opposed to the Gospel, they having no answer for the supernatural transformation of a sinner's life into that of a Christlike life.

by means of which [glory and virtue] there have been generously given to us the precious and exceedingly great promises in order that through these you might become partakers of the divine nature, having escaped by flight the corruption which is in the world in the sphere of passionate cravings.

Jesus' personal presence in His second Advent will be the proof and vindication of all moral and spiritual effort in the Holy Spirit, He having promised forgiveness to the sinful, rest to the weary, comfort to the sad, hope to the dying, and life to the dead, being promises given not only in word but also in deed. In Jesus' character and deeds we have a revelation that is itself a promise, His very life among men with its glory and virtue being the Promise and the Life. And in the expectation of His future personal presence is also a faith that He lives and reigns in grace. Through these promises you have become partakers of, and sharers of, the divine nature. So the divine nature implanted in your inner being becomes the source of your new life and actions, its energy in you giving you both the desire and the power to run from the corruption that is in the world system of evil.

And for this very cause, having added on your part every intense effort, provide lavishly in your faith the aforementioned virtue, and in the virtue experiential knowledge, and in the experiential knowledge self-control, and in the self-control patience, and in the patience godliness, and in the godliness an affection for the brethren, and in the affection for the brethren the divine love;

Bring in, alongside to the divine nature, which nature gives you the desire and power to do God's will, your own responsibility of seeing to it that the Christian virtues are included in your life, since the divine nature works at its best efficiency when you cooperate with it, in not only determining to live a life pleasing to God, but by definitely stepping out in faith and living that life in dependence upon the new divine life which God has implanted in you, not casually, but making an intense effort to do so in the energy of the Holy Spirit Who is in you. In exercising your faith develop and provide room in your inner being for this energy of the Holy Spirit to operate to a copious measure, going beyond the need, and more than generously, so as to supply your own needs and to guide you along life's way, and so that you may exhibit His energy in vigorous action, as God exerts His energy upon you. Develop a knowledge gained through experience as you allow Him to exercise His energy in you, it springing out of your energised life, as you attempt and perfect your Spirit-led walk. Develop a holding back of your sensual passions and desires in the exercise of this knowledge gained, your self-control springing out of your increasing wisdom, as you attempt and perfect your learning as a Christian. Develop a heroic and brave patience that bears and contends, which patience is perfectly submitted to the divine will resulting in you having an entire command over your passions and an excessive love toward mankind as God requires, develop all this in the exercise of this self-restraint, your forbearing springing out of your self-discipline, as you attempt and perfect your dominating of the sinful nature. Develop godliness generously in the exercise of this patience, your reverence for God springing out of your long-suffering, as you attempt and perfect your forbearance. Develop a brotherly affection and a fondness that is saturated with love in the exercise of this godliness, your care for one another springing out of, and as you attempt and perfect, your godliness. Develop divine and self-sacrificial love which is for the benefit of those loved in the exercise of this brotherly affection, your love springing out of, and as you attempt and perfect, your affection for one another.

for if these things are your natural and rightful possession, and are in superabundance, they so constitute you that you are not idle nor unfruitful in the experiential knowledge of our Lord Jesus Christ,

Your possession of these virtues is assured by reason of the fact that you have become a partaker of the divine nature i.e. they were yours from the beginning, attached to you as characteristics of a child of God, so they should be present in your conduct every day. If they are not present in your life, what is there to back your claim of being His child? Rather you should overflow in these virtues, since that is the purpose of the Spirit's presence in you; to be a source of spiritual refreshment to others. If you overflow in them, that means that you are full, and therefore not idle in pressing-on and developing toward, and finally reaching, the knowledge of Jesus.

for he to whom these things are not present is blind, being short-sighted, having taken forgetfulness of the cleansing of his old sins.

Though these virtues are your possession, if they are not present with you, you are near-sighted spiritually, having screwed up your eyes so as to see only things present and worldly, and not heavenly things. And you have wandered far from the sanctifying work of the Holy Spirit which results in victory over sin and growth in the Christian life now, day by day, by His power and by His working in you. You are thus carrying around with you your justification by faith in Jesus, but not availing yourself of the Spirit's enablement so as to resemble Jesus more. You are not completely blind since you have some spiritual light, but the penetrating light of the Word dazzles your sin-sick soul which sadly, in your case, causes you to turn your dimmed spiritual eyes away from Heaven.

Wherefore, brethren, exert yourselves the more, and bend every effort to make for yourselves your divine call [into salvation] and your divine selection [for salvation] things that have been confirmed, for doing these things, you will never stumble,

Therefore satisfy yourselves that you are saved and that you have a legally binding guarantee of your calling and election by cultivating the virtues of a Christlike life since, though you are unable to penetrate into the counsels of God, nevertheless your holiness of life establishes your security and certainty in His purpose for you in that your Spirit-led conduct proves your vision and apprehension of your salvation i.e. make sure of the fact that you are saved by seeing to it that the Christian graces superabound in your life. Whilst you do assuredly possess your salvation, since I am in no way saying that only by conducting yourself well do you retain your salvation, nevertheless do not stumble in your living, resulting in your falling into misery and becoming wretched.

for in this way the entrance shall be richly provided for you into the eternal kingdom of our Lord Jesus Christ.

By following in Jesus' example, a road into His Kingdom is made for you as you walk in His pathway, He being the Road and the Truth and the Life, the Road to Heaven by virtue of His precious blood. Then shall you be richly rewarded by Him, in the fullness of the future and eternal blessedness of His Kingdom.

Wherefore, I intend always to be reminding you concerning these things even though you know them and have become firmly established in the truth which is present with you.

I am prepared to remind you in the future of the truths you know, as I do now and have done in the past, whenever the necessity arises. I know that you have now indeed become stabilised in your knowledge of the Word and in the Christian doctrines that you received from your teachers, these truths being deposited in your thinking and placed firmly and set fast within your minds.

Indeed, I consider it due you as long as I am in this tent to keep on arousing you by means of a reminder, knowing that very soon there is the putting off of my tent, even as also our Lord Jesus Christ gave me to understand.

It is my solemn duty to stir you up in your thinking, you who read this, by reminding you of what you have been taught from the Word of God, each time repeating old truths that you know well, in addition to also bringing fresh, new truth to you that has the dew of Heaven upon it. I repeat the teaching since much of it you have yet to put into practice, so this repetition gives the Holy Spirit an opportunity to make it experiential in your lives. Jesus told me of the manner of my death, and now that I am old, that death approaches me speedily, which death I am glad to suffer, being a result of my following my Lord, and in His service, since by it God will be glorified.

Indeed, I will do my best also that on each occasion when you have need after my departure you will be able to call these things to remembrance,

I bend every effort to give you as complete a picture as I can of all that Jesus is and of all that comprises your calling as His followers, for example, by teaching you about the practice of the Christian graces which I mentioned earlier, and in my reminiscences of Jesus, in particular as contained in the Gospel of Mark, so that, after I have taken the road out of this earth to Heaven, you may have a knowledge of His glory and virtue in your memory.

for we did not follow out to their termination cleverly devised myths when we made known to you the power and personal coming of our Lord Jesus Christ, but became spectators of that One's magnificence.

We did not pursue the lines of thought of Jewish myths or of rabbis' embellishments of Old Testament history, nor of heathen myths about the descent of the gods to earth. Rather we taught you about Jesus' second Advent, when His powerful presence will be seen by all. And I personally had a foretaste of that when, along with Jacob and John, I was lifted to the highest stage of initiation in that we saw Jesus transfigured on the mountaintop, and we beheld Him in His glory and greatest splendour. What an honour that was for us!

For having received from the presence of God the Father honour and glory, there was borne along by the sublime glory such a voice, My Son, the beloved One, this One is, in whom I am well pleased.

On that mountaintop the Father's voice was carried along by the cloud of His glory which overshadowed us, surrounding us with His greatness and splendour and magnificence and majesty.

And this voice we heard borne along, out from heaven, when we were with Him in the holy mountain.

Thus was that mountain, on the lower slopes of Hermon, rendered sacred by His divine presence. And this place is now ascribed a special holiness, since such solemn testimony was given there to the divinity of Jesus, so it is considered to be a holy mount of God, as was Mount Sinai, where God appeared to Moses.

And we have the prophetic word as a surer foundation, to which you are doing well to pay attention as to a lamp which is shining in a squalid place, until day dawns and a morning star arises in your hearts;

The Old Testament, which contains a long line of prophetic Scriptures concerning Jesus, is a more certain and trustworthy confirmation of God's truth than that which we saw ourselves, being even more convincing than the voice we heard on that singular occasion, since those prophecies were fulfilled in so many ways in the life of Jesus. It is not the miracles of Jesus by which I came to know Him, but through His Word as interpreted by the Holy Spirit. Those prophecies shine like a light in a rough and murky place, in that they afford at least some knowledge relative to Jesus' life and glorious return from Heaven, until the time when, by the Holy Spirit, the light which enlightened the prophets shines upon your hearts, allowing you to perceive the true meaning of their prophecies.

knowing this first, that every prophecy of scripture does not originate from any private explanation [held by the writer], for not by the desire of man did prophecy come aforetime, but being carried along by the Holy Spirit men spoke words from God who is the ultimate source [of what they spoke].

When considering Old Testament prophecies, remember that the prophets themselves sought to explain them, since the messages were obscure and hard to fully understand. The prophet's calling was to interpret the working of God, as given to him and inspired in him by the Holy Spirit, to his own generation, as the Spirit spoke His words of revelation through him, and the prophecy's interpretation that was specific to his own time he saw clearly by the Spirit's illumination. But prophecies can have meaning outside of their own time, as do those concerning Jesus, and the prophets, since they could not limit the meaning of their prophecies to their own time, sought to grasp a future meaning, the full implications of their prophecies being a private interpretation known only to the Holy Spirit. Thus the Holy Spirit is the source of prophetic inspiration, He being an Agency rather than an agent, since He impels and men speak, and only He knows what is in God's heart.

But there arose also false prophets among the people, even as also among you there shall be false teachers, who will be of such a character as to bring in alongside [of true doctrine] destructive heresies, even denying the Lord who purchased them, bringing upon themselves swift destruction.

So far in this letter I have dealt firstly with divine provision so as to enable you to live a holy life, close to Jesus and controlled by the Holy Spirit, in order that you may powerfully refute any false doctrine that is opposed to the Gospel, and secondly with the need for your rigid adherence to the doctrine of the full, divine, verbal inspiration of the Old Testament, since this proves the Christian system to be from God, as it is clearly and repeatedly emphasised in the holy Scriptures, in particular the truth of Jesus' deity, of His virgin birth, of His suffering on our behalf to make atonement for our sin, and of His bodily resurrection. Now I want to deal with the issue of false teachers in the Church, as opposed to the true prophets of God who wrote the Old Testament Scriptures and who rebuked Israel because of its sins as well as pointing the way to righteousness, and in contrast to New Testament prophets who preach the Gospel of Grace to the unsaved and explain and interpret the Word to the believers. In what I now say I refer to all who teach the Word, whether pastors, evangelists, or teachers. In the past there were self-appointed prophets who taught much true doctrine, but who would cleverly include false teaching with it, so betraying the way of truth and bringing it into disrepute, and whose heresies led to the loss of all that is good and worthwhile, in this life and the next. The most serious of the heresies that are now taught is to deny Jesus' substitutionary death, in which His precious shed blood paid the ransom so as to redeem us from our slavery to sin. These teachers have an inadequate view of the Person and work of Jesus, and of their relation to the problem of sin, so, as such, are unsaved. They are not misguided believers, but unbelievers who stand in opposition to the Gospel, and so are destined for eternal misery, separated from a holy God.

And many will follow their licentious conduct to its consummation, on account of whom the way of the truth will be reviled.

These teachers will attract many, being those who choose to jointly pursue their lines of thought, which thinking leads these teachers into excess and wantonness and insolence. The fact that they gain a following will cause the road of truth, as exhibited in the life, behaviour, and manner of those who sincerely follow Jesus, to be spoken against by the world, by reason of the ungodly lives of those merely professing to be Christians.

And in the sphere of covetousness, with fabricated words they will exploit you, for whom from ancient times their judgment has not been idle [i.e., it is being prepared], and their destruction is not sleeping.

These teachers have a greedy desire to always be having more, making money out of those who are duped by them. Their words are moulded at will to suit their vain imaginations and, by such words, they go to trading, exploiting their hearers so as to gain wealth from them. For them, the judgment has started on its destroying path toward them, its power illustrated in the fate of fallen angels, in the Flood, and in the overthrow of Sodom and Gomorrah, and it still advances, as strong and vigilant as when it left God's presence, and it will not fail to reach the mark to which it was appointed from of old, damning and destroying them.

For, in view of the fact that God did not spare angels who sinned, but having thrust them down into Tartarus, committed them to pits of netherworld gloom, being reserved for judgment,

Since God did not spare angels, being a higher order of being than man, when they sinned by fornicating with women, surely He will neither spare human beings. These angels are now imprisoned in chains and in densest darkness in Tartarus, from where they will be sent to the Lake of Fire at the final Judgement, there to suffer everlasting misery.

and did not spare the ancient world, but preserved Noah as the eighth person [to be preserved], a proclaimer of righteousness, having let loose the deluge upon the world of those who were destitute of reverential awe towards God,

And all those who were impious in the world were not spared from the Flood, since they maintained their sinful ways despite Noah announcing the coming judgment and showing them the way of personal salvation, he warning them over a period of 120 years. Noah and his family were physically saved, they being spiritually saved before they entered the Ark, kept from the overwhelming waters that were released onto the world.

and the cities of Sodom and Gomorrha having reduced to ashes, He condemned them to destruction, having constituted them a permanent example to the ungodly of things about to come;

Neither did God spare those two sinful cities, but destroyed them and threw them down, covering them with ashes, as a warning to all ungodly people.

and righteous Lot, completely worn down by the manner of life of the lawless in the sphere of unbridled lust He delivered,

The vile lives of those citizens exhausted Lot as his soul rebelled against the filth he saw always about him, since they constantly broke the divine ordinances and fundamental laws given to humanity, and were given to pursuing all that their sinful natures prompted them to do.

for, in seeing and hearing, the aforementioned righteous one, having settled down permanently among them, day in, day out, tormented his righteous soul with their lawless works.

Lot permanently settled amongst the people of Sodom and constantly viewed their evil conduct, though he never participated with them in their sin. Thus did he distress his righteous soul every day, though he realised that it was of his own selfish choosing that he had ended up living there, since the land of that plain was fruitful and fertile and had appealed to his eyes as being a good place to live.

The Lord knows how to be delivering the godly out of testing and temptation but to be reserving the unrighteous for the day of judgment to be punished.

Both Noah and Lot lived in the midst of the ungodly and the unbelieving, so in surroundings that tried their fidelity and integrity. In such an atmosphere, faith can be brought to its full development, though such a place is not to be sought lightly nor entered into carelessly, and it may indeed be one where a believer is brought as a result of their own sin. Nevertheless it can be a joyous opportunity for the development of spiritual and moral strength, as long as the believer's will maintains an opposition to the situation, otherwise it becomes an opportunity to sin.

But [He knows how to reserve for the day of judgment to be punished] especially those who proceed on their way, hot in pursuit of the flesh [the totally depraved nature] in the sphere of the passionate desire of that which defiles, and who disdain authority. Presumptuous, arrogant, they do not tremble when defaming those in exalted positions.

As with those in Sodom, today, in the Greek culture in which we live, there are those who teach others to run after whatever things they lust for, in full agreement with their evil nature. These teachers despise the Lordship of Jesus, reviling Him and speaking disdainfully of His supreme authority and dominion. And they have no fear that would cause them to dread their speaking lightly about spirit beings, as they scoff at the idea both of angelic help and of diabolic temptation. This making light of the unseen world is in order to foster their teaching which denies the reality of sin and of goodness, and consequently they permit and even encourage conduct that is given over solely to the pursuit of pleasure, since that, according to their doctrine, is man's moral duty; to gratify his pleasure-seeking instincts and dispositions.

Whereas angels, being greater in power and might, are not bringing against them from the presence of the Lord reproachful judgment.

Even holy angels, being greater in influence and ability than the false teachers, do not speak reproachfully of fallen angels so as to pronounce judgment on their wrongdoing.

But these, as irrational creatures, [destined] for capture and destruction, uttering blasphemies in the sphere of those things concerning which they are ignorant, shall in their [acts of] destroying surely be destroyed,

These false teachers are alive but have no sense of moral issues, so are like mere animals that exist to be taken and destroyed, being governed by the irrational instincts of nature. They dismiss things of which they have no knowledge, and will themselves be destroyed by their lack of knowledge.

receiving unrighteousness as the hire for unrighteousness, deeming luxurious living in the daytime a pleasure; moral blemishes and disgraceful blots, revelling in their deceitful cravings while they are feasting with you [at the Christian love-feasts],

For their unrighteous living, these teachers are rewarded with the state of being unrighteous. They lead a soft, comfortable life, funded by the money that they get from their followers who they are leading astray into false doctrine and who themselves have to strive to earn a living. When you all meet together as believers before celebrating the Lord's Supper, where the poorer of you partake of the food in common with, and as provided by, the wealthier of you, these teachers feast gluttonously and sumptuously, behaving disgracefully, and turning your spiritual gatherings into drunken revelries.

having eyes full of an adulteress and which are unable to cease from sin, catching unstable souls with bait, having a heart completely exercised in covetousness, children of a curse.

These teachers cannot look at a woman without having lustful, sexual thoughts toward her, unable to stop themselves from sinning, and they are able to deceive those who are not anchored securely, they having no solid foundation either doctrinally or experientially. These teachers have trained their hearts i.e. their reason their will and their emotions, to be covetous and greedy, so that that is now their permanent state, comprising their very nature and character. Therefore they are under a divine curse.

Abandoning the straight road, they went astray, having followed assiduously the road of Balaam, the son of Bosor, who set a high value upon and thus came to love the hire of unrighteousness, but was the recipient of an effectual rebuke for his own lawlessness; the inarticulate beast of burden, having spoken in a man's voice, restrained the insanity of the prophet.

These teachers have completely abandoned the right way of living so have gone astray, treading in the steps of that Old Testament prophet and imitating his ways; by being a 'man of God' for the money that they can get out of it. They do this since they have a love for the world and consider the things in it as precious. That prophet had a rebuke by a means that was contrary to natural law, spoken to by a dumb beast, and forbidding his own law breaking in the pursuit of greedy gain.

These are springs without water, and mists driven by a tempest, for whom the blackness of the darkness has been reserved.

These teachers are ever-upleaping, living fountains that disappoint, since, as the expression has it, "though you can see green growth near to them, they produce no water" i.e. when you look to them for the clear, living Word of God, you are disappointed to find no words of life and truth, since they are devoid of the Holy Spirit and, as such, have no spring of eternal life within them. Their words are like a fog blown by furious gusts of wind, with storm clouds and floods of rain, in that they throw everything into a state of chaos and destruction. Apt then is the everlasting destruction that is reserved for them.

For when they are uttering extravagant things that are in their character futile, they are alluring by means of the cravings of the flesh [the totally depraved nature], by means of wanton acts, those who are just about escaping from those who are ordering their behaviour in the sphere of error.

These teachers speak, like that donkey, with sounds designed to impress their hearers, with an oratorical flare, using immoderate, overblown, and arrogant words, in speech full of high-sounding verbosity but without any substance, they being morally insincere and conveying no accurate or true information. Nevertheless they beguile and entice those who listen to them, since they speak to people's evil nature, finding thus a connection with their audience in encouraging depraved manners, filthy words, indecent bodily movements, and the illicit sexual handling of males and females. Those who are in the early stages of their escape from error and not yet safe from it, nor confirmed in the truth, being those who have been impressed with the Gospel but not yet being strong enough to separate themselves from their old ways, these are led to return to sin through the compromises suggested by these false teachers, which teachers conduct themselves in error, wandering about in wrong opinions and straying from whatever is good morally and spiritually.

While they are promising them liberty, they themselves are slaves of corruption. For by whom a person has been overcome with the result that he is in a state of subjugation, to this one has he been enslaved with the result that he is in a state of slavery.

In promoting lawlessness, these teachers offer a freedom to their hearers, this being a perversion of the teaching of grace, but there is a difference between liberty and license. Abolishing religious legalities and statutes, being part of the Christian doctrine, is open to abuse, and might easily be dangerous to recent converts from a life full of sinful practices. Freedom from the law of Moses does not mean that you can do as you please, rather, divine love, as ministered by the Holy Spirit, regulates your life with a stronger and more effective compulsion than the law ever could. So the conscience needs to be trained simultaneously with, and enabling, a growth in the Christian character. The false teachers, since not saved and so not knowing grace, misrepresent the Gospel as being a license to sin, and have themselves, in this 'liberty' that they teach, been overcome by sin, so that rather than experiencing freedom, they end up becoming sin's abject, servile slaves.

For if, having escaped the pollutions of the world by an experiential knowledge of the Lord and Saviour Jesus Christ, in these moreover again being entangled, they have been overcome with the result that they are in a state of subjugation, the last things have become to them worse than the first ones; for it were better for them not to have known the way of righteousness than, having known it, to turn back from the holy commandment which was delivered to them.

These teachers deny the substitutionary death of Jesus, so they are not saved but merely profess to be Christians. They gave a mental acquiescence to the facts about Jesus, as an unbeliever might, which thinking resulted in their escaping the sacrilegious passions of the world system, and their severing their intercourse with the ungodly mass of mankind, as the moral and ethical influence of the Word of God cleansed their outward lives to a degree, and deterred them from some of their sinful habits. But as they persisted in their false teaching that grace gives license to sin, they gradually became entangled again in their former promiscuous ways.

But it has happened to them according to the true saying: a dog returns to his own vomit, and a sow, having been bathed, to its rolling in mire.

These unsaved teachers were cleaned up on the outside and experienced an outward moral reformation, but there was no inward regeneration, being the new birth which comes through heart-faith in Jesus as Saviour. Hence they went back, as a pig does, to wallowing in the gross forms of sin from which they had been outwardly delivered by the cleansing action of an intellectual knowledge of the Word of God.

This already, divinely loved ones, is a second letter I am writing to you, in which I am stirring up your unsullied mind by way of remembrance, that you should remember the words spoken previously by the holy prophets and the commandment of the Lord and Saviour spoken by your apostles;

As there are false teachers now so, throughout these last times, there will always be. So I exhort you to be sincere in your remembrance of the Gospel that you have heard and have been taught.

knowing this first, that there shall come in the last of the days mockers with mockery, ordering their manner of life according to their personal desires,

These teachers will trifle with truth, playing with it, so as to manipulate it according to their evil desires.

and saying, Where is the promise of His coming? For since the fathers fell asleep, all things are remaining permanently in that state in which they were since the beginning of the creation.

They will mock the promise that Jesus will return in judgment and to rule the world at His second Advent. This is because they deny that Jesus came in the flesh i.e. that the Jehoshua of the Old Testament, being the Anointed One of the New Testament, would ever become incarnate and assume a human body, putting Himself under human limitations but without man's sin. They argue that there has never been an introduction of anything from without into the affairs of the human race, and that since no judgment was meted out upon the ungodly in the past, neither will it be in the future. They say that the promise of Jesus' return was made to those who have now died, and that from that time things have continued as we now see them, even as things continued from before that time, indeed from the beginning of the Creation.

For concerning this they wilfully forget that heavens existed from ancient times, and land [standing] out of water, and by means of water cohering by the word of God, through which the ordered world of that time, having been deluged by water, was ruined.

These teachers deliberately choose to ignore what happened in the past and shut their eyes to the facts, so their denial of Jesus' second Advent is due to a culpable ignorance on their part. In the beginning, God spoke a perfect material universe into being, the surface of the world being made up of land masses surrounded by water. This earth was subsequently overwhelmed with water and perished, becoming without form and void and dark. This was the judgment on the fall of Lucifer and on the consequent apostasy of the race that existed before Adam. The land and water on the perfect earth were placed close together with contrasting effect, the earth being brought out of water, since the waters under the firmament were gathered together into one place so that dry land appeared, and by means of water, since the waters below the firmament, by supplying moisture and rain, were the means by which the moist earth held together.

But the present heavens and the earth by the same word have been stored with fire, being kept so guarded with a view to the day of judgment and misery of men destitute of reverential awe towards God.

And now a judgement of fire has been stored up and is waiting to be released by a word of God's same judgment against those who persist in opposition to Him, with a view to the final Judgment at the end of Jesus' Millennial reign, when the wicked dead, fallen angels, and demons will be judged and sent to everlasting suffering, banished from the presence of a holy God.

But this one thing, stop allowing it to be hidden from you, divinely loved ones, that one day in the sight of the Lord is as a thousand years, and a thousand years as one day.

Do not let this one thing escape you, and be no more ignorant of the fact; that God does not think of the passing of time as men do. So His delaying of judgment is only a delay according to how we view it, nevertheless it is within His chosen time, He being eternal whilst human life is short i.e. there is an impatience of human expectation about Jesus' second Advent and about the day of judgment as being 'at hand'. His judgement may come tomorrow, but what is tomorrow in God's timing? It may be in a thousand years' time. In the timing of His judgment, infinite compassion overrides, in the divine Mind, all finite reckoning. The false teachers argue that since Jesus' second Advent has not occurred after so many years of delay, therefore, it will not occur, ignoring the fact that to God, the passing of a thousand years is no different to Him than the passing of a day, as far as His predicted actions are concerned, so their argument is based on a mistaken belief.

The Lord is not tardy with regard to the appointed time of His promise, as certain consider tardiness, but is long-suffering toward us, not having it as His considered will that certain should perish, but that all should come to repentance.

So the idea of these false teachers is that God made a promise but has not kept it. But God is better than His promise, and as such has additionally allowed His patience with man to have full play, so that for those who have a purely mechanical view of the universe, God shows Himself greater than their conception of Him. This is our Christian hope in Him; that His delay does not spring from His unwillingness or impotence to judge, but rather is so that not even some should perish, though in actuality this is inevitable. Some will indeed perish and be lost, but that is not God's will for man, rather it is that all should turn to Him as they see His goodness to them, but He is bound by man's free will and He will not violate it, and some are not willing to be saved. God shows infinite patience with sinners who put Him to the test and provoke Him so that, generation after generation, he gives men an opportunity to accept His salvation as wrought by Jesus on the Cross.

But there will come the day of the Lord as a thief, in which the heavens with a rushing noise will be dissolved, and the elements being scorched will be dissolved, and the earth also and the works in it will be burned up.

We are in the last age. The next prophetic event will be the Day of Christ or the Rapture of the Church, followed by the Day of the Lord, comprising the seven-year Tribulation, being the seventieth week spoken of by the Old Testament prophet Daniel, and then the one-thousand-year world empire when Jesus will reign. At the conclusion of this period will be the Day of God comprising the Great White Throne judgment, when the wicked dead will be judged, and the great conflagration and renovation of the earth and its planetary heavens, then merging into eternity. In the Day of the Lord the second half of the Tribulation, when the Antichrist turns against the human race to become the ruthless dictator, will come suddenly and catch everyone unawares, with God's judgments falling upon a Jesus-rejecting world. Similarly the judgments of the Great White Throne and of fire, marking the end of the Day of the Lord, will come unexpectedly on those who are not saved. There will be a great harvest of souls saved during the Millennium when Jesus rules the earth, it being a period of universal righteousness, peace, and prosperity, during which the nation of Israel will be saved and only true doctrine will be preached, but despite this, there will be masses of humanity still unsaved at the end of the thousand years. Then, with a sound like the whistling of an arrow in flight, will the earth, water, air, and fire, of which the universe is composed, be dissolved and melted in a violent, consuming heat.

All these things in this manner being in process of dissolution, what exotic persons is it necessary in the nature of the case for you to be in the sphere of holy behaviours and pieties, looking for and hastening the coming of the day of God, on account of which [day] heavens being on fire shall be dissolved and elements burning up are being melted.

Since all these things that we now see are to be destroyed, you are obligated to maintain the holy life of separation in which you started in the Christian life, you being set apart for service to Jesus and separated to God. Desire earnestly therefore and hasten on by faith and prayer, the day of God, helping to fulfil the conditions for its arrival.

But heavens new in quality and an earth new in quality according to His promise we are looking for, in which righteousness is permanently at home.

We await a replacement for this outworn and marred universe, since, though beautiful, it remains under the curse placed upon it because of Adam's sin. The new heavens and earth, free from any curse, will surely be beautiful beyond the wildest expectation of man.

On which account, divinely loved ones, since you are looking for these things, do your best to be found with reference to Him irreproachable and unblamable, in peace.

You are loved by God with an infinite love. Since you are looking to Him and to His return, hurry on with intense effort in order to be living at peace with one another, so that when He returns you will be free from censure and with no fault found by Him.

And the long-suffering of our Lord, consider it as salvation, just as our beloved brother Paul according to the wisdom given to him, wrote to you, as also in all his letters, speaking in them concerning these things, in which letters are certain things difficult of being understood which those who are unlearned and lacking stability distort [from their proper meaning] as also the rest of the scriptures to their own destruction.

So Jesus patiently waits for all to receive Him as Saviour, He being in union and co-equality with the Father, Who rules all things after the counsel of His own will. As I speak with wisdom, so does Paul, whose letter, being part of the Scriptures, you have also read, and who I have affection and respect for. Beware of those who torturously twist and dislocate the meaning of his letters, as they do the meaning of other Scriptures.

As for you, therefore, divinely loved ones, knowing [these things] beforehand, be constantly on your guard, lest having been carried away by the error of unprincipled men, you fall from your own steadfastness. But be constantly growing in the sphere of grace and an experiential knowledge of our Lord and Saviour Jesus Christ. To Him be glory both now and to the day of eternity.

But you know these things that I am telling you, so you have no excuse for misunderstanding me and Paul on this subject. See to it that you are not carried away along with others by erroneous teaching, being seduced by those who stray doctrinally and who roam hither and thither, behaving in ways that break through the restraints of law in order to gratify their own lusts. Rather, you, remain steadfast in the Faith, and be so firmly rooted as to throw out branches and yield increase, within the circle of your spiritual knowledge and experience of Jesus as your Saviour, Friend, and Companion, and of His grace for daily living, this grace being the sanctifying work of the Holy Spirit in conforming you to the likeness of Jesus. Glory be to Jesus now and always.

Appendix

Having completed these ten letters, I remembered what the three writers had said in my imagined words.

How John said, "I want you to have our same joy of intimate, intelligent companionship with Jesus, to see, hear and touch Him through these words, as the Holy Spirit ministers my writing to you".

And how Paul said that we, possessing the mind of Christ are to purpose, "in thought, feeling, and action to resemble Him, that you reproduce the life He lived".

And how Peter made mention of "my reminiscences of Jesus, in particular as contained in the Gospel of Mark".

So I decided to add, as an appendix, a super-expanded translation of Mark's good news.

This Gospel reflects Peter's teaching, due to Peter being Mark's mentor in Rome.

Mark was not an eye-witness of Jesus' life, but certain details in the writing show that he would have had to have had contact with an eye-witness to Jesus as a source of information.

And there are some details not in the other Gospels which show Peter's perspective of some of the events in Jesus' life.

So Mark's Gospel is probably a collection of Peter's discourses and preaching as recalled by Mark and as inspired by the Holy Spirit.

Mark's Gospel, being based on Peter's reminiscences of Jesus' life

The beginning of the good news concerning Jesus Christ, Son of God,

I start from the beginning of the facts of the Gospel of the Kingdom, as announced by John the Baptizer, being the message about Jesus; 'Yahweh saves', He being deity and humanity, the One Who brings atonement for man's sin, the Anointed of God, and Israel's Messiah. He is Son of God by nature, proceeding by eternal generation from God the Father in a birth which never took place because it always was, so that He possesses co-eternally the same essence as God, being absolute Deity.

according as it stands written in Isaiah the prophet: Behold, I send my messenger on a mission before your face who will make ready your road,

The appearance of John the Baptizer was an accurate fulfilment of what was spoken in the Old Testament prophecies, being a permanent record of what God said and what is forever settled in Heaven; "See, I have commissioned John for a purpose, as my ambassador to represent Me, to prepare a road for My Son Jesus."

a voice of One shouting out in the uninhabited place, Prepare the Lord's road. Straight and level be constantly making His paths.

"Having heard My mouthpiece, John, the strong Voice that people need to listen to is that of My Son, Jesus, since He says only what I bid Him say. My words through Jesus are those of My longing for My chosen people, words from My heart, full of love and entreaty. John is commanded to prepare their minds so that they give Jesus a fit reception and so secure His blessings, and John is to do this with strong, curt, no-nonsense preaching. Thus is a road fit for Me to be prepared in their hearts that they might give entrance there to Me, Yahweh, incarnated in humanity, growing from a child to manhood, and offering Myself to Israel as its Messiah and King. I therefore call My sons and daughters in Israel to habitually welcome Me as a natural expression of their hearts, and I call each of them to a right way of life."

There came upon the human scene, John the Baptizer, in the uninhabited region, making a public proclamation with that formality, gravity, and authority which must be heeded and obeyed, of a baptism which had to do with a change of mind relative to the previous life an individual lived, this baptism being in view of the fact that sins are put away.

Then John appeared, in fulfilment of the prophecies and to usher in a new regime in God's dealings with mankind. John was placing people into water, administering the ritual of water baptism, as a testimony to their change of heart and mind with respect to their conduct and their relation to God. This baptism was a testimony that they had been saved, and also a sign of Israel's acceptance of its Messiah since John heralded, with an official proclamation from the coming King, the Messiah of Israel. In submitting to John's baptism, people were giving testimony that their sins were set aside, having shown the work of salvation in their lives, this baptism pointing to the One Who would take away the sin of the world at the Cross.

And there kept on proceeding out to him in a steady stream all the Judaean region and all the people of Jerusalem. And they were being baptized by him in the Jordan river as they were confessing their sins.

So people from all the local area were going out to him in great numbers, drawn by who he was and by what he proclaimed, each of them individually and deliberately acting in a way that showed that they meant to do real business with a God against whom they had sinned. John was continuously baptizing them, one after another, submersing them in the river. As they were baptized, they were each openly confessing their sins to John and to those waiting to be baptized, agreeing with God and looking at their sin from His point of view, and being determined to be done with that sin, having already had a change of heart before coming to John for baptism, their confession then being the outward indication of that change.

And there was this John, clothed habitually in a camel's hair garment, a leather belt about his loins, his diet locusts and wild honey.

John's usual clothing, similar to that of the Old Testament prophet Elijah, was made of rough sackcloth woven from camel's hairs. And his chief source of food was the honey produced by the swarms of wild bees, such as is sold in Jerusalem, and also dried locusts, which are considered palatable.

And he made a proclamation, saying, There comes He who is mightier than I after me, the thong of whose sandals I am not worthy to stoop down and unloose.

John, as the King's forerunner, was announcing the coming of his Sovereign, formally and with authority. He proclaimed the coming of 'the One', being the unique, outstanding Person, even the Yahweh of the Old Testament Who was to come. And John was careful to divert attention from himself, putting himself beneath even the most menial of slaves in comparison to the One coming after him, and was declaring that he must be constantly growing inferior and fading into the distance, while Jesus must be constantly growing greater and coming into the foreground, in dignity, authority, and popularity, he himself being only the herald of Jesus, the King Whom he was announcing.

As for myself, I baptized you by means of water. But He himself will baptize you by means of the Holy Spirit.

John's baptism was ceremonial and had to do with water only and was limited to that locality of the Jordan river, whereas, as John told them, Jesus' baptism would be supernatural, having to do with the Holy Spirit, the Spirit Himself placing the recipient of that baptism into Jesus and thus into His Body, the Church, the fulfilment of John's words being Pentecost, on that day fifty days after Jesus' sacrificial death on the Cross, when the Church was formed.

And it came to pass in those days that Jesus came from Nazareth of Galilee and was baptized in the Jordan by John. And immediately, while He was coming up out of the water, He saw the heavens being rent asunder and the Spirit in the form of a dove descending upon Him.

Then was Jesus baptized into the river by John. When Jesus was coming up out of the water He had no sins to confess, nevertheless He had taken His place with the righteous of Israel in submitting to this baptism. In answer to Jesus' submission, as soon as He was coming up out of the water, the close connection between Father and Son, and between Heaven and earth during the earthly life of Jesus was made visible, in that the Holy Spirit was descending, with the appearance of a dove, to take up residence in Jesus, anointing Him as Prophet, Priest, and King, and enabling Him to discharge the duties of these offices.

And a voice came out from within heaven, As for you, you are my Son, the beloved one; in you I am well pleased.

A voice was heard from within the boundaries of Heaven declaring Jesus to be the unique Son of God, therefore Jesus having God as His own private, personal, unique Father. Jesus is the Son of God and the beloved Son, being infinitely precious to the Father, so calling a love out of His heart for Jesus, the Father taking delight and pleasure and satisfaction in Him, indeed always having been pleased with Him and always being pleased with Him, in a delight that never had a beginning and will never have an end.

And immediately the Spirit thrusts Him out into the uninhabited place.

Then, straight away, the Spirit throws Him out from within, casting Him out into the inhospitable desert wilderness by force of thought, so as to bring Jesus to the place of testing and temptation.

And He was in the uninhabited region forty days, being constantly put to the test, being solicited to do evil by Satan; and He was with the wild beasts; and the angels were constantly ministering to Him.

During forty days Jesus was continuously tempted by Satan, he being the Adversary and the Devil, his temptations increasing in intensity as the time of testing neared its close, he all the while seeking to find a weakness in Jesus and to discover the extent of His power. The purpose of this testing was to show that Jesus was indeed equipped and ready for His ministry. The universe was looking on; God the Father, the holy angels, the fallen angels, and the demons, as Satan pressured Jesus to do evil. And Jesus was also tempted to terror by the presence of boars, jackals, wolves, foxes, leopards, and hyenas in that region, the environment being a hostile one and devoid of supplies. No human beings were near, only angels, as detailed by the Father to continuously care for His Son spiritually. Thus was this a spiritual crisis, characterised by Jesus' intense preoccupation, by His instinctive retreat into unpleasant and grim solitudes, by His temptation, and by the fierce and protracted struggle, resulting in His weakness and calling for supernatural aid so as to be bearing Him up and strengthening Him.

And after John was put in prison, Jesus came into Galilee, making a public proclamation with that formality, gravity, and authority which must be heeded and obeyed of the good news of God, and saying, The time has been fulfilled with the present result that the present moment is epochal in its significance, and the kingdom of God has drawn near and is imminent. Be having a change of mind regarding your former life, and be putting your faith in the good news.

Then Jesus went to Galilee announcing the good news that comes from God; that the older order of things was giving place to a new order i.e. the dispensation of law was being superseded by the coming Kingdom of Heaven in His earth-rule as Messiah. But since Israel would soon reject Him as their Messiah, the new order would be that of the Gospel of Grace and the Age of Grace, brought in with the Church, which order would prevail until Israel's re-gathering for the Millennial Kingdom of Jesus on earth after the Tribulation. The Kingdom of God, being God's rule over all moral intelligences that are willingly subject to His will, comprising holy angels and all believers of all ages, was 'at hand' in that events were at that time moving towards a speedy and final conclusion. The Age of Grace and the Millennial Kingdom will then be followed by a perfect earth with the saved of the human race dwelling upon it for all eternity, so answering Jesus' prayer, "Let Your Kingdom come, let Your will be done, as in Heaven, so on earth".

And while He was walking along the sea of Galilee, He saw Simon and Andrew the brother of Simon, casting their net about in the sea; for they were fishermen.

Jesus was walking along the seashore, near the edge of the water, this being the best way He could reach the men that He was after, they being those whom He had observed often and studied carefully in preparation for making His choice of disciples, men who were busy and energetic. Simon, who was later named Peter, and Andrew were throwing their net, now to one side, now to the other, casting and hauling.

And Jesus said to them, Come, after me, and I will make you to become fishers of men.

Jesus said to them, "Come here, join with me, and I will begin the long, slow process of making you soul catchers".

And immediately, having put away their nets, they followed with Him as His disciples.

So straight away they were leaving their nets and sending them away, and they separated themselves completely and permanently from the fishing business and from their former life to now being those who learnt from Jesus, walking side-by-side with Him on the same road as Him, and following with Him in fellowship and joint-participation of living, attaching themselves to Him and conforming themselves to His example.

And having gone on a little further, He saw James the son of Zebedee and John his brother, and they were in the boat mending their nets. And immediately He called them. And having left their father Zebedee in the boat with the employees, they went off after Him.

And Jacob and John were in their large fishing boat, moored some distance from the shore, putting their nets in order so as to be ready for future use. And Jesus quickly called across the stretch of water to them in a loud voice. And they too separated themselves from their business and joined themselves to Jesus.

And they go into Capernaum. And immediately on the sabbath, having entered the synagogue, He went to teaching.

Some time later, having called other disciples and having performed healings and having taught great crowds, Jesus goes to the city of Capernaum, to where the Jews congregate for worship, this worship comprising prayer and praise and the reading of the Word of God followed by an explanation of it by the rabbi or another competent person. Jesus, as soon as He entered the synagogue, began to teach, and at some length, this being an extended piece of work in His teaching ministry.

And they were completely amazed at His teaching, for He was teaching them as one who possesses authority, and not as the men learned in the sacred scriptures.

The people there were struck with astonishment and shocked, and they listened to Jesus in prolonged amazement as He was teaching with an authority that was within Himself, unlike the rabbis who, while knowing well the law of Moses and how to interpret the scriptures, merely explain Jewish tradition, and who in their teaching just quote other rabbis. The people quickly saw that Jesus was teaching differently, and they marvelled at His remarkable personality, resulting in a buzz of excitement at this new teacher.

And immediately, there was in their synagogue a man with a spirit, an unclean one. And he cried out, saying, What is there in common between us and you, Jesus, Nazarene? You came to destroy us. I know you who you are, the Holy One of God.

No sooner had Jesus finished speaking than a demonised man, who was not a member of that synagogue, stood, and the spirit that had entered the man's body and taken up residence in it so as to control him whose body it was, started to speak. This spirit was a demon; a disembodied being of a race that existed before Adam, a race that had inhabited the first perfect earth but which had then followed Lucifer into sin and was judged by God, the members of which race now comprise the kingdom of Satan in the earth's atmosphere. This spirit raised a cry from the depths of the man's throat, having in its tone the fear of impending doom, since the demon recognised and acknowledged the deity of Jesus and feared that He would send it, along with other demons, to their destruction ahead of time.

And Jesus rebuked him, the rebuke not resulting in any conviction or confession of sin, saying, Shut your mouth and come out of him at once.

Jesus rebuked the demon, though, as with all of Satan's angelic and demonic followers, it did not acknowledge its sin, commanding it to be muzzled and silent.

And when the unclean spirit had torn him with convulsions, he screeched with a loud voice and came out of him.

The spirit vindictively caused the man's stomach to spasm at being ordered to come out of him.

And they were all amazed, so that they kept on inquiring and demanding of one another, saying, What is this? Fresh teaching backed by authority. And the unclean spirits He commands, and they obey Him.

The people were astonished, their amazement mingled with fright and terror to the point of panic. They were disputing with one another in an animated, prolonged discussion what to make of the whole appearance of Jesus in their synagogue that day, since His teaching was new in quality and had power, in contrast to the stilted, dry, and staid teaching of the rabbis. Jesus' words were fresh and given with heavenly authority, and, most astonishingly, Jesus Himself was able to command the hosts of Satan as subordinates, and at will, so that they obeyed Him.

And there went out the report concerning Him immediately throughout the whole region of Galilee.

The report of this new Teacher spread with lightning speed by word of mouth.

And immediately, having come out of the synagogue, they entered the house of Simon and Andrew, with James and John.

Straight after this they went to Simon's house, where he lived with his wife, with Andrew, and with his mother-in-law, this also being where Jesus made His home when He was in Capernaum.

And Simon's mother-in-law had been bed-ridden for sometime, burning up with fever. And immediately they speak to Him concerning her.

As soon as they entered the house they tell Jesus about Simon's mother-in-law who is down sick, prostrate in bed, having been laid up with a fiery fever for some time.

And having come, He went to lifting her up, having taken hold of her hand. And the fever left her, and she went to serving them.

Jesus came to her couch and was facing her, standing over her as a physician would do. Her recovery was instant, with no need for convalescence, so that she immediately began to serve and wait on those assembled in the house, cooking a meal for Jesus and those with Him.

And evening having come, when the sun had gone down, they kept on carrying in a steady procession to Him all those having ailments, and those who were demonized. And all the city was gathered together, seated, and facing the door.

At the close of the Sabbath, the people were at liberty to bring their sick ones, and so they were carrying and bearing these in a steady stream to Jesus, Capernaum being in the midst of a great health resort country with the hot, healing mineral waters of Tiberius not far away. So were the sick and demonised come, settled down together in a group at the door of Simon's house, determined to wait there until their purpose for coming was accomplished and they were healed.

And He healed many who were afflicted with various kinds of diseases, and demons, many of them, He ejected, and He kept on refusing the demons permission to be speaking, because they knew Him.

So were all healed by Jesus of variegated ailments, He all the while hushing the demons who clamoured to be heard.

And in the last watch of the night between three and six, in the early part of the watch while it was still somewhat dark, He arose and went out, and went off into a deserted place, and was there praying.

After this, and while it was still a little dark, Jesus left Simon's house and went out of the city, since He was eager to preach throughout Galilee and was aware that the people of that city would oppose His leaving them. All through the early morning hours He was praying, decidedly directing His prayer to His Father, and being conscious of His Father's presence and attention.

And Simon and those with him hunted Him out.

It was Simon who led a group in pursuing Jesus so as to track Him down, with the intention of bringing Him back to Capernaum, his thought being to make the most of this opportunity to teach and heal all those who would be drawn to the city by news of His being there.

And they found Him and say to Him, All are seeking for you.

Simon tells Jesus, "All men are seeking you, not just those in Capernaum, but those in all the world".

And He says to them, Let us be going elsewhere into the nearby country towns in order that also there I may preach. For this purpose I came out.

Jesus tells the group that it is time to be going, and to keep on going, emphasising the length and arduousness of His preaching mission, and that He had left Capernaum in order to preach elsewhere, beginning with the unwalled village cities close to Capernaum.

And He went preaching in their synagogues all over Galilee and casting out the demons.

Thus He went, accompanied by His disciples, teaching and healing in the cities of Galilee.

And there comes to Him a leper, begging Him and kneeling, saying to Him, If you are willing, you have power to cleanse me.

A leper confronts Jesus face to face, and begs Him urgently to please heal him, appealing to Jesus' tender-heartedness. He has heard of Jesus' ministry in Capernaum and knows that Jesus has the power to heal his leprosy, although such a thing has never been heard of before, but he is not sure whether Jesus has a desire to heal him.

And having been moved with compassion, having stretched out His hand, He touched him and says to him, I desire it. Be cleansed at once.

The pitiful state of the leper aroused feelings of pity and love in Jesus' heart so that He healed him. Then He put His hand on the leper and says, "I am willing", as He is touching him. Jesus placed His hand on the leper in order to show him and the people around that he was immediately cleansed of his leprosy since Jewish law, which law Jesus lived under and fully obeyed, prohibited the touching of a leper. So it is with all who put their faith in Jesus as Saviour; He cleanses men from sin before He touches them i.e. justification precedes being born again as a child of God since mercy can only be given once justice has been satisfied, which justice, in the case of all of man's sin, was satisfied through Jesus' outpoured blood on the Cross.

And immediately the leprosy left him completely, and he was cleansed.

And as when men's sins are put away in a moment by Jesus, so was this man instantly and completely separated from his leprosy.

And sternly charging him, He immediately thrust him out, and says to him, See to it that you say nothing to anyone, but go, show yourself as evidence to the priest, and present that offering with reference to your cleansing which Moses commanded for a testimony to them.

Then Jesus was warning the man sternly and quickly ejected him from the crowd that was there, and tells him to go straight to the priest first and not to tell anyone else about his healing, in order that he do what the law requires and so be recognised and received by all as being one who was no longer a leper. In coming face to face with leprosy, itself a symbol of sin and all its train of evils, Jesus expresses powerful emotion in overcoming it. Jesus also desires not to awaken a premature violence of His enemies, who would require an official priestly pronouncement of the man's healing if they were not to become hostile in their denying of the validity and truth of His cleansing of the leper.

But having gone out, he began to be proclaiming in public a great deal and to be blazing abroad the account, so that no longer was He able to enter a city, but was outside in uninhabited places. And they kept on coming to Him from everywhere.

But the man went off and was continuously speaking to crowds who repeatedly gathered to hear his testimony about this Jesus and of how he had been healed of leprosy by Him, though he neglected to obtain the required priestly proof so that he could be socially recognised as cured. As a result Jesus could no longer enter any city, since the healing and the popularity it afforded Him abruptly ended His synagogue ministry due to the envy of the Jews. Jesus' warning to the man had had a double purpose; for the man's good, and for the placating of the law experts and synagogue rulers. But still the crowds were coming to Him from all over the country.

And having again entered Capernaum, after some days He was heard of as being at home.

Some months later, after His preaching tour, Jesus was discovered to have quietly returned to Capernaum by its city dwellers a few days after His arrival there, and was heard to be living at Simon's house.

And there were gathered together many, so that no longer was there room to receive them, not even at the door; and He was talking to them about the Word.

As soon as Jesus' presence was known, a phenomenally large crowd gathered to hear Him, so that no one could even get near to the door of the house. Jesus was speaking to the crowd in a conversational tone, with a beauty in His voice, His manner charming, His facial expression one of tenderness and love, all of which came as a breath of Heaven to this weary, sick group of people, as He was preaching the Gospel of the Kingdom.

And they come, bearing to Him a paralytic who had been picked up and was being carried by four men.

And now there comes a paralysed man being borne by four men, they having taken him up from the ground on his mat and carrying him to the house on it, and with him his friends accompanying him, which group causes a stir amongst the crowd.

And not being able to bring the paralytic to a place before Him because of the crowd, they took off the surface of the roof where He was, and having dug through, they lowered the pallet upon which the paralytic was lying prostrate.

The only way for them to get the man to Jesus was to carry him up the outside stairs to the veranda of the house and then to unroof the roof. They dug through the grass and earth and then removed some of the roof tiles to create an opening. Then, using four ropes, they lowered the man's padded mat into the room where Jesus was teaching.

And having seen their faith, Jesus says to the paralytic, Child, your sins are put away.

When Jesus saw the faith of the men who carried the paralytic, their digging up of the roof being its visible evidence, he addresses the state of the man, whose physical condition was due to his sinful life, and speaks kindly to him, telling him, "Your sins are dismissed and removed from you". Jesus could say this given the man's belief in Him as Saviour, He looking ahead to His outpoured blood which would remove the man's sin in a judicial way, and, having been so justified, that God would then remove the guilt of that sin and bestow His righteousness, being Jesus Himself, in Whom the believer stands justified forever.

Now, there were certain of the men learned in the sacred scriptures sitting there and reasoning in their hearts, Why is this fellow speaking in this manner? He is by contemptuous speech coming short of the reverence due to God. Who is able to put away sins except one person, God?

The learned men, who were there early enough to take a spot where they could see and hear Jesus distinctly, were seeking to cause trouble and to pick flaws in His teaching, since they were jealous of this new Teacher's popularity and power. They were deliberating Jesus' words in their minds, and the looks on their faces and their actions and their very personalities created a hostile atmosphere in the room which Jesus sensed. They were reasoning, "Surely it is blasphemous of this Man to assume this divine right and privilege of the forgiveness of sin", in which thinking they were logically correct. The flaw in their argument was that Jesus did indeed hold a peculiar relation to God which justified His claim, so it was Jesus' deity that was the point of contention.

And immediately, Jesus having become fully aware in his inner being that in this manner they were reasoning within themselves, says to them, Why are you reasoning these things in your hearts?

Straight away Jesus knew, and was clearly and completely conscious of what they were thinking, so He questions their motives for having such a mind.

Which of the two is easier, to say to the paralytic, Your sins are put away; or to say, Be arising and pick up your pallet at once and carry it away, and start walking and keep on walking?

And Jesus says to them, "If I command this man to walk, will that satisfy you as to Who I am?"

But in order that you may have absolute knowledge of the fact that the Son of Man possesses authority to forgive sins on the earth, - He says to the paralytic, To you I say, Be arising, pick up your pallet at once, and be going away into your home.

So Jesus says to them, "That you may know, with absolutely no doubt, that I have such authority to forgive sin, delegated to Me by God, this paralytic being healed at My command now shows My deity". Then He bids the man get up and leave the room and not remain with Him any more, lest he attract unnecessary attention to Jesus by his being there, so increasing even more the antagonism of the religious leaders, thus hindering Jesus' preaching ministry.

And he arose, and immediately, having picked up his pallet, went out before all of them, so that all were astonished, and were glorifying God, saying, In this manner, never have we seen it.

With no hesitation the man stood and left, carrying his mat. The crowd were ecstatic, and intensely amazed, and beside themselves, feeling they might just as well be out of their own bodies so far as registering their sense impressions was concerned, they being so taken up with the sight of this man walking that they noticed nothing else, being overwhelmed with wonder at the miracle they had just seen.

And He went out again along the seashore. And all the crowd kept on coming to Him, and He went to teaching them.

Jesus loved to walk along the seashore, for quiet and rest, and for the opportunity to be alone with His Father, taking in the freshness of the air and the quieting influence of the sound of the waves and the long view over the sea, all as a tonic to His human nature, since His human body needed recreation and rest just as our bodies do. And He kept on teaching the crowd as they kept coming to Him.

And as He was passing by He saw Levi, the son of Alphaeus, sitting at the tax collector's desk. And He says to him, Start following with me, and continue to do so as a habit of life. And having arisen, he followed with Him.

Jesus saw Levi at the customs office in Capernaum, at the landing place of the many ships that cross the Sea of Galilee, Levi being one of those who collected taxes for Herod Antipas, so in the employ of the Roman government, and thus hated and despised by the Jews and considered by them to be a sinner. Levi loved money more than the good regard of, and fellowship with, his countrymen, so his soul was in an immoral state. But Jesus had long observed him at his tax collector's desk and noted his intensity of purpose. Similarly Levi had seen Jesus before, since the whole city was flooded with His fame and reputation. Jesus calls Levi, with an authoritative, commanding tone of voice, to start walking the same road with Him, and to join Him as an attendant and disciple and companion, and thereafter to continue as a habit of life to follow with Him. Levi left his business, which afforded him a life of affluence and luxury, and embarked on Jesus' road of self-sacrifice and concern for others, and of separation, suffering, and holiness.

And it comes to pass that, as He was dining in his house, many tax collectors and sinners stained with vice and crime were dining with Jesus and His disciples, for there were many, and they were following with Him.

And so now, Jesus was eating in Levi's house, along with His disciples and with Levi's associates, all of them reclined on couches as they ate a great feast. This crowd was not one that Jesus could have taught in a synagogue since they would all have been excluded from there, and this meal was Levi's gesture of introducing his fellow tax collectors to his new-found Saviour. Also Jesus was attracting a following from the tax collectors who swarmed the trade markets in Capernaum, and some of those present at the meal were not formally invited but were those who followed this fascinating new Jewish Teacher Who, unlike their countrymen, befriended them. The disciples of Jesus were those who learned from Him, but who were not necessarily saved, some later deserting Him or, in the case of Judas, betraying Him.

And the men learned in the sacred scriptures belonging to the sect of the Pharisees, having seen that He was eating with the sinners and tax collectors, were saying to His disciples, With the tax collectors and the sinners stained with vice and crime is he eating?

The students of the Pharisees, being those who study the law of Moses and adhere to its statutes strictly, having followed Jesus into the large hall where He was feasting, went to questioning His disciples as to why He would be so intimate with sinners as to eat with them.

And having heard, Jesus says to them, No need do they have who are strong, for a doctor, but those who are ill. I did not come to call righteous ones but sinners.

Jesus replies to them, saying that He was not there because He enjoyed that kind of company, since He did not, for there was sin all about Him and His righteous, sensitive soul shrank back from it, but that He was there in order to reach their souls for salvation, since these sinners had a sense of their need to be saved.

And John's disciples and those of the Pharisees were observing a fast. And they come and say to Him, Why are John's disciples and the disciples of the Pharisees fasting, but your disciples are not fasting?

And later that day the followers of John and the strict Pharisees come to Jesus and question Him about observing the set fast that was then happening, since here He and His disciples were feasting instead. John's disciples were not following their teacher in saying this, he being in prison at the time, and they would have been aware of John's deference to Jesus, and of John referring to the Pharisees as 'the offspring of snakes' because of their deluded religious snobbery and because of their zealous observance of mere ceremonial and ritualistic practices while not having a heart for justice.

And Jesus said to them, The sons of the bridechamber are not able to be fasting while the bridegroom is with them, are they? As long as they are having the bridegroom with them, they are not able to be fasting.

Jesus replied to them saying, "How can guests invited to a wedding be fasting, since mourning does not befit a marriage scene?" Thus was Jesus challenging the cherished beliefs of the religious leaders, with His emphasis on the spiritual rather than on the ritualistic and ceremonial.

But there shall come days when there shall be taken away from them the bridegroom, and then they shall fast in that day.

And Jesus alluded to His crucifixion, at which time, given the events and atmosphere, His disciples would indeed, on that day, fast and mourn.

No one sews a patch consisting of cloth which has not been pre-shrunk upon a worn-out garment. Otherwise that which fills it up takes away from it, the new from the worn-out, and the tear becomes worse.

Jesus then gave them another parable with the analogy that if the fuller does not correctly use new cloth to mend old; by cleansing, shrinking, and thickening, through the use of moisture, heat, and pressure, but rather puts unfulled cloth onto fulled cloth, the worn-out cloth will not furnish the patch with enough of a grip to keep both together. The 'new' refers to Jesus' ministry and preaching of grace, as compared to the 'old' law of Moses, it being ready to be set aside. His meaning being that one should not retain the law of Moses, which God would set aside at the Cross, and put upon it the patch of grace since, in attempting to mix law and grace, both lose their true identity.

And no one puts newly-made wine into worn-out wineskins. Otherwise, the wine will burst the wineskins, and the wine and the wineskins are destroyed. But newly-made wine is put into wineskins which are just beginning to be used.

And Jesus then gave a third parable with the same meaning as the previous one, this analogy being that of the animal skins that are used to store wine, with the example that already expanded, so worn-out, containers would burst under the pressure of newly-fermenting wine being put into them. Rather, new, just-made wine must be put into new, unused skins. So again, co-mingling new with old renders both useless.

And it came to pass that on the sabbath He was proceeding along a path through the fields of grain. And His disciples began to be making their way, picking off the grains as they were going along.

On another occasion, Jesus and His disciples began to be walking along a path with fields of grain on either side. As they were making their way through the grain field they were plucking the ears of grain.

And the Pharisees kept on saying to Him, Observe that, will you. Why are they doing on the sabbath that which is not lawful?

Now the Pharisees pressed Him repeatedly, demanding that He rebuke His disciples for, in their legalistic interpretation of the law, reaping the grain, and so working on the day set aside for resting from work, as specified by God in the law of Moses.

And He says to them, You have read, have you not, what David did when he was having need and was hungry, he himself and those with him, how he entered the house of God when Abiathar was high priest, and the loaves that were set forth, he ate, which are not permitted to be eaten except by the priests, and he gave also to those who were with him?

Jesus appeals to their knowledge of the Old Testament Scriptures, a familiarity with which was their source of pride, and gives them an example where David, whose descendant was to be the Messiah, broke the law of Moses, by eating food that was purely and exclusively to be consumed by the priests i.e. David entered the tent that was a holy place and took of the old loaves of the face, being the loaves that had previously been set forth before the presence of God, and which were only to be eaten by the priests when they were thus removed from the holy table.

And He was saying to them, The sabbath for the sake of man came into being, and not man for the sake of the sabbath.

Jesus was explaining to them, since it took some talking to get the idea across to their minds which were warped with an over-attention to details of religious practice, that the purpose of the Sabbath was only a means to an end, being for the good of mankind. The Pharisees, with all their petty rules, have made the Sabbath into a set of statutes that must be followed, so that the rule of the day is upheld and maintained regardless of the welfare of men.

So that the Son of Man is Lord even of the sabbath.

This dialogue gave Jesus opportunity once again to affirm His deity, stating that while, in His incarnation and being manifest in human flesh He identified with mankind in the way He referred to Himself, nevertheless He also declared His deity in being the Creator and Lord of the Sabbath that He had brought into being for the sake of mankind. Since in His deity Jesus had made the Sabbath, in His humanity He would not break it, though, in the eyes of the excessively scrupulous Pharisees who denounced the sanctity of the Sabbath ever being broken, infringed, or dishonoured, He had. Jesus prioritised doing good to a fellow human on the Sabbath, in opposition to those who forbade the doing of good to others on the pretext that it was work, for example Jesus was glad to heal the sick on the Sabbath, though the Pharisees told the people to come back for healing on another day.

And He again entered a synagogue. And there was there in that place a man whose one hand had withered.

Another clash over Sabbath observance occurred when Jesus, as was His custom, attended a synagogue service where there was a man present whose right hand was withered due to accident or disease.

And they kept on spying upon Him closely, whether He would on the sabbath heal him, in order that they might bring a formal accusation against Him before a tribunal.

The Pharisees were now intent on laying charges against Jesus before the authorities, constantly watching Him carefully and closely, while maintaining an aloof distance from Him, so as to find Him at fault with reference to the Sabbath. They considered themselves the watchdogs of Israel's religion and as such were attempting to discredit this Man's claim to be the Messiah by finding Him violating its regulations. They sat there, hoping that Jesus would heal the man, not for the benefit of the man, but that they might accuse Jesus of Sabbath-breaking with many witnesses present.

And He says to the man having the withered hand, Be arising in the midst of everybody around you.

Jesus says to the man, "Stand where everyone can see you", thus answering the spying attitude of the Pharisees by this daring act, bringing matters out into the open at once, and throwing out a challenge to them.

And He says to them, Is it lawful on the sabbath to do good or to do evil, to save life or to kill? But they kept on being quiet.

Jesus demands of the Pharisees, "On this Sabbath day, shall I do that which is ethically good, since the Sabbath is made for the good of man, or are religious duty and benevolence divorced, with the former taking precedence over the latter? If I can not do this good deed today then I am omitting to do good and therefore doing evil. If a life is not saved when it can be, that life is destroyed. So what would you have me do?" The Pharisees could not answer and so theirs was a painful and embarrassing silence. Their legal point of view was wholly different from Jesus' ethical one. There was nothing in common between them and Jesus.

And having looked round about on them with a righteous indignation, being grieved at the callousness of their hearts, He says to the man, Stretch out your hand at once. And he stretched it out. And his hand was restored to its former state.

Jesus' momentary look of anger at them flowed from His settled state of mind, and which this occasion demanded, since God loves good and therefore hates evil, the two being inseparable, and so with Jesus, God's Son. His anger was tempered with a continuous grief at the sins of these people, the Pharisees having a blunted moral and spiritual discernment, and an increasingly dulled perception of God's ways. The instant healing of the man signalled an immediate exodus of these champions of orthodox Sabbath-keeping, they being full of wrath that not only had the Sabbath been broken, but that it had been broken by a miracle which then brought fame to the One Who was breaking it.

And having gone out, the Pharisees at once with the Herodians were giving counsel against Him, in order that they might destroy Him.

The Pharisees were then holding talks with their enemies the Herodians. The Herodians are not of proper Jewish descent and try to please their Roman patrons, so they were in direct antagonism with the Pharisees who considered it abhorrent that Israel was ruled by Gentiles. Nevertheless the Herodians were in unity with the Pharisees in that they also feared Jesus, their concern being that He looked ever more likely to lead a popular uprising against the Roman rule of Israel. Setting their differences aside the Pharisees and the Herodians discussed how they might together solve the problem of this Man and rid themselves of Him, the Pharisees needing the Herodians' influence at court so as to facilitate the process of having Jesus killed legally. So, on the holy Sabbath, the legalistic Pharisees were plotting to kill, oblivious to the words of Jesus that they had just heard; "Is it lawful on the Sabbath to save life or to kill?"

And Jesus with His disciples withdrew to the sea, and a vast multitude from Galilee followed. And from Judaea, and from Jerusalem, and from Idumaea and across the Jordan, and about Tyre and Sidon a vast multitude, hearing constantly of such great things which He was continually doing, came to Him.

So Jesus took His disciples to the safety of the open beach because of the size of the exceptionally large crowd which had gathered together, His following accumulating and increasing over a period of time, since the people were continually hearing of the many miracles which He was always performing.

And He spoke to His disciples to the effect that they should always keep a small boat in readiness for Him because of the crowd, in order that they might not crush Him, for He healed many, so that as a result, they kept on jostling Him in order that they might touch Him, as many as were having a distressing bodily disease.

And Jesus requested His disciples to have a small row boat constantly ready since the crowd, in their desperation of need, pressed hard upon Him. And some people in the crowd were dangerously falling against Jesus, knocking against Him in their eagerness to be healed. Jesus stayed with the crowd because of their need for Him, but He took this precaution lest they crush Him unintentionally, that He might be taken into the boat at a moment's notice. So the boat kept up with Him as He moved down the shoreline, some of the disciples rowing it near to the shore, they keeping a watchful eye on their Master.

And the spirits, the unclean ones, when they set eyes on Him, kept on falling prostrate before Him, and kept on crying out with a loud voice, saying, As for you, you are the Son of God.

When the demons critically inspected Jesus they understood Who He was, they looking at Him with a practiced eye long used to the measuring of the good and the true as exhibited in the character of God. And they were recognising in Jesus the embodiment of the holiness out from the presence of which they had been driven when they shared in the downfall of Lucifer, the one who is now called Satan. These demons were then causing the persons they inhabited to cry out loudly in evil, throaty, raucous voices, so that there was a constant sound of those possessed declaring Jesus to be the unique Son of God, equal with the Father.

And He kept on rebuking them and charging them under penalty that they should not make Him known.

Jesus was severely censuring these demons to be quiet since He did not wish to have the testimony of demons as to His deity, wanting no advertising from that source.

And He goes up into the mountain and calls for himself and to himself those whom He himself was desiring, and they went off to Him.

Then Jesus, in His own interest, calls those that He had chosen, being more than the twelve that He would soon choose. These separated themselves from the crowd and followed Him up the hill.

And He appointed twelve in order that they might constantly be with Him, and in order that He might send them forth as ambassadors with credentials, representing Him, to accomplish a certain task, that of making a proclamation with such formality, gravity, and authority as must be heeded and obeyed, being equipped with delegated authority to be casting out the demons.

Of those that Jesus had called, He formed twelve of them into a compact body, to be trained by Him so as to be His representatives in declaring the Gospel of the Kingdom, and He gave them authority to declare with a word that demons were cast out, God's power then casting them out.

And He appointed the Twelve, and added to Simon's name, the name Peter;

The first of the twelve that Jesus chose was Simon, on whom He also placed the name Peter, referring to his rock-like firmness and strength of soul, though before he was filled with the Sprit he had a tendency to vacillate and to behave unpredictably at times, and occasionally to fail, especially in a crisis. Thus Jesus foresaw that, after Pentecost, Simon would be dependable and immovable, equal to the emergencies and crises that would then confront him.

and James the son of Zebedee, and John the brother of James, He surnamed Boanerges, which is, sons of thunder; and Andrew and Philip, and Bartholomew, and Matthew, and Thomas, and James the son of

Alphaeus, and Thaddaeus, and Simon the Canaanite, and Judas Iscariot who also handed Him over.

Upon the brothers Jacob and John, Jesus also placed the name which means impetuous, zealous, and thunderous, indicating Jacob's character, which led to him being one of the first martyrs, and also predicting the thunders of John's revelation of the Apocalypse. Andrew and Philip, though Jewish, had Greek names. Thaddaeus was also known as Judas, not the one who betrayed Jesus. Simon the Zealot was much changed; from being a member of that revolutionary, fierce war-party that, like the Pharisees, considered it treason against the majesty of Yahweh that Rome ruled the Holy Land and who were also fanatical in their Jewish restrictions and exclusiveness, from all of that to being a follower of Jesus Who proclaimed peace with God and acceptance of the Roman rule. Judas, the man of Kerioth, betrayed the Saviour, handing Him over to the Jewish leaders.

And He comes home. And there comes together again the multitude, so that they are not able even to eat bread.

Then Jesus comes home to house-life from hill-life, since He had been in the hills for some days. The crowd from before that had partially dispersed, reassembles, they having lingered in the region in order to see and hear more of Jesus. This mass of people, now crowding about Peter's house and seeking Jesus' presence so that He might meet their needs, was of such intensity that Jesus and His disciples could not find leisure to rest or even eat, nor could Jesus teach His disciples.

And having heard, those nearest to Him among His kinsfolk went out for the purpose of taking Him by force, for they were saying, He is out of His mind.

When Jesus' mother and brothers heard all that was being said about Him; the demons being cast out, the healings, the contentions with the Pharisees, and the vast crowds that followed Him, they left their home in Nazareth in order to seize Him by force, for they were saying to each other, "He is in such an unhealthy state of excitement it is bordering on insanity", and they put it down to His great learning and to the adulation of those following Him, since they themselves did not believe that the things that they were hearing about His healing ministry were true.

And the men learned in the sacred scriptures, the ones from Jerusalem, having come down, kept on saying, He has Beezeboul, and by means of the ruler of the demons He is casting out the demons.

The local Pharisees who had made an alliance with the Herodians to kill Jesus, had sent word to the Jerusalem authorities in order to enlist their aid against Jesus. The charge brought by these scribes was that He was possessed and was being used by a Satanic incarnation, in particular the god of dung, so as to cast out demons, thus denying the work of the Holy Spirit and, in their thinking, disproving Jesus' claim to be the Messiah. This sin of theirs, committed when Jesus was on earth, He being in humiliation and attempting to gain a foothold for His claims and teaching by means of attesting miracles, was beyond pardon.

And having called them to himself, He was speaking to them in the form of illustrations: How is Satan able to be casting out Satan?

Jesus invited the Pharisees over so as to talk with them and reason with them. He spoke to them in parables, throwing concrete illustrations alongside a truth so as to explain it, here using figures of a kingdom, a house, and a strong man. He thus showed to them the impossibility of Satan casting his own out, since, though he has the strength to do so, what would be his purpose in depleting his own forces?

And if a kingdom be divided against itself, that kingdom is not able to stand. And if a house be divided against itself, that house will not be able to stand. And assuming that Satan arose against himself and is divided, he is not able to stand but has an end.

Since the Pharisees' reasoning made no sense with respect to any normal, rational, observable agents, for example a kingdom or a house, neither did it make any sense with respect to Satan, who is very rational.

But no one is able, having entered the house of the strong man, thoroughly to ransack his equipment, unless first he binds the strong man, and then he will thoroughly plunder his house.

How could Satan cause damage to his own demons, being the very tools by which he carries on his business, and the equipment he uses to further his ends?

Assuredly I am saying to you, All sins shall be forgiven the sons of men, and all malicious misrepresentations, as many as they use to defame, but whoever maliciously misrepresents the Holy Spirit never has forgiveness, but he is guilty of an everlasting sin: because they kept on saying, He has an unclean spirit.

Having reasoned with the Pharisees, Jesus now solemnly warned them that since they obviously did not believe their own theory, it being absurd, and since He therefore must be casting out demons by a very different spirit from Satan, that they were not mere mistaken theorists, but rather men in a very perilous moral condition, since their speech intentionally came short of the reverence that is due to God and sacred things. In attempting to break the attesting power of Jesus' miracles, knowing full well that they were done in the power of the Holy Spirit but deliberately and knowingly attributing them to Satan, they were committing an unpardonable sin, everlasting in its guilt.

And there come His mother and His brethren, and standing outside, they sent to Him, calling Him.

Jesus' mother and brothers arrive from Nazareth, thinking He is beside Himself and desiring to take Him home, and they sent word to Him via the crowd that they want to speak with Him.

And a crowd was sitting in a circle around Him, and they say to Him, Behold, your mother and your brothers and your sisters outside are seeking you.

Jesus' disciples were sitting, encircling Him, in Peter's house, and there was a large crowd around them, seated and standing. His mother and brothers had spoken to those at the edge of the crowd to pass their message on to Jesus, and by the time the message reaches Him it has been embellished to also include His sisters.

And answering them He says, Who is my mother and my brethren? And having looked round about upon those sitting in a circle around Him, He says, Behold, my mother and my brethren. Whoever does the will of God, this one is my brother and sister and mother.

Jesus knew why His family had come, and He answers graciously, looking at all of those listening to Him, and with a gentle smile. Jesus' answer, when relayed back to His mother and brothers, confirmed to them that He was in an abnormal and unhealthy state of mind, and they left for home without seeing Him.

And again He began teaching along the seashore. And there gathers together to Him a crowd, the largest one up to that time, so that He entered a ship in order to occupy a place on the sea. And the whole crowd was on the land facing toward the sea.

After spending time with His disciples, Jesus was resuming His wider ministry among the people at various points along the coast line, His teaching being simple but often repeated, in order that the people might understand. Due to the size of the crowd, the largest that has yet gathered, He spoke to them from a larger boat that was moored in close to shore, seated on the deck, so that all on land heard Him from across the water.

And He was teaching them many things by means of illustrations, and was saying to them in His teaching,

Jesus was explaining to them the Word of God. To do so He was using parables with familiar illustrations, so as to adapt the simplicity of His teaching to the limitations of His hearers, though still many of His words were falling on dull ears, hard hearts, and unresponsive wills.

Be listening. Give attention to this.

Jesus, with kindness and humility, entreated the crowd to listen, since many of them had come for healing rather than for salvation. He says to them, "Look, ponder and see the meaning of this illustration".

The sower went out to sow. And it came to pass that while he was sowing, some indeed fell alongside the road, and the birds came and ate it up. And other seed fell upon the ground full of rocks, where it was not having much earth. And immediately it sprang up because it was not having any depth of earth. And when the sun arose, it was burnt, and because it did not possess rootage, it withered. And other seed fell into the midst of thorns and the thorns sprang up and utterly choked it, and it did not give fruit. And other seeds fell on ground that was good, and it kept on yielding fruit, growing up and increasing, and it kept on bearing, up to thirty-fold and to sixty, and to one hundred. And He was saying, He who has ears to be hearing, let him be hearing.

The illustration was of the same seed which fell upon different types of ground, the ground determining the amount and kind of fruit that would result. The ground looked the same on the surface, since the rock layers were just underground and the thorns were just seeds which then sprang up with the good seed and pressed round it and thronged and strangled it so as to almost suffocate it.

And as soon as He was alone, those about Him, with the Twelve, went to asking Him concerning the illustrations.

After the crowd dispersed, Jesus' disciples were immediately asking Him to explain the parables, they all having a common theme, since they did not want the multitude to see that they did not understand His teaching.

And He was saying to them, To you the mystery of the kingdom of God has been given, and it is in your possession. But to those who are outside, in the form of illustrations are all the things given, in order that seeing they may be seeing and may not perceive, and hearing, they may be hearing and may not understand, lest haply they turn again and it should be forgiven them.

Jesus was explaining to them that the secret counsels of God are hidden from the ungodly, but when revealed to the godly they are understood by them, the parables' interpretation only being possible when their meaning is revealed, so that they then become plainly understood. And He was telling His disciples that it was for them to come gradually into a clear understanding of the truth, since His parables were open to them, while being shut to the Pharisees due to their hostile minds. Thus the parables were a condemnation on the wilfully blind, while being a guide and blessing to the enlightened. Light resisted, blinds, so those who wilfully reject Jesus and the truth will never reverse their position.

And He says to them, Do you not understand this illustration? Then how is it possible that you will understand all the illustrations? The sower sows the Word. And these are those alongside the road where the Word is being sown; and whenever they hear, immediately there comes Satan and snatches away by force the Word which has been sown in them. And these are, on the same principle of interpretation, those who are being sown on ground full of rocks, who, whenever they hear the Word, immediately with joy receive it; and they do not have rootage in themselves, but last only for a time; after that, affliction or persecution having come because of the Word, immediately they are displeased, indignant, resentful. And others are those who are being sown in the midst of the thorns. These are those who heard the Word, and the anxieties of the present age, and the deceitfulness of wealth, and the passionate desires with reference to the rest of the things not in these categories entering in, choke the Word, and it becomes unfruitful. And those are they which were sown on ground that is good, which are of such a nature as hear the Word and receive it, and bear fruit, some thirty-fold, some sixty, and some one hundred.

Jesus, before explaining the parable, gently reproaches them that He should need to be explaining it, He being surprised at their dullness, even though they had been initiated into the mysteries of the Kingdom of God, and leading Him to question if they had understood any of the parables He had given them and whether they would understand those that He would give them in future. But He implies that understanding this particular parable would be key to them then understanding all of the parables, whereas not understanding this particular one would make it impossible for them to understand all the others. As to the first type of people, Satan, the Adversary and the evil one, being he who is in active opposition to the good and who is seeking to drag everyone down to destruction along with himself, straight away steals the Word from these careless people's hearts as it is beginning to grow, so as to prevent it from becoming a plant. The second type of people instantly accept something of the Word but have only a superficial experience of divine truth. These trip and fall easily since they straight away disapprove of any persecutions that acceptance of the Word brings, so that they do not permit it full access into their soul, they not acknowledging its proper authority in their lives. The third type of people, lacking the thoughtlessness of the first and the shallowness of the second, have some depth and earnestness for the Word, so could be expected to be fruitful, but they are distracted and drawn in a different direction by those same cares and worries of the earthly life that the unsaved have who live apart from God. The fourth type understand the Word and produce fruit and yield, some thirty per cent, some sixty per cent, and some one hundred per cent of their potential fruit.

And He was saying to them, The lamp does not come, does it, in order to be placed under the peck measure or under the reclining couch? Does it not come in order to be placed upon the lampstand?

Then Jesus was giving them an illustration to show them the purpose of His teaching and explaining of the Word to them, and thus how, and why, they should be the fourth type of people in the seed parable. To put the lamp under a peck measure will put out the flame so that it gives no light. To put the lamp under a couch will set the couch on fire. Thus Jesus was instructing His disciples that since they have more insight than the multitude, they must employ it for the common benefit i.e. they must share His teaching with others since that was His purpose in teaching them.

For there is not anything which is hidden, except it be in order that it might be made known, nor has anything become hidden but in order that it might come into full view.

Jesus, in explaining about the mysteries of the Kingdom, was saying that things are only temporarily concealed from men in order that they may be finally revealed, and that those who He was charging with the things then secret, were to be given the responsibility of proclaiming them after His Ascension.

Assuming that a person has ears to be hearing, let him be hearing.

He was also exhorting them to use their ears, since some of them were inattentive to His words.

And He was saying to them, Keep ever a watchful eye on what you are hearing. In the measure by which you are measuring, it will be measured to you; and it will be measured to you not only according to that measure, but there will be some added on top of that. And he who does not have, even that which he has shall be taken away from him.

And Jesus was warning them to be careful how they listen and study, since they will be rewarded in proportion to their degree of virtue and knowledge, and their reward will exceed that which is due them if they go beyond mere listening and rather think on what they hear. The more a man thinks, the more he will understand and knowledge will be given to him, the less a man thinks, the less his power of understanding will become and the seed of knowledge in him will not grow but rather be taken from him and destroyed.

And He was saying, In this manner is the kingdom of God, as if a man should throw the seed upon the earth, and should be sleeping and arising night and day, and the seed should be sprouting and lengthening; how, he does not himself know.

Jesus was then giving them another illustration to do with their being the fourth type of people in the seed parable, that they, His disciples, being fertile soil, would only gradually produce fruit, and that their growing process demanded time. In this He was also saying that only in them had His ministry so far produced any promise of fruit. As seed is cast about by a man, who then just patiently waits for results, results which come in a way that is a mystery to him, and which operation of growth is a secret but reliable process of nature, so is the mysterious growth of the Kingdom in the heart and life of a believer which, when man has done his part, is an operation which is a secret but reliable process of the Holy Spirit.

The earth bears fruit spontaneously, first, herbage, then a covering for the grain, then the fully-developed grain in its covering. And whenever the fruit permits, immediately, he sends forth the sickle, because the harvest stands ready.

Totally by itself, the earth, automatically and without external aid, with a way and a will of its own which must be respected and waited for, brings forth fruit. The nature of the soil, the weather, and the cultivation of the plant are all factors, but the secret of the growth is in the seed itself. Thus when the seed of God's Word is sown in the soil of a soul who gladly receives it, the Holy Spirit works on the heart of that sinner, using the seed sown and causing it to germinate and grow. So this parable illustrates, using the law and order in nature, the law and order of grace in the Kingdom of God. And in this law and order of grace was Jesus' confidence in the ultimate establishment of His Kingdom, in spite of any obstacles which would obstruct its progress, when there would be a final harvest of souls won, at the time of the Father's choosing, the time being the instant that the harvest is full.

And He was saying, In what way shall we liken the kingdom of God or by what illustration shall we set it forth?

Jesus' previous two parables having alluded to the Kingdom; only a few being fruitful and even in them the fruit only appearing after a passing of time, He was now asking them how they could illustrate the Kingdom itself, how best to show the state of things, thus bringing His hearers into consultation as He was teaching them; "With what parable shall we put it?".

It is like a grain of mustard seed, which when it is planted in the earth, is less than all the seeds which are upon the earth; and when it is sown, it grows up and becomes greater than all of the herbs, and puts out great branches, so that the birds of the heaven are able to find shelter under its shadow.

Jesus was then giving the illustration of the tiniest of seeds, which springs up and becomes greater than all the garden herbs, six to twelve feet high with branches an inch or more in thickness, its wood sufficient to cover a potter's shed.

And by means of many illustrations of this kind He was speaking to them the Word as they were able to be understanding. But without an illustration He was not in the habit of speaking to them; but in private, He was in the habit of fully explaining all things to those pupils who were peculiarly His own.

So was Jesus adjusting His discourse to His hearers' capacity to understand, by the habitual use of illustrations to explain the Word to them in order to make the truth plain, even to the point of revelation, He privately teaching His own twelve chosen disciples fresh revelations concerning the mysteries of the Kingdom of God.

And He says to them on that day, evening having come, Let us go over to the other side.

At the end of that day, a day of blasphemous accusation, the visit of His mother and brothers to lay hold of Him, the leaving of the crowded house to teach on the seaside, and then teaching in the house again, Jesus now bids His disciples go out again with Him, headed for the open sea in crossing the Sea of Galilee, as a delightful and refreshing change for the weary Lord Jesus, and His only way to escape the crowds.

And having dismissed the crowd, they take Him under their care just as He was, in the boat, and there were other boats with Him.

The disciples take the exhausted Jesus in the larger boat and set sail.

And there arises a great windstorm of hurricane proportions, and the waves kept on beating into the boat, so that already it was being filled.

As they crossed the sea, a sudden, furious, powerful storm breaks forth, with great gusts of wind and floods of rain, throwing everything violently into chaos, and there is an earthquake under the sea, so that its waters are stirred to their depths, and so that wave after wave was being thrown into the boat, filling the boat full, to the point where the boat was being covered with the waves.

And He himself was in the stern of the boat, sleeping on the steersman's leather cushion. And they arouse Him from sleep and say to Him, Teacher, is it not a concern to you that we are perishing?

Jesus was sleeping still, He worn out from the toil of the day, the need of His body for rest overcoming the demands of the noise and tumult and cold and wet on His senses. They wake Him, saying, "O, Teacher, do You not care that Your disciples are drowning?"

And having awakened, He rebuked the wind and said to the sea, Be getting calm; hush up and stay that way. And the wind ceased its raging, and there was a great calm.

Jesus spoke with sharp disapproval to the wind, "Be being calmed", and He commanded the sea, "Be muzzled and stay muzzled". The wind immediately ceased from violence as if suddenly weary and tired, and the waters became completely calm, so that there was a great stillness.

And He said to them, Why are you such timid, fearful ones? How is it that you do not have faith?

Jesus asked them, "How is it possible that you are afraid? Where is your faith in Me?" The Creator and Sustainer of the universe was with them in the boat, but, as yet, His disciples had an inadequate view of Him, not recognising all the implications that His office of Messiah carried with it.

And they feared a great fear, and were saying to one another, Who then is this person, that even the wind and the sea obey him?

The shocked disciples suddenly feared this Man who stood before them. He could command the wind and waves at will, drive out demons, heal diseases, and speak such deep mysteries in parables, which led to them voicing their thoughts amongst themselves; "Given what we have seen today, what is His identity and what is this power He exhibits? What type of Person is this? This surely is no mere man."

And they came across the sea into the country of the Gerasenes.

So they arrived at the city of Gerasa in the district of Gadara on the southeast shore of the Sea of Galilee.

And having come out of the boat, immediately there met him out of the tombs a man with an unclean spirit who had settled down there, making his home in the tombs; and no longer was anyone able to bind him, not even with manacles, because he often was securely bound with shackles and manacles, and the manacles were snapped in two by him, and the shackles crushed together, and no one had sufficient strength to restrain him. And throughout all the night and the day, in the tombs and in the mountains, he was constantly screaming and shrieking, and was constantly lacerating himself all over with stones.

And straight away a demon-possessed man came to Jesus, the demon having settled in him permanently, forcing the man to live among dead men's bones where only outcasts from society find shelter, also giving him superhuman strength so that no one could subdue or restrain him, even when he was thoroughly and completely chained hand and foot, and tormenting him, causing the man to cry out in anguish night and day and to hack at his own flesh, leaving him covered in scars.

And having seen Jesus from a distance, he ran and prostrated himself on the ground before Him, and he cried out with a great voice, and says, What is there in common between me and you, Jesus, you Son of the most high God? I adjure you, by God, don't begin to torment me. For He was saying to him, Come out of the man, unclean spirit.

The naked man ran towards Jesus screaming at Him, but when the man got to Jesus he fell down in worship before Him, the personality of the Son of God in His power and grace quieting the hostile, violent spirit, and causing the man to fall on his face in reverence. Jesus was commanding the spirit to leave the man, so the demon, destined to be damned for all eternity, put Jesus under oath not to torment it ahead of time.

And He kept on asking him, What is your name? And he says to Him, Legion is my name, because we are many. And he kept on pleading much with Him to the effect that He should not send them off outside of the country.

Jesus had to repeatedly ask the spirit its name before it responded, and when it does it declares that there are thousands of demons in the man, and it kept on begging on behalf of all of them that they could stay in that region of the ten cities where the demons loved to be, since there they found many to possess among the Greek-influenced Jews who had renounced their religious beliefs.

Now, there was there near the mountain, a herd of hogs feeding, a great herd. And they begged Him, saying, Send us at once into the hogs in order that we may enter them.

The demons, in their panic, grasped quickly at this convenient, practical end, lest a worse fate befall them at that time, they needing a physical body to reside in, whether that body be human or animal.

And He gave them permission. And having gone out, the unclean spirits entered the hogs, and the herd rushed impetuously down the steep place into the sea, about two thousand, and were drowned one after another in the sea. And those feeding them fled and brought away tidings into the city and into the farms. And they came for the purpose of seeing what it was that had taken place. And they come to Jesus and view with a critical, searching eye the demoniac sitting, clothed and in control of himself, the one who had had the legion. And they became afraid. And those who saw, related fully and in detail to them how it happened to the demoniac and concerning the hogs. And they began to be begging Him to go away from their boundaries.

Jesus allowed the spirits their request. The herd of hogs were stirred up and incited, then running rapidly as one to their death. The terror-stricken swineherds ran away and told everyone what had happened, leading many people from the area to see for themselves, which sight astonishes them as they scrutinise the well-known possessed man now completely changed, he being clothed and sane. The power that had caused this change in him aroused in them a new fear of this same man, and that fear was increased when they saw the two thousand dead hogs in the water. The man once controlled by demons now had self-control, no longer wild and uncontrollable, but become quiet and docile. Having seen and heard the whole story of events, they determined that Jesus was a dangerous person, since His curing of the man had caused a catastrophe for their property, so they were requesting that He retire from that region, in accordance with which wish of theirs, Jesus withdrew.

And while He was going on board the boat, the one who had been demon-possessed kept on begging Him for permission to be with Him. and He did not permit him, but says to him, Be going into your home, to your own relatives, and bring back tidings to them of such great things which the Lord has done for you, and of the fact that He had a sympathy for you which issued in action in your behalf. And he went off and began proclaiming publicly in the Decapolis such great things which Jesus did for him. And all were marvelling.

As Jesus was leaving, the man was pleading with Jesus to let him go with Him as a disciple, fearing a return of the demons if he stayed there. Jesus tells the man to testify to his own flesh and blood as to the results of the complete, finished, permanent cure that he had received from God. This time Jesus was glad for the healed one to proclaim what had taken place, given the people's lack of enthusiasm and rejection of Him, meaning they most certainly needed to hear the Gospel message. The man went through the ten cities proclaiming how he, the famous madman of Gerasa, had been transformed by Jesus.

And when Jesus had crossed over in the boat again to the other side, a great crowd was gathered together after Him, and He was at the seashore.

As soon as Jesus arrived at the other side of the sea, a great crowd gathered on the shore, controlled by an irresistible longing to see Him and avail themselves of His help.

And there comes one of the synagogue rulers, by name, Jairus; and having seen Him, he falls at His feet, and begs Him earnestly, saying, My little daughter is at the point of death. Come, place your hands upon her in order that she might be healed and live.

One of those who administered the synagogue pleads with Jesus to come to his house and save his young daughter from impending death, she being in the last gasp of life.

And He went off with him. And there kept on following with Him a large crowd, and they kept on pressing upon Him almost to the point of suffocation.

Jesus immediately went off with Jairus, and the crowd kept following Him, thronging and pressing round Him on all sides.

And a woman having come who had a flow of blood for twelve years, and had endured much suffering under the hands of many doctors, and had spent all of the things which she had, and was not even one bit improved but rather grew worse, having heard the things concerning Jesus, having come in the crowd behind, touched His garment, for she kept saying, If I touch even His garments, I shall be made whole. And immediately there was dried up the fountain of her blood, and she suddenly came to feel in her body that she had been healed of her plague and was at that moment in a state of health.

A woman who had suffered and been in pain for twelve years due to her physical condition, and also due to the efforts of many doctors to heal her, had only just heard of The Jesus Who healed many, since she was not a resident of that area, and she thought to steal a cure by touching Him, since it was forbidden for her to touch anyone given her ceremonial uncleanness. Pushing through the crowd that was following Jesus, she kept believing that by just touching Him she would be saved from her physically ill condition. Having finally managed to touch His clothing she felt her ailment to be completely and permanently healed, sensing that the blood had, in that instant, stopped flowing out of her body, and that she had entered into a new condition of health, and she joyfully knew, "I have been healed of this scourge".

And immediately, Jesus, having had a personal and clear knowledge in himself of the experience of power going out of Him, having turned around in the crowd, was saying: Who touched me on my garments? And His disciples kept on saying to Him, You are seeing the crowd pressing hard around you from all sides; yet you are saying, Who touched me? And He kept on looking round about to see the woman who had done this. And the woman, fearing and trembling, knowing that which had been done for her, came and fell down before Him, and told Him all the truth. And He said to her, Daughter, your faith has saved you. Be going into a state of peace, and be continually sound in body, healed of your affliction.

From His knowledge gained by experience, Jesus straight away knew, and also felt in Himself, that power to effect a change had gone out from Him. The disciples could see the eager, crushing pressure of the crowd on Jesus, so were surprised at His sensitiveness to a single touch, unconscious as they were of the tremendous drain on Him from all this healing that tugged away at His tender heart and exhausted His nervous energies. Jesus, in His own interest, kept on scrutinising the crowd in answer to the protest of the disciples, looking for a woman, it having been a gentle, cautious, and sensitive touch, since a man would rather have caught hold of His clothing. The woman was fearing publicly relating her action and motive, given the stigma attached to her previous condition, and thinking that Jesus might disapprove of her secrecy and disregard of ceremonial law. But He spoke to her tenderly, as a Father to a child, expressing His exquisite sympathy for her in His manner, and He assured her that the healing was permanent and that the peace stemming from health of body and soul would now be hers.

While He was still speaking, they come from the home of the ruler of the synagogue saying, Your daughter died. Why are you still bothering the Teacher? And Jesus overhearing the word being spoken, says to the ruler of the synagogue, Stop fearing, only be believing. And He did not permit anyone to follow with Him except Peter, and James, and John the brother of James.

Right while Jesus was still speaking to the woman, messengers arrive from Jairus' house, attracting attention away from her, and telling Jairus that his daughter had died. And they chide him to the effect that he should not worry and annoy Jesus any more on this matter. Jairus immediately felt fear in his heart, but Jesus commands him to desist from this feeling and rather to continue believing for his daughter's life, even in the presence of death. Jesus chose three from His chosen twelve to witness, as a unit, the great miracle that He was about to perform within the confines of Jairus' house.

And they come into the home of the ruler of the synagogue, and He looks carefully and with an understanding eye at the tumult, and at those who were weeping audibly and at those who were wailing greatly. And having come in He says to them, Why are you wailing tumultuously and weeping? The little girl did not die, but is sleeping. And they went to laughing and jeering at Him. But after He himself had thrown them all out, He takes the father of the little girl and her mother and those with Him, and proceeds in where the little girl was. And having taken a strong grip on the hand of the little girl, He says to her, Talitha koum, which being interpreted is, Little girl, to you I say, be arising. And immediately the little girl stood up and went to walking about, for she was twelve years old. And they were amazed with a great amazement. And He charged them sternly that no one should know this. And He gave orders that she be given something to eat.

They arrive at Jairus' house and enter in to find a great uproar, which Jesus critically examines, their ears being filled with the monotonous wailing of "Alala" by the hired mourners. Jesus tells them that she is just sleeping, meaning that she is not to stay dead, at which they started ridiculing Him and laughing, showing their lack of sympathy with the family employing them. Jesus forcefully ejected them, taking on the role of Master of this house, though it was the house of a stranger, and takes the father and mother under His care, they, being grief-stricken, needing someone to guide them. His disciples also needed His reassurance given that they were now confronted with death. He journeys with them all, the harrowing and seemingly long walk into the child's death-chamber. He firmly takes the girl's hand, having given her back her life, speaks to her in the language of the ordinary people of that region, and helps her up, since she had been ill before dying and so needed some help. The girl instantly rose from her bed and started walking and kept on walking, to her mother, then to her father, and then to Jesus. Her parents were overwhelmed and ecstatic, as if removed out of their senses. Jesus warned them not to tell anyone that she had been raised from death, desiring that expectations of such acts should not be awakened amongst the people. As the girl was completely well, Jesus told them to prepare her some food.

And He went out from there and comes into His own country. And His disciples follow with Him.

Then Jesus goes back home, to Nazareth where He had lived for nearly thirty years before His anointing with the Holy Spirit, to a place of comparative quiet and rest, so as to escape from the crowd.

And when the sabbath had come, He began to be teaching in the synagogue. And the many hearing were completely flabbergasted, saying, From where does this one get these things? And what wisdom is this which has been given to this fellow? Even such great exhibitions of supernatural power take place through the medium of His hands?

When invited to speak, Jesus gladly took the opportunity to be giving out the Word in their synagogue. His hearers were struck very forcibly by His teaching and by the miracles which followed, to the point of losing control of themselves, and then continuing to be amazed for some time, their astonishment so great that their self-possession was completely exhausted, as they witnessed the supernatural power exerted in these miracles. The people, who knew Jesus as being the son of Mariam and Joseph, were impressed by the unworldly miracles He performed and by His divine wisdom, but wondered as to where both had come from.

Is not this the carpenter, the son of Mary, and brother of James, and Joses, and Jude, and Simon? And are not His sisters here with us? And they saw in Him that of which they disapproved and which kept them from acknowledging Him.

The people remembered Jesus as the builder and craftsman Who used to live among them with His family, and could not reconcile this image of Him with what they were now seeing and hearing, which caused them to be offended with Him so that they would not recognise His authority i.e. they could not explain Him so they rejected Him. Even His own brothers and sisters disbelieved His claim to be their Messiah, His singularly beautiful life lived out before them their whole lives making no effective impression on their dull, cold hearts.

And Jesus was saying to them, A prophet is not without a correct evaluation and the due respect and deference which that evaluation demands except in his own country and among his own kinsfolk and in his own home. And He was not able to do there even one work of power, except that He laid His hands on a few sickly ones and healed them. And He marvelled because of their unbelief. And He kept going around the villages in the encircling country, teaching.

Jesus' claim to be One Who speaks out God's message as His mouthpiece should have afforded Him with honour and reverence, and it did elsewhere, but not in His home city. Even His offer to heal the sick among them was spurned, with only a very few weak ones coming to Him, such that Jesus was disappointed and taken aback, He being unprepared for their senseless lack of reception of Him given the response He had had elsewhere with crowds of people following Him. Leaving there He was teaching in the villages that circled Nazareth.

And He calls to himself the Twelve. And He began to be sending them forth as His ambassadors with credentials on a mission to represent Him, sending them forth two by two. And He was giving them authority over the unclean spirits.

Jesus then summons His chosen twelve disciples and started sending them out in pairs to proclaim the Gospel of the Kingdom, in pairs so that they might help and encourage each other, and also so as to give a fuller testimony. And He was delegating to them the authority to command demons to leave the individuals in which they were operating, which command God's power would then enforce.

And He commanded them not to be taking even one thing for the road except only a walking stick, not bread, nor a begging-bag, nor money in their belt, but to wear sandals, and not to clothe themselves with two undergarments.

Jesus ordered them not to collect any money, either for His support or for their subsistence, nor to take any money with them. And He also directed them against any luxury in their equipment and against taking anything that they could procure from the hospitality of others.

And He was saying to them, Wherever you enter a home, there be abiding as a guest until you go out from there, and whatever place does not welcome you nor hear you, when you are going on your journey out from there, shake off the dust that is underneath your feet as a testimony against them.

On being welcomed by a place, whether it be a city or a village, they were to take care in choosing where to stay, and then to remain there in that house, so as to avoid exhibiting a restless, dissatisfied manner. If they were met with hostility, so that none in a place would receive them or invite them in, nor anyone talk with them nor offer any friendship, Jesus was telling them to show their refusal to have anything more to do with the people of that place.

And having gone out, they made a proclamation to the effect that they should be repenting. And demons, many of them, they were casting out, and they were massaging with oil many who were sick, and were healing them.

The disciples preached that all should have a change of mind about their life and course of action, to turn from the sinful to the good, and to be determined to maintain that change. This change, they announced, would be accompanied by salvation from sin, as provided by God through His Son and Messiah, Jesus. The disciples were setting free many demon-possessed ones and anointing many sick ones with oil who were then healed, giving testimony and weight to their message.

And the king, Herod, heard, for His name became known, and they were saying that John the Baptizer had been raised out from among those who were dead, and because of this, the miraculous powers are operative in him. But others kept on saying that He was Elijah. But others were saying that He was a prophet like one of the prophets. But Herod, having heard, kept on saying, Him whom I decapitated, John, this man was raised.

This tour of Galilee by the disciples resulted in news about Jesus spreading among the people, until even King Herod in his Palestinian palace heard about Him. Herod was troubled in his conscience since he had ordered that John, a good man in his own estimation, be beheaded, so he reasoned with himself and came to the conclusion that this John, having now been put in touch with the unseen world of the dead, had come alive again and was utilising supernatural powers from that world. Whilst among the people it was said that Jesus was a new prophet like those of old, or one of those prophets come to life again, Herod, not being able to put out of his mind the image of John's severed head dripping with blood being brought to him on a gold platter in his banqueting hall, was positive and emphatic, often repeating his pronouncement that this was John raised from the dead.

For Herod himself, having commissioned an official representative, apprehended this aforementioned John and bound him in prison for the sake of Herodias, the wife of Philip his brother, because he had married her; for John had been saying to Herod, It is not lawful for you to be having the wife of your brother. Therefore, Herodias set herself against him and was desiring to kill him. But she was unable to do so, for Herod was fearing John, knowing him to be a man, righteous and holy; and he kept him constantly out of harm's way, and, having heard him often, he was in a continual state of perplexity, and he was in the habit of hearing him with pleasure.

It was only recently that Herod had killed John, news of which, when brought to the disciples, abruptly ended their preaching circuit of Galilee. Herod had personally imprisoned John in the grim fortress of Machaerus, since his wife held a grudge against him, never letting up in her fury towards him. She desired to kill John but did not have the power to do so, so she waited her time for revenge. Herod was in a continual state of fear of John, so kept on keeping him safe from the evil plots of his wife, he maintaining a constant watch over him. When Herod heard John speak he grew embarrassed, not knowing which way to turn, yet he repeatedly visited him in prison, which left him, on each occasion, at his wit's end, due to his life with Herodias, his guilty conscience, and the insistent demands of his wife.

And a strategic day came, when Herod on his birthday made a supper for his great men, and his military commanders, and the chief men of Galilee. And the daughter of Herodias herself, having entered and danced a rapid-motion, leaping, lewd dance, it pleased Herod and those who were dining with him. And the king said to the young woman, Ask me at once whatever your heart desires, and I will give it to you. And he put himself under oath to her: Whatever you ask me I will give you, up to the half of my kingdom. And having gone out, she said to her mother, What shall I ask for myself? And she said, The head of John the Baptizer. And having come immediately with haste to the king, she made a request for herself, saying, I desire that you give me at once on a dish the head of John the Baptizer. And though the king became exceedingly sorrowful, yet because of his oaths and because of those who were dining with him, he did not desire to frustrate her. And immediately, the king, having sent off one of his bodyguards, issued the order to bring his head. And having gone off, he beheaded him in the prison, and brought his head upon a dish and gave it to the young woman, and the young woman gave it to her mother. And having heard, his disciples came and took up his corpse and laid it in a tomb.

Herodias chose Herod's birthday as the opportune moment to spring her trap and force her husband to put John to death. At the banquet were lords, commanders of a thousand, and prominent dignitaries, so all the men of Galilee's government, military, and civil life. Herodias' own daughter degraded herself in performing a sexual dance that only professional actors of loose morals would do, being an unprecedented act for a woman of such rank and respectability. This immoral spectacle catered to the totally depraved natures of the drunken men and Herod offered her a reward, so stepping into Herodias' trap. The daughter was totally unprepared for the gruesome request of her mother, she then being sent by her mother straight back to the banquet with it before the king could change his mind and before the spell of her dancing had passed, nevertheless the way in which the daughter expressed her wish showed a cool impudence almost outdoing her mother. The drunken king became regretful that he was being pressured into killing the prophet whom he feared and respected, nevertheless he did not wish to break faith with the young woman and slight her by treating his oath as a joke, so, in his intoxicated state, he quickly ordered one of his nearby protectors to carry out the grim deed.

And the missionaries gathered themselves together to Jesus and brought back news to Him of all things whatever they did and whatever they taught.

Having ended their preaching circuit of Galilee, the disciples returned to Jesus and related to him all that they had achieved in their announcing of the Gospel of the Kingdom to the people of that region.

And He says to them, Come here, as for you, yourselves, into the privacy of an uninhabited place, and rest yourselves a little. For there were those who were coming and those who were going, many of them, and not even was there an opportune time to eat.

Jesus acknowledges the need of His disciples for some rest, since they had worked hard and been in constant activity during their preaching tour so that they were now near to exhaustion. They needed some time in private, away from the crowd, the demands of which left them no good time when they could even eat. So He leads them off into the wilderness that they might recover their strength.

And they went off in the boat to the privacy of an uninhabited place. And they saw them going away, and many understood, and on foot from all the cities they ran there with one another and preceded them.

They took the larger of the boats that was always kept in readiness for Jesus lest the crowds crush Him. When the crowd saw them rowing away thus they reasoned that they were leaving them to go to a place of privacy, but, rather than allowing Jesus and His disciples some much needed rest, in their excitement, and as an exciting thing to do, they ran along the shore, rushing in frenzied hurry, and gathering yet more people as they passed near to other cities, so that the crowd grew to many thousands of people. They ran around the foot of the lake and met the boat as it landed.

And having come out, He saw a large crowd, and He was moved with compassion for them because they were as sheep not having a shepherd. And He began teaching them many things.

Tired as they were, Jesus' compassion led Him to give Himself to the crowd, teaching them and continuing to teach them, since the people were weary of the powerless teaching of the rabbis and were eager to hear Him.

And when the day was already far gone, His disciples came to Him and were saying, Uninhabited is the place, and already the hour is late. Dismiss them in order that, having gone off to the neighbouring farms and villages, they might purchase for themselves something to eat. And He answering said to them, As for you, you give them to eat. And they say to Him, Having gone off, shall we purchase two hundred denarii worth of bread, and give them to eat? And He says to them, How many loaves do you have? Be going and see. And having found out, they say, Five, and two fish.

Jesus taught until sunset was approaching, so His disciples were telling Him to send the crowd away since this was a deserted region. When Jesus was telling them to feed the crowd, they argue that even all the money they have with them would not be enough to feed such a large crowd.

And He commanded them to make all recline in open squares like oriental diners, upon the green grass. And they reclined in squares that looked like flower-garden plots, by hundreds and by fifties.

Jesus ordered His disciples to get the crowd to recline on the fresh grass, like party guests, in open-ended squares, and to wait to be served. With their clothing of red, blue, and yellow, the people looked like flower-beds in a garden.

And having taken the five loaves and the two fish, having looked up to heaven, He invoked a blessing, and broke the loaves, and kept on giving to the disciples in order that they might continue setting them beside them, and the two fish He divided to all.

As Jesus broke the loaves they multiplied in His hands and He was continuously giving them to His disciples.

And all ate and were filled. And they took up twelve wicker baskets full of broken pieces, and from the fish. And those who had eaten the loaves were five thousand men.

Once all had eaten as much as they wanted, the leftover bread filled twelve variously sized baskets. The number of men that were fed was five thousand, in addition to the women and children that formed the crowd.

And immediately, He constrained His disciples to go on board the boat and precede Him to the other side, to Bethsaida, while He himself dismisses the crowd. And having taken leave of them, He went off into the mountain to pray.

Straight away Jesus compelled His disciples to cross the sea again in the boat while He bids farewell to the crowd and separates Himself from them.

Then He withdrew to the hill so as to spend time in prayer directed toward God, seeking His face, and being aware of His Father's presence and of His listening ear.

And evening having come, the boat was in the middle of the sea and He himself alone upon the land. And having seen them constantly distressed in their rowing, for the wind was against them, sometime between three and six in the morning He comes to them walking directly on the sea. And He was desiring to go to their side. But having seen Him walking directly upon the sea, they supposed that it was an apparition. And they screamed, for they all saw Him and were agitated. But He immediately spoke with them; and He says to them, Be of good courage. It is I. Stop being afraid. And He went up to them into the boat, and the wind ceased its violence. And exceedingly beyond measure, in themselves they were amazed,

At sunset Jesus came down from the hill and returned to the seashore. Some hours later he could see that His disciples were harassed and making torturously slow progress in their rowing due to the strong wind beating against them. Jesus goes toward them, walking on the surface of the sea as if it was hard pavement, aiming to come to the side of the boat so as to help them in their difficulty. When they saw Him walking on the water they assumed it was a disembodied spirit from the realm of Satan and they shrieked in terror. But straight away Jesus calms their inner commotion with friendly and encouraging words, "Cease your fear. It is I and nobody else". Like before when Jesus calmed the storm, as He now climbed up into the boat the wind grew suddenly weary of blowing and ceased from its raging, and the sea, exhausted by its own beating, sank to rest, so that all was immediately calm, to the amazement of the disciples.

for they did not reason upon the basis of the loaves. In fact, their heart was in a settled state of callousness.

The disciples didn't bring together in their mind this miracle with that of the feeding of the crowd, failing to reason that the supernatural power that enabled Him to multiply loaves and fish would mean that He could also exert this power to quiet the wind and still the sea, and to walk on the surface of the water. Their reasoning was dull and their heart grown to become hard, so that they lacked understanding.

And having crossed over, they came to the land, to Gennesaret, and they cast anchor off shore. And when they had gone out of the boat, immediately, having recognised Him, they ran around throughout that whole countryside, and began to be carrying around on pallets those who were afflicted, where they were hearing that He was. And wherever He kept on proceeding, into villages, or into cities, or into farming districts, they laid those who were sick in the market places, and they kept on begging Him if they might touch even the fringe of His cloak. And as many as touched Him were being made whole.

When they arrived at the other side they moored the boat close to the shore. Straight away the people on land recognised Jesus, since He had now become well-known in the region. They ran around in circles, finding all who were in need of a healing touch and carried these to Him. And this practise continued as the people were following Jesus from place to place. Also, since they had heard about the healing of the woman, they were pleading with Him that they might just touch His cloak's fringe so that all the more of them might be healed, and all who did so were made well.

And there gather together to Him the Pharisees and certain ones of the men learned in the sacred scriptures who came from Jerusalem.

In contrast to His phenomenal popularity with the people, there now come to Him the hostile religious leaders from Jerusalem.

And having seen certain ones of His pupils, that with unhallowed hands, that is, unwashed hands, were eating the loaves, they found fault,

These criticised some of Jesus' disciples for eating with hands that, while physically clean, were not ceremonially clean, in eating some of the leftover loaves from when He had miraculously fed the crowd.

for the Pharisees and all the Jews, unless they wash their hands meticulously in a ritualistic fashion, do not eat, habitually keeping, carefully and faithfully, that which was delivered from the elders to be observed. And from the market place, if they do not wash, they do not eat; and many other things there are which they received for the purpose of keeping, washing of cups and pint measures and copper vessels. Both the Pharisees and the men learned in the sacred scriptures went to asking Him, Why are not your pupils ordering their manner of living according to that which was delivered from the elders to be observed, but with unhallowed hands are eating their bread?

These wash themselves with one fist clenched, rubbing the other hand and the arm up to the elbow, according to the tradition handed down from previous generations so as to be closely observed by the succeeding generation, therefore being a man-originated observance and not from the Word of God. Also, after mingling with Gentiles, they practise this washing. And there are numerous other washings that are required so that all items used in connection with food preparation are clean ceremonially. The rabbis hold that disobedience to such observances of oral law is a mortal sin. So the religious leaders keep asking, "Because of what do Your disciples not observe that which was delivered from the elders?"

And He said to them, Well did Isaiah prophecy concerning you, the hypocrites, as it stands written: This people is constantly honouring me with their lips. But their heart holds at a great distance from me.

Jesus said to them, "Beautifully did the prophet Isaiah describe you", and then He quoted from the Old Testament scriptures, a precise knowledge of which was a source of great pride to these leaders. And Jesus Himself described them as those who hide behind a mask, assuming a character of which they are not, and He emphasised how outstandingly adept they were at this not being, on the inside, what they pretended to be, on the outside. The prophecy declares them to be holding their hearts a great way off from where they should be, so much so as to be found to be absent in their ritualistic worship of God.

But in vain are they worshipping me while they are teaching as doctrines, commandments of men. Having abandoned the commandment of God, you are carefully and faithfully keeping those things which men delivered to you to be observed. And He was saying to them, In a very beautiful way you are constantly making the commandment of God null and void in order that that which has been delivered to you for observance you may keep.

The prophecy warns that worship of God should be characterised by fear and respect and reverence, not by vain and empty pride, its foundation being a life based on the Word, and not on man-made practises. The Word, these Pharisees have left behind and are finished with, while the practises that are passed down, these zealously grip on to with all their strength. And Jesus was bitingly and ironically telling them, "Excellently do you do away with the Word, thwarting its effectiveness in its soul-saving work, in order to keep your own tradition."

For Moses said, Be paying due respect and reverence to your father and your mother. And the one who is constantly reviling father or mother, let him come to an end by death. But as for you, you are saying, If a man should say to his father or his mother, Korban, which is a gift, whatever from me you may be profited; no longer are you permitting him to do anything for his father or his mother. You are rendering void the authority of the Word of God by that which has been delivered to you to observe, which in turn you are delivering over to another to keep. And many things of this kind you are constantly doing.

Jesus continued rebuking them for their hypocrisy, "Moses taught that parents must be honoured, and that the one who continually speaks evil of his parents should be killed as a punishment for breaking this law. But you, contrary to what the Word of God says, say that a man can withhold money from his parents if he declares it to be a gift to God, in defiance of God's command which requires him to honour his parents by providing for their necessities where they are in need. And this law-breaking tradition you pass on to your posterity, adding yet more weight and importance to it."

And having again called to himself the crowd, He was saying to them, Hear me, all, and understand. There is not even one thing that from the outside of the man, which entering him, is able to defile him. But the things proceeding out from the man are those that defile the man.

Jesus called to the crowd who had withdrawn a little out of respect for the Jerusalem grandees, and was revealing to them the Pharisees' hypocrisy so that the people could see the true character of their religious leaders. He was showing the fallacy of their argument; that disobedience to their man-made regulations results in ceremonial defilement. He was saying, "What enters into a man is just food, which does not make him ceremonially unclean, no matter what be the manner in which he eats it. Teaching what is in direct opposition to God's Word in words that come out from a man, this makes him unholy and not set apart for God.

And when He entered into residence away from the crowd, His disciples went to asking Him about the illustration. And He says to them, In this manner also, as for you, are you without understanding? Do you not know that everything which from the outside enters into the man is not able to defile him, because it does not enter his heart but his intestines, and goes out into that which is designed to receive it? This He said making all the foods clean.

When Jesus went into Peter's house, Peter lost no time in asking Him many questions regarding the interpretation of the parable. Jesus replies, "You also, as well as the multitude?" showing His disappointment that His own chosen pupils were still under the spell of the traditions and theological outlook of the Pharisees. They could not understand a statement that did away with the distinction between clean and unclean, so ingrained was it in their thinking as they had been so taught in Judaism. Jesus explains, "Ethical defilement alone is of importance. All other defilement, whether it be the subject of Moses' ceremonial law or of the Pharisees' traditions, is a trivial matter. Food just passes through the digestive system and ends up in the toilet." So did Jesus abolish the ceremonial distinctions in the law of Moses, as He reiterated to Peter in a vision some time after Pentecost where, following Peter's objection to Jesus' command to kill at once and eat of creatures presented to him from out of Heaven but which creatures are considered unclean by the law, Jesus responded, "The things which God cleansed, as for you, stop calling them unhallowed."

And He was saying, That which is constantly proceeding out of the man, that thing defiles the man. For from within, out of the hearts of men are constantly proceeding the depraved thoughts, fornications, thefts, murders, adulteries, covetousness, perniciousness, deceit, wantonness, a malicious, mischief-working eye, malicious misrepresentation, pride, folly. All these pernicious things from within are constantly proceeding and are constantly defiling the man.

Jesus then was explaining the things that actually bring defilement; things in the area of evil thoughts and desires, being dangerous, destructive, and actively opposed to the good, by nature lawless, unpredictable and foolish, insolent and proud, due to a heart uplifted against God and man.

Now from there, having arisen, He went off into the region of Tyre. And having entered a home, He was desiring that not even one should know. And He was not able to be hidden.

Jesus now entered Phoenicia, which territory borders Israel, and He went deep into the heart of the country, having failed to find recuperative quiet and leisure among the Jewish people and time to teach His disciples, and also so as to have relief from the antagonism of the Jewish leaders. But news about this Teacher and Healer had spread beyond the borders of Israel so that neither here was there an opportunity for privacy.

But immediately, a woman having heard about Him, whose little daughter had an unclean spirit, having come, fell at His feet. And the woman was a Gentile, a Syrophoenician as to her race. And she kept on begging Him to cast out the demon out of her little daughter.

Once it was known that Jesus was there, straight away a woman, whose religion, language, and race were not Jewish, came to Him, and kept right on requesting Him to heal her little daughter, that He would throw out the demon at once and by one act.

And He was saying to her, Let first the children be fed, for it is not right to take the bread of the children and to throw it to the little pet dogs. But she answered and says to Him, Yes, Sir, yet the little pet dogs under the table are constantly eating from the little morsels of the little children. And He said to her, Because of this word, be going; the demon is gone out of your daughter. And having gone off into her home, she found the little child quietly upon her couch and the demon gone out.

Jesus spoke to her in Greek, being the international language of the day, explaining that His commission was to the Jew first, and then to the Gentile, this being the chosen Old Testament method; reaching the large number through a selected smaller group, the Jew being the chosen channel through which God elected to reach the Gentiles, and that therefore, as the Messiah, He was sent to Israel, and so needed to be careful to preserve that order. Though His compassionate heart went out to this Gentile, He desiring to help her, He reminded her that she came second, not first, in the great salvation plan of God, illustrating this by the example that it is only seemly and proper to see to it that the children are fed first, and not to give their food to the little dogs, their pets. The woman answered by expanding on Jesus' illustration and says that the little children secretively drop little morsels of food to their beloved little pet dogs. She knew nothing of Jesus' deity but knew that He had the power to decide on whether the demon would be cast out or not. Jesus acknowledged the woman taking her place as being a Gentile i.e. second in line behind the Jews, so was now free to minister to her according to His commission, and He told her that the demon had gone out of her daughter permanently. When the woman arrived home she found her daughter permanently set free, relaxed and resting on her bed.

And again, having gone out of the region of Tyre, He went through Sidon to the sea of Galilee in the midst of the region of Decapolis.

Jesus then travelled south east and around the eastern shore of the Sea of Galilee to reach the Decapolis region.

And they bring to Him one who was deaf and who spoke with difficulty. And they beg Him to place upon him His hand. And having taken him away from the crowd, in private He put His fingers into his ears, and having spit, He touched his tongue. And having looked up into heaven, He groaned and says to him, Ephphatha, which is, Be opened. And his ears opened, and immediately that which bound his tongue was loosed, and he began to be enunciating correctly.

A deaf man is brought to Jesus Who, desiring to focus on His preaching and teaching and meeting of the spiritual needs of the multitude rather than encourage a wide healing ministry, took the man aside from the people. Jesus thrust one finger of each hand into the man's ears and spat and touched his tongue, so as to capture his attention and encourage his faith since he couldn't hear anything that Jesus was saying to him. Jesus sighed, both in sympathy with the man, and due to the exhausting nature of His healing ministry. The man heard and straight away spoke in clear and distinct words.

And He in His own interest commanded them to be saying not even one thing. But the more He kept on commanding them, they themselves kept on proclaiming it publicly so much the more to a greater degree. And they were completely flabbergasted, and that in a superabundant degree which itself was augmented by the addition of yet more astonishment, saying, He has done all things well. He makes both the deaf to be hearing and the dumb to be speaking.

Jesus charged them to be keeping quiet about this, for His sake and for the future welfare of His ministry. But they were telling abroad more and more what had happened, since they were completely out of themselves with an amazement that more than greatly surpassed overflowing, and they were settled in their conviction as to how great and deserving of praise was the miracle that they had just seen and heard.

In those days again, there being a great crowd, and they not having anything to eat, having called His disciples to Him, He says to them, My heart goes out to the crowd, because now for three days they are staying with me and they do not have anything to eat. And if I send them off fasting to their homes, they will faint along the road. And some of them are from a distance.

On another occasion, Jesus' heart goes out to the crowd, they having been facing Him in fellowship continuously for three days.

And His disciples answered Him, How can it be that anyone will be able to satisfy these with loaves of bread here in the uninhabited region? And He went to asking them, How many loaves of bread do you have? And they said, Seven. And He commands the crowd to recline on the ground. And having taken the seven loaves of bread, having given thanks, He broke them, and kept on giving them to His disciples in order that they might keep on setting them forth. And they served the crowd. And they had a few little fish. And having prayed that God might bless them to their intended use, He directed them to set these also before them. And they ate and were satisfied. And they took up that which was left over of broken pieces, seven baskets. And there were about four thousand. And He sent them away.

The disciples objected saying, "How could all these people be filled and satisfied out here in the wilderness?" they having quickly forgotten how the five thousand had been fed before. As before, Jesus broke the loaves and they multiplied in His hands, so that He was continuously giving them to His disciples to give to the crowd. This time the surplus consisted of larger fragments of bread.

And immediately, having gone on board the boat with His disciples, He went to the region of Dalmanoutha. And there came out the Pharisees and began to be disputing with Him, demanding of Him an attesting miracle from heaven, putting Him to the test. And having groaned deeply in His spirit, He says, Why is this breed of men seeking an attesting miracle? Positively I am saying to you, There shall no attesting miracle be given to this breed.

Straight after this Jesus went to Decapolis again. The Pharisees, in their zeal against Jesus, left their seat in Israel to travel into this heathen region which they normally carefully shunned. They began to question Jesus and kept on questioning Him, putting Him under cross-examination, which then led to them being in open dispute with Him. Jesus took part in the dispute, defending His position absolutely, so that they resorted to then demanding that He perform some sign in order to confirm to them the validity of His claim to be the Messiah, or, if He failed their test, to show them that He was an impostor. Jesus' human spirit was stirred to its depths due to the hard-hearted rejection of His ministry by Israel's religious leaders, they entrenched in their strict adherence and over-attention to the details of religious practice, they who would later demand that He be killed even though they had actually seen Him perform attesting miracles, since they attributed these to Satan rather than to God. His sigh was one that expressed His spiritual sense of irreconcilable enmity, invincible unbelief, and coming doom. The miracles Jesus performed were to attest that His claim to be the Messiah was true and that His message was from God, not to satisfy the whims of demanding unbelievers who He knew would not accept their attesting value, so He refuses their demand, on this or any future occasion.

And having sent them away, again having embarked, He went off to the other side. And they had completely forgotten to take loaves of bread, and except for one loaf, they did not have any with them in the boat.

Jesus then bid the Pharisees leave and go away from Him, bringing the dispute to an abrupt end with His refusal to perform a sign for 'such as you who have renounced the principles of your faith'. The disciples, in preparing to journey across the Sea again, put no importance on what they would eat, having just the one loaf left for the day.

And He repeatedly charged them, saying, Be taking heed. Constantly be keeping a discerning mind's eye upon, and ever be on the lookout for the yeast of the Pharisees and the yeast of Herod.

In the boat Jesus kept warning them to think carefully and watchfully and critically about the teaching of the Pharisees and the Herodians i.e. that practising what they taught would ultimately lead to corrupting the true message of the Gospel of the Kingdom, with their emphases on religious externalism and on worldliness.

And they kept on discussing among themselves, saying, Because we do not have loaves of bread.

The disciples did not understand that Jesus was using bread as an illustration for the leaders' false teaching i.e. He was warning them not to feed on and swallow their doctrines. They kept on quietly discussing His words and reasoned that He was actually talking about their forgetting to bring bread.

And having come to know, He says to them, Why are you reasoning as follows: Because you do not have loaves of bread? Not yet are you perceiving, nor even understanding? In a settled state of callousness do you have your hearts? Having eyes, you are not seeing, and having ears, you are not hearing? And you are not remembering, when the five loaves I broke among the five thousand, how many baskets full of broken pieces did you take up? They say to Him, Twelve. When the seven among four thousand, how many baskets of broken pieces did you take up? And they say, Seven. And He kept on repeating to them, Not yet are you understanding?

Jesus then questions His pupils, showing His disappointment at their intellectual and spiritual dullness, rebuking them for their preoccupation with things transient and temporary, as if there were nothing higher to be thought of than bread. Currently their hearts were like the hard path of the seed parable, since Jesus' higher truths were not sinking down so as to germinate. These were the kind of men Jesus had to train as His disciples, who would preach the Gospel after He had ascended to Heaven, hence Jesus' desire to spend more time alone with them so that He could properly train them before it was necessary for Him to leave this earth. And, in spite of this training, Peter, the foremost of them, would later desert Him and go back to his fishing business, taking six other disciples with him. Jesus repeatedly says, "How is it that you do not yet understand?" half speaking to them, half to Himself, given the tremendous issues at stake. He finally had to explain to them that He was talking about false teaching.

And they come into Bethsaida. And they bring to Him a blind man. And they beg Him to touch him. And having taken the hand of the blind man, He brought him outside of the village, and having spit upon his eyes, having placed His hands upon him, He kept on asking him, Do you possibly see anything? And having looked up, he kept on saying, I see the men; as trees I see them walking around. Then again He placed His hands upon his eyes; and he looked steadfastly; and he was restored to his former state; and he was seeing all things at a distance and clearly. And He sent him off to his home, saying, Do not even go into the town.

Jesus conducted the blind man away from the crowd that He might perform the cure in secret, so as to avoid a stampede of sick ones. His compassionate heart went out to the sick, but He always kept His chief mission in mind, the cure of souls, not bodies. Spitting on the man's eyes was to encourage his faith, since this practice is considered to be a means of cure by many. The man looked up tentatively, firstly seeing the darkness pierced, then seeing objects as if through a mist, and finally seeing everything clearly. Again to avoid a sensation, Jesus directed the man not to return to the people who brought him, but to go back to his family. In this gradual healing Jesus was illustrating the slowness of the disciples in attaining spiritual sight.

And He went out, Jesus and His disciples, into the villages of Caesarea Philippi. And along the road He kept on asking His disciples, saying to them, Who do men say that I am? And they told Him, saying, John the Baptizer, and others, Elijah, and others, one of the prophets. And He himself kept on questioning them, But as for you, who are you saying that I am? Answering, Peter says to Him, As for you, you are the Christ. And He strictly charged them that they should not tell even one person concerning Him.

Jesus desired solitude with His disciples, so avoided the larger towns with their Herodian passion for ambitious architecture, and thus was safe from the annoyance of Herod and the Jewish leaders. He needed to prepare His disciples for His impending crucifixion, just a little over six months ahead. On one occasion Jesus held an important dialogue with them since it closely concerned them. He began by drawing out from them what they had heard of Him as gleaned from the surrounding opinions of the crowds. Then He was asking them directly and repeatedly, "But you, having heard Me and having walked with Me, who do you think I am?" Peter answers, "You, you are the Messiah, the Anointed One, the coming King of Israel, sent by God to occupy the throne of David forever". Jesus sharply admonished them, threateningly, not to disclose this to anyone, as if anticipating premature or foolish talk about this on their part, since His time was not yet ripe. Only when He entered Jerusalem would He permit widespread and rightful adulation of Himself.

And He began to be teaching them that it was necessary in the nature of the case for the Son of Man to suffer many things, and, after having been put to the test for the purpose of being approved should He meet the specifications, to be rejected by the elders and the chief priests and the men learned in the sacred scriptures, and to be put to death, and after three days to arise.

Then Jesus began to be solemnly teaching them about the inevitability and rationale of the Cross. Since God is love and man is a sinner, He will provide a salvation for him, but, since God is also just, it is necessary for Him to die on the Cross so as to pay the penalty that will satisfy the demands of that justice; that man's sin be paid for. Jesus was teaching them that His death would result from His being rejected as the Messiah of Israel by each of the Jewish authorities. But the disciples' hearts were still hard, and the announcement of His resurrection made no impression on them at all.

And with utter plainness of speech He was speaking this aforementioned word. And having taken Him aside to himself, Peter began to be rebuking Him. But having wheeled around, and having looked on His disciples, He rebuked Peter, and says, Be gone under my authority and keep on going. Behind me, out of my sight, Satan, because you do not have a mind for the things of God but for the things of men.

Jesus repeatedly and in detail gave them what He had to tell them, at length, and making it plain and unmistakeable, this time with no hints or veiled allusions, unlike before when He had said, "But there shall come days when there shall be taken away from them the bridegroom". Peter took hold of Jesus, aside from the other disciples, and made Him face him so as to rebuke Him regarding this unwelcome news about His death. Having heard what Peter said to Him, which words the other disciples also heard, Jesus turned His back on Peter and subjects him to a lesson before them all, Peter not realising at this time the dreadful thing he did. Now, as in the wilderness previously, Satan was tempting Jesus to go around the

Cross and receive the rulership of the world empire from his hands, the price, worship of him, but this time using Peter as his spokesman. So Jesus speaks directly to the Tempter, but also including Peter in His rebuke, which rebuke would not bring Satan to repentance, but which, in time, Peter would agree with; that his words here were inspired by Satan. Then would Peter side with the ways of God, rather than with those of man.

And having called the crowd together with His disciples to himself, He said to them, If anyone is desiring to come after me as a follower of mine, let him at once begin to lose sight of himself and his own interests, and let him at once begin to take up his cross and carry it, and let him start taking the same road that I travel in company with me, and let him continue to do so moment by moment.

To the crowd Jesus said, "Many will not come to Me that they might have life, but to those who do come to Me I say; Enter into fellowship with Me now. And die to self now, coming into a new state where you forget your own interests. Having made these two once-for-all decisions, namely, one, that your whole life be permanently directed and characterised by a habitual coming to Me, and, two, that you habitually set aside your life so that it is counted as given over to Me and that you consider that you are no longer your own but are owned by Me and are My own property, having so decided, accompany me on My road, and live your life walking by My side every moment of every day".

For whoever would desire to save his soul-life, will lose it. But whoever will lose his soul-life for my sake and the gospel, will save it. For what shall it profit a man to gain the whole world and lose his soul? For what shall a man give in exchange for his soul?

Jesus continued, "Those who desire to save their own soul, with its will and hopes and emotions, will indeed find self-gratification, but they will lose that which alone makes the activity of these things worthwhile and satisfying, since man is so created that he does not find complete rest and satisfaction until his entire being is swallowed up in God's sweet will for him. Not that God gives salvation as a reward for a life well lived, since self-denial alone can never save a soul from sin nor make a man into a child of God. Nevertheless, a lack of self-denial, together with self-satisfaction, will result in a man going into eternity a lost sinner, even though he gain all the pleasures and power that the world system, of which system Satan is the head, has to offer. Such a man will suffer total and everlasting loss since he did not want God."

For whoever is ashamed of me and my words in this generation which is adulterous and sinful, also the Son of Man shall be ashamed of him when He comes in the glory of His Father with the angels, the holy ones.

So Jesus warned the crowd, "Your conduct and attitude toward Me now will determine My future conduct and attitude toward you at my second Advent."

And He was saying to them, Assuredly, I am saying to you, there are certain ones of those standing here who are such as will not taste of death until they see the kingdom of God having come in power.

Jesus concluded by saying that some of them would soon see His Millennial Kingdom. Peter, Jacob, and John were indeed about to see Jesus' Millennial glory, being part of an anticipatory picture of this Kingdom that He would shortly show them on the mount of His transfiguration. In this picture those three disciples represent Israel, cleansed and restored at Jesus' second Advent, Moses represents the saints from Adam's time until the Rapture, raised to life at the Rapture and part of the Millennial Kingdom, Elijah represents those saints, alive on earth at the Rapture, who will be glorified and translated without dying, and the crowd below the mount represents the Gentile nations in the Millennium, being the recipients of the renewed ministry of Israel.

And after six days, Jesus takes with Him Peter, and James, and John, and brings them up into a mountain, a high one, in private, alone. And the manner of His outward expression was changed before them, that outward expression coming from and being truly representative of His inner nature. And His garments became glittering ones, exceedingly white, such as a fuller on earth is not able thus to whiten.

It was six days later that the three disciples were shown this picture of the Kingdom. On that mount, for a brief time, no longer was Jesus seen as a travel-stained, itinerant preacher claiming to be the Messiah, but with the radiant glory of the essence of deity shining right through the flesh of His humanity and through the clothing that He now wore, which glory He had in His pre-incarnate state. His radiant appearance came from within, shining actively, as sunshine flashing on reflective shields or on a sword, intensely dazzling, being a picture of what He will be like in the Millennium.

And there appeared to them Elijah and Moses, and they were holding a protracted conversation with Jesus. And Peter giving off his judgment, says to Jesus, Rabbi, it is an excellent thing for us to be here. And let us make three booths made of tree branches, for you one, and for Moses one, and for Elijah one; for he did not know what to give as his judgment, for they were terribly frightened.

Peter, having listened to Jesus' lengthy discussion with Moses the law giver and Elijah the Old Testament prophet, offers his judgment as to what ought to be done, "Jesus, my great One, my honourable Sir, it is beautiful for us to be here. Allow me and Jacob and John to build three leafy tents, one each for You and for Moses and for Elijah" because he did not know what to say given his violent fright, though he may have done better to keep silent.

And there came a cloud which enveloped and surrounded them. And there came a voice out of the cloud, This is my Son, the dearly-beloved One! be constantly hearing Him.

Suddenly a new condition entered, with the appearance of a remarkable shining cloud having a definite form, being the Shekinah Glory Cloud, such as had guided Israel out of Egypt and which rested above the Mercy Seat in the Temple's Holy of Holies. This cloud enveloped the disciples and surrounded them with brightness. A voice from the cloud then declared Jesus to be God's Son and God's dear and precious One, and charged them to obey whatever they hear Him say.

And suddenly, after they had looked round about, no longer did they see anyone but Jesus only with them. And while they were coming down out of the mountain, He charged them that they should narrate the things which they saw to not even one person, except when the Son of Man should arise out from amongst the dead. And the aforementioned matter they kept carefully and faithfully to themselves, all the while discussing with one another what that particular thing, namely, to arise out from amongst the dead, was.

Immediately the cloud disappeared and the disciples were left alone with Jesus. He told them not to disclose to anyone what had just happened, and this charge they strongly obeyed, mastering their instinct to relate their experience, though they disputed among themselves trying to discover what 'rising out from amongst the dead' might mean, since this would involve Jesus' death, the concept of which they could not fathom or receive.

And they kept on putting the question to Him, saying, How is it that the men learned in the sacred scriptures are constantly saying that it is necessary in the nature of the case for Elijah to come first? And He said to them, Elijah, it is true, having come first, restores all things. And how it stands written concerning the Son of Man, that He will suffer many things and be set at naught. But I say to you that indeed Elijah has come, and they did to him whatever things they were desiring to do, even as it stands written of him.

On the way down the disciples were repeatedly asking Jesus about what the Scriptures say about Elijah. He replied that in looking for Elijah to appear before the Messiah the teachers were correct. But 'Elijah' had appeared, unbeknown to them, being John the Baptizer, in the spirit and power of Elijah, to prepare the hearts of Israel for Him in His first Advent. Elijah himself will appear to prepare Israel for Jesus' second Advent. Elijah was persecuted by Queen Jezebel but ascended to Heaven without physically dying, while John was beheaded at the request of Herodias, and Elijah himself will be killed in the Tribulation period by the Wild Beast who ascends out of the bottomless place.

And having come to those who were following Him as their teacher, they saw a great crowd around them, and men learned in the sacred scriptures wrangling with them. And immediately, the entire crowd, having seen Him, was completely amazed, and running to Him, welcomed Him. And He asked them, What is it that you are discussing with them?

When they got to the bottom of the mount they saw the nine disciples who, having failed to heal a boy, were being taunted by the scribes, these suggesting the waning power of their Master, Jesus, in Whose authority they had attempted to perform the cure. All the while the gathered crowd listened. When they saw Jesus, the crowd was amazed to the point of exhausting their supply of amazement, having no further stores of amazement from which to draw, and straight away they ran to Jesus. The crowd was surprised and shocked, since Jesus was not looked for but needed, they being confused at the failed healing but exceedingly glad at His appearance. And His disciples, ashamed at their failure to heal the boy, were yet delighted to see their Teacher. And Jesus asked the crowd, "About what were you disputing?" seeking to find out what the contention was about.

And one of the crowd answered Him, Teacher, I brought my son to you, who has a spirit that has rendered him incapable of speech. And wherever he takes possession of him, he throws him into convulsions, and he foams and grinds his teeth and falls into a motionless stupor. And I spoke to your disciples that they should cast him out, and they did not have the power to do so.

The father of the boy replied to Jesus that he had thought He was with His disciples so had brought his son to be healed by Him. This demon controlled the boy's tongue and vocal organs so that he could not speak, and would seize his body and pull him down and cause him to fit in convulsions and to gnash his teeth, finally draining his strength so that he became as if dead. And the man told Jesus that the disciples were not able to exert any power over the demon.

And answering them, He says, O unbelieving generation, how long shall I have to do with you? How long must I bear with you? Be bringing him to me.

Jesus rebukes His disciples, given their relation to Him, and laments that He is still having to bear their weakness of faith.

And they brought him to Him. And, having seen Him, the spirit immediately threw him into a complete convulsion, and having fallen upon the ground, he was being rolled and was foaming. And He asked his father, How long is it that this came to him? And he said, Since he was a little boy. And often also he threw him into fire, and into water in order that he might destroy him. But if you are able to do anything, help us at once, having had compassion upon us.

Jesus parted Himself from the crowd and the boy was brought, and straight away the demon, knowing that his control over the boy would soon be ended, made a last attack. The father told Jesus about the boy's condition; how he would be thrown into life-threatening situations in a suicidal mania induced by his intermittent demon possession. And he pleaded that Jesus help him and his son right now given His compassion for them. But he was now wondering if Jesus had the power to overcome the demon, his own faith having been shaken by the failure of the disciples to cast it out and by the increasing severity of the attacks, as he was now seeing before his eyes.

And Jesus said to him, As for those words of yours, If you are able: - all things are possible to the one who believes. Immediately having cried out, the father of the little boy was saying, I am believing. Be helping my weakness of faith.

Jesus held up the man's own words, 'If You can', for the man's consideration and for His own comments. Jesus replied, "If you can, … all things can be", contrasting the man's plea for 'anything' with His ability to do 'all things'. Instantly, in response, the father of the boy was piercingly crying out with eagerness and fear, "Help me to believe more constantly and stronger".

And Jesus, having seen that a crowd was gathering together on the run, rebuked the foul spirit, saying to him, Dumb and deaf spirit, I order you, be coming out of him, and no longer enter him. And after crying out and throwing him into severe convulsions, he came out. And he became as one who is dead, so that many were saying that he had died. But Jesus, having taken a strong grip of his hand, went to raising him up. And he stood up.

The piercing cry of the father attracted the attention of the crowd so that they came running towards them, the sight of which interrupted Jesus' conversation since privacy would no longer be possible. Jesus rebuked the demon which, not willing to repent, came out with one last vengeful and fatal attack on the boy in response to Jesus' sharp and firm command to, "Come out and stay out". But Jesus firmly took the boy's hand, having given him back his life, and the boy instantly rose from the ground.

And having entered into a house, His disciples kept on asking Him privately, As for us, why were we not able to cast him out? And He said to them, This kind is able to come out by nothing but prayer.

Jesus again left the crowd, seeking privacy so as to be able to teach His disciples. The nine were asking Him to explain their failure to cast out the demon. Jesus told them that the heart and spirit need to be prepared for such encounters, since evil spirits of that kind are able to discern any lack of moral power in their opponent and will yield to no other kind of power, and that the disciples had instead trusted solely in an almost magical power with which they thought they had been permanently invested i.e. their failure was due to prayerlessness, resulting in a lack of moral power.

And going out from there, they went on their way through Galilee. And He was not desirous that anyone should know it, for He was constantly teaching His disciples. And He was saying to them, The Son of Man is being betrayed into men's hands, and they will kill Him, and having been put to death, after three days He will arise. But they were not understanding the word. And they were fearing to ask Him.

Jesus and His disciples then travelled south, He now fully occupied with training them, they occasionally splitting into smaller groups so that He could focus on quietly teaching them two or four at a time. He was telling them that He was imminently to be handed over to the Jewish authorities and that the process was already underway, in that He could see His betrayal already lying as an undeveloped thought in the heart of Judas Iscariot.

And they came into Capernaum. And having come in the house, He kept on asking them, What along the road were you disputing about? But they kept on being quiet, for with one another they had discussed along the road who was the greatest. And having sat down, He called the Twelve and says to them, If, as is the case, anyone is desiring to be first, let him be last of all and a servant of all. And having taken a little child, He stood him in their midst; and when He had taken him in His arms, He said to them, Whoever receives one of such little children in my Name, receives me. And whoever receives me, does not receive me but the One who sent me.

When they had all arrived at Peter's house, Jesus was asking them about their conversation on the way, they not realising that He had heard them. This discussion was about what rank each of them would have in their Master's Kingdom that they expected to be set up soon, this topic being in light of three of them having been taken up the mount with Jesus and of Peter's prominence among those three. The disciples were ashamed and were maintaining a long silence. Jesus then schools them in humility, taking His seat as their Master, and pointing out to them that the way to true greatness, since they were wanting to be first, was through servanthood and in ministering to others. He illustrated His teaching with a child, since such are trusting, and the least self-conscious and self-sufficient. To exhibit these same qualities would result in a character approved and recognised and welcomed by Jesus Himself, making one a great, true, and loyal disciple of His.

John said to Him, Teacher, we saw a certain individual casting out demons in your Name who does not follow with us. And we kept on forbidding him because he was not following with us. But Jesus said, Stop forbidding him, for there is no one who will perform a miracle upon the basis of my Name who will also soon be able to speak ill of me, for whoever is not against us is in behalf of us.

John interrupted, in response to this teaching, now frankly confessing and questioning his previous prohibiting of a non-disciple from using Jesus' Name in exorcising demoniacs. Having been taught about true greatness, John now believed that possibly he should rather have welcomed him as a brother rather than being jealous for the honour of the twelve disciples? Jesus, noting his sincerity, corrected John, saying he should have at least been neutral, since the one that he had rebuked was practically committed to a course of action that was incompatible with hostile thought or speech of his Teacher.

For whoever will give you to drink a cup of water in my Name because you belong to Christ, truly I am saying to you, he will positively not lose his reward. And whoever will cause one of these little ones who believe to stumble, it is good for him rather if a millstone is hung around his neck and that he has been thrown into the sea.

Jesus continues His teaching on greatness by saying that, in ministering to others, there is a most definite spiritual significance in the act of serving that is independent of the material value of that service. And conversely, that a disservice done that causes harm to the least of His followers, being an act that causes that one to trip or to fall, whether that be through a careless disregard for their infirmities or by a wilful creation of impediments to them, will bring incalculable evil upon the evil-doer, more so than their being weighed down so as to be trapped at the bottom of the sea.

And if your hand causes you to stumble, cut it off at once. It is good for you to enter life maimed, rather than having two hands to go off into hell, into unquenchable fire. And if your foot causes you to stumble, cut it off at once. It is good for you to enter life maimed, rather than having the two feet to be thrown into hell. And if your eye causes you to stumble, throw it out at once. It is good for you to enter the kingdom of God one-eyed, rather than, having two eyes, to be thrown into hell where their worm does not come to its end in death and the fire is not quenched. For everyone will be salted with fire. Salt is good. But if the salt loses its pungency, with what will you restore the saltness to it? Be having salt in yourselves, and be being at peace with one another.

Jesus then warns His disciples that a man may also place impediments in his own path, the temptations proceeding from some part of his own nature. As men submit to the loss of a limb in order to preserve their physical body as a whole, so is it better to live under a sense of incompleteness of soul than to perish in the enjoyment of all one's powers. The eye for instance, designed to develop a love of visible beauty, may look upon the sinful and so be a cause of temptation. By the same reasoning it is in a man's interest to sacrifice powers and functions of his spiritual nature which have been found to be inevitable occasions of sin i.e. better to live the worthwhile life having an eye only for the spiritual and eternal beauty, than to indulge the lower, worldly taste to the loss of all. The spiritual wounds inflicted on a man by his own sins, causing the degradation and deterioration of his being, have no limitations of time, but will cause him everlasting misery. Everyone must be salted, either with the fire of Hell or with the fire of self-discipline. So keep the fire of self-discipline burning and do not let it go out. Then Jesus centres in on their own recent behaviour, "If you, My chosen disciples, become selfish, wrangling about who is the greatest, the fire which I brought is clearly not burning in you, so what will cause your love to be rekindled? Disputes about precedence among you endanger the very existence of the new life, the first condition of which is; be at peace with your brethren."

And from there, having arisen, He comes into the regions of Judaea and across the Jordan, and again crowds journeying along with Him come constantly to Him, and as was His custom, He again was constantly teaching them.

Now Jesus starts out on a considerable journey, finally quitting Galilee and Capernaum, His face now turned towards Jerusalem. Others who are also going to Jerusalem, many of whom are followers of Jesus or kindly disposed toward Him, join with Him and His disciples along the road. As they are journeying along together, He was continually teaching them.

And having come to Him, Pharisees kept on asking Him whether it is lawful for a man to dismiss a wife, putting Him to the test. And He answering, said to them, What did Moses command you? And they said, Moses permitted a writing of a bill of divorce and to dismiss her.

As Jesus was resuming His public teaching, the Pharisees were returning to their attacks on Him, now venturing to find an error in His orthodoxy by asking Him a leading question so as to get Him to commit Himself on the law of Moses. They did this, hoping to put Him in an unfavourable light with the people, since they thought that He would say that it was not lawful to divorce and, in their interpretation of the law, Moses allowed for it. Also, such an answer from Jesus might excite the anger of Herod, who had put away his first wife and married again. Jesus' counter-question was referring to Moses' first book of the law, where Moses declared marriage to be the ideal state of things and not to be broken, rather than to when Moses subsequently made provision for divorce, which Scripture the Pharisees now demanded Jesus make a judgment on.

And Jesus said to them, On account of your hardheartedness he wrote this commandment for you. But from creation's beginning, a male and a female He made them. On account of this a man shall leave behind his father and mother and the two shall become one flesh, so that no longer are they two but one flesh. That therefore which God yoked together, let no man separate.

Jesus explained to them that Moses did not command divorce, but that he commanded regulations tending to limit it and to prevent its abuse. These regulations were only necessary due to the harsh and stern hearts of the first Hebrew people, and in clinging to this temporary recognition of a necessary evil, the Pharisees showed that they had not outgrown the moral stature of their fathers, but were still maintaining a condition of indifference to the call of God, their moral nature withered under the power of practical unbelief. Jesus appealed to the principle clearly pronounced in the original composition of man; a man is to forsake his parents' nurturing of him so as to cleave closely to his wife and remain joined to her, yoked together with her and united with her in the marriage tie, which tie, in God's purpose, should not be parted.

And in the house again the disciples kept on asking Him concerning this. And He says to them, Whoever puts away his wife and marries another woman commits adultery against her. And if she herself, having put away her husband, marries another man, she commits adultery.

When they came into the privacy of a house, the disciples kept questioning Jesus about divorce. He now adds that to marry after divorcing is to commit adultery against the divorced person, except in the case of unfaithfulness by either party in the marriage relation, since mere formal divorce does not annul an actual marriage consummated by the physical union of a man and his wife.

And they kept on bringing to Him young children in order that He might touch them. And His disciples kept on rebuking them unjustly and without effect. But Jesus having seen this, became indignant, and said to them, Be permitting the little children to come to me. Stop preventing them, for of such ones is the kingdom of God. Truly, I am saying to you, Whoever does not receive the kingdom of God in the same manner as a little child, will positively not enter it. And having taken them up in His arms, He kept on fervently blessing them, placing His hands upon them.

After this teaching on the sanctity of married life, children kept on being brought to Him at the house, being a sign of the growing reverence of the people for this great Teacher as shown by their even bringing infants and older children to this wonder-working Prophet for Him to bless and to dedicate, He in their view being greater than any of the local synagogue rulers. The disciples kept trying to stop them, intent on protecting their Master's dignity, but their efforts were ineffective given the constant stream of people coming in and out of the house. Jesus was pained by the actions of His disciples and entered into a state of indignation, since they still misunderstood the nature of His Kingdom and were hindering those who were seeking to come to Him. And more, the little children, being trusting and with a simple and loving obedience, represent those who constitute His Kingdom in their trusting and simple reception of the salvation that God offers, while those lacking in such qualities will never never enter it. Jesus took each child in succession and kept on blessing them all emphatically, His hands laid on each of them individually.

And when He was going out into the road there came one running toward Him, and having fallen on his knees before Him was asking Him, Teacher, you who are intrinsically good, what one act shall I do in order that I might inherit eternal life? And Jesus said to him, Why do you say that I am intrinsically good? No one is intrinsically good except One, God. The commandments you know: Do not commit murder, do not commit adultery, do not steal, do not bear false witness, do not defraud, honour your father and mother. And he said to Him, Teacher, these things, all of them, I carefully guarded and obeyed from my boyhood.

And carrying on the journey, a rich man, of dignity, was running to Jesus and was paying homage to Him, zealously seeking spiritual advice from this good Teacher. Jesus questioned the man's use of the word 'good' since he had used it lightly, out of mere courtesy and politeness, revealing the poverty of his moral conceptions. Jesus called him to consider the absolute goodness of God and to measure himself by that supreme standard, not desiring that He Himself be ascribed goodness by one who knew not what he was saying. And also Jesus directed the man to think carefully about the competing types of goodness to choose from, whether it be that of the Pharisees or that exhibited in His own teaching. Having fixed the standard of goodness, Jesus then rehearsed the divine precepts which the Jews considered to be the highest expression of the good will of God, citing those which regulate a man's duty to his neighbour, and comprising a relatively simple application of the lawful conduct of life. The man said that he had obeyed these commandments and held them to be precious and, as such, had honoured them throughout his life, taking care not to violate any of them, and so he was relieved to hear that the eternal inheritance could be secured by his simply obeying the Ten Commandments and that therefore eternal life was already his, the deeper meaning and larger requirements of the law being as yet hidden from him.

And Jesus, having fixed His searching gaze upon him, fell in love with him, and said to him, One thing you are lacking; go, whatever you have sell at once and give at once to the poor, and you will have treasure in heaven, and come, make a beginning of following with me on the same road that I am taking, and continue to do so. And he, saddening at the word, went off, being grieved, for he was in possession of great wealth.

Jesus looked intently at the man and entered into a new condition of self-sacrificial love for him, seeing the virtues and seeds of virtues in him. In answer to the man's question of 'What do I lack?' Jesus saw that, in his case, a necessary test of faith and obedience was for him to sell and distribute his property, and thereafter to follow with Him on the road of self-renouncing, of self-sacrifice, of separation, and of service to others. This step of obedience would lead to his becoming a disciple of Jesus and to him receiving salvation in answer to his faith in Jesus as Saviour. But his love of wealth kept him from making this step i.e. the 'one thing' that he needed to do he was not willing to do. The man's previous optimism broke down and his mood clouded over, so that his face became sad and gloomy with the disappointment and grief that he now felt. It pained him that his hopes were dashed, the one thing he wanted being beyond his reach since he was not willing to pay the price, it being too great a price to pay even for eternal life. So he went off, for the time being his love for the world prevailing, though a seed had been planted in his heart and his current sorrow was maybe just the birth-pains of a struggling spirit about to be released.

And Jesus, having glanced swiftly around, says to His disciples, How with difficulty will those who keep on holding on to wealth enter the kingdom of God. And the disciples were astonished at His words. And Jesus again answering, says to them, Children, how difficult it is to enter the kingdom of God. It is easier for a camel to go through the eye of the sewing needle than for a wealthy man to enter the kingdom of God. And beyond measure they were amazed, to the point of almost losing their self-possession, saying to one another, Then who is able to be saved? After having swiftly glanced around them, Jesus says, With men, impossible, but not in the presence of God, for all things are possible in the presence of God.

After the man had gone, Jesus looked around the circle of the twelve disciples and speaks to them so as to draw a lesson from this incident; "How hard it is for those who cannot release their worldly wealth, to release their faith so as to inherit eternal and true wealth in God's Kingdom." Since the disciples were thrown into consternation by these words i.e. by His adding to the condition of becoming as a child, the difficulty also of men of substance entering the Kingdom, Jesus then speaks tenderly to them, "Children, it is hard for anyone to enter the Kingdom. And impossible for anyone whose love of riches keeps them from trusting in Me in order to be saved." Now the disciples were astonished so as to be beside themselves, so He reassures them, "While it is impossible to be saved by standing with men on the question of riches, if you take your stand beside God on this matter, the impossible becomes possible."

Peter began to be saying to Him, Behold, as for us, we abandoned all once for all and have followed with you, and this as a permanent thing. Jesus said, Truly I am saying to you, There is no one who abandoned house or brothers or sisters or mother or father or children or lands for my sake and for the sake of the gospel, but that he will receive one hundred times as much now at this time, houses, and brothers, and sisters, and mothers, and children, and lands, with persecutions, and in the age to come, life eternal. But many who are first shall be last, and the last ones, first.

Peter started to be responding to this teaching, "See, we decided irrevocably to yield up everything and bid it go away permanently so as to follow You?" with the unspoken question, 'What reward will we get for having become poor for You?', showing that he was still thinking in terms of material rather than spiritual riches, and indeed later, after Jesus' resurrection, he would abandon his preaching commission to go back to his fishing business. Jesus said to them that the relations of home, relatives, and property given up for Him, would be recompensed handsomely by the spiritual affinities which bind the members of God's family. Accompanying this would come persecutions, since it is in this world that the moral compensation takes place. In the Millennial Age, the Jews who accept Jesus at His second Advent will be rewarded with eternal life. And Jesus warned them against sacrifice purely in the hope of reward, which spirit Peter did not have the courage to put into words.

And they were on the road, going up to Jerusalem. And Jesus was going on before them, and they were amazed. And those who were following along were fearing. And having taken again the Twelve, He began to be speaking to them concerning the things that were about to be converging upon Him. Behold! We are going up to Jerusalem, and the Son of Man shall be delivered up treacherously to the chief priests and to the men learned in the sacred scriptures, and they shall condemn Him to death and shall hand Him over to the Gentiles, and they shall deride Him and spit upon Him and scourge Him and kill Him, and after three days He shall rise again.

Jesus and His disciples were heading to Jerusalem and to the Cross. As often before, Jesus was walking alone, ahead of His disciples, but now he was walking with a solemnity and determination as He set His face firmly against the danger ahead. Given Jesus' disposition, the disciples were now beginning to anticipate an impending disaster, and the following crowd were fearful, with a sense of foreboding. As the atmosphere was so tense and as there was a real danger of panic, Jesus stopped and was waiting for the disciples to come up to Him, and then was telling them clearly what they were walking into.

And there come to Him James and John, the sons of Zebedee, saying to Him, Teacher, we desire that whatever we ask of you, you will do for us. And He said to them, What do you desire me to do for you? And they said to Him, Grant us at once that, one on your right hand and one on your left hand, we might sit down in your glory. But Jesus said to them, You do not know what you are asking for yourselves. Are you able to be drinking the cup which I am drinking, or with the immersion with which I am to be overwhelmed, are you able to be immersed? And they said to Him, We are able. And Jesus said to them, The cup which I drink, you will drink. And the immersion with which I am to be overwhelmed, with that immersion you will be overwhelmed. But the sitting on my right hand or my left is not mine to give. But it is for those for whom it has been prepared.

Jacob and John, prompted by their mother, and acting like spoiled children in trying to get Jesus to commit to their desires before He knows what they are, approach their King with a request to be given the places of highest honour in His Kingdom, in marked contrast to Jesus' self-denial, self-sacrifice, and courage in going to the Cross, He having no sense of self-ambition, they having self-interest, self-advancement, and ambition on their mind. Jesus gently rebuked their self-seeking, "Are you able to drink the unique, special, and unusual cup of the ordeal that is already beginning for Me and will conclude on the Cross? Are you able to be placed into the calamities that are about to overwhelm Me when I will be made sin and be abandoned by God?" Given the crucial and terrible moment that was fast approaching for Jesus, how patient and kind and loving was He in His response to these two disciples who had asked such a question. Their reply to Jesus, that they were able, was eager and showed their loyalty and moral courage as exhibited in their readiness to share in His lot, whatever that might be. And they would indeed later die, Jacob by the sword and John through hard labour in exile, both as martyrs, but their response here lacked any clear understanding of Jesus' repeated warnings about His own death. While Jesus will distribute eternal rewards at the Judgment, nevertheless He will only do so in accordance with the Father's wishes.

And when the ten heard, they began to be indignant concerning the matter with reference to James and John, and kept it up. And having called them to himself, Jesus says to them, You know that those who are accounted as ruling over the Gentiles, rule with absolute power over them, and their great ones domineer over them. But not thus is it among you. But whoever desires to become great among you, he shall be slave of all. And whoever desires to be first among you, he shall be your slave. For even the Son of Man did not come to have service rendered Him but to render service and to give His life a ransom for many.

Once again a spirit of jealousy was aroused among the disciples. Jesus shows them the difference between greatness as expressed in the world and greatness as expressed in His Kingdom. In the Kingdom there is to be no pomp and privilege, rather lowliness and slave-like servitude, as shown by Him, the King, and God incarnate in human flesh, who came to serve mankind, and to pay with His own precious blood the ransom money so as to free men from their slavery to sin, taking their place as a substitutionary sacrifice to procure their atonement, a Lamb without spot or blemish.

And they come into Jericho. And as He is proceeding out from Jericho, and His disciples and a sizable crowd, the son of Timaeus, Bartimaeus, blind, a beggar, was sitting as was his habit alongside the road. And having heard that it was Jesus, the Jesus from Nazareth, he began to be crying out and saying, Son of David, Jesus, have sympathy with me in my affliction and help me at once. And many kept on censuring him severely to the effect that he should become silent. But he kept on crying out all the more, Son of David, have sympathy with me in my affliction and help me at once. And having come to a standstill, Jesus said, Call him at once. And they call the blind man, saying to him, Be of good courage, be arising, he is calling you. And having thrown off his outer garment, having leaped up, he came to Jesus. And answering him, Jesus said, What are you desiring that I shall do for you? And the blind man said to Him, Rabboni, that I might recover my sight. And Jesus said to him, Be going on your way. Your faith has healed you perfectly. And immediately he recovered his sight and was following with Him on the road.

As Jesus is on His way to Jerusalem and the Cross, He enters Jericho in a public way, accompanied by the crowds who are going to the Passover, thus placing Himself in the power of the Roman and Jewish authorities. On leaving the city there was sitting by the road one of the many blind beggars in the region. Hearing the increasing noise of the crowd and having been told that it was The Jesus Who was approaching, he began to be shouting for the 'Son of David', that being the title of the Messiah since all the Jews of Judaea and Jerusalem consider themselves to be sons of David, he pleading to be healed at once. The crowd preceding Jesus entered into a state of censure, demanding him be quiet so as not to spoil the triumphant and harmonious mood by bringing his misery to the attention of the great Prophet. But the man carried on, shouting even louder. From within the crowd, Jesus asked that they call the man to come to Him now, and they in turn call him, their words of rebuke now turned to those of friendliness, "Courage, He calls you!" The man abandoned his large garment that he slept in and sprang up, and ran to Jesus. Then, respectfully and reverently, he asked his Master that he might see again. Jesus told him that he was now permanently physically healed. Straight away the man's sight was restored and he joined with the crowd that was following Jesus to Jerusalem.

And when they were getting near Jerusalem, Bethphage and Bethany, at the Mount of Olivet, He sends two of His disciples on a mission, and says to them, Be going off into the village opposite you, and immediately upon proceeding into it, you will find a colt securely tied, upon which not even one man ever sat. Loose it at once and be bringing it. And if anyone says to you, Why are you doing this? say, The Lord is having need of it and forthwith will send it here again. And they went off and found a colt tied securely to a door outside in the open street, and they loose it. And certain of those who were standing there went to saying to them, What are you doing, loosing the colt? And they spoke to them even as Jesus had said. And they gave them permission. And they bring the colt to Jesus and throw upon it their outer garments, and He sat upon it.

As Jesus was approaching Jerusalem, He sends Peter and another disciple to bring to Him a particular unbroken donkey foal from Bethany. They found it, exactly as He described, tied at the entrance of a house's passageway from its open court onto the street. The owners of the colt, who had tied up their animals while they were involved in a discussion, were satisfied when they heard that it was the well-known Prophet who needed to borrow it, since they did not need it at that particular time, but rather were proud that it was Jesus Himself Who would be using it. The colt is brought to Jesus and they throw some spare clothing on its back since, being unbroken, it has no saddle.

And many spread their garments into the road, and others, soft foliage, having cut it out of the countryside. And those who went before and those who followed kept on crying out, Hosanna, praised be He who comes in the Name of the Lord. Praised be the coming kingdom of our father David. Hosanna in the highest.

Some of the crowd threw their garments into the road and spread them there, while others placed straw and rushes and leaves so as to form a carpeted way for Jesus, riding on the donkey, this being His formal presentation of Himself as the Messiah. The crowd, realising this, were entering into the spirit of the occasion with their shouts, they expecting

Him to now set up His rule in opposition to that of Rome and thus deliver them from the yoke of their oppressors. Hearing the shouts, another crowd was pouring out from the city of Jerusalem, meeting with the previously assembled crowd, they then turning and going on ahead of Jesus, so He riding in the centre of these two crowds. Together they unite to shout Jesus' praises, "Praise the One Who has come to save us and bless us".

And He entered Jerusalem and the temple. And after He had given all things a comprehensive inspection, it being already the evening hour, He went out to Bethany with the Twelve.

Jesus came into the city and went to the Temple, where He closely and keenly observed all that was going on in its porches and outer courts, inspecting this part of God's house in a serious and judicial manner. It being late now, He postponed His proposed action until the next day. He left the city with His chosen disciples and headed for Bethany, spending the night on the Mount of Olives, which mount offered comparative security against the danger of sudden arrest, and where conditions were favourable for meditation and prayer.

And the next day, they having come out of and away from Bethany, He became hungry. And having seen a fig tree a long way off having leaves, He came, assuming that He would find something on it. And having come to it, He found not even one thing, except leaves. For it was not the season of figs. And answering, He said to it, Hereafter forever, from you no one eats fruit. And His disciples were listening.

Early the next day, being Monday, the second day of the week, and three days before the Cross, at around six in the morning, Jesus and His disciples set out to return to Jerusalem. He was looking for food on a tree which was prematurely in leaf, and that therefore should also be bearing a premature crop of figs. But the tree did not fulfil its promise, so Jesus was condemning it, not only because of its fruitlessness, but because of its fruitlessness in the midst of a display which promised fruit. Thus was Jesus pronouncing God's judgment on Israel's fruitless religiosity.

And they come into Jerusalem. And having entered the temple, He began to be throwing out those who sold and those who bought in the temple, and He threw down the tables of the money-changers and the seats of those who sold doves, and was not permitting anyone to carry household gear through the temple. And He went to teaching and was saying to them, Does it not stand written, My house shall be called a house of prayer for all the nations? But as for you, you have made it a den of robbers.

Jesus came into the Temple courts and started clearing out the market stalls. This market was a recognised institution under the protection of the chief priests and referenced in the writings of the rabbis, whose stalls comprised those selling various Temple requirements, for example animals for the sacrifices, and wine, oil, and salt as used in the rituals. And there were stalls where Greek and Roman coins could be exchanged for Jewish half-shekels so that the Jew could pay his Temple-tax, which business brought in much profit. To have their tables turned over and their money thrown all over the floor on the eve of Passover was to deal their business a serious blow at this time when money traffic was at its height. And Jesus was also preventing those using the courts as a short-cut for transporting goods between Jerusalem and the Mount of Olives, a practice forbidden by the Jewish authorities, but not enforced by them. A crowd gathered to see all the commotion, which gave Jesus an opportunity to be teaching, "Who can pray in a place which is a cattle market and an office of exchange, where dealers haggle and commit wholesale robbery as they conduct their operations on a large and systematic scale, and where people come merely to purchase things?"

And the chief priests and the men learned in the sacred scriptures heard. And they went to seeking how they might destroy Him, for they were fearing Him; for the entire multitude was struck with astonishment at His teaching.

In response to Jesus' actions, the chief priests now joined the scribes in their hostility to Jesus, His attack on their market incensing them. Together they now set their minds on how they might kill Him. But they feared the crowds, who being mostly from Galilee and the Gentile countries, were captivated by Jesus, and beside themselves on hearing His teaching, it being in such contrast to that of the Jewish leaders, and so any attempt to arrest Jesus on the part of the authorities might result in their being stoned by the people.

And when evening came they were going forth out of the city. And passing by in the morning they saw the fig tree completely withered from the roots. And being reminded, Peter says to Him, Rabbi, see, the fig tree which you cursed is withered away.

Jesus taught in the Temple all day until the city gates were about to be closed. Then He and His disciples headed back to the Mount of Olives. Early the next day, being Tuesday, the third day of the week, and two days before the Cross, they were heading back to Jerusalem and passed by that same fig tree, now shrivelled up. Peter noticed it and brings Jesus' attention to it, almost blaming Him for cursing the tree.

And answering, Jesus says to them, Be constantly having faith in God. Truly, I am saying to you, Whoever says to this mountain, Be lifted up and be thrown into the sea, and does not doubt in his heart but believes that that which he says comes to pass, it shall be his.

Jesus' reply does not explain the state of the tree. Rather He gives them an important teaching arising from the prompt fulfilment of His prayer. He had exercised faith in His Father in cursing the tree, so He now emphasises their need to always have faith in God. The figure of speech He uses about faith cooperating with the Divine Will resulting in the basin of the Dead Sea being filled with the mass of limestone of the Mount of Olives, was in use among the rabbis. This metaphor is symbolic of true faith, being the normal attitude of the heart and not an isolated emotion or action, it always contemplating, without any wavering doubt, its effect as potentially accompanying its exercise, though its actual fulfilment may be delayed i.e. real and living faith sees the future result as being a present reality.

On this account I am saying to you, All things whatever you are praying and asking for, be believing that you received them, and they shall be yours. And whenever you are standing, praying, forgive, if you have anything against a certain person, in order that your Father also who is in heaven may forgive you your trespasses.

Jesus continues, "Since faith is the criterion of success in spiritual matters, faith should be your constant attitude of mind when you pray to God asking Him for something to be given you, so that you always see your request's fulfilment before it happens, your faith guaranteeing the answer to your prayer before you are in possession of it. Given your Father's constant attention to your requests, hold no ill will against any other, that you may enjoy His cleansing of your false steps which would otherwise weaken your faith due to your guilty conscience".

And they come again into Jerusalem. And when He was walking about the temple, there come to Him the chief priests and the men learned in the sacred scriptures and the elders, and they kept on saying to Him, By what sort of delegated authority are you doing these things, or, who gave you this authority to be doing these things? And Jesus said to them, I will ask you concerning one point, and answer me, and I will tell you by what sort of delegated authority I am doing these things. The baptism of John, from heaven was it or from men? Answer me. And they were reasoning with themselves, saying, If we say, From heaven, he will say, Then, why did you not believe him? But if we say, From men, - they were fearing the people. For all were holding John actually to be a prophet. And answering Jesus, they say, We do not know. And Jesus says to them,

Neither am I telling you by what sort of delegated authority I am doing these things.

As Jesus was walking among the colonnades of the Temple teaching the people, representatives of each of the three groups of Jewish leaders approach Him, they coming together in agreement with one another due to their mutual indignation that He had ejected those engaged in business from the Temple, which Temple was their responsibility. Jesus was claiming a superior official power, so they were demanding that He now produce His credentials in public; the nature of His authority and the person from whom He had received this authority. Jesus replied with a question for them, "What was John the Baptizer's source of authority?", since John had testified to the divine source of Jesus' mission. If they answered 'God', they would then be charged guilty since they had rejected John's baptism, but if they said that John's authority was of human origin, they feared being stoned by the crowd, since the people held John's words to be of God, their regard for him only deepened by his martyrdom. In humiliation, they, the learned ones, have to say, "We do not know".

And He began to be speaking to them in the form of illustrations. A man planted a vineyard, and set a hedge about it, and digged a place for a wine-press, and built a tower, and let it out for his own advantage to vineyard men, and went away to foreign parts. And he sent off to the vineyard men at the season a slave, in order that from the vineyard men he might receive some of the fruit of the vine. And having taken him, they beat him severely and sent him off empty. And again he sent off to them another slave. And that one they knocked about the head and grossly insulted. And another he sent off. And that one they killed, and many others; some, on the one hand, beating severely, and others, on the other hand, killing.

Jesus now started speaking to these leaders in a story that accused them of being the future murderers of the Messiah, also exposing the true character of the hostility of the Jewish ruling council, and this in the presence of the crowd. The vineyard, as they and the better-taught among the crowd knew, represented Israel, the covenant people. The man who planted the vineyard was God, and the vineyard men these leaders. The hedge represented God's protective care over Israel and His blessings upon the Chosen People. The rent was to be paid in kind i.e. a stipulated portion of the wine. The slaves sent to collect the rent were the Old Testament prophets sent to Israel. The beating and killing of the slaves represented the failure of Israel to heed the preaching of the prophets.

Yet one he had, a son, a beloved one. He sent him off last to them, saying, They will reverence my son. But those vineyard men said to themselves, This is the heir. Come. Let us be putting him to death, and ours shall be the inheritance. And having taken him, they killed him and threw him out of the vineyard.

Jesus now alluded to Himself in the story; the beloved only son. So improbable was his fate in the story, it pointed to the absolute hardness of heart of these leaders towards Jesus, and also, more generally, to the utter and complete depravity of mankind, of which depravity the fallen race has no proper conception, so that it will go to any lengths to hold onto its sin. The story's accusation was that the leaders of Israel actually recognised Jesus for what He was, the Son of God and Messiah of Israel, and that He had come to claim the vineyard, Israel, for Himself. But the fact that the people received Him in a friendly recognition aroused a senseless jealousy in these leaders, and, seeing their own power over the people waning, led to them now seeking to kill Him. The story predicts what the people did not yet know; that the leaders were about to excommunicate Jesus by condemning Him as a blasphemer, and hand Him over to the Romans to be executed, by whom He would be crucified outside of the walls of Jerusalem, symbolising this expulsion from the community of Israel.

What will the master of the vineyard do? He will come and destroy the vineyard men, and will give the vineyard to others. And did you not even read this scripture, A stone which the builders rejected after having put it to the test for the purpose of approving it, and finding that it did not meet their specifications, this became the head of the corner? From the Lord came this. And it is marvellous in our eyes. And they were seeking to seize Him, but were fearing the crowd, for they knew that with reference to them He had given the illustration. And having left Him, they went off.

The story now moves into prophecy; Jerusalem will be destroyed, the Jews dispersed around the world, the Gentiles will be called, and the Church of Jesus will be the new channel through which God operates while Israel is temporarily dispersed, and until Israel is re-gathered at Jesus' second Advent and restored to fellowship with, and usefulness, to God. Then Jesus questioned the leaders' knowledge of a Scripture, showing that it refers to Him, the rejected Stone, rejected by them, the builders, not rejected because they found His claims to be false, the miracles He performed proving His validity, but rejected because He did not meet their requirements. They were looking for a Messiah who would deliver Israel from the despotism of Rome, not from the dominion of sin. Despite their rejection of Him and killing of Him, Jesus will nevertheless become the King of kings and Lord of lords over the earth as the Head of the

Millennial Empire, the Headstone of the Corner. The leaders again had to admit defeat, not able to act in defiance of the crowd, so returned to their council chamber to refine and mature their schemes.

And they sent to Him certain of the Pharisees and of the Herodians with a commission to snare Him in a statement. And having come, they say to Him, Teacher, we know positively that you are true and that you do not kowtow to anyone, for you do not pay regard to the outward appearance of men, but upon the basis of the truth you are teaching the way of God. Is it permissible to give poll tax to Caesar or not? Shall we give, or, shall we not give?

Following their defeat, the leaders broke into separate parties again, each to formulate its own plans. First came the Pharisees with a pretended enquiry, knowing that either a 'Yes' or 'No' answer from Jesus would leave Him open to accusations of either betrayal of Israel or of rebellion against Rome. They purpose to catch Him like some wild animal, He entangling and trapping Himself in His talk. They skilfully prepare for their question by praising Jesus for His speaking of the truth whatever the consequences i.e. since He had shown little consideration for the learned of Israel, also He should show the same indifference to the authority of Caesar himself where the truth was concerned. Thus, they declare to all, His answer to their question will be given with fearless impartiality, and will be the truth, since He cannot lie. The payment of tax was objectionable to both patriotic and religious Jews since it was a sign of subjection to a foreign power and also since the image on the coin with which the tax was paid was that of the ruler whom they were required by Roman law to worship as a god. So the question they pose is; should a Jew pay this tax in view of his theocratic relationship to God? They hoped Jesus would reply 'No', since that would involve Him at once with the Roman authorities and, given the mood of the crowd, might put Him at the head of a rebellion. On the other hand, a reply of 'Yes' would greatly displease the Jewish crowd and undermine His popularity with them.

But He, knowing their hypocrisy, said to them, Why are you putting me to the test? Be bringing me a denarius in order that I may see it. And they brought one. And He says to them, This likeness and title belong to whom? And they said to Him, To Caesar. And Jesus said to them, The things belonging to Caesar pay off to Caesar, and the things belonging to God, to God. And they were marvelling at Him.

Jesus was well aware of their craftiness and wickedness, detecting their character intuitively, that they were not seeking the truth on this matter but rather trying to find an accusation to bring against Him, and so He was demanding that they find such a coin and bring it to Him. The crowd waited in silence, speculating internally as to what the response of Jesus would be. Having brought the coin, Jesus asks a question that they could not this time answer with 'We do not know', even if they suspected the purpose behind it. They had asked 'Shall we give?' Jesus' reply talked about paying a debt. "Let Caesar have his own coin, since the fact that it circulates in Judaea shows that it is in the ordering of God's providence that you be under Roman rule. Paying that debt to a human is not incompatible with you paying your debts to God, and both are to be discharged, the two spheres of duty being at once distinct and reconcilable." The Pharisees were standing there, amazed at Him, since there was nothing in His reply on which they could lay hold.

And there come Sadducees to Him, that class which says there is not a resurrection. And they kept on questioning Him, saying, Teacher, Moses wrote us, If a brother of a certain man should die, and should leave a wife and should not leave a child, his brother should take the wife and raise up offspring for his brother. There were seven brothers. And the first took a wife, and dying, did not leave offspring. And the second took her, and he died, not having left offspring. And the third likewise. And the seven did not leave any children. Last of all the woman died also. In the resurrection, when they are raised, of which of them shall she be wife, for the seven had her as wife?

Next come those of the party which are rationalists, who do not believe in angels or spirits or in the possibility of a resurrection of the dead, and who are few in number and not held in as much esteem by the people as the Pharisees. They were questioning Jesus according to their own particular viewpoint and were claiming to want to know what position this new Teacher took on a point-of-issue between themselves and the Pharisees, but they had not come to learn, their purpose also being one of hostility toward Jesus. Their questioning began, "This resurrection of which so much is heard", and went on to give a crude example involving the legislation to prevent a family inheritance from being broken up.

Jesus said to them, Is it not because of this that you err, namely, that you do not know the scriptures nor even the power of God? For when they arise out from among the dead, neither do they marry nor do they give in marriage, but are [in this respect] just as angels in heaven. But concerning the dead that they arise, did you not read in the book of Moses, at the bush how God spoke to him, saying, I am the God of Abraham, and the God of Isaac, and the God of Jacob? He is not a God of the dead but of the living. Greatly do you err.

Jesus explained to them the fundamental errors that they made in their reasoning, showing them their two-fold ignorance, this being inexcusable given their membership of the priesthood. In the matter of marriage and the future life, the thinking of the Sadducees and Pharisees was that either God could not raise the dead, or, that He could raise them only to a life which would be a counterpart of the present one, it being even more filled with the material pleasures that are experienced in this life. Jesus said, "Since in the future life there will be no propagation of human beings, your question has no relation to the resurrection of the dead. The example you gave only applies to the present life". Jesus then proved the truth of the resurrection by showing God's real and continuing relation to those long dead, and that therefore these people must still exist, being alive to Him though dead to the visible world. It might be argued that this just refers to men's souls, but resurrection of the body is also implied, since the body is a true part of human nature, and God would not leave men with whom He maintained relations in an imperfect condition. The living soul, of necessity, in due time would recover its partner, the death of the body being a mere suspension of vital activities which, in some form, would in future be resumed.

And having come, one of the men learned in the sacred scriptures having heard them questioning together, knowing that He had answered them well, asked Him, Of what sort is the first commandment of all? Jesus answered, The first is, Be hearing O Israel, the Lord our God is one Lord, and you shall love the Lord your God with your whole heart, and with your whole soul, and with your whole mind, and with your whole strength. The second is this, You shall love your neighbour as yourself. Greater than these, another commandment there is not.

Then came one of the scribes, impressed with Jesus' answers, and he asked Jesus which class of commandments in the law was of the greatest quality, was it those to do with rituals like Sabbath-keeping and circumcision, or was it those to do with morality and love for others? Jesus replied by quoting the Scripture which is recited daily by every Jew and which the scribes carried with them at all times, so already considered to be of prime importance by all. "Your intellect, desires, and affections are to be wholly given over to God, with a self-sacrificial love for God and for your neighbour. These commandments reveal the ultimate principle of morality, which the law is there to enforce, and on which the highest teaching of the prophets depends. These fundamental laws of human life are second to none."

And the man learned in the sacred scriptures said to Him, Right! Well! Teacher, truthfully you said, He is One, and there is not another except

Him. And to be loving Him with your whole heart, and with your whole understanding, and with your whole strength, and to be loving your neighbour as yourself, is much more than all the whole burnt-offerings and sacrifices. And Jesus, having seen him, that he answered intelligently, said to him, Not far are you from the kingdom of God. And no one any longer was daring to ask him a question.

The man heartily agreed with Jesus' reply, and showed in his response his own sincerity and independence of thought. Jesus was refreshed by the man's mind and thinking. He could see that the man recognised that God's judgment rests on the superiority of moral over ritual obligations, showing that he was to some extent intellectually qualified for admission to the Kingdom, he having grasped one of its fundamental principles.

And answering, Jesus was saying as He was teaching in the temple, How is it that the men learned in the sacred scriptures say that the Christ is David's son? David himself said by the Holy Spirit, The Lord said to my Lord, Be seated on my right hand until I make your enemies the footstool of your feet. David himself calls him Lord, and how can it be that He is his son? And the great crowd was hearing Him gladly.

And Jesus was questioning the scribes' interpretation of the Scriptures concerning the nature of the Messiah and future King of Israel Who will one day sit on the throne of David. They believed the Messiah would be a human descendant of David, but Jesus shows how David spoke of the Messiah as having power over him, David recognising Him as deity, even Yahweh of the Old Testament. This posed a problem for those listening to Jesus; how, since the Messiah is Yahweh, deity, can He also be human? The answer is the Incarnation. But the Jewish leaders rejected this teaching, and also rejected Jesus' claim to deity; He calling God His own private and unique Father and thus making Himself equal with God, which claim they considered to be blasphemous. They believed God to be one Person since He said that He is one Lord, but David here recognises Father and Son, and Jesus was saying that this was revealed to David by the Holy Spirit, so putting the Triune Godhead in an Old Testament setting, the Three operating in unity, as One.

And in His teaching He was saying: Be constantly bewaring of the men learned in the sacred scriptures who are fond of parading about in stately robes, and are fond of reverential and deferential greetings in the market places, and the seats of honour in the synagogues, and the chief places at the feasts, those who devour the houses of widows and for a pretence make long prayers; these will receive greater condemnation.

Jesus was then warning the people against the scribes. Whilst He recognised their official character and their position as authorised teachers, nevertheless their conduct was to be condemned; fond of ostentatiously wearing long, priestly and royal robes, fond of public salutations, fond of sitting on the front benches reserved for officials and persons of distinction that faced the congregation in the synagogues, and fond of the uppermost places of highest honour at social gatherings. The scribes were employed to make out wills and conveyances of property and were in the practice of persuading widows, by deception and flattery, to give their homes to the Temple, proceeds from the sale of which they and the Pharisees would take a good part of for themselves. They would encourage widows to do so by offering long prayers for them in their homes, a pretence done with an ulterior purpose. Their sentence will thus be greater than that of a simple robber, since they added a pretence to piety to their offence, so earning for themselves the sentence on the hypocrite in addition to that on the robber.

And having sat down opposite the treasury, He was viewing with a discerning eye how the crowd throws money into the treasury. And many wealthy ones were throwing in much. And one having come, a poverty-stricken widow, threw in two very small brass coins which make a farthing. And having called His disciples to himself, He said to them, Truly, I am saying to you, This widow, and she, poverty-stricken, threw in more than all those who are throwing into the treasury, for they all threw in out of their abundance, but she out of her poverty threw in all, as much as she had, the whole of her life's necessities.

Jesus finished His teaching in the Temple courts and passed within the wall which fences off the inner precinct of the Temple from the Gentiles, being now in the Court of the Women. And He was sitting across from the offering chests in the Treasury colonnade. In stark contrast to a greedy, hypocritical scribe stealing from widows, He was carefully observing an obviously impoverished widow, given her clothing and wasted look, throwing in two of the least value coins, totalling one fortieth of a denarius. It was all that she had to live on yet she willingly put in both of them, making her gift incomparably greater than all the others, she withholding nothing, so giving her all to God.

And while He was proceeding out of the temple, one of His disciples says to Him, Teacher, see what manner of stones and what manner of buildings. And Jesus said to him, Do you see these great buildings? There shall positively not be left a stone upon a stone which is not torn down.

As they were leaving the Temple, one of the disciples calls Jesus to observe the magnificence and glory of its buildings, the edifices, enclosures, colonnades, halls, and sanctuaries which Herod had had built for the Jews, the largest of the stones of which weighed over one hundred tons. Jesus in turn called this disciple to indeed fix his attention on those very buildings, whose greatness He acknowledged, since their complete destruction would not be long in coming, when all of the Temple estate would be loosed down stone by stone until completely and utterly demolished, with not so much as one stone left on top of another, but only the foundation remaining.

And being seated on the Mount of Olivet opposite the temple, there were asking Him privately Peter and James and John and Andrew, Tell us, when will these things be, and what will be the attesting miracle which will indicate when these things, all of them, are about to be consummated? And Jesus began to be saying to them, Keep ever watching lest someone lead you astray. Many will come in my Name, saying, I, in contradistinction to others, am he, and will lead many astray. And when you hear of wars and reports of wars, stop being terrified. It is necessary in the nature of the case for these things to take place. But not yet is the end. For there will rise up nation against nation and kingdom against kingdom. There shall be earthquakes in various places; there shall be famines. A beginning of intolerable anguish are these.

Having left the city they ascended the steep road over the Mount of Olives. While sat resting, the disciples were questioning Jesus as to the signs warning of this destruction. He began by warning them of false Messiahs who would arise, and of the danger of following them in their error, those falsely claiming that they alone are the one that Israel is looking for, and pretending to possess powers which only belong to Him. Jesus then went to warning them of imminent political troubles and national upheavals and was telling them not to let these distract them from the work of spreading the Gospel, since they were issues solely for the world system of evil headed up by Satan, and of no concern to the Kingdom of God i.e. no matter what happens in the world, the people of God must carry on toward the God-ordained and predicted consummation. He was telling them to stop being troubled about the political unrest that they could see around them in Palestine, since such things were necessary events, man's total depravity being the root of all war and itself making wars inevitable. Each of the next three Caesars would make threats of war against the Jews, and the Jews would be singled out for persecution in Seleucia and Joppa. And there would be earthquakes in Crete, Rome, Phrygia, and Campania, as well as four famines, all of these things during the next forty years, after which time the Temple would be destroyed as Jesus predicted.

But as for you, be constantly paying heed to yourselves. They will deliver you up to councils, and in the synagogues you will be beaten, and before rulers and kings you will be placed for my sake, as a testimony to them. And to all the nations first is it necessary in the nature of the case for the gospel to be proclaimed. And whenever they may be leading you, delivering you up, do not continue to be anxious as to what you will say, but whatever will be given you in that hour, this be speaking. For, as for you, you are not the ones who are speaking, but the Holy Spirit.

And Jesus was then warning the disciples of what would happen to them personally. They would be summoned to appear before both Jewish and Gentile authorities on a charge of loyalty to the Name of Jesus, in order to be a means of proclaiming His Name to those who might not otherwise hear the Gospel. Also, further into the future, Jewish believers will be similarly persecuted during the Tribulation, and their persecution will intensify as that period approaches. Then Jesus was assuring His disciples of the Holy Spirit's assistance in the giving of their defence which they will offer before their judges, and that they are therefore not to worry as they are being led away to court as to what to say to their accusers.

And a brother will deliver a brother to death, and a father, a child, and children will rise up against parents, and will cause them to be put to death. And you will be those who are being hated by all for my Name's sake. But he who has persevered to the end, this one shall be preserved from destruction.

Jesus went on to be predicting treachery from friends and relatives within the Jewish community. And this will be more intensely fulfilled in the Tribulation when Jews will be forced to choose between the coming Jesus and the then present Antichrist, and also when the Jewish nation will be hated by all people around the world. Those Jews who survive to the end of that period will be physically protected and so saved in their well-being to enter into the Millennium.

But when you see the object of religious nausea and loathing who has to do with the desolation, standing where he ought not; the one who reads, let him understand; then those who are in Judaea, let them flee into the mountains; the one who is on the housetop, let him not go down, neither let him enter to take anything out of his house; and the one in the field, let him not turn back to take his garment. But woe to those who are with child, and to those who are nursing their young in those days. But pray that it may not be winter.

Jesus now was focusing His predictions on the Tribulation to come when the Antichrist, after three-and-a-half years of that seven year period, will violate his covenant of friendship with the Jewish nation by stopping the Temple worship in Jerusalem and by entering the Holy of Holies, showing himself to be not the nation's reputed friend and protector, but rather its bitter enemy, at which time Israel must flee. Mothers with young children will not be able to escape, such will be the haste needed to evade the Antichrist.

For those days will be characterised by tribulation such as has not been from the beginning of the creation which God created until this particular time, and will positively not be. And unless the Lord had shortened the days, no flesh would be saved. But for the sake of the chosen-out ones whom He chose out for himself, He shortened the days.

The days following this will be a tribulation, evil days, when the judgments of God which will fall upon unbelieving Israel and the Gentile nations will have no precedent in all past history, and will have no counterpart in all succeeding history. In these days, the preaching remnant of Israel, who announced Jesus' second Advent during the previous three-and-a-half years, are no more present, they having lost their lives due to the Antichrist's persecution. But God, in His mercy, has shortened this period, so that His chosen nation of Israel might be spared and not cease to exist.

And then, if anyone says to you, Look, here is the Christ; look, there; stop believing him. Moreover, there shall arise false Christs and false prophets, and they will perform attesting miracles and miracles that arouse amazement in order to be leading astray, if that were possible, which it is not, the chosen-out ones. But, as for you, be constantly taking heed. I have told you beforehand all things.

Then Jesus was predicting that there will come false claimants to being the awaited Messiah and King of Israel, they having the ability to perform supernatural signs and wonders. Israel must not accept the claims of these persons based on the miracles they perform, since their character and message will show them to be deceivers, and since He has now forewarned Israel of their coming.

But in those days, after that tribulation, the sun will be darkened and the moon will not give its light, and the meteors will be falling out of the heaven, and the natural powers that control the heavenly bodies will be disorganized. And then they will see the Son of Man coming with clouds, with much power and glory. And then He will send off the angels and will gather together His chosen-out ones from the four winds, from the outermost border of the earth to the outermost border of heaven.

After the end of the seven years of the Tribulation, the sun, moon, and stars will be disturbed. Jesus Himself will then return, His second Advent, together with clouds of glorified believers and angels, to defeat the Antichrist, and to set up His Millennial Kingdom on earth. All Israel will be re-gathered, saved in sovereign grace and restored to fellowship with, and service to, God, as Jesus rules the world for a thousand years.

Now, from the fig tree be learning the meaning of the illustration. When already its branch becomes tender and is putting out the leaves, you know from experience that the summer is near. Thus also, as for you, when you see these things coming into being, you know that He is near, at the doors. Truly I am saying to you, This race will positively not pass away until these things, all of them, take place. The heaven and the earth will pass away, but my words will not pass away. But concerning that day or hour no one knows, not even the angels in heaven nor even the Son, only the Father. Be constantly taking heed, be constantly on the watch, for you do not know when it is the strategic season.

Jesus was then re-emphasising the need to be aware of the signs during the final days of the Tribulation that told of His soon coming, and He was re-affirming that the Jewish nation was indestructible and would remain on earth as a nation through the time of the fulfilment of these events. In His Incarnation, even Jesus Himself did not know the hour of His second Advent, nor the timings of these other things grouped around that event.

It is as a man gone off to another country, having left his house, and having given his slaves the authority, to each his work; and to the doorkeeper he gave orders to be constantly alert and watching. Therefore, be constantly alert and on the watch, for you do not know when the master of the house comes, whether at evening time, or at midnight, or at cockcrowing, or in the morning, lest having come unexpectedly, he find you slumbering. And that which I am saying to you, I am saying to all, Be constantly watchful and alert.

Jesus was then giving an illustration referring to that period when He, having departed back to His Father in Heaven, had left His disciples and apostles with the responsibility of guarding the 'house' and of being ready to open the 'door' to Him on His return, charging them to keep watch and remain wakeful as they awaited Him. The parable used the examples of the

Temple's night guards, any of whom found sleeping by the captain when on his rounds were beaten and their garments set on fire, and of those servants whose job it was to arise early in order to prepare for the Temple's morning service, for the performance of which the superintending priest might knock at the door at any moment.

Now, it was the feasts of the passover and the loaves baked without yeast, after two days. And the chief priests and the men learned in the sacred scriptures were seeking how, having seized Him by craftiness, they might put Him to death. For they were saying, Not during the feast, lest at any time there be an uproar on the part of the people.

It was now two days before the Feast of Passover when lambs were sacrificed. This was done in remembrance of Israel's deliverance from slavery in Egypt, in advance of which the angel of death had seen the lambs' blood on the Jews' doorposts and refrained from killing their firstborn children whilst killing the Egyptians' firstborn. Jesus now appeared as the true Lamb, of whom those other sacrificial lambs were symbolic, and by His death He would pay for man's sin and defeat death itself. The Jewish council were convening, now agreed that Jesus must be killed by handing Him over to the Roman authorities, but undecided as to the timing of their action. They were reasoning that the Passover was neither an opportune nor safe time, due to Jesus' popularity with the people.

And while He was in Bethany in the house of Simon the leper, as He was reclining at table, there came a woman having an alabaster cruse of ointment, nard, pure, very costly. Having broken the alabaster cruse, she was pouring its contents upon His head. Now, there were certain there who were moved with indignation among themselves. To what purpose has been this waste of the ointment? For it was possible to have sold the ointment for more than three hundred denarii and to have given these to the poor. And they bristled with indignation against her.

That evening, while Jesus was eating, a woman came and, having broken a jar of genuine Indian ointment, was quickly pouring all of it over His head. Judas and the other disciples were affronted at such an extravagant waste of this rare perfume. At Passover time many of the poor were given alms, so, very angrily amongst themselves, they murmured, 'How many could have been helped if this ointment had rather been sold?'

And Jesus said, Let her alone. Why are you causing her trouble? A munificent service she rendered me. For the poor you always have with you, and whenever you desire, you are able to do them good; but me you are not always having. That which she had, she used. She took occasion beforehand to anoint my body for the entombment. And truly I am saying to you, Wherever the gospel may be proclaimed in the whole world, also that which she herself did will be spoken as a memorial of her.

But Jesus praised her act as being beautiful and pleasing to the eye, having a true moral beauty, her helping of Him being equivalent to helping the poor. And it was a timely act, since helping Him would very soon be impossible, while opportunity for helping the poor would abound to the end of time. The woman, Mariam, could not understand Jesus' death, but she showed sympathy for Him, unlike the others there. The anointing of a dead body was done after it had been washed, but when the women came to do this to Jesus' body after His death they could not do so, so this was the only such anointing that Jesus received, by the hands of Mariam.

And Judas Iscariot, the one of the Twelve, went off to the chief priests for the purpose of betraying Him to them. And they, having heard, rejoiced inwardly and promised to give him money. And he went to seeking how he might betray Him when the opportunity presented itself.

Judas was the one who betrayed Jesus. He knew who to go to and agreed to hand Jesus over to them. The chief priests hid the delight that they felt, the burden of finding a way to kill Jesus so that the Passover crowds would not see, now definitely on Judas' shoulders, his position in the inner circle of disciples giving him an advantage which they did not have.

And on the first day of the feast of loaves baked without yeast, at which time it was the custom to kill the passover, His disciples say to Him, Where do you desire that we go and prepare in order that you may eat the passover?

The next day, being Wednesday, the fourth day of the week, and the day before the Cross, the disciples ask Jesus about where in Jerusalem they are to celebrate Passover, commemorating the time when Israel was passed over, God being enabled to withhold the judgment of death on its people on seeing the symbolic blood sprinkled on their homes.

And He sends off two of His disciples, and says to them, Go into the city and there will meet you a man carrying an earthenware pitcher of water. Follow him, and wherever he enters, say to the master of the house, The Teacher says, Where is my guest-chamber where I may eat the passover with my disciples? And he himself will show you an upper room, large, in a state of readiness, prepared. And there make ready for us. And the disciples went out and came into the city, and found even as He told them. And they prepared the passover.

Jesus commissions Peter and John to procure the room where He and His disciples will eat the Passover. The two disciples find the slave and the house and the room exactly as Jesus tells them they will. The owner of the house was a follower of Jesus and himself showed the disciples the furnished room, large enough to accommodate them all, and already prepared for the Feast, with couches around the table.

And evening having come, He comes with the Twelve. And while they were reclining at table and eating, Jesus said, Truly, I am saying to you, one of you will betray me, the one eating with me. They began to be grieved and to be saying to Him, one after another, It is not I, is it? And He said to them, One of the twelve, the one who dips with me into the deep dish. The Son of Man indeed goes even as it stands written concerning Him. But woe to that man through whose agency the Son of Man is betrayed. Good were it for him, if that man had not been born.

After sunset Jesus and the disciples come to the room. He told them that it would be one of them, being those closest to Him, who would betray Him, pointing to one aspect of the enormity of the offence, in that Jesus, the Son of God, would be betrayed by a friend and associate. Each disciple in turn was seeking reassurance from Jesus that they are not the one. The fate of the betrayer would be a misery which even Love itself could not prevent.

And while they were eating, having taken bread, having offered a blessing, He broke it and gave to them and said, Take. This is my body.

During the meal Jesus took a bread-cake, gave thanks for it, and distributed it to His disciples to eat, symbolising His body of flesh; that to eat of the bread is to partake of His great sacrifice, and that it also represents the spiritual nourishment on which a believer may feed and have eternal life.

And having taken a cup, having given thanks, He gave it to them, and all drank from it. And He said to them, This is my blood of the testament which is being poured out in behalf of many. Truly, I am saying to you, I will positively no longer drink of the product of the vine until that day when I drink it new in quality in the kingdom of God.

Jesus then took a cup, gave thanks for it, and passed it to them, its contents symbolising His blood being shed on the Cross, His sacrifice being the fulfilment of the Old Testament animal sacrifices with the shedding of their blood. The next time Jesus would drink would be in the Millennial

Kingdom, when the Messiah would sit on David's throne in Jerusalem, reigning over the world for a thousand years, drinking superior spiritual wine with His cleansed and restored Israel.

And having sung a hymn, they went out into the Mount of Olivet.

Then, as was their habit, Jesus and His disciples left Jerusalem and headed to the Mount of Olives.

And Jesus says to them, All of you will fall away, because it stands written, I will smite the shepherd and the sheep will be scattered. But after I have been raised I will go before you into Galilee. But Peter said to Him, Even if all will fall away, certainly not I. And Jesus says to him, Truly, I am saying to you, that, as for you, today, on this night, before a rooster crows twice, three times you will deny me. And he kept on saying with more vehemence and iteration, If it should be necessary for me to die with you, I will positively not deny you. Moreover, in like manner also all kept on saying.

Jesus tells them that, in fulfilment of an Old Testament prophecy, they will all desert Him when He is attacked and struck, but that that will be a preface of better things, namely, an early reunion, He contrasting the gloom of the immediate future with the hope of His resurrection. Peter conceded that the others would likely flee, but not him, to which boast Jesus pointedly tells him the precise time before which Peter himself will indeed deny Him, not once but three times. Peter would not accept this prediction and kept on passionately and forcefully declaring his undying allegiance to Jesus.

And they come into a place called Gethsemane: and He says to His disciples, Sit here while I shall pray. And He takes with Him Peter and James and John. And He began to be thoroughly alarmed and distressed. And He says to them, My soul is encompassed with grief even to the point of death. Abide here and be watching.

Jesus now spends time in prayer before the coming ordeal. He had long foreseen this time, but now its terrors exceeded His anticipations. Jesus throughout His time on earth learned upon the basis of the things He suffered, but this last lesson in obedience to His Father was beginning with a sense of inconceivable awe and anguish, bringing Him an overpowering mental distress and causing Him to become confused and distracted and to experience unfamiliar feelings, His consciousness enveloped and saturated with grief and sorrow, "So that I almost die".

And having gone on ahead a little, He fell repeatedly upon the ground, and was praying that if it were possible, the hour might pass from Him. And He was saying, Abba, [namely] Father, all things are possible to you. Cause this cup to pass by and from me. But not what I desire, but what you desire.

In the desperateness of His struggle, Jesus repeatedly fell on His face in prayer, continuously asking that He might be spared the dread of the Cross. Jesus was speaking to His Father intimately and emotionally and naturally, in His mother tongue. He was conscious that while His Father had the power and ability to do all things, that nevertheless He was constrained by His righteousness and love, so Jesus was asking if the Cross really was according to the divine will. Jesus was requesting release because of who He was and what He was. Firstly He, the holy Son of God, was to be made sin and charged by the High Court of Heaven with the guilt of all human sin, from which prospect He drew back, given the infinite hatred of sin that was His. Secondly Jesus was to be deprived of the fellowship of the Father while He was on the Cross, which fellowship had had no beginning, so that He would be losing something that He had always known, resulting in infinite suffering for Him. Shrinking away from these two things, dreading them with all His heart yet counting the awful cost, Jesus was saying to His Father, "Not what I Myself desire, but what You Yourself desire".

And He comes and finds them sleeping, and He says to Peter, Simon, are you sleeping? Did you not have strength to watch one hour? Be constantly watching and praying in order that you might not enter a place of testing that will present to you a solicitation to do evil. The spirit indeed is willing but the flesh is weak. And again, having gone off, He prayed, having said the same thing. And again, having come, He found them sleeping, for their eyes were heavy, and they did not know what they should answer Him. And He comes the third time and says to them, Keep on sleeping now and taking your rest. It is enough. The hour has come. Behold, the Son of Man is being betrayed into the hands of sinners. Be arising. Let us be going. Behold, the one who is betraying me has come near and is at hand.

Jesus returns and finds that His three disciples have not remained watchful but rather have fallen asleep. He personally addresses Peter, calling him 'Simon', and rebuking him that he who was ready to die with Him has been proved not to possess the strength of will needed so as to even resist sleep during only a third of a single watch. Their spirit, Jesus says to them, is willing and eager, being under the influence of the Spirit of God through their fellowship with Him, but their spirit's willingness was not a match for the inertia of their frail flesh. Jesus left them again to pray and once more returned to find them sleeping through grief and again speechless when questioned by Him. And the third time after going off to pray He finds them yet again having submitted to sleep. This time Jesus ironically gives them permission to sleep and tells them to rest if they can, now that His betrayal is imminent. The disciples, now aroused, Jesus no longer chastises them for their lapses since His enemy is near. With the disciples still lying on the ground, as Judas approaches Jesus goes out to meet him and those with him. This was Jesus' hour and He was ready to meet it.

And immediately, while He was still speaking, there approaches Judas, one of the Twelve, and with him a crowd with swords and cudgels who came personally from the chief priests and the men learned in the sacred scriptures and the elders. Now, the one betraying Him had given them a prearranged signal, saying, Whomever I shall kiss, it is He himself. Seize Him and lead Him away safely. And having come, immediately approaching Him he says, Rabbi, and kissed Him. And they laid their hands upon Him and seized Him.

Straight away Judas and the crowd arrives, comprising a hastily gathered group of armed men; some from the Jewish council, some of the Temple police, some Roman soldiers, and some personal servants of the High Priest. Judas had instructed that they seize the One he kiss and securely capture Him, since he had seen Jesus previously evade those trying to attack Him, and since Jesus had many followers, some of whom might attempt to rescue Him. So as soon as Judas arrived, he goes straight to Jesus without delay, and affectionately and fervently kissed Him.

And a certain one of those who stood by, drawing his sword, struck the slave of the high priest and took off his ear. And answering, Jesus said to them, As against a robber you came out with swords and cudgels to seize me. Daily I was with you in the temple, teaching, and you did not seize me. But the scriptures must be fulfilled. And having forsaken Him, they fled, all of them.

Peter was drawing his sword and slashed at one of the crowd, cutting off his ear. Having restored the man's ear, Jesus questioned the crowd as to why they were arresting Him now when previously, in public, they had not, since He was not a night-time robber but a Teacher Who had taught in the daylight for three consecutive days that week. But, He said, this treachery and secrecy of arrest was in fulfilment of Old Testament prophecy. The disciples all fled.

And a certain young man was following with Him who had thrown a linen cloth around his nakedness. And they seize him. And having left the linen cloth, he fled unclothed.

On hearing of Jesus' arrest I got out of bed and ran to see, with just a sheet wrapped round me, and I was following the crowd until they seize me, so that then I too fled and deserted Jesus.

And they led Jesus off to the chief priest. And there are gathered together all the chief priests and the elders and the men learned in the sacred scriptures. And Peter followed Him at a distance even into the uncovered courtyard of the house of the chief priest. And he was sitting with the officers and warming himself at the fire.

Jesus was led away to the Chief Priest's house where the council members are gathered. Peter stealthily followed right into the courtyard of the palace and, venturing further and further in, was finally near to, and seated by, the charcoal fire which was used for light and warmth in the cold early morning air of that season, meaning also that his face could be seen.

Now, the chief priests and the entire council were seeking testimony against Jesus with a view to putting Him to death; and they were not finding any, for many were repeatedly bearing false testimony against Him, but their testimonies were not in harmony. And certain, having arisen, were bearing false testimony against Him, saying, As for us, we heard him saying, As for myself, I will destroy this temple which is made with hands, and after a period of three days another one made without hands I will build. And not even in the way described did their testimony harmonize.

The full Jewish council were set on finding a charge for which they could pronounce a sentence of death on Jesus, which sentence could then be validated and enacted by the Roman procurator. Attempts at bringing forward two witnesses who could agree on the essential details of a charge against Jesus were repeatedly failing, their testimonies always not fully corresponding, so not warranting a conviction. Two of them were misquoting Jesus, since He never said that He would destroy the Jerusalem Temple, rather He had said, "You destroy this inner sanctuary and in three days I will raise it up", predicting that their actions against Him in killing Him would result in His bodily resurrection.

And having arisen, the chief priest in the midst questioned Jesus, saying, Do you not answer even one thing? What is this that these are testifying against you? But He kept on maintaining His silence and answered not even one thing. Again, the chief priest went to asking Him, and says to Him, As for you, are you the Christ, the Son of the Blessed? And Jesus said, As for myself, in contradistinction to all others, I AM. And you will see the Son of Man sitting on the right hand of the power and coming with the clouds of heaven.

The High Priest then arose from his seat and advanced into the semi-circle of the council and towards Jesus, irritated at the lack of evidence against Him. Jesus was maintaining His silence, neither denying the charge against Him nor justifying the words that were misquoted as being His, since these men could not be profitably addressed, nor could He admit the authority of an assembly which was following up an unjust arrest with the employing of perjured witnesses. The High Priest puts Jesus under solemn oath in order to force Him to incriminate Himself, a method forbidden in Jewish legal practice. To refuse to answer his question, "Are You the Messiah, the Anointed of God?" would be tantamount to Jesus denying His deity, so Jesus answered by declaring Himself to be Yahweh, God, and referenced the words of both David and Daniel in asserting Himself to be the Messiah. Jesus' words also included a warning that one day their roles will be reversed i.e. that He will one day be their judge, this warning being a final and ineffectual summons to their repentance and to their having faith in Him, ineffectual since they were wholly intent on His being crucified.

Then the chief priest, having torn apart his tunics, says, Why do we still have need of witnesses? You heard his blasphemy. What is your view? And they all condemned Him to be guilty of death. And certain ones began to be spitting upon Him and to be covering His face and to be pummelling Him and to be saying to Him, Prophesy. And the officers caught Him by blows with the flat of the hand.

The Chief Priest tore both his tunics as a customary expression of horror at any blasphemous utterance being made in his presence. There is no further need for witnesses since Jesus has incriminated Himself, and he asks the council for their verdict, that being a foregone conclusion. The sentence was unanimous and immediate. Having blindfolded Jesus, they were all punching Him frenziedly with their fists.

And when Peter was down in the courtyard, there comes one of the female slaves of the high priest, and having seen Peter warming himself, having gazed intently at him, she says, And as for you, with the one of Nazareth you were, that Jesus. But he denied, saying, Neither do I know nor do I understand what you are saying. And he went outside into the forecourt. And the female slave having seen him, began again to be saying to the bystanders, This man is one of them. But again he kept on denying. And a short time afterwards, again the bystanders were saying to Peter, Truly, one of them you are. In fact, you are a Galilaean. But he began to be putting himself under a divine curse, and to be putting himself under oath, I do not know this man concerning whom you are speaking. And immediately a second time a rooster crowed. And Peter was brought to a remembrance of the word as Jesus spoke it to him, Before a rooster crows twice, three times, me you will deny. And having put his thought upon it, he began to be weeping audibly.

While this trial was being held in an upper storey Peter waited below. One of the domestics employed by the High Priest, being on duty with reference to the early morning events, was looking intently at Peter and recognises him as a follower of Jesus, which he was twice denying, showing his weak point of a lack of moral courage. When accused a third time Peter was subjecting himself to a divine curse should he be lying when he was again denying knowing Jesus. At once a rooster crowed, the sound of which caused him to throw his thoughts upon Jesus' words and, remembering them, he went to tearful sobbing.

And immediately at daybreak, the chief priests convoked a council with the elders and men learned in the sacred scriptures and the entire Sanhedrin; having bound Jesus they took Him away, and handed Him over to Pilate. And Pilate asked Him, As for you, are you the King of the Jews? And answering him He says, As for you, you are saying it.

As soon as it was light, it now being Thursday, the fifth day of the week, and the day of the Cross, the council brought Jesus to the Roman governor of Palestine, they having craftily put a political viewpoint on His confession, since none of the other charges would interest the Roman authorities but only Jesus' claim to be the King of Israel. Pilate had to address this charge since it asserted Jesus to be setting Himself up as a King in opposition to Caesar.

And the chief priests kept on accusing Him of many things. And Pilate again went to asking Him, saying, Are you not answering even one thing? See how many things there are of which they are accusing you. But Jesus still answered not even one thing, so that Pilate was in a state of amazement.

Jesus maintained the silence that He had kept before as false witnesses were being brought before the council to testify against Him. His silence was astounding Pilate who had never before known a prisoner to act in this way. He did not believe Jesus to be a political pretender but rather saw a remarkable man, and decided to proceed with caution until he might make some sense of the passions amid the parties of this strange people, Israel.

Now, at the feast, it was his custom to release to them one prisoner whom they would be desiring. And there was the one commonly known as Barabbas, who was in chains with those who had participated in an insurrection, those being of that class that had committed murder in the insurrection referred to. And, having gone up, the crowd began to be asking him to do just as he had always been accustomed to do for them. And Pilate answered them, saying, Are you desiring that I release to you the King of the Jews? for it was gradually dawning upon him that because of envy the chief priests had delivered Him up.

As happened every Passover, the crowd was forcing its way up to Pilate's headquarters to ask him to release one prisoner. The most notorious prisoner that year was one who had led a revolt against Rome and who had murdered. Pilate suggested to the crowd that Jesus should be the one released, referring to Him in a way that was a mortal offence to the council. Pilate was now beginning to realise that Jesus' real offence against the Jewish authorities was rooted in their envy of His great influence with the people, so Pilate was trying to play off the people against the priests.

And the chief priests stirred up the crowd that he should rather release Barabbas to them. But Pilate again answering, was saying to them, What then shall I do to him whom you are calling the King of the Jews? But they again cried, Crucify him at once. But Pilate was saying to them, Why, what evil did he do? But they cried out with an indescribable uproar, Crucify him at once. Then Pilate, desiring after reflection to satisfy the crowd, released Barabbas to them,

The authorities moved to influence the crowd; Barabbas was a local man, a citizen of Jerusalem, Barabbas was a man dedicated to freeing Israel from Roman rule, Barabbas should be released. The crowd having decided on Barabbas, Pilate was asking them what he should do with their 'king'. The fickle crowd were incensed that this Roman, having attempted to dictate to them his choice of prisoner to release, should now be lauding his power over them, so they repeatedly and with ever increasing fervour demanded that the One Pilate had sought to release, the One they had previously praised, be killed, despite not having an answer to Pilate's question to them as to what offence He had committed.

and having scourged Jesus, delivered Him to be crucified. And the soldiers led Him off into the courtyard which is the Praetorium, and they call together the entire band. And they clothe Him with a purple robe, and having woven together a victor's crown of thorns, they place it upon Him. And they began to be saluting Him, Hail, King of the Jews. And they kept on beating His head with a staff made of a reed, and they kept on spitting upon Him; and bowing their knees, they were doing obeisance to Him. And when they had mocked Him, they took off from Him the purple robe, and put on Him His garments. And they lead Him out in order that they may crucify Him.

Jesus was handed over to the soldiers in charge of the prisoners. He was first scourged by them and His back was so lashed by the leather whips that contained bone and metal that His veins were laid bare and His inner muscles, sinews and bowels were exposed. Then Jesus was conducted into the barracks where all the contingent of soldiers are gathered to cruelly ridicule Him as being supposed royalty and therefore their superior, their sport of Him leaving His flesh extremely and dreadfully disfigured, and His face, now unrecognisable, crowned with long, sharp thorns. And on His bleeding, lacerated back is laid the Cross to which He is to be cruelly nailed.

And they commandeer the services of a certain Simon of Cyrene who was passing by at the time, coming from the surrounding farmland, the father of Alexander and Rufus, in order that he might carry His cross. And they bring Him to the place, Golgotha, which interpreted is, a place of a skull. And they offered Him wine mixed with myrrh. But He did not receive it.

A Jewish man from Libya is pressed into service by the Roman soldiers to carry Jesus' cross when He could no longer do so. Indeed, barely being able to walk, Jesus was brought to the site of His crucifixion, as the sick had previously been brought to Him. Before being nailed to the Cross, Jesus was offered a stupefying drink so as to deaden the sense of pain, but He refused to drink it.

And they crucify Him and distribute His garments among themselves, throwing a lot upon them, who should take what. Now, it was the third hour, and they crucified Him. And there was the inscription of His accusation written above, THE KING OF THE JEWS. And with Him they crucify two robbers, one on His right and another on His left. .

Jesus is crucified at 9 a.m. with the charge written above His head that had been carried before Him on His way to the Cross.

And those passing by kept on reviling Him, wagging their heads and saying, Ah, the one who is destroying the inner sanctuary and building it in three days, save yourself, having come down from the cross. In the same way also, the chief priests, mocking, were saying to one another with the men learned in the sacred scriptures, Others he saved, himself he is not able to save. The Christ, the King of Israel, let him come down now from the cross in order that we may see with discernment and believe. And those crucified with Him were reviling Him.

Passers-by were expressing ironic admiration that Jesus had ended up on a cross, unable now to rescue Himself. Also the council members, separate from the crowd, were mockingly discussing Jesus' fate amongst themselves, they not acknowledging the wording of the charge written against Him, but nevertheless professing that they would believe Him to be the Messiah should He now miraculously release Himself.

And the sixth hour having come, a darkness came upon the whole land until the ninth hour. And at the ninth hour Jesus shouted with a loud voice, Eloi, Eloi, lama, sabachthani? which interpreted is, My God, My God, why did you let me down?

From 12 p.m. until 3 p.m. there was a supernaturally-caused darkness over the land. At the end of this period Jesus cried out that He had been abandoned by God. On the Cross, the Holy Spirit also abandoned Jesus just as surely as did the Father, withdrawing His sustaining presence while Jesus was suffering on the Cross. Thus the Holy Spirit ceased keeping alive in divine life the human spirit of Jesus, which spirit, though sinless, became dead, the life-giving power of the Holy Spirit having ceased to energise it. So in the day time of His sufferings, from 9 a.m. until 12 p.m., and in the night season of His sufferings, from 12 p.m. until 3 p.m., when a darkness came upon the whole land, His human spirit was devoid of the life-giving ministry of the Holy Spirit, and the Father would not hear Him.

And certain ones of those standing by, having heard, were saying, Behold, he is calling for Elijah. And, having run, a certain one, having filled a sponge with sour wine, having put it upon a reed, was giving Him a drink, saying, Hold off. Let us see whether Elijah comes to take him down.

Those near to the cross were heartlessly theorising that Jesus was asking Elijah, a past deliverer of Israel, to rescue Him. On hearing this, one compassionate spectator was offering Jesus some of the Roman soldiers' drink in an effort to prolong His life, so that Elijah would indeed have an opportunity to take Jesus down from the Cross.

And Jesus, having cried with a loud voice, breathed out His life. And the curtain of the inner sanctuary was torn in two from the top to the bottom. And the centurion standing by opposite Him, having seen that thus He breathed out His life, said, Truly, this man, Son of God He was.

Sin having now been paid for by Jesus' sinless sacrifice of Himself, so that the atonement was looked upon as complete, Jesus was praying that He might be raised from the dead, and the Holy Spirit returned to make alive again His human spirit, since that prayer could now be answered by Him, and fellowship between Jesus and the Father was restored. Then Jesus was triumphantly shouting "It has been finished and stands complete! The price has been paid! Father, into Your hands I entrust my spirit", and He laid down His head, and His human body died on the Cross. The thick veil, which separates the Holy of Holies from the Holy Place within the Temple, was torn apart by the unseen hand of God, showing that the way into the earthly Holy of Holies was no more, and that now, access into the Father's presence was to be through His Son Jesus, He having fulfilled all of the Old Testament sacrifices and so done away with them. Seeing the way that Jesus died caused the centurion in charge of the executions to marvel at this innocent, extraordinary, and possibly supernatural person.

Now, there were also women looking on carefully and with interest, viewing attentively from a distance, among whom were also Mary, the Magdalene, and Mary the mother of James the younger and of Joses and Salome, who when He was in Galilee, were accustomed to follow with Him and minister to Him the necessities of life, and many other women who came up with Him to Jerusalem.

Some others, as well as the centurion, viewed Jesus' crucifixion with seriousness. The women from Jesus' home region of Galilee watched from a distance, safe from the coarse and irreverent behaviour of the crowd.

And already evening had come. Since it was the time of making ready, which is the day before the sabbath, Joseph, the one from Arimathaea, having come, an honourable member of the council, who also himself was waiting for the kingdom of God, having taken courage, went in to Pilate and asked as a personal favour for the body of Jesus. But Pilate wondered whether He was already dead. And having called the centurion, he asked him if He had just died. And having come to know it from the centurion, he freely gave the corpse to Joseph.

Since the Passover lambs were to be sacrificed at 6 p.m., Joseph, a devout and godly man, came in haste to Pilate and boldly requested that he might take Jesus' body down from the Cross so that it could be buried in his own grave, and not the common grave provided for criminals, before the start of the Sabbath. In doing this, Joseph was risking the wrath or indifference of Pilate, and risking causing offence to the Jewish authorities by showing sympathy to this obnoxious One, even though Jesus was now dead. Since death by crucifixion could take two or three days, Pilate asked the centurion whether He had been dead a little while. Having had Jesus' death officially confirmed to him, Pilate released the body to Joseph, glad that this inconvenient and troublesome affair was now over.

And having purchased fine linen in the market place, having taken Him down, he wrapped Him with the fine linen and placed Him in a tomb which had been hewn out of rock, and rolled a large stone against the door of the tomb. And Mary, the Magdalene, and Mary the mother of Joses were attentively observing where He was laid.

Joseph purchased linen on his way back to the Cross. Together with Nicodemus, another godly council member, he took Jesus' body down, wrapped it in the linen between the folds of which, spices which Nicodemus had brought were freely crumbled, and finally bound the hands and feet with strips of cloth and covered the face with a face cloth. Then they carried the body to an adjacent garden in which was a new tomb which Joseph had prepared for his own burial, and they sealed it shut with a large stone. Two of the women who had remained at the Cross were carefully watching all that was done.

And the sabbath being past, Mary, the Magdalene, and the mother of James, and Salome, purchased aromatic spices in order that, having come, they might anoint Him. And very early in the morning of the first day of the week they come to the tomb, the sun having risen.

The women rested on the Sabbaths, then purchased anointing oil after the sunset that closed the Saturday Sabbath. Very early on Sunday, being the first day of the week and three days after the Cross, while it is still dark, they leave Bethany, which is two miles away, and arrive at the tomb just after sunrise.

And they kept on saying among themselves, Who will roll away for us the stone out of the door of the tomb? And, having looked up, they saw clearly that the stone had been rolled back, for it was exceedingly great.

All through their journey from Bethany the women were discussing how they would move the stone completely away from the entrance to the tomb. From a distance they could see that the very large stone had already been moved out of the place from where it had been set into the entrance.

And having entered the tomb, they saw a young man sitting on the right, clothed in a long stately garment, white. And they were utterly amazed. And he says to them, Stop being utterly amazed. Jesus you are seeking, the Jesus of Nazareth, the One who has been crucified. He was raised. He is not here. See the place where they laid Him. But be going; say to His disciples and to Peter, He is going before you into Galilee. There you will see Him just as He told you. And having gone, they fled from the tomb, for there had come upon them trembling and astonishment: and they said not even one thing to anyone, for they were afraid.

In the tomb they found a man dressed in a solemn, rich, and beautiful robe, he having the appearance of an angel, so that the women wondered at him in amazement. He tells them the good news that Jesus is no longer there in the tomb and that they will see Him soon, just as He had predicted before His death.

Now, having risen early, on the first day of the week, He appeared first to Mary, the Magdalene, from whom He had cast seven demons. That one, having proceeded, brought word to those who had been with Him, who were mourning and were weeping audibly. And those, having heard that He lives and was seen by her, disbelieved. And after these things, to two of them while they were walking He appeared in a different outward appearance as they were proceeding into the country. And those having gone off, brought word to the rest. Neither did those believe them.

Jesus appeared to Mariam as a gardener, making Himself known to her on calling her by her name. And He appeared to two disciples who were leaving Jerusalem as a stranger and fellow-traveller, making Himself known to them when breaking bread with them. But neither of these encounters with Jesus, resurrected and alive, was believed by the other disciples.

And afterward He appeared to the eleven themselves as they were reclining at table, and He reproached their disbelief and hardness of heart because they did not believe those who viewed Him attentively after He was raised. And He said to them, Having proceeded into all the world, make a public proclamation of the good news to the whole creation. The one who believes and is baptised, will be saved, but the one who disbelieves will be condemned.

Jesus, after rebuking the disciples for their doubting His resurrection of which He had told them about on numerous occasions, charged them to be going out and announcing the Gospel message, being the offer of salvation and eternal life to all who will believe in Him as Saviour, together with the accompaniment of baptism as a picture of this new life in Him, but not as a means of securing it. Those who reject the Gospel message will be condemned for their refusal to believe in Jesus as their Saviour.

And these attesting miracles will accompany those who believe these things. In my Name they will cast out demons. In new languages they will speak. Snakes they will pick up. And if they drink anything deadly, it will positively not harm them. Upon the sick they will lay hands, and they will recover. So then the Lord Jesus, after He had spoken to them, was received up into heaven, and sat on the right hand of God. And those having gone forth, preached everywhere, the Lord working with them, and confirming the Word through the attesting miracles which accompanied them.

After appearing to the disciples over a period of forty days, Jesus was taken up in a cloud and ascended to Heaven, there interceding for believers until His return for the Church at the Rapture. As the disciples went to preaching the Gospel message, the Word was accompanied by supernatural signs; casting out of evil spirits, speaking in other languages, protection from snake bites, protection from physical imprisonment, healing the sick, and raising the dead.

Bible chapter finder

Printed in Great Britain
by Amazon

46063686R00249